Shore Chronicles

*Diaries and Travelers' Tales
from the Jersey Shore
1764 - 1955*

*Edited by
Margaret Thomas Buchholz*

Foreword by John T. Cunningham

Down The Shore Publishing
Harvey Cedars, New Jersey

For information, address:
Down The Shore Publishing Corp.
P.O. Box 3100, Harvey Cedars, NJ 08008
www.down-the-shore.com

The words "Down The Shore" and the Down The Shore Publishing logo are a registered U.S. Trademark.

Printed in the United States of America. First printing, 1999.
10 9 8 7 6 5 4 3 2 1

Book design by Leslee Ganss.

Library of Congress Cataloging-in-Publication Data
Shore chronicles : diaries and travelers' tales from the Jersey shore,
   1764 - 1955 / edited by Margaret Thomas Buchholz ; foreword by
John T. Cunningham.
        p. cm.
      Includes bibliographical references (p.   ) and index.
      ISBN 0-945582- 58-7 (hardcover)
        1. Atlantic Coast (N.J.) -- Description and travel. 2. Atlantic Coast (N.J.) --
History, Local.   3. Atlantic Coast (N.J.) Biography. 4. American diaries -- New
Jersey -- Atlantic Coast. 5. Travelers' writings. 6. New Jersey -- Description and
travel. 7. New Jersey -- History, Local. I. Buchholz, Margaret Thomas, (date).
F142.A79S56   1999
974.9--DC21   99-13119
                                                                                       CIP

*Dedicated to the memory
of Marion Figley...
friend, colleague, inspiration.*

Contents

Foreword

In 1764 Carl Magnus, a pastor of the Swedish Lutheran Church in Philadelphia, rode 220 miles on horseback from Philadelphia to Great Egg Harbor and back; not for beach bathing, surfing or casino-hopping, but to save souls. He found precious few on the unnamed, tree-covered island he visited, but even in his somber diary can be found his excitement over the birds, the oysters and the power of the waves.

In 1809 Sarah Thomson, a Philadelphia maiden, made the trip from Philadelphia to Tuckerton aboard a stagecoach, which "had more the appearance of an old Jersey waggon." Sarah recorded a romantic vacation — flirtations, eating, long walks, sea bathing and playing cards with an incomplete deck. Sarah's atrocious spelling and syntax fail to lessen the charm of her thoughts.

In 1875 Olive Logan, an actress, journalist, playwright and lecturer, came by train to spend the summer in Long Branch, considered then to be America's "gayest, sportiest, most fashionable" shore vacation spot. In a long, insightful essay, she observed that Long Branch "is perhaps better in accord with the spirit of American institutions than any other of our watering places."

These are but three of the diarists, journalists, naturalists, authors and inspired non-professionals whom editor Margaret Buchholz has assembled to give first-hand accounts of visits to the Jersey Shore between 1764 and 1955.

While Shore Chronicles encompasses a broad period of time and a wide variety of visitors, these people were not the first inhabitants to know the values of the restless waters that edge our coast. The Lenape Indians trekked to the shore each summer, perhaps as many as 9,000 years ago, for the utilitarian purpose of gathering shellfish for winter food. One doesn't have to be much of a romantic to believe they also frolicked in the surf, picked up shells, chased girls across the dunes or sat in the sand to ponder waves splashing across the strand in the eternal rise and fall of the tides. None of those original people left an account; the Lenape had no written language.

A fascination of this book is that Margaret Buchholz found so many visitors who spent so much time writing in diaries or journals when they might have been soaking up sun or wading in the surf. Today's average visitor might scribble an occasional postcard, or possibly an e-mail note from a laptop.

I consider myself a Jersey Shore chronicler —although not a diarist — after more than six decades of tramping up and down the coast, in all seasons of the year, at every time of day, from pre-dawn to long past midnight. Since the early 1950s I have written hundreds of thousands of words about the shore, including a book unimaginatively titled The New Jersey Shore. I did not see the Atlantic Ocean until I was a teenager in high school, and I came not to surf or to swim but rather to experience the ocean in one of its foulest moods.

The wild winds, towering waves and cold, lashing rain of a late summer northeaster ravaged the coast on September 8, 1934, the night of my first visit. My older brother, a reporter for the small-town Morristown Record, and I were tooling around Morristown when we heard on his car radio that a burning ship was being swept ashore near Asbury Park. It was, of course, the stricken Morro Castle. By midnight, as we walked through the Asbury Park Casino, the doomed passenger liner had beached a few hundred feet from the boardwalk. Smoke still rose from the ship but the fires had been subdued.

We stood in the intense darkness of the night, awed by the towering ship and, although I did not know it then, I was overwhelmed as well by the power and majesty of the sea. That storm-swept night became the base point for all that I have learned since about the Jersey Shore. No one can begin to understand the ocean's incredible wrecking force until he sees it in the grip of a mighty storm.

Since the night of the Morro Castle I have been up and down the 127 miles of New Jersey seacoast on hundreds of nights and days, perhaps as many as three or four full years in total.

Unwittingly I had become one of the peripatetic visitors whose shore peregrinations form the basis for this book. No matter what most of us profess, in past or in present, the essential lure is the ocean in all its mood swings, from docile pussycat on most summer days to sullen beast in wintertime. Even some of Atlantic City's modern slot-feeders wander out on the boardwalk for an occasional breath of sea air and a view of the ocean.

The Jersey Shore has been transformed almost beyond recognition or remembrance in the past half century. The Garden State Parkway has metamorphosed much of the northern portion to year-around living. Sandy Hook is no longer the mystery that it was when I first sought admission there in the 1950s. The portion surrounding Toms River has year-round traffic, mainly because of the proliferation of nearby senior citizen complexes.

When I first saw Long Beach Island in the early 1950s, I was so enthralled by its beauty and open spaces that I wrote: "A lover of Long Beach Island is like the teenage boy who has a new, beautiful girl friend. He is just bursting to introduce her to the world, but he has the vague, uneasy feeling that to do so is the surest way to lose her."

Sadly, many visitors have introduced that island to the world. Too many lovers crowd the place that my family and I enjoyed for 15 summers in the 1950s and early 1960s. As we enjoyed vacations there, Long Beach Island's seasonal population grew to five times the number of admirers that I first knew. I realize that I helped bring them there with my unbridled praise.

When I first began frequenting the shore, Route 9 was a two-lane road much of the way, but it was the only road south. Getting to Atlantic City from Morris County took at least four hours. Cape May was about six hours distant; staying overnight was mandatory — and by late September not even Wildwood had a decent overnight room for rent.

Casinos have turned the Jersey Shore topsy turvy. There is often as much traffic headed south to Atlantic City on a late Friday afternoon in February as there was once on a Saturday morning in July. But it isn't all casino traffic; the huge rise in year-round populations in Monmouth and Ocean county towns often creates near-gridlock.

None of this is by way of lament. Shore-bound automobiles are filled with happy-faced people who believe that today is the acme of Jersey Shore summertime. They happen to be right, for they claim neither past nor future. Perhaps in the year 2055, one of them will write of the "old days" in 1999, when he recalls traveling to Atlantic City by automobile.

Is there anything that might link that raconteur of 2055 with today, and with the more than 300 years of New Jersey's coastal history?

Obviously a book such as Shore Chronicles is resource number one.

The stories have several common threads with today — the need for a place where a person can get away from daily life, the belief that the sea air is "good for you," the sea itself; and an awareness that no matter how antiquated or tiresome the modes of travel, the trip is worth the effort. Anyone stuck in today's traffic on a hot summer day might well ponder that his forebears made the trip in a springless stagecoach whose air-conditioning was whatever winds chanced to blow.

I am lucky. I have walked from Sandy Hook to Cape May, many times. I have known the shore at all hours of the day — from pre-dawn, when professional fishermen in seaside towns rise to earn their livings, to late night, when casino optimists stay awake to prove the odds can be beaten.

I have known it in the mixed excitement and dread of fall hurricanes; in winter's doldrums when softly flapping, faded posters tell of last summer's joy; in spring's awakening when the waves become meek and permissive; and in summer glory when beach umbrellas and the slightly-coconut smell of sunblock lotions fight the battle of too much vs. too little sun.

I am sure that if I could talk to any of the individuals whose first-person accounts appear in these pages, we would quickly get back to the fundamentals, to the wonder that waves have been breaking on this shore since time began, to the awareness that a wave retreating on ebb tide leaves the strand different from how it was at high tide. We would talk about the migrating birds that fly over the bays and gather every spring and every fall at Island Beach, Cape May Point or at the Edwin B. Forsythe National Wildlife Refuge.

We would talk of summer romances, of nighttime dancing, of day-time strolls along the beach in quest of shells. We would talk of climbing up through the lighthouses; of riptides and jellyfish and seasickness aboard a fishing boat. We would talk of our shore — and cherish the thought that we know it well.

Margaret Buchholz gives us the chance to hear of distant days. We can't talk back, but we can understand.

— John T. Cunningham

Introduction

The writers of the stories in this book — famous authors, pioneering naturalists, journalists, sailors, sportsmen, and ordinary people on vacation — all visited the New Jersey seashore between 1764 and 1955. They walked along the beaches and boardwalks, sailed on the bays, swam in the ocean, climbed the lighthouses, beachcombed, gathered shells, fished, sketched, hunted and, in the hundred years before 1850, were fascinated with the novelty of lobsters, jellyfish, sand crabs and shipwrecks. Some founded the early resorts. Others lived in them year 'round. Their experiences varied as much as their individual points of view. But what binds them together, and brings them to us, is the fact that they all picked up a pen and recorded their impressions.

The journalists who came before the railroads were built, when a trip to the Jersey Shore was equivalent to today's adventure travel, published reports of their journeys in magazines and newspapers. Foreign visitors such as Arthur Conan Doyle, on a grand tour of the United States, included the Jersey Shore on their itineraries and recounted their thoughts in books. Both fun-seeking vacationers and enthusiastic youngsters working at summer jobs came, relished life at the shore, then went home and wrote about it, leaving us with vignettes of weeks, months or summers by the sea. And the diarists — those scribblers who, by recording their everyday comings and goings, reflections and ideas, documented a time and space, and in so doing left us with a glimpse into the past.

Reading these varying accounts from such different eras, I realized that the energy and excitement, the sounds and sights, and even some of the entertainments, have a surprising resonance. In 1896 the author Stephen Crane described the "observation wheel, a gigantic upright wheel of wood and steel, which goes around carrying little cars filled with maniacs, up and down, over and over." Those summer maniacs are still riding Ferris wheels in Seaside Park, Beach Haven, Ocean City and Wildwood.

A hundred years ago in Atlantic City, Lilyan West and her girlfriends donned "different colored dresses and linked arms and promenaded down and up the Boardwalk." Today's teenage girls may not know the meaning of "promenade," but they choose their shorts and T-shirts very carefully before they cruise today's boardwalks and resort streets.

Visiting Cape May in 1850, the Swedish novelist Frederika Bremer observed, "More than a thousand people, men, women and children, go out to the sea in crowds, and leap up and down in the heaving waves, or let them dash over their heads amid great laughter and merriment." The scene on the gently sloping Cape May beach is the same today; but 150 years ago the men were covered from neck to knee and the women wore "dresses of all colors and shapes" with pantaloons and yellow straw hats, not bikinis or skintight maillots. Did the 1850 bather enjoy the surf any less? I doubt it.

In 1833, when the taxonomist Constantine Rafinesque sailed across Barnegat Bay to Long Beach, he noted that the island was "frequented for the sea air and the sea baths." Sea breezes and swimming are, and always have been, the essentials of a visit to the shore. Our visceral response to being immersed in the water or deeply breathing the salt air expresses our elemental affinity to the sea, and is what attaches us so securely to the shoreline. This is as true now as it was when Sarah Thomson wrote in 1809: "All went in the surfe. Find myself very much refreshed. The white foaming waves all seemed combined to add to the buty [sic] of our walk."

Or in 1879 when Walt Whitman drove in a carriage on the hard-packed Atlantic City beach: "How the main attraction and fascination are in sea and shore!"

Or in 1917 when Van Campen Heilner cast a surf rod into Little Egg Harbor Inlet: "The fascination lies in the sea, the birds, the whispering dunes, and the loneliness and wildness that goes with the pounding surf and the gray sands."

Or in 1919 when Christopher Morley ducked under the waves in Wildwood: "To splash and riot in that miraculous color and tumult of breaking water seems an effective answer to all the grievances of earth."

The loyalty of some summer visitors to their own special beach had an amazing longevity. Four generations of Richard Atwater's family came to Sea Isle City after he built a home there in 1881 and started his house diary. Dorothea Sjostrom, for years a renter, built an oceanfront cottage in Harvey Cedars in 1935; her great-grandchildren still vacation on Long Beach Island. Jim Doyle's childhood summers in Townsends Inlet in the 1920s colored the rest of his life, and he still returns.

Although most of these narratives are set in the summer, I have included the Cape May diary of Frank Leach (1870 to 1871) and the Tuckerton diary of Eleanor Price (1915 and 1917), both of which give the flavor of those coastal towns year round. Likewise, Barnegat Bay is not the same sparkling, sun-kissed expanse of water during duck-hunting season, and November 1864 was no exception, as is evident in T. Warren Robinson's earthy tale. Also, Robert Louis Stevenson wrote briefly of his preseason visit to Manasquan (1888).

Yet these glances into the past only serve to underscore how the Jersey Shore has changed with the passage of time. The most dramatic difference, of course, is the physical look of the coastline. In 1878, when Dr. Theophilus T. Price wrote *The History of the Beaches*, the major resorts of Long Branch, Asbury Park, Atlantic City and Cape May were firmly established, but most of the 127-mile shoreline was guarded by rows of sand dunes. Price observed: "Several successive ridges are found on these old beaches, separated by long narrow valleys, in which are found coarse grasses, rushes, low bushes and vines, in addition to oak, cedar and holly timber."

Indeed, naturalists were drawn to the region as early as 1750, when the Swedish botanist Peter Kalm journeyed to South Jersey where he lived with Scandinavian colonists for several months, gathering specimens from the Pine Barrens to the shore. An eminent ornithologist, Alexander Wilson, identified abundant wildfowl here beginning in 1808. The taxonomist Rafinesque came at various times between 1802 and 1836 and recorded: "In July I took an excursion of fifteen days through New Jersey to the sea shore and sea islands to study them better still. I went by Burlington, Mount Holly, Vincentown and Buddtown to the Pine Barrens, which extend here about 30 miles to the sea, intermingled with cedar swamps of *Cupressus thyoides*. I stopped at Cedarbridge to botanize and found many plants. I went to Manahawkin, which has sixty houses and a fine pond of clear water three miles around. I remained five days in the neighborhood to explore the woods, swamps, salt marshes, meadows, etc., and six days on the great Island of Long Beach, twenty-four miles long, but often cut up by the sea in storms."[1]

When the ornithologist Charles Abbott arrived in Wildwood in 1892 the town was developing but still aptly named, with 50 acres of primeval forest intact. Probably the saddest of all the thoughtless annihilation of the coastline's natural beauty was that untold centuries of nature's work, including hundreds of huge holly trees and cedars, some as large as 12 feet in circumference, were destroyed within the next two decades in the name of progress.

In 1940 Cornelius Weygandt, in his classic book *Down Jersey*, expressed his fear that boardwalks and rows of bungalows would eventually cover the "beautiful stretches of dune-land." He predicted that "in another generation the barrier islands off the Jersey coast will have wholly lost their glory. It is too much to hope that the State or the Nation will intervene and preserve certain stretches of strand and dunes, bayberry flats and stands of red cedar, holly thickets and salt marsh, as representative of the beauty our coast had for miles on miles down to a generation ago." Fortunately, the vagaries of fate spared Island Beach, described later in these pages by the nature writer Shirley Briggs; that nine-mile stretch of shoreline remains as pristine as when the very first visitors saw it.

Several of the earliest diarists described their trips but often told us little about the shore itself. Consider Bordentown resident Edward Shippen's loop through central New Jersey about 1835: "The canal was then finished, and we went to New Brunswick in a passenger boat, which was a cabin built upon two cigar-shape cylinders with which the horses trotted along briskly. As one was not much in a hurry then, it was a very pleasant and favorite way of travel, although we were eight or ten hours in reaching New Brunswick... and then [we] drove in Murat's barouche across the country to Long Branch. There were then only one or two rather primitive hotels or boardinghouses there. From Long Branch we drove to Barnegat, where we took a large sailboat and went round to Somers Point in Great Egg Harbor, passing out to sea around Absecon, the first time I ever felt the motion of the ocean. This took two or three days, and we lived on board the boat. At Somers Point Murat's carriage again met us and we drove slowly up through the heart of 'the Pines.' We spent one night at the Blue Anchor tavern [then] went on, by Long-a-coming, to Camden and Philadelphia, and then by steamboat to Bordentown."[2]

Young Shippen was traveling for his health, for the fresh, briny air, but today's seeker of sun and relaxation would most likely find the traffic-clogged trip more exhausting than refreshing.

The communities fronting the water, whose worlds of the past we visit in this collection, are the same as those whose names are on the green-and-white signs that today dot the Garden State Parkway; but the long-gone writers who chronicled the Jersey Shore's developing years had no express highway to bring them here. Those early adventurers traveled by stagecoach, sailboat or steamboat, until trains and then automobiles eased the journey. The rapid access to the shore provided by the parkway, described in the final chapter by a travel writer as a "miracle ride," so altered the unhurried, measured development of the Jersey Shore that I chose to end my book the year the parkway opened.

I first envisioned this book as a collection solely of diaries written by visitors and residents. Journals have an immediacy not equalled by reminiscence. For me, finding a yellowed, handwritten diary is the prize in a treasure hunt. I see more than just the words on the page. I feel the age of the thick rag paper, the emotion behind the smartly inked swirls and affirmative exclamation points. I can speculate about the writer holding the pen or pencil.

The first diary I uncovered was Sidney Townsend's 1868 daybook. Then the Tuckerton historian Steve Dodson shared Eleanor Price's and Sarah Thomson's diaries with me. (After Steve showed me Sarah Thomson's diary, my colleague Edward Brown reminded me that we had published it in the newspaper *The Beachcomber* in 1972.) These three finds stimulated my search for more diaries and, after combing through historical society archives and placing ads in newspapers, I found the others included in this volume. I actually came upon many more, but most offered only brief daily entries — bits and pieces of interesting information but no developing narrative.

I was tempted to include Townsend's reports of cutting blocks of ice from Ludlam's Bay, his catches of game — the phrase "thick with ducks" was penned in equally thick ink strokes — and his irritation with the incessant northwest wind. Townsend's joy at the return of warm weather was expressed by elaborate curlicues at the end of each day's entry as he wrote of such events as "hunting water and mush melons" or catching "three quarters of a bushel of hake and five drums." He told of "green flies and mosquitos about as thick as they was ever known" and hinted at the commerce between mainland farmers and resort merchants when he wrote on July 11, 1868, that "Elmer Young has just returned from Atlantic City this evening with an empty boat and pockets lined with greenbacks, I spect."

But finally, I decided that the brief entries didn't tell us enough about Townsend himself.

Robert Juet's journal, written on board the *Half Moon* as Henry Hudson coasted past these shores between April 4 and November 7, 1609, was an obvious choice, but I rejected it as being too well known. However, I will cite here the paragraph that has warmed the hearts of New Jersey publicists since it was first brought to their attention: "Then the Sunne arose, and we steered away North againe, and saw the Land from the West by North, to the Northwest by North, all like broken Ilands. [The coast between Atlantic City and Little Egg Inlet], and our soundings were eleven and ten fathoms. Then wee looft in for the shoare, and faire by the shoare, we had seven fathoms. The course along the land we found to be Northeast by North. From the Land which we had first sight of, untill we came to a great Lake of water, as wee could judge it to bee, being drowned Land, which made it to rise like ilands, which was in length ten leagues [Barnegat Bay]. The mouth of that Lake hath many shoalds, and the Sea breaketh on them as it is cast out of the mouth of it [Barnegat Inlet]. And from that Lake or Bay, the Land lyeth North by East, and wee had a great streame out of the Bay; and from thence our sounding was ten fathoms, two leagues from the Land. At five of the clocke we Anchored, being little winde, and rode in eight fathoms water, the night was faire. This night I found the Land to hall the Compasse 8 degrees. Far to the Northward off us we saw high Hils [Navesink Highlands, Staten Island hills, or even Harbour Hill on Long Island]. For the day before we found not above 2 degrees of Variation. This is a very good land to fall with, and a pleasant Land to see."[3]

Charlotte Turner, a young bride summering in Seaside Park in 1910, left a brief handwritten record of the first time she went to the shore with her seven-month-old baby: "I coped with the problems of no conveniences, no lights, no transportation except one train a day, and worst of all, no milk for the baby. Early one morning I heard the mooing of a cow. Determined to locate that cow I walked down the railroad tracks to a large grey clapboard house called the Bond House, a boarding house for fishermen, and there was the cow. I bargained with the owner for a quart of milk. This I pasteurized and for lack of ice we dug a pit under the kitchen floor in which we kept the milk and other perishables. Adequate and ingenious." I regret that Charlotte didn't tell us more about her life in the fledgling resort.

Ultimately, well-written diaries with a striking sense of time and place were few and far between, so I broadened my quest.

Early on in my research Bill Kelly, a writer in Ocean City, offered me Ray Hansen's unpublished manuscript from which I excerpted his harrowing escapade during the hurricane of 1944. (What's a book about the Jersey Shore without mention of a hurricane?) Fellow Long Beach Islander Deb Whitcraft gave me a box of unsorted ephemera in which I discovered Theophilus Price's 1874 letter about the opening of the Parry House in Beach Haven. (The Parry House burned down just eight years after its inaugural dinner and was rebuilt as the Baldwin Hotel, which in turn burned down the night I got married, so this chapter has a warm, personal resonance.) Knowing I enjoy reading diaries, my friend Annsi Stephano suggested I might want to see her mother's World War II journal, not knowing it contained an account of their summer trip to Mantoloking in 1945. Then Carroll Sheppard, a Philadelphia writer who summers in Beach Haven, kindly sent me a copy of the 1828 Long Beach story she'd found while doing her own historical research. And so it went. I decided to take an empirical approach and see what I could come up with as I followed leads from New England to Hawaii to an isolated house deep in the Pine Barrens, and gently plundered historical archives and libraries up and down the coast.

Personally, the most satisfying find was artist and sailor Will Lathrop's log. I'd read the New England portion of it in *Yankee* magazine in the early 1980s and reasoned that if *Widge* had been launched in the Delaware River, Lathrop had to sail along the Jersey coast to get to Long Island. Through friends in New Hope, Pa. and Florida I located his grandson in New Hampshire. It took more than a year, but I finally got to read Lathrop's log. I love his spirit and vitality, and after slowly reading five years of his combination log and diary I felt really connected to him, and cried at the end. Now, each time I drive past his studio on River Road just north of New Hope I picture the old man, white beard flapping, rolling his boat toward the Delaware River and his destiny.

For the past two years I have been intimately involved with these writers and their stories about this shore I love so well. I hope you will find, as I do, that each is somehow graced with the power of the ordinary, which makes each individual so extraordinary.

NOTES

1. Constantine S. Rafinesque, *A Life of Travels and Researches,* Philadelphia, 1836. Reprinted in Chronica Botanica, VIII, 1944.

2. Edward Shippen, "Reminiscences of Admiral Edward Shippen: Bordentown in the 1830s," *Pennsylvania Magazine of History and Biography,* LXXVII, 1954.

3. *The Voyage of the Half Moon from 4 April to 7 November 1609* by Robert Juet, New Jersey Historical Society, Newark, 1959, edited by Robert M. Lunny.

Editor's Note

*This collection encompasses a wide variety of
writing styles and I have allowed each writer to retain
his or her own style, without editorial intrusion,
except for the substitution of italics for quotation
marks, where appropriate. I have corrected the
peculiarities of each author's spelling — especially in
the earliest entries, before spelling rules were fixed —
only when it interfered with the meaning. Also, I have
added punctuation where necessary for ease of
reading. In the case of magazine articles and
chapters of books I have made no changes except for
obvious typographical errors.*

*Several of the diaries were excerpted from longer
manuscripts. Although I have silently pruned some
material, I have chosen not to use ellipses; any words
added for clarity are surrounded by brackets. The
notes at the end of each chapter are intended to
explain relationships between people, to define
obsolete words and allusions, and to elaborate on the
fascinating minutiae of history.*

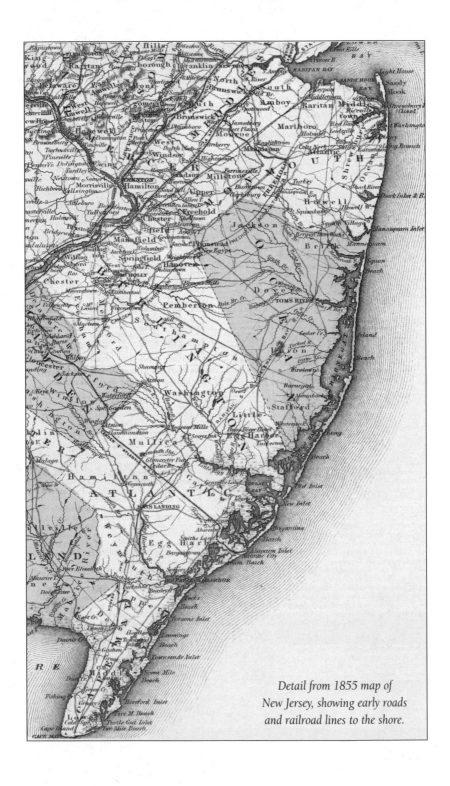

*Detail from 1855 map of
New Jersey, showing early roads
and railroad lines to the shore.*

Shore Chronicles

1764
Pastor Wrangel's Trip
To the Shore

Rev. Carl Magnus Wrangel

This 1740 Dutch map shows no towns and indicates nothing but "sterile land" along Pastor Wrangel's route, although Glocester (Gloucester City), Waldbury (Woodbury) and Raccon Creek (Swedesboro) are in place.

The Rev. Carl Magnus Wrangel was dean of the Swedish Lutheran congregation in America from 1758 to 1768. In October 1764, he and his companion, Gloucester County Sheriff Robert Price, made a ten-day, 220-mile trip on horseback from Philadelphia to Great Egg Harbor and back, including a jog north to Little Egg Harbor. Pastor Wrangel was concerned about the souls of pioneers living in isolated settlements far from centers of civilization. He lamented, "These Swedes[1] lived at the seaside, at a place called Egg Harbor, abandoned and completely without the means of grace." According to Carl Magnus Anderson, who translated the pastor's diary from the Swedish in the 1960s, Wrangel was responsible for a significant awakening among the spiritually neglected coastal immigrants. Although Pastor Wrangel's highly readable journal is primarily a record of sermons preached and souls saved, his description of the barrier island as it was in the mid-18th century is one of the earliest known.

OCTOBER 7: I left my house at eight o'clock in the evening and crossed the Delaware River in glorious moonlight. At ten o'clock I arrived at my companion's house, two English miles on the other side of the river, from whence we were to leave early the next morning.

OCTOBER 8: Early in the morning, after we together had invoked God's merciful blessing upon us during the journey, and had eaten breakfast, we betook ourselves to the road and traveled ten miles to a German by the name of Nyman, where we rested. After we had been there for an hour we continued our journey a further ten miles to a tavern owned by a man named Scull[2], a member of the English Church; he moved here from Egg Harbor. Little or no knowledge of God appears to dwell in this house; however, the people showed themselves to be attentive to my address on man's obligation to so care for the body that he does not thereby completely forget the soul.

We continued our journey another nine miles to another tavern called The Blue Anchor[3], where we arrived at one o'clock. These people received me with great joy. When I inquired about the condition of their souls, they answered with tears in their eyes that here they lived in a parched land where water was not to be found. I explained to them how a Christian ought to try to make up for the lack of hearing God's word by its diligent reading at home and by prayers to God.

The country hereabouts has been inhabited only during the last twenty years. Previously there had been only wild, barren ground between Philadelphia and Egg Harbor, so that travelers had to provide themselves with food for both their horses and themselves when they came this way. The land sells for $10 a hundred acres and the soil consists mainly of drift sand, which, however, produces reasonably good crops of maize and rye; but wheat does not grow especially fast. There are no meadows, but good wooded pasturage is available for the cattle throughout the summer. In the winter they bring their herds to the seaside in Egg Harbor, where they pay ten shilling a head for the winter; they fetch hay for the horses from the same place. They have to depend principally on the woods, which consist here of spruce, pine and cedar, for a livelihood; several sawmills are therefore located here, where boards and building lumber are sawed and shipped, partly by the river and partly by wagon, to Philadelphia. They also make shingles here (of Cedar *Cupressus Thyoides*) and charcoal. They also extract some tar. Oak also grows here but there is no hickory.

After dinner we continued our journey and traveled ten miles over a barren land, which is uninhabited since the soil is very poor. The road is completely level without even the smallest hills. Nor are there any rocks or other stones, except small pebbles which lie among the sands. These are white and very fine. It seems very probable that all this land was once part of the sea; this is supported by the fact that when they dig wells here they often find oyster shells deep in the ground. In this land there are found more conclusive proofs of the theory that the water is still receding than anywhere in the world. We crossed a *Ceder Kiärr*, which in English is called a cedar swamp. Inasmuch as such a swamp consists of moss-grown mud with a great many rivulets, sawmills are commonly built beside such cedar swamps if there is adequate water for them.

We finally caught sight of the Egg Harbor River, where there was a loading site for planks, boards and shingles. Toward evening we arrived at the home of a Swede named Carl Steelman, who lived by the highway. Around his house were high fences, on which were hung a considerable number of deer antlers; like trophies, they witnessed that here dwelt a mighty hunter. Here we were received with much love and feasted on Swedish venison. The man lamented, with tears in his eyes, that they here were ignorant as heathens of the only thing needful and that he had not seen a Swedish minister for twenty years.

October 9: Early Tuesday morning we received a message from a Swedish family that lived nearby. They asked whether the Swedish minister who had been expected had arrived; if so they dearly wished to see him that morning. I set out with my companion for their house, about an English mile away. When we reached the house the man met me and received me with tears of joy. His name was Carl Streng; he was born into the Raccoon[4] congregation. I then betook myself to the house where I was to preach; they also went, in a boat, down a small river that flows by here, called the Great Egg Harbor River.

A Swede by the name of James Steelman[5], who was present with his wife and children, invited me after the service to his home, which was located down by the seashore. So, after we had eaten dinner, we left in company with him for his house. On the way we stopped to see a man named Blackman, who was married to this Steelman's sister. She was sincerely glad to see me and talked with me about the condition of her soul with great candor. I marvelled at finding her in the middle of a barren land, a soul who had come so far in her Christianity. She had sought God in His holy word and had also read edifying books, combining her search with diligence in prayer.

OCTOBER 11: After dinner I went in company with James Steelman and Mr. Price to a place called Little Egg Harbor, where a sermon was fixed for the following day. We arrived late in the evening at the home of an Irishman named Elisha Clark, by religion a Presbyterian. We were affectionately received and well treated in this house. He lived in the middle of the forest where, by the river called Little Egg Harbor, he had built a saw and flour mill. What especially delighted me here was to find that the man with his entire household feared God. He had built a small wooden church on his property, near the house, and two or three times a year there was preaching by Presbyterian or other ministers.

OCTOBER 12: In the morning, after prayers and after we had eaten breakfast, we went out to see the place and the mills. About half a mile away we saw the loading site on the river, where more than twenty ships now lay to receive the products of the district. There was a tavern[6] run by an Irishman by the name of Wescott, who appeared to be making money to the harm of others and with little concern about God.

We traveled over a sand barren, which was overgrown with a plant the English call Mirtell[7], but is a kind of *pors*. They use its berries to make the beautiful green Mirtell wax. We came back finally at ten o'clock in the evening.

OCTOBER 13: Early in the morning we went out to the ocean where we first rowed over a bay formed by a long narrow island which lies out in the ocean, about half a mile from the mainland. Providence seems to have intended this island as a protection for the mainland against the ocean waves, which otherwise would make their homes insecure, since the loose sand of which the soil is composed would soon be washed away by the violence with which the waves strike the land. This island, which is overgrown with trees, also holds off the chill winds from the ocean which in winter would make their seaside houses more than a little uncomfortable. However, now in the intolerable heat of summer they have a pleasant coolness from the ocean.

Out of the bay we took oysters, which are found here in such abundance that in half an hour we had half filled the boat. We also took quantities of clawed crayfish[8] with a specially prepared scoop. The sea was nearly covered with all kinds of sea fowl such as wild geese, wild ducks, sea gulls, etc., etc. One is permitted to shoot as many as he wants. After we landed on the island and walked about a quarter of a mile, the width of the island, we came to the great ocean and drank of its salt water; it is considered healthful and therefore a great many people, with various illnesses, come here in the spring and summer for two or three weeks to bathe in the water and to drink it. The beaches were covered with mussels, snails and coral, of which I gathered a whole pile. We also saw a kind of crayfish that was one-and-one-half feet in diameter. It was similar to the clawed crayfish, but the shell had the form of a horseshoe, wherefore it is also called the hoof by the people around here. They use the shells as scoops to bail out their punts and boats, but the meat is not eaten. By the seaside we saw a kind of snipe[9]. When the waves receded these ran down to catch the insects that were thrown up; as soon as the waves came back again they ran before them out of the way, and so continued for several hours. This was very amusing to watch.

After we had strolled with the greatest pleasure for two hours and had slaked our thirst with the wild grapes that grow on the island, we betook ourselves homeward. We caught several fish called Sheeps Head[10], so called because the head greatly resembles a sheep. They have functional teeth, otherwise the body resembles an ide[11]. The meat is very white and tastes good. We also shot two wild geese and several other feathered creatures, so that after four hours' absence we came home with a rich supply of foodstuffs.

Thus does the merciful God raise His hand in blessing over these inhabitants, although they know Him so slightly. Oh, that the time may come when His blessing over them may be equally rich in spiritual measure!

NOTES

1. *These Swedes*: The Swedes arrived in Delaware Bay in 1638 and established their headquarters near what is now Wilmington, Delaware. A second colony followed quickly and settled at Raccoon Creek on the east bank of the Delaware River, now Swedesboro. New Sweden eventually covered the present state of Delaware, southeastern Pennsylvania and southwestern New Jersey. Under pressure they ceded their lands to the Dutch in 1655; a decade later the English superseded the Dutch. Colonization continued, however, and Swedish immigrants spread out over South Jersey.

2. *Tavern owned by a man named Scull*: Samuel Scull operated his tavern in Long-a-Coming, now Berlin, on an old Indian trail to the seacoast that later became the Egg Harbor Road.

3. *The Blue Anchor tavern*: The Blue Anchor was further along the old Indian trail.

4. *Raccoon*: Wrangel consistently refers to Raccoon, although the name had been officially changed to Swedesboro the year before.

5. *James Steelman*: His father, James, was the first Swede known to have settled on the Atlantic Coast. The Steelman name survives in Steelmanville and Steelmantown. According to James Steelman, a descendant, the original homestead was near the Linwood-Somers Point boundary, and the island to which they rowed was probably what is now Ocean City.

6. *Wescott's Tavern*: Col. Richard Wescott kept his tavern at a settlement known as The Forks, now Pleasant Mills, near Batsto, from about 1761 until 1781.

7. *Mirtell*: Bayberry, *Myrica pensylvanica*.

8. *Clawed crayfish*: Crayfish is a popular Scandinavian food, but the pastor probably never saw a lobster.

9. *Snipe*: The sanderling, *Crocethia alba*.

10. *Sheeps Head*: A deep-bodied, black-banded food fish, *Archosargus probatocephalus*, living along the Atlantic Coast.

11. *Ide*: A freshwater carp-like fish of northern Europe.

"Pastor Wrangel's Trip to the Shore" first appeared in *The Magazine of New Jersey History*, 1969, 87:5-31. Reprinted with the permission of the New Jersey Historical Society.

1809
Long Branch

Anonymous

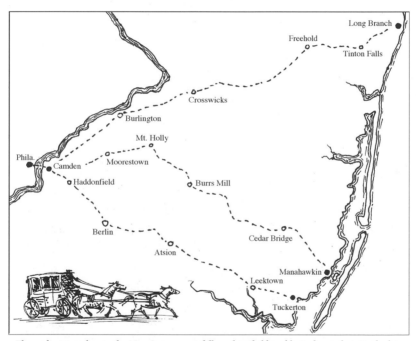

The earliest travelers to the New Jersey coast followed trails blazed by Indian tribes. By the late 18th century these had been widened to accommodate wagons and stagecoaches, and served until the railroads extended service to shore resorts.

The sandy soil near the Long Branch oceanfront was regarded as practically worthless by the farmers who first settled there. They chose to go one mile inland where the land was richer and where homesteaders were protected from northeast storms. The earliest record of a house accepting board-

ers there was about 1790, although the accommodations were casual in that guests were obliged to bring their own beds and bedding. In 1793 the boarding house was improved and promoted as "a watering place." Its proprietor announced in the Philadelphia Dunlap Advertiser *its "good waters, spacious stables and large supply of liquors."*

By 1809, when the anonymous New York Herald *reporter who penned the following critique visited Long Branch, stagecoaches were making scheduled runs from Philadelphia and New York. The resort was gaining a reputation as a spa, and doctors often recommended the waters to their wealthy patients. There was little frivolity in Long Branch hotels: the atmosphere was sedate, with hymn singing, prayer meetings, and grace offered at each meal.*

Mixed bathing in the ocean was strictly forbidden. Men were permitted to swim in the buff at around sunrise — "the gentlemen had the only privilege of disporting themselves in natural abandon" — and an unwritten rule forbade women from coming to the beach before six A.M. *Later in the morning a white flag would be raised to signal that women could swim; a red flag alerted the men.*

Four years ago I took a trip to Long Branch, a bathing place on the shore of the Atlantic sea, chiefly resorted to by the opulent citizens of Philadelphia, etc. I was then much pleased with the charming situation and conveniency of the place for bathing — the salubrity of the sea air — the magnificent view of the ocean, and shipping almost constantly in sight, sailing from or making their way to this and other Eastern Ports — the respectability and sobriety of the company resorting thither; the majority of whom, I was persuaded, came for the improvement of their health and relaxation from the cares of business, at the most leisure season of the year, rather than to spend their money and time in dissipation — falsely called pleasure!

I could not then help thinking it a pity that this inviting place was not more known and resorted to by the New Yorkers[1], being a little more than fifty miles from our city, whilst the Philadelphians have to travel nearly eighty miles to it.

On the beach are three large frame buildings, or boarding houses, each capable of entertaining one hundred boarders which are continually fluctuating — some going, others coming; and considering that the season, on an average, lasts but three months in a year, the terms of board, eight dollars per week, appear to me to be very reasonable. The tables are excellent, plentifully covered with the delicacies of the season; variety of the fish, fresh from the sea — the wines, etc., good and genuine — the proprietors and waiters very attentive — but, the lodging, at all of them, capable of improvement. Among other changes they should substitute Windsor Chairs for the straight backed rush bottom ones in use.

I also suggest a steamboat be started from this city to Long Branch; or one or two packets built for the purpose, furnished with sweeps to row if becalmed in the creek. The price of passage in the present homely packets is three shillings. They stop at Red Bank, six miles from Long Branch, but might easily get within a mile of it, where there is a good landing.

I am an utter enemy to gaming — the ruinous pursuit of the idle and vicious, also to resorts at watering places to trap the unwary, but am a friend to innocent and reasonable amusements, many of which the visitors to Long Branch already have: the sedentary or serious enjoy riding, walking, reading, social converse — a cheerful cigar and a half pint of wine after dinner; the young and gay have dancing and tea parties — excursions to the neighboring villages; and lately horse racing has been introduced which, by the by, I don't like much, but hope it will be hereafter on the Brighton Hotel plan, where there is to be no gaming — which would tend to keep off that corroding disease of the mind, "ennui," and send the visitors and bathers back to their homes and firesides with improved health and fresh relish for the solid comforts of domestic happiness.

NOTE

1. *Resorted to by the New Yorkers:* Steamboat service between Manhattan and Long Branch didn't start until 1828.

From undated clipping, *New York Herald*, 1809.

1809
Tuckerton

Sarah Thomson

The stagecoach Sarah Thomson took on her overnight journey from Camden to Tuckerton was probably similar to this one. Aggressive drivers could lash their team up to 40 m.p.h. on a flat trail.

Sarah Thomson left Philadelphia and crossed the Delaware River to Cooper's Ferry, now Camden, where, with her mother and brother, she boarded a stage-coach for the overnight journey to Tuckerton. Their host in this bustling coastal town of about a thousand persons was Judge Ebenezer Tucker, in whose honor the seaport had been named 23 years earlier. The "beach" to which Captain Gale sailed was Tucker's Island, where the judge's son, Reuben, kept a large house catering to paying guests. Joseph Horner, in whose chair Sarah surreptitiously sat, was the manager. Nothing more is known of Sarah except that which the sprightly young woman reveals in her diary — a fun-loving, adventurous spirit, an awareness of human nature, and the more mundane concern about putting on weight.

Sarah's journal was discovered 106 years after she penned it, tucked in the cubbyhole of a desk in the Tuckerton home of Georgiana Page, daughter of the Eliza in the diary. Eleanor Price, a Tuckerton resident and lifelong diarist, transcribed the original in 1939 and deposited a typescript in the archives of Rutgers University. The final disposition of the original is not known. Though Sarah's mastery of syntax is comparable to her idiosyncratic spelling, I have kept editorial intrusions to a minimum in order to preserve her unique qualities as a diarist; and although it is difficult to read, I have left the first sentence as it appears in the typescript.

JUNE 22: Started for Tuckerton the weather very damp met with a smart Beau in my walk down to the Ferry he immediately joined and escorted us safe over We bid him Adieu walked up to the House to take our passage the stage as they called it for to me it had more the appearance of an old Jersey waggon[1] such as they go to market in but there was no use in complaining we started, nine passengers in all, the back part of the stage was stuffed full of bags banboxes bags without number one poor old man about 80 years of age the poor soul was cramed in among them to beshure he had a soft seat but the Ban Boxes they were flat enough and their contents wich were principlely Sunday Bonnets for the Tuckerton Bells.

Stopted at Haddonfield, saw Mrs Bolton and was very much pleased with her. She made many inquiries after Mr West's family. We was very sociable and dined at Eves Ham. Pewter plates and Wooden spoons. Landlady rather short. Had very good peas and pretty good Lam current pie Sweet with molasses. Left and got pretty well in the Pines and heavy sand and got caught in a Thunder storm lightning, one says, "O dear, O my O, I wish I was with the old man among the Band Boxes." The stage leaked, spoiled my pretty Bonnet. Blessed the stage and its proprietors and the old ragged curtains.

Arrived safe through all our troubles at Quaker Bridge, had a very good supper with clames in abundance, good coffee and very good beds. Landlady very kind. Charles complained of the rats, said they bit his ear, could not discover any mark; he must of drempt it, swears he did not. Started next morning at daylight, a very pleasant ride after the rain. The driver polite he stopted several times to pick us magnolies, water Lily, etc.

Arrived at Tuckerton to dine and found them all well. Aron's[2] eyes as large as ever, too large for my comfort some how, made my mind up not to look at them but had the misfortune to get oppossit to him at table. Changed my position, Judg[3] monsterous polite, Susan and Josephine[4] sweet children, fine fine weather, fine sperits, fine every thing that is fine and clever.

JUNE 23: Took it out in resting and talking, no mosquitoes, great appitite that day.

JUNE 24: Take my turn in drumming at the piano, walk in the evening, very serene walk around Hanover Square[5], very fine wheat, the Judgs land very highly cultivated.

JUNE 25: Charles and Aron go a guning, not much luck, great fatigue and little game. Poor fellows had to cream their faces so blistered with the sun. Charles tore a great hole in his back and Sally had to mend it. Had a dance in the evening. C&A did not come home till 2 oclock, staid out sparking[6]. Sad fellows, Mama scholded, did not mind it.

JUNE 26: Fine day, took a ride down to the salt works.[7] The Horse very troublesome would not go, sulky Devil, however, conquered him at last and had a fine view of the bay. Returning back saw a 4 footed animal sticking in the mud up to his neck, he seemed to sit very composed. He fell through the railing of the Bridge and it was impossible for him to extricate himself without assistance. The alarm was given pretty quick and the poor creature relieved.

JUNE 27: Very cool, put on our flanin peticotes, sewed a little. That day introduced to some fine girls in the evening, had a dance, enjoyed myself very much. Mama and the Judg led down the dance. Aron was my pardoner, he dances very well. Eliza looked very pretty.

JUNE 28: Invited to a quilting frolic, 20 round the frame, looked at them a little while and come home to bed and had a nap. Dreamed of Arons eyes and cryed because I had not them. Most crazy with the pain in my face, staid out too long in the night air, dose it up with garlic. Had a fine ride in Judg Cranes carriage and tandam, rode up to see Mr. Deacons country seat, fine prospect but nothing else to recommend it. Mama taken very ill with the cholic, all very much frightened, hot oil, laudanum, etc., much better, able to ride out, must not eat any more radishes. Had a fine walk in the wood, find tea berry leaves, love them dearly. See a great Black Snake, got off before we could kill it. Magnolies in abundance, C&A picked a fine parcel to decorate the chimney.

JUNE 29: Embarked for the Beach, Judgs family, mama, Charles and myself. Fine breeze but notwithstanding met with some trouble on our road such as getting a thump with the oar now and then, low and behold we all got batared. My pretty silk peticote is gone to the shades. Blessed Capt Gale from the bottom of my heart, got safe to the Beach and found the landlady in the straw, set about to get breakfast. Eliza made the short cake, Margrett[8] the coffee, I opened clames and laid the table. C&A split some wood to make the kittle boil. Made up a very good breakfast.

Went to take a nap, dreamed of the *Shaddow*[9], thought we picked L[?] and John up half drowned on our Beach. Give them some coffee and short cake. Just agoing to look at the wreck when up comes Mag and wakes me. The *Shaddow* and all is gon, not a vestage left not even poor L. All a dream, blame it, so it was.

JUNE 30: Very bad back ake, tryed to clean my peticote. Got the stomack ake and could not do any thing with it. Prepared to take a ride. The Horse got into a mulish fit and the Devil could not move him. Four at his head and C at his tail, beat, punched and poaked in every quarter, all would not avail. Give up the ride when low and behold the Judg knocked him down for dead. He did not lay long, got up pretty quick and started spanish[10] round Hanover Square and so round about till we was tired.

JULY 1: Took a walk in the afternoon. Called to see old Dinah, clever old soul but she did not give us any cheries, Josey was a bed, could not see him, continued our walk. Aron and me lost our company some how or other, obliged to walk home alone. Found my walk very agreeable notwithstanding.

Introduced to Dr Garrison, very tall, fine eyes, commanding figure. No fault excepting his pantiloons being different couler and coat tail too short and looked too much at Margrett. Got jelious. She too, to crown all, looked uncomonly hansome that evening. He loves her I do think but I suspect she dont care too much for him. Had the honner of his company to dance. Very good spring, jumps admirable, had like to upset Miss Deacon in one of his springs. He lodged with us that night, snored very well, prevented me from sleeping.

JULY 2: Sweet day, all went to meeting, very much pleased with Mr Budd who preched with moderation. Some of the good folks growned very much. Come home wrote some poetry on Dr Garrison and Margrett. He left us in the afternoon. Margrett sighed and I went to bed, dremp nothing. Walking in the evening. Charley still at Deacons. Mother dont like it, sends over for him, he wont come. Sent Margrett for him, he through cherry stones at her, give Charley a pinch and brings him off. The Deacons swear vengenace. Charles not a bit pleased. Margrett is scolded for interfearing and me too for taking Charleys part. All this work for a little innocent sparking, poor fellows, how I pity them.

JULY 3: Notwithstanding all this went over to Deacons again for our strings. Sally Deacon tied Charlie. Our mother looked very Grim. Took a walk down to the launch, was chased by a mad Bull, was deprived of our walk. Met the Judg and wanted to get on behind him. He would not let me because the Horse would kick up. Of course, I would meet with the same fate and that would not be so clever. Came home just time enough to set down to a capital dinner, Turtal soup, dessert, cold coustard, fritters, drank to the *Francis* and the *Shaddow*. Wished them safe home. Thought of Miss Nixon and Maria, determined not let my sweetheart go to sea, that is wen I get one. Swoarn enemy against engagement. If you love each other, that is enough.

JULY 4: Rather dull, damp, rainy. The people seemed to caught the infection and appear sleeping away the most glorious day, a day that gave them Freedom. Cleared up in the afternoon, and people began to stir. I here the cannon, the Tuckertonians begin to shew themselves. This day must be remembered, oration was read, toast was drank, got quit over there lethergy and the 4 of July was celebrated quit in style.

Took a ride over a great stump, had to get out, began to put up a prayer. Horse began to be mulish, began to pray in earnest how to get home, fortune smiled got on again, arrived safe, spent the afternoon at the Deacons. Mrs Deacon a fine old woman, one of her daughters very hansome. Had dance in the evening, Eliza looked butifull, dance till 12 oclock, had plenty of cherry pie, looked up me and Aron in the dark, took it out in dancing.

JULY 5: Sweet day. Walked in the morning, got a rideing the saplings in the afternoon, took a ride on horseback and went to meet C & A. Did not see but one tract. Nancy Deacon greatly distressed about it, found two tracts at last, give our nags a cut and tore through the woods like two furies. Met the gentlemen at last and low and behold they got speechless, thought we was some crazy girls. Soon convinced them to the contrary and returned home. Our ride lay through a beautiful woods, violets, magnolies and roses. The evening very mild. Went a sparking.

JULY 6: Went to Hawken[11] in the afternoon. The Judg and mama, Charles, Margrett & Miss Deacon rode in the waggon. Aron and my pretty self went in the gig. Very pleasant ride, just got in the door and it began to rain. Arrived at Mr Grays, very much pleased with the family indeed. Quaker, but so kind and every body so fat. Fine prospect from the bay. Staid all night, room too close, had like to smothered, 4 of us in one room, too close, knocked my elbow against the petitions, for the first time found the mosquitoes troublesome.

JULY 7: Left Grays ferry, called at Judg Cranes. Very good kind of a man. Called at Hawken, went a shopping, seen Kaly Wright, bought a pair of shoes of him and a thimble. He looked quit smiling, grown very fat. Got some string and started for Tuckerton. Took some cake and wine. Too tired to dance in the evening. Set ourselves down to a dish of Politics. As we were all Demoes could not of had much argument. Stage arrived, flew to hear the news, did not get any letters, read the papers.

JULY 8: Introduced to Mr Dean, monsterous man to beshure a second Goliah. He talked much of Kaly Wright, runed down Samy Smith, did not thank him for it. Tooked Samys part, soon got in a good humer again for he told me Caly and Dr Gant was coming the next day to see us. Margrett dashed away at cleaning house, suds began to fly, brushes and soap, Dear O Dear every thing begin to change couler, even the very brick, in fact where ever she touched her hand it began to shine.

JULY 9: Fine day indeed. We have the finest weather in the world here. Went to Quaker Meeting, got the back ake, no wonder, had no back to there benches, no preaching. People got to nodding. Come to a very good dinner. Got low-spirited for low and behold the doctor and Caly never come. They had quarterly meeting in there town, no wonder. Staid to see the pretty girls I suppose. Had Aunty Chases company in the afternoon, took a walk, in the evening went over to Mr Deacons, saw Danny Shin, right clever little fellow. Looks very hard at Sally Deacon. Sally looked quit interesting.

JULY 16: Sunday morning, fine day. Went to here Mr Mills preach.

Liked him pretty well, quit refined in some of his ideas but people did not understand him, some went to sleep. Had preaching at Quaker meeting, had a walk in the afternoon. Aron, Miss Deacon and myself lost the rest of our company so we bent our way to old Josey Ridgway. Found him sitting up and a young man reading the Bible to him. Did not stay long. Went to see old Dinah, nice old creature, came home. Went to get some dew berrys, could not find any. We all walked round Hanover Square about 20 times.

JULY 17: Got a making cards to play wist[12]. Had a sort of a pack but not enough. Aron made king and Queen, did very well. Plaid wist. Got teribley beet.

JULY 18: Ceres, goddess of plenty, must not be forgoten, she is reeping in her favors. The reepers are crowding in for there diner, seemed to like there rice pudding very much. Took a peep at them through the window, round went the can, the jest, the glee. Took a liking to one with the blue jacket. He cleverest looking I think but I have heard parted from his wife, dont like that much and she was a mighty pretty woman too, what a pity.

JULY 19: Most terible day, got the Blue Devils, not only me but mother. Aron would not smile, no not for a kingdom, got mad at last, went upstairs. Got to singing, the only way to forget myself. Had some talk in the evening, got so mad went to bed. Mama very uneasy about the boys. The wind blew very hard, thought of the *Francis* and the *Shaddow*.

JULY 20: A death. Poor old Jack fell down in the night, could not get up again, took a spasm, ended up with the lock jaw, poor creature. Drawn off to the woods for the crows to pray on. Quit a loss to the Judg. Walked in the afternoon for huckleberries, musquitoes plenty and Ticks O Ticks by thousands, scratch all night. Ran over to see Sally Deacons bed quilts but the best of all was brought me, a quart bowl full of huckleberries and milk. Quit a treat.

JULY 21: Receive letters, great joy. One from Brother Sam. Delighted to here he visits with his cousin Anthony at Fyall[?]. Mad at Joe for not writing, so taken up with partys. Got a letter from Cousin Dick, he thinks I am going to be married, very much mistaken. Took tea at Dr Towers. Very clever family, there house very pleasantly situated, fine view of the bay, dance in the evening, taken with a very bad headake, leave the dance. Fever in my head, get frightened, come home go to bed, take some cordial. Sleep pretty well.

JULY 22: Saturday find my head much better, crimp shirt and darn stockings. Look hard for Dr Garrison, dont come, try the woods again for huckleberrys, get enough to eat but the woeful insects wont let us alone, come home most bit to death. Spent very quiet evening, somehow felt myself happy that evening, dreampt a queer drame about aunty Streitches[?] family.

JULY 23: Lovely day, talk of going to Quaker Meeting, changed our minds & all go to here Mr Jenkins preach. Disappointed, Mr Jenkins sick, great many of the good folk prayed most terible loud. Was ready to come out several times. Mr Wardell brought us a fine parcel of dew berries in the evening.

AUGUST 10: A party of us went over to Bass River, had a walk on the river. Fine supper, boiled chicken, coffee and short cake. Went after a fiddler but mans wife not let him come. All tearing mad, had a great notion to go and tye the woman and fetch the husband off, concluded to dance by our own music. Started for home at nine, kept it up a dancing after we got home until 11 oclock.

AUGUST 11: Started for the Beach, mama, Eliza, myself, Aron and Charles. Pleasant sailing. Found the landlady runing about as well as ever. Coffee, short cake and shell fish for dinner. All went in the surfe but me. How funny mother looked when she com from behind the white hills in her white flanin peticote, put me in mind of one of the witches in Macbeth.

AUGUST 12: Very cool, did not go in the surfe, went a rideing in the ox cart, hunted birds eggs. Charley got a handkerchief full, fetched them home to make egg nog, found them all full of young ones. Ha ha ha. Had a great laugh upon Charley. Poor mother, as I got out the cart tilted up, and down went mother with her head in the sand. Her eyes turned up, we all thought she was gone to Davy Jones locker. She was stuned at the time but soon recovered, very bad pain in her head that night. Was very uneasy about her, was afraid her brain was affected but it appeared to be Rhumatism.

AUGUST 13: Mama much better. C and A went a fishing, no luck. Took a long walk on the beach, come home with wonderfull apitite. Drank a quart of butter milk, they called me Miss Guzzel, break my peticote string every day. Shall certainly get too fat.

AUGUST 14: Fine day, all went in the surfe. Find myself very much refreshed. Went to sleep, got up with a great apitite. Aron and me went a walking on the Beach, the sea looked grand, the roaring of the waters and the white foaming waves all seemed combined to add to the buty of our walk. Meet Charley agoing again in the surfe, his suspenders broke and he seemed to be in such trouble about his small cloths that I turned about and walked homeward. Was agreeable supprised, found some of our acquaintance from the city. Very glad to see them tho we did not know where to put them. Great consultation. Agreed to put C and A on the floor to sleep. I could not sleep for thinking what a heard birth they must of had, great mind to give them a piece of my bed.

AUGUST 15: Give up our place at the Beach for our city friends. Detained by a sloop to take some groceries for some of the Tuckertonians, mama did not like it a bit. Set in one of Mr Horners chairs, hope nobody dont tell Mr Horner. Arrived safe to dinner, found the greene yard decorated with the Harvest table. Glad of it. Put my mind upon carrying the Luntion. Heard that Reuben Tucker was married, dont believe it.

AUGUST 24: Nothing particular excepting my being very much troubled with the headake occationed by my eating too much milk — cant help it, I do love it so.

AUGUST 25: Still bad headake. They tell me about takeing salts, blame the salts, and I must be bled and pucked[13]. Begin to think about coming away.

AUGUST 26: Fine weather, Tuckerton is certainly a very healthy place, never hot here. They have such fine sea breezes. Sick stomach, it is the milk, I have give it up. They wont give me a drop to save my life. They say cannot think of taking medicine after being so hearty.

AUGUST 27: My head much better, getting out of the notion of pucking. Mr Evens family and Deacons are all gon to the Beach. Talk of bringing the violin over and having a dance up at the Tavern.

AUGUST 28: Could not get the fiddle so all the danceing knocked in the head. Had a little kick up of our own in the evening, danced fishers hornpipe and what beet all, the Judg can tire us all out at dancing. I could not join in there dance so went to bed sick.

AUGUST 29: A lovely day, everybody in a good humer. See Nathan Willis. Nathan clever looking fellow. Saw Obediah Squeek just come. Skunks misery, Lord help him I say, it is enough to make him squeek to some purpose.

Sarah's diary ends suddenly. Eleanor Price, in a note appended to her typed copy, says that the diary became more illegible toward the end and speculates that Sarah might have died in Tuckerton or was too ill to remember to take her diary when she returned to Philadelphia.

NOTES

1. *Jersey waggon:* The original Jersey wagon was designed in the 1730s to transport farm produce and other goods. It was heavy and cumbersome, requiring four to six horses to pull it. Eventually, the colonists cut it down in size, making it suitable for passengers; but the springless ride over rutted roads would have been jarring.

2. *Aron:* Aaron was Judge Ebenezer Tucker's son. He became a physician and married Elizabeth Carroll, granddaughter of Charles Carroll, a signer of the Declaration of Independence.

3. *Judg:* Judge Tucker had his fingers in every imaginable pie. During his 88 years he was a merchant, ship owner, real estate agent, surveyor, collector at the Customs House, district judge, postmaster, member of the House of Representatives and Tuckerton's wealthiest citizen.

4. *Susan and Josephine:* Children of the Judge's second marriage to Phoebe Ridgway.

5. *Hanover Square:* The only full square in town, bordered by Main, Green, Church and Wood Streets.

6. *Sparking:* An obsolete term for hugging and kissing.

7. *Salt works:* Marine Street was formerly known as Salt Works Lane. The salt works was thriving during the American Revolution; its ruins below Bartlett's Landing were still visible in the early part of the 20th century.

8. *Margrett:* Margaretta Tucker was Reuben's daughter; she married Daniel Budd of Pemberton.

9. *Shaddow and Francis:* These were probably two coastal schooners on which Sarah's friends were seamen.

10. *Started spanish:* Spanish was a style of riding.

11. *Hawken:* Manahawkin is about eight miles north of Tuckerton.

12. *Wist:* The card game whist was an early form of bridge.

13. *Bled and pucked:* Sarah probably meant cupping and bleeding, a medical practice widely used until the end of the century. To be bled, according to Harry B. Weiss in *Life in Early New Jersey*, a patient was seated in a chair with his arm on the back of another chair. A tourniquet was applied and a superficial vein in the elbow was lanced. An assistant caught the blood in a basin. When the patient became lightheaded a compress was placed over the wound and the arm was put in a sling for 24 hours. Cupping involved producing a vacuum in a cup by heat, then placing the cup over the skin. In wet cupping, the swelling produced by the vacuum was scarified and blood was taken.

The diary of Sarah Thomson is in the Special Collections and University Archives, Rutgers University, New Brunswick, New Jersey. It was first printed in *The Beachcomber*, July 1972.

1828
Long Beach Island

Unknown

Casks, masts, sails and cables were salvaged from a barque that had run aground. The merchandise was auctioned off on the beach by the wreckers who had recovered it.

Many of New Jersey's barrier beaches were originally named for their length: *Two-mile Beach (north of Cape May City), Five-mile Beach (the Wildwoods), and Seven-mile Beach (Stone Harbor to Avalon) along the southern coast and Short Beach (Tucker's Beach), Long Beach, and Nine-mile Beach (Island Beach). The usage has been dropped by all of them except Long Beach Island, and until well into the 20th century "Island" was not always appended to*

Long Beach. When the anonymous writer of this tale first visited Long Beach, its southern end was called Horner's Beach since some names of the coastal islands referred to their original settlers, as in Ludlam's Beach (Sea Isle City) and Peck's Beach (Ocean City).

Boarding houses had also sprung up behind the dunes further north on the island. Two small establishments offered rooms across the bay from Manahawkin as early as 1820, and five years later James Cranmer completed a large hotel on the edge of the "Great Swamp."

Joseph Horner knew a good opportunity when he saw it and left his managerial position on Tucker's Beach to start his own place on Long Beach, just across the inlet. By 1821 he had sold to a Philadelphia consortium — some of whom were former guests — who upgraded the old building and established the Philadelphia Company House as one of the finest on the coast.

The following impressions seem to be a composite of the reporter's two trips, and he was fortunate to arrive when wreckers were conducting an auction on the beach, after a British barque had run aground.

Long Beach, situated midships between Sandy Hook and Cape May, is a sea island twenty miles long, and at the south end one mile broad. It is separated from its neighbour, Tuckers Beach, by an inlet to Egg Harbor Bay. These islands, or sand bars, thrown all along the coast form a natural breakwater defending the mainland from the direct fury of the "vexed sea," at the same time giving shelter to the coasting vessels which slip in through the inlets to the different bays, where they ride in safety from the NE storms until a change of weather. They may then be seen edging away, Indian file, towards Cape Cod, as far as the eye can reach. Separated from the mainland, Long Beach can be approached only by water, across the bay, seven miles from Tuckerton (the emporium of the Egg Harbor world), and sixty miles ESE from Philadelphia. It is now a place of considerable resort during the bathing season, and yet known only to those who have penetrated the Pines on their way to this "end of the earth."

In search of health and novelty, a few years ago we took stage at Camden before daylight; arrived at Clem's, through Longacoming[1], passed through the then deserted village of Atsion, and having rattled over various corduroy bridges, we arrived at our last stopping place on the road to Tuckerton. While the horses took their bite of hay, we walked on just before evening to Bass River bridge while the silvery moon, riding high, struggled with day light through the tops of the pines. There, in the midst of deep silence, [we saw] a twilight fairy scene broken only by the swift rush of the pure stream of living water against the washed and tangled roots of red cedar, and the beautiful shrill note of bob-white from a startled partridge. We dipped, each of us on bended knee, a drink, with a mammoth clam shell, from the cedary stream, holding on to the tangled roots with one hand, while drinking out of the shell with the other.

Emerging from the pines, a change of atmosphere was perceptible and [we] were informed that now we sniffed the ocean air. One of the passengers exclaimed, now for Clam Town![2] This being the original name of the place we were rapidly approaching. We very readily imagined some dozen log huts, the largest one an inn with clam shells stacked behind the oven. What was our surprize, when, after passing a kind of suburb and under a row of willows bending over a bridge or dam thrown across the outlet, to a large sheet of water or mill head on the left, and up a handsome straight street — we beheld in the distance two elegant hotels lighted up in front, and an assembled crowd awaiting the arrival of the mail and passengers.

The appearance of Tuckerton next morning was as agreeable as unexpected. Directly opposite was seen the mansion house of Judge Tucker. Standing back from the main street, and deeply shaded by the willow and lombardy poplar, it was evident some considerable person resided there. As is his custom, he came after breakfast and gave us, as strangers on our way to the surf, the civilities of the place. Being First Day, we went along to Friends Meeting (near the bridge), shaded by venerable oaks, with the usual accommodations for carriages that Friends have in country places every where. After the meeting, we observed the Judge mingling among, and shaking cordially by the hand, his friendly country neighbours.

After dinner, about twenty passengers embarked in a small sloop, which, by the aid of two men with a long rope, was towed along the bank against the tide, down a serpentine salt water creek two miles to Egg Harbor Bay. Taking leave of the mainland, we stretched across with a fair wind and a gentle swell. After a miniature sea voyage of seven miles over a bay studded with small islands of salt-grass, we anchored at Horner Beach.

The house at that time [before 1821] was only of limited accommodation, and considering circumstances, was excellently well kept by Mr.

Horner, aided by a widow relative, highly respected, well known to visitors as Aunt Becky. The property has been since purchased by a company of gentlemen of the city; their additions and improvements have been such, that on going over there the last season, it seemed as though Alladen's Lamp had been at work. Instead of the sunburnt leafless sea coast, we found a spacious sea shore hotel with all the requisites of ball room, excellent bar, well furnished table and comfortable lodging for one hundred persons. The company of well dressed persons of every shade of fashion seemed thrown together like cabin passengers on board a ship at sea — in number about enough not to make a throng — and civility and good humor the order of the day.

Persons visiting this portion of the sea coast the first time are struck with the strange wilderness of the scenery around, so very different from that of the deep valley or mountaintop. On entering within the Pines, the attention is arrested by the visible remains of fire on each side of the road. The standing trunks of pine, scathed and black from fire which had devoured the underbrush, and mould — leaving all bare to the white sand, giving to the eye the appearance of winter in August, and the ground covered with a deep snow. Then may be, the chance view of a wild deer crossing the road at a single bound. Then, after you embark at Tuckerton, the muddy sides of the creek are alive with a whimsical marine animal about the size of one's thumb, called Fiddlers, retrograding rapidly about crab fashion, each one with a large claw folded above him, looking like a boy with a bass viol on his back.

Then the variety of aquatic birds observable in crossing the bay. Flocks of willets, sheerwater and brown backs on the wing, in wheeling order — presently broken and dispersed by a quick shot from the deadly level of a gun. Snow-white, and then blue sea cranes[3], wading about on some passing island in the slimy mud. The fish hawk[4] high aloft in air, looming large on extended, motionless wing — moving in curved lines to and fro. An immense pile of pine wood, cut and corded, lying on a small island in the centre of the bay.

Then the singular appearance of Long Beach ahead, like a long black streak with Wickham House upon it, looming gradually from the waterline as you now approach rapidly from the boat — the crowd from the house, pressing forward on the landing-place, to get a sight of the new come's — the hearty welcome, good cheer at the house, and plenty of everything but sand! Then the first pilgrimage through the green-topped sand hills on a plank causeway to the edge of ocean, now seen the first time. The interminable din from a strong surf rolling forever along the beach, eastward as far as you can see. The snow-white sea gull screeching just over head. The black hog-backed porpoises, emerging in quick succession along the outer surf. The distant ship with all sail set, stretching off to Europe, and gradually sinking below the horizon. The breakers far at sea like flocks of white sheep gamboling on the dark hill side.

Groups of umbrellas and parasols on the sand hills, small parties, generally ladies, intently occupied in looking about the sand for beautiful marine shells cast up by the sea — picturing the while to their imaginations the eager delight with which they would be viewed by some little favorite left at home, to whom they had promised to bring shells from the sea shore.

Then the surf dearborn[5], emerging from the sand hills, drawn securely slow by oxen, and well loaded with invalids on their way to the bathing house. Then again, the moonlight view at night, along the sea-beat shore, the moon reflected and lying for hours in a log line of harmless fire stretching leagues on leagues to the rim of the Ocean. Then from the piazza on the bay side, beholding in a dark night the Vesuvius appearance twenty miles off in Jersey, caused by a fire in the pines — then nearer hand in the bay, the lighted torch looming large and blazing from the bow of a boat anchored off bobbing for eels.

Last not least the dancing room lighted up after supper with lights placed in a circular wooden chandelier, characteristically and fancifully decorated with green bayberry leaves and chalk white clam shells by way of glass drops and reflectors. The cook, one of Johnson's Band giving the tuning scrape on a deep toned violin with an occasional bravura touch, and "coming through the rye" indicating his readiness to accompany the "light fantastic toe."[6] The regular cotillion occasionally broken in upon by the three and six handed reel, danced with all their might and main by three wild, but merry young bucks (wearing large leghorns[7]) with their girls, come over on a frolic from the main — funds vanishing between the bar and the fiddler like a straw fire. Eleven o'clock all lights out, the cook snoring.

Next morning, may be, the piled baggage on the piazza gives rise to the friendly enquiry of "who is going." Then the cavalcade to escort the departing good fellows with the ladies under their care down to the bay side, headed by the great Captain and music from the gunner and the cook with haut-boy[8] and violin in marching order. The repeated adieus — the silent waiting to see them all on board the anchored sloop — the hoisting sail — the three cheers from those on board echoed by those on shore. The departure of a large portion of such a company leaves a vacuum not immediately replenished.

Hearing that a British barque bound from Liverpool to Brazil had so far missed her reckoning as to go quietly ashore at the next island, a boat load of us sailed across the inlet to see the wreck sale on the strand. From the landing place on the bay side we beheld on the piazza of the house, quarter of a mile off, a dense crowd of persons — at our approach they filed away in a long line towards the sheer hulk — high and dry two miles off.

Under the balcony in front, clam shells nailed to bear a name and white washed so often as to appear part of the woodwork, indented with some hundred names, cut time out of mind. Three parasol looking cedar trees shading a small group of the wrecked sailors who were smoking by turns their only pipe, while jawing over their strange disaster. The Old Tritons of the neighbourhood forming on the route part of the rear group, headed by the old shipwrecked British captain seated in a chair fixed on a cart, drawn along the strand by oxen. He was lamed, probably by his exertions while the ship was driving ashore. The shore a way ahead, all alive with busy bodies moving to and fro near the wreck. The whole affair similar to the whale ashore scene near the residence of Magnus Troil in the Orkneys[9], as described by the "great known" in his novel of the pirate. Coming up to the hulk, a sudden notice from Col. Tucker, the wreckmaster, caused a quick huddling together of the wreckers[10] around the camboose — old sheathing copper, casks, masts, sails and chair cables, dragged ashore on the sand, and now to be knocked off to the highest bidder. As is usual at all such gatherings every where, there are generally those who go for fun, and one of those plays clown to the company. The old British captain sat in his chair at a little distance from the sale, leaning on his cane. Tumbling about in the sand, the one playing clown, in friendly scuffle, came head over heels near the lame legs of John Bull — with reddened visage he raised his cane, but did not strike.

The long, thin, good natured looking "native" being fired at the sight of the uplifted cane, sprung instantly on his feet — then advancing with steady eye and clench'd fist he informed the Captain, with suppressed breath and tone, he was not on board his ship now, but on shore. The thing passed away like a shadow — only exhibiting for a moment the living posture of a real John Bull sea captain — and a genuine bay-shore spirited Jonathan.

The flotsam and jetsam, it seems, all went off at fair wreck prices. Prejudiced by a name, we expected to see wreckers with savage aspect — rain wetted, sundried, and murder in each eye. We are compelled by observation and just feelings to declare the miserable prejudice we laboured under. At this wreck sale at sea — seven miles from any main-land on an island and on sand, we observed among the mainland throng no noise or clamour other than of real business.

When all was over, they separated quietly into groups, discussing their probable loss or gain. People living near the sea coast are always excited by the stranding of a vessel, especially a large one. It is all at least a novelty, equal to the appearance of "the Garcia"[11] or any other star on the boards of the theatre. And when the proceedure is well regulated, as it is at Tuckerton district by the authority of a wreckmaster appointed by the government of the United States — these wreckers are always a ben-efit to the stranded property and never an injury — as had been hereto-fore impressed on the mind.

NOTES

1. *Longacoming:* An early name for Berlin, in Camden County.

2. *Clam Town:* A colloquial name for Tuckerton, which was originally called Little Egg Harbor; in 1786 the name was officially changed.

3. *Snow-white and blue sea cranes:* Snowy egret or little blue heron in white plum-age and great blue heron.

4. *Fish hawk:* A local name for osprey.

5. *Dearborn:* The *Oxford English Dictionary* defines a dearborn as "a kind of light four-wheeled wagon. U.S. 1841." From this 1828 reference we can see that it was in use earlier than 1841. The Dearborn Historical Museum in Dearborn, Michigan, told me that this sturdy wagon was invented for the overweight General Henry Dearborn, Secretary of War under President Thomas Jefferson.

6. *Light fantastic toe:* A line from the poem "L'allegro" by John Milton. "Come and trip it as ye go, on the light fantastic toe."

7. *Leghorns:* Finely woven straw hats.

8. *Haut-boy:* Oboe.

9. *Magnus Troil in the Orkneys:* Magnus Troil was a character in Sir Walter Scott's novel *The Pirate.*

10. *Wreckers:* Men who were licensed to salvage and sell bounty gathered from shipwrecks, in contrast to those who intentionally caused a wreck by misplacing lights, leading mariners to mistakenly head for inlets that weren't there.

11. *The Garcia:* Garcia (1778-1836) was an internationally famous Spanish opera singer who made his American debut in 1825.

Poulsen's Daily Advertiser, May 16, 1828, volume 57, no. 16,052. Reprinted with the permission of the Historical Society of Pennsylvania.

1829
Great Egg Harbor

John James Audubon

During his visit to Great Egg Harbor, Audubon sketched this osprey clutching a weakfish. He observed upwards of 50 nests in one day.

A despairing business associate of John James Audubon complained that he neglected his material interests, "Forever wasting his time, hunting, drawing and stuffing birds, and playing the fiddle. We fear he will never be fit for any practical purpose on the face of the earth."[1]

Nonetheless, what Audubon did exceedingly well was roam the North American frontier, from the Florida Keys to Newfoundland, observing, identifying, collecting and drawing the birds of this continent. During the summer and fall of 1829, the 44-year-old naturalist made his headquarters in Camden, gathering specimens on field trips around the state and into Pennsylvania. At Great Egg Harbor he made drawings of the bay-winged bunting, the yellow-breasted chat, the warbling fly-catcher, the golden-crowned thrush, the small green-crested fly-catcher, the rough-legged falcon and an osprey clutching a weakfish. All of this original artwork was reproduced in his monumental Birds of America, *which was published in four volumes of plates and five volumes of text between 1827 and 1839.*

Some years ago, after having spent the spring in observing the habits of the migratory warblers and other land birds, which arrived in vast numbers in the vicinity of Camden in New Jersey, I prepared to visit the sea shores of that State, for the purpose of making myself acquainted with their feathered inhabitants. June had commenced, the weather was pleasant, and the country seemed to smile in the prospect of bright days and gentle gales. Fishermen-gunners passed daily between Philadelphia and the various small seaports, with Jersey wagons, laden with fish, fowls and other provisions, or with such articles as were required by the families of those hardy boatmen; and I bargained with one of them to take myself and my baggage to Great Egg Harbor.

One afternoon, about sunset, the vehicle halted at my lodgings, and the conductor intimated that he was anxious to proceed as quickly as possible. A trunk, a couple of guns, and such other articles as are found necessary by persons whose pursuits are similar to mine, were immediately thrust into the wagon, and were followed by their owner. The conductor whistled to his steeds, and off we went at a round pace over the loose and deep sand that in almost every part of this State forms the basis of the roads. After a while we overtook a whole caravan of similar vehicles, moving in the same direction, and when we got near them our horses slackened their pace to a regular walk, the driver leaped from his seat, I followed his example, and we presently found ourselves in the midst of a group of merry wagoners, relating their adventures of the week, it being now Saturday night. One gave intimation of the number of "Sheep-heads" he had taken to town, another spoke of the Curlews which yet remained on the sands, and a third boasted of having gathered so many dozens of Marsh Hens' eggs. I inquired if the Fish Hawks[2] were plentiful near Great Egg Harbor, and was answered by an elderly man, who with a laugh asked if I had ever seen the "Weak fish" along the coast without the bird in question. Not knowing the animal he had named, I confessed my ignorance, when the whole party burst into a loud laugh, in which, there being nothing better for it, I joined.

About midnight the caravan reached a half-way house, where we rested a while. Several roads diverged from this spot, and the wagons separated, one only keeping us company. The night was dark and gloomy, but the sand of the road indicated our course very distinctly. Suddenly the galloping of horses struck my ear, and looking back we perceived that our wagon must in an instant be in imminent danger. The driver leaped off, and drew his steeds aside, barely in time to allow the runaways to pass without injuring us. Off they went at full speed, and not long after their owner came up panting, and informed us that they had suddenly taken fright at some noise proceeding from the woods, but hoped they would soon stop. Immediately after we heard a crack; then for a few moments all was silent; but the neighing of horses presently assured us that they had broken loose. On reaching the spot we found the wagon upset, and a few yards farther on were the horses, quietly browsing by the roadside.

The first dawn of morn in the Jerseys in the month of June is worthy of a better description than I can furnish, and therefore I shall only say that the moment the sunbeams blazed over the horizon, the loud and mellow notes of the Meadow Lark saluted our ears. On each side of the road were open woods, on the tallest trees of which I observed at intervals the nest of a Fish Hawk, far above which the white-breasted bird slowly winged its way, as it commenced its early journey to the sea, the odor of which filled me with delight. In half an hour we were in the center of Great Egg Harbor.

There I had the good fortune to be received into the house of a thoroughbred fisherman-gunner, who, besides owning a comfortable cot[3] only a few hundred yards from the shore, had an excellent woman for a wife, and a little daughter as playful as a kitten, though as wild as a Sea-Gull. In less than half an hour I was quite at home, and the rest of the day was spent in devotion.

Oysters, though reckoned out of season at this period, are as good as ever when fresh from their beds, and my first meal was of some as large and white as any I have eaten. The sight of them placed before me on a clean table, with an honest and industrious family in my company, never failed to afford more pleasure than the most sumptuous fare under different circumstances; and our conversation being simple and harmless, gayety shone in every face. As we became better acquainted, I had to answer several questions relative to the object of my visit. The good man rubbed his hands with joy, as I spoke of shooting and fishing, and of long excursions through the swamps and marshes around.

My host was then, and I hope still is, a tall, strong-boned, muscular man, of dark complexion, with eyes as keen as those of the Sea-Eagle. He was a tough walker, laughed at difficulties, and could pull an oar with any man. As to shooting, I have often doubted whether he or Mr. Egan, the worthy pilot of Indian Isle, was best; and rarely indeed have I seen either of them miss a shot.

At daybreak on Monday, I shouldered my double-barrelled gun, and my host carried with him a long fowling-piece, a pair of oars, and a pair of oyster-tongs, while the wife and daughter brought along a seine. The boat was good, the breeze gentle, and along the inlets we sailed for parts well known to my companions. To such naturalists as are qualified to observe many different objects at the same time, Great Egg Harbor would probably afford as ample a field as any part of our coast, excepting the Florida Keys. Birds of many kinds are abundant, as are fishes and testaceous animals. The forests shelter many beautiful plants, and even on the driest sand-bar you may see insects of the most brilliant tints. Our principal object, however, was to procure certain birds known there by the name of Lawyers[4], and to accomplish this we entered and followed for several miles a winding inlet or bayou, which led us to the interior of a vast marsh, where after some search we found the birds and their nests. Our seine had been placed across the channel, and when we returned to it the tide had run out, and left in it a number of fine fish, some of which we cooked and ate on the spot. One, which I considered as a curiosity, was saved, and transmitted to Baron Cuvier.[5] Our repast ended, the seine was spread out to dry, and we again betook ourselves to the marshes to pursue our researches until the return of the tide. Having collected enough to satisfy us, we took up our oars, and returned to the shore in front of the fisherman's house, where we dragged the seine several times with success.

In this manner I passed several weeks along those delightful and healthful shores, one day going to the woods, to search the swamps in which the Herons bred, passing another amid the joyous cries of the Marsh Hens[6], and on a third carrying slaughter among the White-breasted Sea-Gulls; by way of amusement sometimes hauling the fish called the Sheep's-head from an eddy along the shore, or watching the gay Terns as they danced in the air, or plunged into the waters to seize the tiny fry. Many a drawing I made at Great Egg Harbor, many a pleasant day I spent along its shores; and much pleasure would it give me once more to visit the good and happy family in whose house I resided there.

NOTES

1. *Forever wasting his time:* This was quoted by Les Line, editor of *Audubon* magazine, in April 1985.

2. *Fish Hawks:* Audubon wrote, "Fish Hawks are very plentiful on the coast of New Jersey, near Great Egg Harbor, where I have seen upwards of fifty of their nests in the course of a day's walk, and where I have shot several in the course of a morning. When wounded, they defend themselves in the manner usually exhibited by Hawks, erecting the feathers of the head, and trying to strike with their powerful talons and bill, whilst they remain prostrate on their back... The largest fish which I have seen this bird take out of the water, was a Weak-Fish, such as is represented in the plate, but sufficiently large to weigh more than five pounds. The bird carried it into the air with difficulty, and dropped it, on hearing the report of a shot fired at it." (*The Birds of America,* Volume 1, Dover Publications, Inc., New York, 1967)

3. *Cot:* cottage.

4. *Lawyers:* Black-necked stilt, *Himantopus mexicanus*.

5. *Baron Cuvier:* Georges Cuvier was a noted French naturalist and paleontologist who had arranged for a show of Audubon's work in Paris the previous fall.

6. *Marsh Hens:* Clapper rail, *Rallus longirostris*.

From *Audubon and His Journals,* Maria R. Audubon. Two volumes, New York, 1897.

1848
Cape May

Rebecca Sharp and Henrietta Roberts

The two young Quaker women stayed on the second floor of Cape May's Ocean House. The 1878 fire that destroyed most of the business district started in the old wooden hotel.

Summer visitors had been going to New Jersey's southernmost tip since at least 1766, when the Philadelphia Gazette *reported that Cape May was the place for healthy sea bathing. On July 1, 1801, Ellis Hughes advertised his Cape Island public house in the* Philadelphia Aurora and General Advertiser *as having a "beautiful situation, just on the confluence of Delaware Bay with the Ocean in sight of the Light-house. The slope of the shore is so regular that persons may wade a great distance. It is the most delightful spot the citizens can retire to in the hot season." The lighthouse was built in 1785 but was destroyed by the 1821 hurricane, which also severed the tip of the cape. The beacon tower that Rebecca Sharp and Henrietta Roberts climbed was completed just the year before their 1848 visit.*

Hughes' son built the grand Congress Hall in 1816. (It was rebuilt after fires in 1818 and 1878 and still stands.) In 1822 a Philadelphia writer observed that the village had about 20 houses and that "all the gentry of Delaware and Philadelphia" had arrived. A decade later, Richard Ludlam opened his elegant, three-story Mansion House. The resort was booming: President and Mrs. Franklin Pierce and other nationally known figures went there to play in the surf or to gamble at the Blue Pig or Jackson's Clubhouse. Three thousand guests were said to have summered there in 1844, and Israel Leaming's stately — though not tightly built against the elements — Ocean House had been open eight years when Rebecca and Henrietta moved into their third-floor front room.

The two young Quaker women penned a record of their July "pleasure excursion" to Cape Island in a flowing script and titled it Sea Side Leaves. The pair were accompanied by "CCR, Hiram R and joined by SWR," probably Henrietta's brothers or cousins. Which girl did the actual writing is uncertain, although it seems to have been Henrietta, who had beautiful penmanship and perfect spelling, even if her writing style was sometimes stilted. Based on the girls' interest in the parade of young men they met at the shore, their age might be guessed as young marriageable, and they probably had been recently presented to society. Many of the names they mentioned (not included in this excerpt) are still known in Philadelphia.

The young women came by steamship from Philadelphia and landed on the bayside of the cape, and in a Jersey wagon bumped eastward for two and a half miles along a crushed-shell road to the barnlike wooden hotels fronting on the ocean.

7th MONTH, 15th: Having safely arrived at this delightful and fashionable watering place, are snugly ensconced in an apartment 6 feet by 8 and corresponding height. Were received with open arms by Mrs. John White who has taken us under her very kind and motherly protection[1] tho' no one would credit her with daughters our age. Ushered into our apartment, found it expedient to mount the bed, the floor having the appearance of a recent deluge. Joined in penning our *Sea Side Leaves*.

After tea a moonlight walk, concluded with a visit to the Columbia[2] to be produced to a party of 8 mostly Misses Binghams. A very satisfactory hours confab, bade good night and wended our way to Mrs. Tompkins' ice cream saloon. Delighted with the events of the day, repaired to our third story front, enjoying for awhile the grand views of the ocean and "Millers" directly before us.

The after part of the Sabbath morning was spent in our chamber, initiating the nails into the wall hanging thereon 13 bonnets and hats, including bathing hats and sun bonnets, arranged circulating library, fixed everything in apple pie order, and mounted our Island Home (the bed). Seriously engaged in the contents of a tract, were aroused by a gale of wind which capsized into the wash basin 2/8 of our circulating library, medicine chest and jewelry.

It would be impossible to describe the perfect splendor of the evening. The moon rising in its glorious majesty from the ocean threw a radiance over Sea & Sand, and our spirits, soothed into a calm, contemplated the scene with reverence & delight.

17th: Arose at 20 of 6 oclock to fulfill an engagement for an early morning walk on the beach. Arriving at the trysting gate, found our last night's escort not punctual, but at the same time, our Wilmingtonian friend appeared & with him we sought the sea. Were very soon joined by the missing one.

At 1/2 past 2 oclock drove off in a carriage to join another party at the Columbia. Had a delightful drive to Cold Spring, there refreshed with mineral water. After tea, not wishing to soil our ball dresses on the beach, remained at home in an animated conversation with the Baltimore widower, Mr. Bradford & Mr. Browning. Then repaired in a large body to the "Kurdall" to witness the trippings on the light fantastic toe. Delighted with the dancing, dressing, refreshments, and numerous attendants.

4th DAY: Took an early morning walk on the beach with Hiram, who we consider A-Number 1, joined by Anne Bingham, escorted her to the Columbia, returned in good time for breakfast. After which a puff from the widower who has put himself to no little trouble to inquire who and what we are. Knowing our untarnished Philada [Philadelphia] fame, we fear no inquiries. In turn we also have made ourselves acquainted with his Baltimore reputation, finding it without blemish, in possession of an emmence establishment, carriage & horses. Have concluded to accept any little attentions he may proffer.

At 11 oclock rigged for our salt bath, joined a large party from the Columbia. Returning met our friend Andrew Miller on the stairs in the act of being carried up by Wm Parrish, [Miller] having been seized with a fit of oppression in the water.

With crimson shawls, bare arms & neck, the Binghams arrived, and our party of six soon crossed to Millers to enjoy the hop. Met there many Philadelphians. At midnight Hen writing and Rebecca fallen into the arms of Morpheus. Then a startling knock at the door to inform us of the intoxicated state of the poet, owing to an overdose of opium & mint juleps — Our nerves were quite unhinged, at 1 oclock retired.

5th DAY: Declined an invite to accompany a crabbing party. Attired for bathing. Rebecca, whilst riding the billows with T Mellor, was conveyed by the undertow with such unresisting sway that she believed herself rapidly on her way to England. T Sharpless kindly offered his life preserver. Hen & the widower floated laughingly in the distance. After dinner drove to the Columbia for our party, rode to Poverty Beach[3] & the contents of the vehicle were soon in the arms of Morpheus in each others laps. Returning passed thro' the Borough for the light house, on the road encountered the boat's 200 passengers. Arrived at our destination, ascended the wearying steps, but at the top were recompensed by the glorious view. Some singing on our homeward journey added much to the enjoyment.

Encountered the widower who inquired if we were in want of a bosom friend. Replied in the affirmative, he drew from the inside of his vest a beautiful sand-crab, which he harnessed and had galloping around, much to the amusement of the gathering household.

Our second Sabbath: Promenaded the balcony before breakfast with Wm Parrish, then repaired at the sound of the bell to the table, our grace being pleasingly interrupted by an epistle from our dear, departed "mother," Mrs. John J. White. [The letter begins] "My dear, delightful darling daughters. I have felt so uneasy about you since I left, that for my own satisfaction must send you a little advice, that may prove a safeguard to you amid the trials and temptations to which you are exposed. How does my substitute make out, does he extend his protecting wing over you? Please tell him I do not intend to have any more sand pets, this poor little one has cost me such a heart ache. It seemed so fine in its box of sand, so to give it a little air & exercise we took it out & attached a string to its leg which we fastened to a post. But it walked itself off, leaving its leg behind. So to ease it of its misery I put it in alcohol & made up my mind as I watched its dying struggles that henceforth sand crabs should be undisturbed by me..."

2nd DAY, 24th: Visited again the light house, recorded names. Home & preparations for bathing, R with Joshua Jeanes, H with Wm Parrish. Were joined by the widower, all floated delightfully. After dinner accompanied Cale to the beach to witness a boat race. Returning stopped at Tompkins to lay in a store of sweet meats. At the gate were met by the widower with a pet curiosity in the shape of a jelly fish.

4th DAY, MORN: Had quite a long stroll thro' the sand, which reminded us of the "great desert," procured some rare plants & our friend the naturalist supplied us with shells & dug up a sand crab, which was gliding gracefully about, much to our diversion. Home in time for bathing. Hen's dear brother Solomon [arrived] laden with epistles for sis Hen, also a joint letter for the both of us from Mother White, viz. "Many thanks, my dear, dutiful daughters for the promptitude & candour with which you answered my carelessly written note. But a pang shot thro' my bosom, as you recounted the many persevering attentions of Pantaloons! Be cautious, be dignified & polite in your intercourse with him, it seems hard to turn the cold shoulder upon one so polished & winning. I fully agree with you that to stroll on the beach with a congenial spirit, to drink in the sublimities of nature with one who appreciates them as you do is indeed delightful. How much more so to walk thro' life by the side of such an one, knowing your feelings are reciprocated, your thoughts — your wishes — your opinions the same. Such is the fate I crave for you my darling daughters.

"But do not, I beseech you, rely too much on passing attentions, remembering that the acquaintances of a watering place are but of the hour. Allow them to make no deeper impression than your foot-prints make upon the sands."

NOTES

1. *Motherly protection:* Mrs. White was, in effect, acting as a chaperone to the two girls. Their male brothers and cousins would also be expected to keep an eye on them and to protect them from unwanted advances.

2. *Columbia, Atlantic, Washington, Millers, Leamings:* All hotels on Cape Island (the name would be changed to Cape May City in 1869). Millers was Congress Hall, owned by Jonas Miller.

3. *Poverty Beach:* This is now the site of the U. S. Coast Guard training base in Cape May City.

————————

Sea Side Leaves, the diary of Rebecca Sharp and Henrietta Roberts, reprinted with the permission of the Greater Cape May Historical Society.

1850
Cape May

Frederika Bremer

In the mid-19th century modest bathers frolicked in the surf while fully dressed.

By midcentury Cape May was vying with Long Branch for the claim of being the most popular resort on the Jersey Shore. A New York publication wrote of the "infinite trail of restaurants, barber shops, ice cream saloons, bowling alleys, billiard rooms, pistol galleries, bathing houses — the little city really grows metropolitan in aspect." New hotels were built and Long Branch experienced remarkable growth, even as the rest of the country was mired in a sluggish economy prior to the Civil War. President James Buchanan visited in 1859, and vacationers from Washington and Wilmington joined the Phila-delphia regulars. Frederika Bremer, a 49-year-old Swedish novelist, had been traveling throughout North America for the previous eighteen months record-ing her impressions. After watching Congress in session in Washington, Bremer journeyed to Philadelphia, from where she took the steamer to Cape May.

AUGUST 1: I went from Philadelphia with Professor Hart and his wife, on a beautiful July day, to Cape May; and beautiful was our journey upon the mirror-like Delaware, with its green, idyllian, beautiful shores. During the day I read Mr. Clay's "Annals" of the Swedish Colony[1] upon these shores, and experienced heartfelt delight in glancing from the his-torical idyll to those scenes, where it had existed in peace and piety. The temerity and the war-like dispositions of two of the leaders, Printz and Rising, were the cause of disturbances which ultimately led to the over-throw of the colony; but the people themselves were peaceful and con-tented. The names which they gave to different places, New Gotheborg, Elfsborg, &c., prove the affection which they bore to the mother coun-try. And how enchanted they were with the New World is shown by the name of Paradise Point[2], which they bestowed upon a point where they landed, on the shore of the Delaware, and by many anecdotes preserved by their Swedish annalist, Campanius. Here, in the Vineland of the old Sagas, did the Swedes find again the wild vine, and many glorious fruits which they mention. Here, amid these beautiful, sunbright hills and fields, they lived happily, even though under a foreign sway; for, says the chronicle, "the new government was mild and just toward them; but it caused them to forget their mother country." The memory of that first colony upon these shores is, however, like the fresh verdure which cov-ers them. I contemplated them with affection. Peace and freedom had been planted here by the people of Sweden.

In the evening we reached Cape May and the sea.

And now for the republic among the billows; not at all "high life," excepting as regards certain feelings. It is now about ten o'clock in the morning; a very parti-colored scene presents itself on the shore at an early hour; many hundreds, in fact more than a thousand people, men, women, and children, in red, blue, and yellow dresses; dresses of all colors and shapes — but the blouse-shape being the basis of every costume, however varied — pantaloons and yellow straw hats with broad brims, and adorned with bright red ribbon, go out into the sea in crowds, and leap up and down in the heaving waves, or let them dash over their heads amid great laughter and merriment. Carriages and horses drive out into the waves, gentlemen ride into them, dogs swim about; white and black people, horses and carriages, and dogs — all are there, one among another, and just before them great fishes, porpoises, lift up their heads, and sometimes take a huge leap, very likely because they are so amused at seeing human beings leaping about in their own element.

It is, as I have said, a republic among the billows, more equal and more fraternized than any upon dry land; because the sea, the great, mighty sea, treats all alike, roars around all and over all with such a superiority of power that it is not worth any one's while to set themselves up in opposition to it, or to be as anything beside it; the sea dashes over them all, dashes them all about, enlivens them all, caresses them all, purifies them all, unites them all.

Among the citizens in the billows you must particularly notice one couple, a citizen in grand flame-colored attire, and a citizeness in a brown, cabbage-butterfly-striped woolen gown. The citizeness distinguishes herself by her propensity to withdraw from the crowd to some solitary place, by her wish to be independent, and her inability to keep her footing against the waves; and these waves hurl her piteously enough upon a sand bank, where she is left alone to her own powers and a trident (a three-tined fork) with which she endeavors to keep herself firm on the ground, but in vain; while the citizen goes back to take out his wife. This couple are Professor Hart and the undersigned. Presently you might see me rise up out of the water, tired of struggling with the waves and being dashed on the bank — now sitting upon it like a sea-mew[3], surrounded by white-crested, tumultuous billows — now contemplating the ocean and infinite space, and now that parti-colored company among the waves by the shore — very unlike that in the Capitol of Washington! Here human beings do not appear great, nor remarkable in any way, and more like ungraceful, clumsy beasts than the lords and ladies of creation, because the garments in which they are attired are not designed to set off beauty.

I was at first almost frightened at the undertaking and the company, and at the unlovely, apparent rudeness of this kind of republic; but I longed for the strength of the sea, and thought, "We are all as nothing before our Lord, all of us sinners, poor wretches all of us!" And I went out among the rest. And though I am not yet as much at home among the waves as I see many others are, yet I am already enchanted with this wild bath, and hope to derive much good from it. It gives me a peculiar impression of a something at once grand and delightful; the waves come on like a giant, strong, but at the same time kind, gentle, and mighty, almost like a god, at least like the power of a god, full of health-giving life, so that when I feel them sweeping over me, I involuntarily seem to think that it would not be hard to die amid them.

With Professor Hart and his wife I get on excellently; they are quiet, kind, earnest people; they let me do as I like. I have a nice little room near theirs, with a fine view over the ocean, which here, without islands or rocks, rolls up unimpeded upon the low sandy shore; I hear its roar day and night from my open window, for I have for several months slept with my window open and the Venetian shutters closed, as people do here generally. I rest and enjoy myself as I have not hitherto done in this country. The restless mind, however, labors still, writes romances and dramas, the scenes of which are all laid in Sweden, although the scenes here have given life to them; but I live for Sweden in all that I do and all that I imagine.

AUGUST 10: How beautiful it is to be here; how pleasant to pause from going out to see things, from the excitement of hearing, and learning, and from social life and conversation! How good it is to be alone, to be silent, and quiet! And the sea! the sea! that grand, glorious sea, how soothing and refreshing it is to contemplate it, to listen to it, to bathe in it! I sit every morning, after my breakfast of coffee, Carolina rice, and an egg, by the sea-side under a leafy alcove with a book in my hand and gaze out over the sea, and into the vast expanse of sky; see the porpoises in flocks following the line of the coast, and hear the great waves breaking and roaring at my feet. The porpoises amuse me particularly; they go, for the most part, in couples, and pop their heads up out of the sea as if to say "good morning," making a curve of their bodies, so that the upper part is visible above the surface of the water; after this curved movement, made slowly and with a certain method in it, they plunge their heads down again and vanish in the waves, but are soon seen up again doing the same as before. They are large fishes, I should imagine about two ells[4] long, and seem in form not to be unlike our largest salmon, and they have something very grave in their movements as they offer us their salutations from the deep; sometimes, however, they give great leaps.

But I must now tell you about my life at Cape May. I pass my mornings in company with the sea and the porpoises. When the tide comes in — as for instance this morning at half past ten — and the waves advance further and further on the sands, I attire myself in bathing costume, and thus go out into the sea, but before the great crowd assembles there, and let myself be washed over by the waves, most frequently having hold of Professor Hart's hand, sometimes in company with a lively Quaker lady, a niece of Lucretia Mott[5]; sometimes also alone, for I have now become quite expert in wrestling with the waves, and in keeping my balance in them. One remains in the water about a quarter of an hour, and it feels so pleasant that one is quite sorry to come out. After this bathing, I go to my chamber, write a little while my hair dries, drink a glass of good ice-cold milk with a piece of excellent wheaten bread, and then lie down on my bed for an hour, where, hushed by the great cradle-song of the sea, I fall asleep directly, as lightly and pleasantly as, I imagine, little children slumber to their mother's lullaby.

When I wake, I dress myself quickly for dinner. The dinner hour is two, and a noisy scene it is! There sit, in a large light hall, at two tables about three hundred persons, while a thundering band is playing, waited upon by a regiment of somewhat above forty negroes, who march in and maneuver to the sound of a bell, and make as much noise as they possibly can make with dishes and plates, and such like things, and that is not a little. They come marching in two and two, each one carrying a dish or bowl in his hands. Ring! says a little bell held aloft by the steward, and the dish-bearers halt. Ring! says the little bell again, and they turn themselves to the table, each one standing immovably in his place. Ring! and they scrape their feet forward on the floor with a shrill sound, which would make me ready to jump up if the whole of their serving were not a succession of scraping, and shrill sounds and clamor, so that it would be impossible to escape from their noisy sphere. The dinners are, for the most part, very good, and the dishes less highly seasoned than I have been accustomed to find them at American tables, and especially at the hotels. Although I here always find a deficiency of vegetables, yet I am fond of one which is called "squash" and which is the flesh of a species of very common gourd here, boiled and served up much in the style of our cabbage, and which is eaten with meat. It is white, somewhat insipid, but soft and agreeable, rather like spinach; it is here universally eaten; so also are tomatoes, a very savory and delicately acid fruit, which is eaten as salad. On the second course I dare not venture to eat anything but sago pudding or custard, a kind of egg-cream in cups, and am glad that these are always to be had here.

One standing dish at American tables at this season is the so-called "sweet corn." It is the entire corn ear of a peculiar kind of maize, which ripens early. It is boiled in water and served whole; it is eaten with butter and tastes like French "petit pois"; they scrape off the grains with a knife or cut them out from the stem. Some people take the whole stem and gnaw them out with their teeth; two gentlemen do so who sit opposite Professor Hart and myself at table, and whom we call "the sharks" because of their remarkable ability in gobbling up large and often double portions of every thing which comes to table, and it really troubles me to see how their wide mouths, furnished with able teeth, ravenously grind up the beautiful white, pearly maize ears, which I saw so lately in their wedding attire, and which are now massacred, and disappear down the ravenous throats of the sharks. When I see that, I am convinced that if eating is not a regularly consecrated act — and is it not so in the intention of the grace before meat? — then it is a low and animal transaction, unworthy of man and unworthy of nature.

After dinner I again sit with my book in my hand, contemplate the sea, and enjoy the life-giving sea-breeze. Some bathing again takes place toward half past five, when the tide again rises, and occasionally I also take a second bath, but in a general way I find that once a day is sufficient, because the wrestling with the waves makes bathing fatiguing. I mostly about that time take a walk, and sometimes call on people who have visited me, either in this great hotel where we are, or in some of the small cottages scattered about. When it gets dark, and it gets dark early here[6], I walk backward and forward in the upper piazza which runs round our hotel — the Columbia House — and contemplate the glorious spectacle produced by the lightning, and the unusual eruptions of light with which the heavens have favored us every evening since I have been here, without being audible. The one half of the vault of heaven during these wonderful lightning-exhibitions will be perfectly clear and starlight; over the other half rests a dense cloud, and from its extremities, and from various parts of it, flash forth eruptions of light such as I never saw before; fountains of fire seem to spring forth at various points, and others they flash and sparkle as from the burning of some highly inflammable substance; gulfs open full of brilliant and colored flames which leap hither and thither; and from the edges of the cloud where it appears thin and gray, spears and wedge-like ashes are sent forth incessantly, while toward the horizon, where the clouds seem to melt into the sea, it is illuminated by far-extended and mild gleams of lightning. In short, it is an exhibition of celestial fire-works which are always new, astonishing, and, to me, enchanting. We have had two magnificent thunder-storms, when the lightnings flashed and crossed each other over the ocean, so that it was a really grand spectacle. The weather just now is perfectly calm, and the days and nights are uninterruptedly delicious and beautiful.

We have frequently music and earthly fire-works on the beach opposite our hotel, so that we do not experience any want of cheerful amusement. To the same category belong the cavalcades of gentlemen and ladies on the beach, driving about in light, little carriages, the crowds of pedestrians wandering along the shore, seeking and finding Cape May diamonds, small, clear crystals, which, when cut, present a remarkably clear and beautiful water. Later in the evening, when the moon rises, Professor Hart and myself may often be seen among the pedestrians; for I like to hear him develop his thoughts on the subject of education; I like to hear his method of awakening and from year to year anew awakening and keeping alive the attention of the boys, and calling forth their peculiar faculties into full self-consciousness and activity. His theory and his practice in this respect seems to me excellent; and the progress of his school, and the ability and the cleverness of the boys in their various ways, when they leave the school, testify to the correctness of the principle and the excellence of the method.

The roar of the sea is generally lower in the evening than in the day, the slumbrous light of the moon seems to lull the restless billows, and their song is one of repose. Sometimes I go to a little distance inland, and listen to the whispering of the maize in the evening breeze — quiet, soothing sound! Thus approach night and sleep to the great cradle-song of the sea. Thus pass the days with little variation, and I only wish that I could prolong each twofold. It is said that the number of bathers here is from two to three thousand persons.

"Miss ——, may I have the pleasure of taking a bath with you, or of bathing you?" is an invitation which one often hears at this place from a gentleman to a lady, just as at a ball the invitation is to a quadrille or a waltz, and I have never heard the invitation refused, neither do I see any thing particularly unbecoming in these bathing-dances, although they look neither beautiful nor charming; in particular, that tour in the dance in which the gentleman teaches the lady to float, which, however, is not a thing to be despised in case of shipwreck.

Very various are the scenes which on all sides present themselves in the bathing republic. Here a young, handsome couple, in elegant bathing attire, go dancing out into the wild waves holding each other by the hand, and full of the joy and the courage of life, ready to meet any thing, the great world's sea and all its billows! There, again, is an elderly couple in gray garments, holding each other steadily by the two hands, and popping up and down in the waves, just as people dip candles, with solemn aspects, and merely observant to keep their footing, and doing all for the benefit of health. Here is a young, smiling mother, bearing before her her little, beautiful boy, a naked Cupid, not yet a year old, who laughs and claps his little hands for joy as the wild waves dash over him. Just by is a fat grandmother with a life-preserver round her body, and half sitting on the sands in evident fear of being drowned for all that, and, when the waves come rolling onward, catching hold of some of her leaping and laughing great children and grandchildren who dance around her. Here a graceful young girl, who now for the first time bathes in the sea, flies before the waves into the arms of father or mother, in whose embrace it may dash over her; there is a group of wild young women holding each other by the hand, dancing around and screaming aloud every time a wave dashes over their heads; and there, in front of them, is a yet wilder swarm of young men, who dive and plunge about like fishes, much to the amazement of the porpoises (as I presume), who here and there pop their huge heads out of the billows, but which again disappear as a couple of large dogs rush forward through the water toward them in the hope of a good prize. Sometimes, when one expects a wave to come dashing over one, it brings with it a great force of ladies and gentlemen, whom it has borne along with it, and one has then to take care of one's life.

Three life-boats are continually rowing about outside this scene during the bathing season, in order to be at hand in case of accident. Nevertheless, scarcely a year passes without some misfortune occurring, principally from the want of circumspection in the bathers themselves, who venture out too far when they are not expert swimmers. The impulse of the waves in the ebb is stronger than in the flowing tide, and it literally sucks them out into the great deep; and I can not, in such case, but think upon the legend of our mythology, about "the false Ran"[7] which hungers for human life, and drags his prey down into his bosom. There is no other danger on this coast; porpoises are not dangerous, and of sharks there are none excepting at the dinner-table.

A shipwreck has lately occurred not far from Cape May, which has crushed the hope of many a heart and has made a deep impression upon thousands of minds in the Northeastern States. One stormy night during July, a brig was stranded upon a rock on the coast of New Jersey. This brig conveyed to her native land the Marchioness Ossoli (Margaret Fuller[8]), and with her came her husband, the Marchese Ossoli, and their little boy. They all perished, after having seen death approach for four hours while the waves dashed to pieces the vessel which had borne them hither.

After the death of the captain, the first mate took the command of the vessel. He seems to have been an expert seaman, and so certainly calculated on bringing his ship safe into port, that the evening before the disaster occurred he assured the passengers that on the morrow they should be in New York. All, therefore, went to rest and were awoke in the early dawn by the vessel being aground. The helmsman had mistaken one beacon in these roads for another. They were not far from land, and the waves were running toward the land, so that several of the passengers had themselves lashed to planks, and thus came to shore, although half dead. This mode of saving her life was offered to Margaret Fuller, but she refused it; she would not be saved without her husband and her child.

Before her embarkation from Italy, she wrote to one of her friends in America, "I have a presentiment that some great change in my fate is at hand. I feel the approach of a crisis. Ossoli was warned by a fortune-teller in his youth to beware of the sea, and this is his first great voyage; but if a misfortune should happen, I shall perish with my husband and my child." And now the moment which had been foreshadowed to her was come, and she would perish with her beloved ones!

A sailor took the little boy and bound him to a plank together with a little Italian girl, and threw himself into the sea with them, in the hope of saving them. They told Margaret Fuller that they had safely neared the shore. They told her that Ossoli also was saved. And then it was that she consented to be lashed to a plank. She never reached the shore. A wave had washed Ossoli from the deck into the deep. The corpse of neither has ever been found; but the little boy was found upon a reef of sand, still lashed with the little Italian girl to the plank, but both were dead.

AUGUST 12: All continues to be delicious and good! The sea, the heavens and their grand show; the warlike games of Valhalla, which take place every evening, in which heroes and heroic maidens hurl their flaming spears; the embraces of the sea during the day; the song of the sea at night; freedom, peace in the open air — ah! how glorious is all this!

Professor Hart enjoys the bathing and the life here as much as I do, and little Morgan flits about like a sea-gull, now on the shore and now in the water, barelegged and brown, and as happy as a free lad can possibly be on the sea-shore.

I have derived pleasure from my acquaintance with an amiable family, or rather two brother-families from Philadelphia, who live in a cottage near here for the benefit of sea-bathing. Mr. F., the elder, is the minister of a Unitarian congregation in Philadelphia, one of the noblest, purest human beings whom God ever created, true, fervent, and full of love, but so absorbed by his anti-slavery feelings that his life and his mind suffer in consequence, and I believe that he would with the greatest pleasure suffer death if by that means slavery could be abolished. And his lovely daughter would gladly suffer with him, a Valkyria in soul and bearing, a glorious young girl, who is her father's happiness as he is hers. This grief for slavery would have made an end of the noble minister's life had not his daughter enlivened him every day with new joy and fascination. She is blonde and blue, like the Scandinavian "maiden" of our songs, and considerably resembles a Swede. The wife of the second brother is a brunette, delicate, beautiful, witty, charming as a French woman, a great contrast to the fair "Skoldmo,"[9] but most delightful. She is the happy mother of three clever lads. The Valkyria has three brothers. The two families live together in beautiful family love. That which I see in this country of most beautiful and best is family-life and nature, as well as the public institutions, which are the work of Christian love.

Among the novelties here at the present moment are some Indians who have pitched their tent in the neighborhood of the hotels on the shore, and there weave baskets and fans according to Indian taste, with other small wares which they sell to any body who will buy them. The men are half-blood Indians, but the women are true squaws, with black, wild elf-locks, and strong features. They are ugly, but the children are pretty, with splendid eyes, and as wild as little wild beasts.

There is a "hop" every week in one of the hotels, that is, a kind of ball, which, I suppose differs only from other balls by people hopping about with less ceremony. I have not had the heart to leave the companionship of the sea and the moonlight to go to a ball and see human beings hopping about; neither have we here been without scenes of a less lively character. We have had a great battle in one hotel between the black servants and the white gentlemen, which has caused some bloody heads. The greatest share of blame falls upon a gentleman who owns slaves. He will be obliged to leave. There have been two attempts at murder in another hotel, but which were prevented in time. The blame of these is laid upon a negro, but still more upon the landlady's treatment of her domestics in this hotel. All the waiters here are negroes or mulattoes.

AUGUST 16: There is now an end to my good time! To-day I set off to New York. I regret leaving Cape May, which is to me so quiet and invigorating; but I must not linger any longer, I have so much yet to see and to learn in this country.

NOTES

1. *The Swedish Colony:* In 1642 John Prinz was appointed governor to the colony by the Swedish queen. In 1656 John Rising became governor and attacked the Dutch fort at New Castle. Peter Stuyvesant retaliated and sailed down from New Amsterdam with seven warships and forced the Swedes to submit to Dutch rule.

2. *Paradise Point*: Most likely Clark's Point, nine miles northeast of Milford, Delaware, where colonists had stopped before reaching what is now Wilmington.

3. *Sea-mew*: A small gull, *Larus canus*.

4. *Ells*: An obsolete unit of measure used most commonly in Europe.

5. *Lucretia Mott*: A feminist reformer and abolitionist who lived from 1783 to 1880. When women were denied status at the 1840 World Anti-Slavery Convention in London, she and Elizabeth Cady Stanton organized the first Women's Rights Convention in Seneca Falls, New York.

6. *It gets dark early here*: At this time of the year in Sweden, Bremer would have been accustomed to an 11 P.M. sunset.

7. *The false Ran*: In Norse mythology Ran was the goddess of the stormy sea and the drowned: she dragged down ships with her bare hands.

8. *Margaret Fuller*: A Utopian Transcendentalist, poet, teacher, critic and writer on social problems. Extremely well educated for a woman, she was fluent in many languages. She went to Italy in 1846, married, and was writing a book about a hero of the Italian war of liberation when she died on her voyage home.

9. *The fair Skoldmo*: This could refer to *Skuld*, one of the three Norns, or fates, usually virgins, who in Scandinavian mythology predestine the life of god and man at birth.

From *Homes of the New World*, volume 1, translated from the Swedish by Mary Howitt, edited by Adolph B. Bensen, New York, 1854. Reprinted with the permission of the American-Scandinavian Foundation.

1857
Long Branch

Anonymous

Steamships had ferried excursionists between Manhattan and Long Branch since 1828, although the iron ocean pier wasn't built until 1879.

Long Branch had become less stuffy by the 1830s: Card playing, billiards, bowling, dancing, and racing horse-drawn wagons on the beach were pulling in a livelier crowd; visitors were not solely interested in "taking the waters" for their health. The majority of tourists were New Yorkers, who came on the scenic steamer voyage described in this account, but Philadelphians still had to put up with the rigorous, dusty, overland journey by stagecoach. That inn-keepers were said to have attempted to "rub the dirt off their faces to see whether they were serving Negroes by mistake" is a reminder of the racial

prejudice of the times, and that the Mason-Dixon line passed through south-
ern New Jersey.

Improved accommodations, obliging hosts, the panorama of passing ship-
ping, good gunning and fishing, and a clean, high shoreline with a gently
sloping beach kept pleasure-seekers coming and stimulated expansion of the
resort. Five new hotels were built along the bluff during the 1840s, and by the
time Mary Todd Lincoln came in August 1861, a more elegant Long Branch
had space for more than 4,100 guests. When the president's wife arrived for a
ten-day visit, the American flag floated all along the beach, from every hotel,
and over front doors for miles around. The First Lady had given Long Branch
her imprimatur, and the resort had arrived.

The anonymous reporter who wrote this article came before Long Branch
had its own landing — when visitors still had to ride in beach carriages along
the sandy shore between the Shrewsbury River dock and "The Branch".

Long Branch, now-a-days, seems to be quite a fashionable watering
place. People flock there to breathe in the delicious sea breezes, and
stroll along the shore, and bathe in the salt waves; and latterly the great
influx of stragglers from the beau monde has brought Long Branch before the public in the decided position of a highly popular resort.

Last week, being thoroughly wearied of the furnace-like atmosphere
and burning streets of this modern Gotham, we determined to set out
on a pilgrimage in search of some cool spot where the fresh winds were
not flavored with smoke, and blasts from close, narrow lanes, and the
sunshine could strike on green grass and white sands, instead of being
reflected from glowing pavements and brick walls. Safely embarked on
board the enterprising little steamer Alice Price, at the foot of Robinson
Street, it was but a short time before we were clear of the forests of
shipping which fill the New York Harbour, and en route for Long Branch.
Three boats leave daily for this watering place, one generally starting in
the morning and two in the afternoon, but the exact hour of their departure is for the most part regulated by the tides.

The deck, protected from the fervor of the sun's rays by an awning,
was dotted with all sorts of groups and parties. Every available inch of
room was crowded with pleasure-seekers, and if one might judge from
their manners and appearance, they were entirely successful in their
search. Portly merchants, fresh from Wall Street and Broadway, reclined

easily on the chairs and settees, and drank in the delicious winds, as if they were so many draughts of hock or champagne; ladies forgot that the sun would brown their lily complexions, and leaned against the railings with utter abandon, while a score of bright-eyed babies and children rolled and reveled on the deck as only young folks can. In secluded corners, pretty girls in a halo of crinoline, French rosebuds and kid gloves, found attractive company in sentimental young gentlemen, who talked of "life on the ocean," and looked unutterable things, while comfortable family groups who had outlived the age of romance ate sandwiches, read the papers, and chatted together in the old-fashioned social style. We were surprised to see the boat so full, and supposed it must be an unusually favorable day, but the captain, a polite and agreeable personage, told us that the Long Branch boats were always crowded — an important evidence of the good taste of the world in general! The scenery along the Bay was exquisite; we glided past the velvet shores of Bellew's[1] and Governor's Islands, the tapering shaft of the Light-house, and the picturesque landings at Staten Island, and almost ere we were aware, had passed the Narrows, and were in the Lower Bay.

But here some of our fellow-voyagers began to look a little doleful, and to experience "singular sensations" as the steamer commenced to rock and heave with the tide. The pretty young ladies grew pale, and retreated precipitately to the "below stairs" regions, the young gentlemen leaned over the rails, and contemplated the water with an air of fixed attention, and the genial-looking old fogies lost their contented aspect in a pitiful expression of discomfort. But some were exempt from this annoying trial, and we, being among that fortunate few, looked on with all the philosophy, which generally characterizes those who are called on to pity, and not to endure.

In the Lower Bay we crossed to Sandy Hook, and entered Shrewsbury River, here separated from the ocean by the long stretch or bar of land of which Sandy Hook forms the extreme point. Here began the sea-swell in good earnest, and the salt breezes, wafted across the bar, blew off gentlemen's hats, set ladies' mantles fluttering, and showed not the smallest respect to rank, age or sex.

We passed any quantity of shoals of fish, darting higher and thither in the shallow water in this neighborhood. "O Look! there's a whale," screamed one of the ladies, clinging to her companion's arm, as one of these scaly creatures leaped into the air with a sudden splash. We all sprang to our feet, expecting to behold some terrific monster of the deep, armed in a complete panoply of teeth and claws — a shark, or leviathan at the very least: but when this frightful creature proved to be merely an insignificant little porpoise, sporting in the water with its comrades, we had a hearty laugh both at the lady's terror and our own panic!

Up Shrewsbury River to the first steamboat landing, at the Highlands of Nevesink, was a short and pleasant progress, but soon after we ran aground and came to a dead stop, much to our discomfiture. However, the captain told us that this was by no means an unusual occurrence. At this point, during certain tides, the water is frequently very shallow, and as we had chanced on one of these periods, all we had to do was to wait patiently until the tide should think proper to help us out of our dilemma again.

Nevertheless, we contrived to elicit a great deal of sport from this embarrassing position. We indulged in plenty of good natured raillery, and cracked several capital jokes over ourselves and our situation, and when again the dilatory tide took us off and "set us afloat" again, there was a general rejoicing.

The Highlands of Nevesink are extremely romantic, and as we glided along a panoramic succession of lovely views met our eyes, such as are to be witnessed in few other localities. The fine light-houses at a short distance from the beach, the cottages scattered along the shores, and the long line of purple woods, which we could just distinguish along the background in the evening twilight, which was beginning to close around the scene, gave a life and animation to the whole picture, which was all it needed to be one of the finest prospects in the United States.

In this neighborhood we passed a fine hotel, called the Sea View House, and the name is singularly appropriate, for it commands a magnificent prospect of the sea, over the narrow neck of land on the other side of Shrewsbury River. Two miles further on we reached the Ocean House, where we were finally landed, and the *Alice Price* pursued her way up the river.

The Ocean House is finely situated on the sandy bar before mentioned, and from the back windows you have a splendid view of the Atlantic. This beautiful situation possesses many attractions — excellent fishing, fine sea-bathing, and capital accommodations. It is easy of access, being only two hours from New York (the fare is but twenty-five cents), and is, consequently, much frequented by New Yorkers, who come there to engage in piscatory sports in the pretty little sail-boats that belong to the hotel, or bring their families for several weeks during the warm season. It is capable of accommodating three hundred persons, and forms one of the most delightful summer retreats we can imagine. Who is there that would not give twenty-five cents to reach such a pleasant resort and enjoy a good day's fishing?

We passed the stations, where are moored one or two lifeboats, with mortars to be used on extreme occasions, and had a passing view of busy fishermen working away in the moonlight at packing fish for the New York markets. They are put in large wooden boxes, and placed on the pier at the Ocean House, where the boat takes them up on its next trip.

Here we found a number of "beach carriages," as they are called, awaiting the arrival of the boat from New York to take its passengers to Long Branch. They are curious-looking but very convenient vehicles, with broad wheels, formed so as to travel with greater ease along the yielding sands.

We had a charming moonlight ride in these beach carriages upon the shore, sometimes grinding along through the moist sands, and sometimes splashing through pools with our carriage-wheels nearly submerged in water. Our progress was necessarily slow, although the horses were spirited and the stages light; but the nature of the beach does not admit of rapid traveling. The journey was nevertheless extremely animated and lively as we were all full of mirth and gaiety, and enjoyed every feature of the scene to its full capacity. In front of us was a seemingly interminable line of these same equipages, all were laden; we counted forty or fifty, and if any conclusions might be drawn from the cheerful laughter and lively conversation which reached our ears from each and all, a merrier party seldom travelled along those gray old sands.

After traveling two miles and a half upon this sandy neck of land we reached the mainland, where the scenery became much more diversified and attractive. One or two quiet, old-fashioned farm-houses, nestling among trees and orchards, presented a delightful image of rest and seclusion to our metropolitan eyes. The fishhawks, with their monster nests, attracted our attention in the neighborhood of these rural spots; they abound in this vicinity, and manifest remarkable trust and confidence in those by whom they are surrounded. You can approach so nearly as almost to touch them before they will take flight, and they sail and eddy around in all directions apparently fearless of danger. As they are very gentle and harmless few molest them, and they are suffered to build where they will; but it is a singular fact that wherever they plant their gigantic nests a blight seems to descend. The tree loses its leaves and dies, and wherever you see a fishhawk's nest it is almost sure to be supported by a dead and splintered tree.

NOTE

1. *Bellews Island:* Bedloe's Island was also known at various times as Kennedy's Island and Gibbet Island.

Frank Leslie's Illustrated Newspaper, August 22, 1857; quoted in *Another Look at Nauvoo to the Hook*, George H. Moss, Jr., Ploughshare Press, Sea Bright, 1990.

1864
Barnegat Bay

T. Robinson Warren

Duck hunters hid in sneakboxes behind blinds on Barnegat Bay's marsh islands.

Except for fashionable watering places like Long Branch and Cape May, most early 19th-century shore hotels and boarding houses catered to sportsmen — individuals from the emerging middle class who had the time and money to spend gunning and fishing on Barnegat Bay. T. Robinson Warren, a Wall Street stockbroker who lived in New Brunswick, was one such man. To Warren, the charm of gunning and other "gentlemanly" sports — he also wrote about yachting — is its "absolute change from conventional city life. To a man who has been caged for months in an office, reduced to a mere machine run for the purpose of turning out so many dollars per diem, whose only excercise has been an occasional walk of a mile or so, the change to a fisherman's hovel on an open beach, with a snow storm driving through its every crack and cranny, could hardly be more radical — there is an indescribable something about it which yearly attracts men of refinement and means. It is manhood asserting its dignity!"

Barnegat Bay is on what is now called the Atlantic Flyway, and its coves and estuaries provide a natural habitat for the wildfowl that stop to rest and feed during migration each fall and spring. In Warren's day the number of different birds was beyond belief: "I sat on the beach on a soft balmy day in November from early morning until night and scarcely saw a break in the continuous line of ducks, geese and brant bound south. None but those who have seen it can conceive of the vast numbers which can often be computed by tens of thousands. I have seen acres of them feeding, and when they rose it was like distant thunder." He observed black duck, widgeon, sprigtail, green and blue-winged teal, spoonbill, canvasback, redhead, broadbill, whistler, dipper, old wife, shelldrake and in late April, "vast flocks of brant congregated around the Barnegat inlet. Indeed, I have in one day shot at all these varieties. I also shoot Canada geese in large quantities, but only occasionally a swan."

Warren wrote the following episode in November 1864 and included it in his 1871 book, Shooting, Boating and Fishing for Young Sportsmen. *He dedicated the book to his sons, reminding them that real sportsmen must combine the intense physical training of the athlete with the intellectual assiduity of the student.*

Last week, having a little spare time on our hands, we resolved to go down to Barnegat Bay and have a shot at the ducks, and we accordingly announced our intention in family council, whereupon our better half immediately had a vision of a week's rollicking, unbecoming a paterfamilias, to be followed by a sharp attack of inflammatory rheumatism. The youngsters, however, received the announcement with demonstrations of evident delight, as being suggestive of long stories for approaching winter's entertainments, and forthwith began to "quack" and "honk," in the most deafening manner, and frantic rushes were made for our boots, over-alls and shooting equipments generally. No. 4, whom we call the General, in his military capacity, seized our gun; No. 3, who, judging from her pugnacious disposition, will be a second Joan d'Arc, joining issue for its possession, while No. 2, rejoicing in the name of Schuyler, and true to his historic antecedents, was bestowing his attention upon the ammunition, and No. 1 (our John) quietly assumed the post of Inspector-General and issued his orders with great dignity. Our preparations made, we proceeded to the steamboat, but found to our consternation, shared by some twenty sportsmen, that she was incapacitated and could not leave.

An hour of awful suspense elapsed, setters and pointers gave forth low growls of dissatisfaction, and gunners, after staring each other in the face and out of countenance, gradually, under the influence of case bottles, grew friendly and breathed vows of vengeance against steamers generally. A substitute was, however, finally furnished, when, shifting our traps, we were soon steaming down the bay,[1] and a picturesque group we formed, in our gunning costumes, with half-a-dozen thoughtful dogs artistically interspersed among us. Away we whisked, passing Owl's Head, Lafayette, through the Swash Channel to Port Monmouth, thence by rail and stage to Toms River, where, having had a capital feed, we got aboard the little *Zouave*, and stretched across the bay to Bill Chadwick's[2].

The little low bar-room looked cosily familiar to us as we peered through a cloud of tobacco-smoke, as did the faces of the various gunners there assembled, Jno. [Jonathan] Harbor, Zeph., Charley Stout, Dave, Lishe, Jno. Gaunt, and the rest of them, as they warmly welcomed us. The style of accommodation is peculiar to the beach, and gunners are generally expected to sleep double. We, ourselves, were too tired to be particular, so we turned in with our boatman, and had hardly, as we thought, got to sleep, when a candle flashed before our eyes and a rough shake of the shoulder brought us to the consciousness that it was three o'clock, A.M., and time to get up. Without waiting to yawn we sprang up, and in a quarter of an hour were arrayed in full shooting costume and were sitting down to a substantial breakfast.

It was still pitch dark when we slipped into our sneak boat,[3] nor indeed had the day fairly broken until we were comfortably sitting in our blind, with our gun at half cock, waiting for a flock of ducks.

By way of digression, let us here state what is, in our opinion, an essential to the comfort of the duck shooter. What we call blinds in the northern part of the bay are simply points of meadow jutting out into the bay, always damp and frequently very wet; on the extreme end of these points, a circular rampart of reeds and sea grass about thirty inches high is thrown up, within which the gunners (two generally) recline, watching their decoys, which float at anchor within thirty yards of the point. Now as the gunner is always exposed to the bleak winds sweeping over the meadows, and is obliged twenty times a day to lie flat on his back in the wet sedge, it becomes necessary to provide the proper clothing to guard against a thorough wetting, with its attendants of cold and rheumatics. We therefore make the following suggestions — heavy woolen stockings and the thickest possible woolen drawers and under-shirts, as well as a worsted muffler for the throat, with a pair of long loose rubber boots, and over these again an oil-skin suit the color of the sedge. We should also advise an India-rubber army blanket or a buffalo robe, and an army satchel for ammunition.

When we broke off into the foregoing digression, we were reclining on our batteries awaiting a shot. Unfortunately for us, however, the wind had been strong from northwest for six weeks past and was then blowing therefrom, the very worst possible direction, and the weather had been so mild that the ducks had hardly begun to migrate and the only ones that we could hope to get a bang at were the regular traders who rarely came to stool, being too knowing by half. Just as day was breaking, however, half a dozen dippers came down and took a look at our stool, but seeing the point, wheeled and shot away, but took with them a couple of charges, killing two and crippling a third. Barely were we loaded again, when "quack, quack," goes the gunner, the stool, giving an answering "quack," but [they] sail out of gunshot. Hardly are they gone by, when down we go again — and up come a bunch of broad-bill, and as they flutter over the stool we give them three barrels and turn them over on their backs; while loading, a flock of mallard poise over us for an instant, answer our "quack," but catching sight of us, are off again. Hardly are we capped before, just over the edge of the horizon, we see a long string of geese heading for us this time, and we as flat as pancakes — a small pool of water trickling down the back of our necks — "Honk, honk" from the stand. "Honk, honk," goes goosey, and down comes the flock within a couple of hundred yards of the stool, then follows a long conversation between the inmates of the stand and the different members of the flock — first, the conventional "honk," which being politely answered is equivalent to "How do you do," "Very well, thank you!" Then comes a low quack, quack, quack. (Not unlike the enunciation of a London cabby on a wet night, when, in shortest and most gutteral tones, he compresses into the smallest possible dimensions the word cab.) This last quack signifies "Walk in if you please," after which, as goosey more nearly approaches, a dialogue in an unknown dialect ensues between fowl and gunner, which generally ends in the slaughter of the victim. Hallo! here come the ducks again, three big black ducks — quack! quack! — bang! bang! — down go two and away swims off the third, badly hit though.

Although we have before described Chadwick's, we will again venture a few passing words upon it. Imagine a sand-spit betwixt bay and ocean, say eighteen hundred yards across, of glittering white sand thrown up into hummocks of all conceivable shapes by the autumnal gales, and midway between the raging surf and the waters of the bay a large, low beach-house, the roof sloping down to within six feet of the ground, sheltering a low corridor surrounding it. The only other building in sight is the life-boat station.[4] Everything is suggestive of desolation as we approach, all the gunners being absent on the various points. Not a soul is to be seen, the only visible object besides the house is the debris of wrecks, here a rudder with its spokeless wheel and torn steering gear, there a spectral looking spar, encircled by the top, looking like the cross which, in Spanish countries, is raised over the murdered man.

As we step ashore, Quango, a Newfoundland bitch who swam ashore from a wreck, comes down to meet us, expressing the most canine affection at our return, and as we walk into the yard everything reminds us even more forcibly of ruin and desolation; and as our eye wanders over the "head-boards" washed ashore from wrecked ships nailed along the corridor, we unconsciously read aloud the names: *Samuel Willets, Pilgrim, T. Hathorn, Darax, Honduras.*

But, though desolate outside, there's no cosier place within than Bill Chadwick's and we defy any one to be gloomy as he sits about the bar-room fire after the day's sport is over, exchanging experiences, cleaning guns, replenishing ammunition and listening to a conversation never outdone since the building of Babel. Every gunner has his say; every phase of duck-shooting is discussed; guns are inspected and compared, and loud above the rest a young man is eloquent upon the beauties of Hakodadi women, appealing, in support of his assertions, to another who had spent years in the China seas smuggling opium.

This polyglot is going on in an atmosphere of tobacco smoke dense as a London fog; indeed in that low murky room scarce six feet high from floor to ceiling, barely lighted by a kerosene lamp, whose flickering flames struggled with the tobacco fumes for mastery, there was a grouping picturesque in costume, noble in form, with surroundings of fowling gear and game that would have delighted Vandyke or Murillo.

NOTES

1. *Steaming down the bay*: Warren and his fellow gunners were coming from New Brunswick so this reference is to Raritan Bay.

2. *Bill Chadwick's*: In 1851 Bill Chadwick bought a boarding house that had been in business since1830. It was located where Ortley Beach is today; at that time the beach between Bay Head and Seaside Park was known as Squan. Warren also mentions other gunning houses along the bay: "There's Jakey's [Jake Herbert in Mantoloking], Bill Chadwick's, Ortley's, Amos Grant's, Martin's at the inlet [Barnegat], Double Jim's [James James' place at Loveladies] and Kinsey's below that." Kinsey's hotel in Harvey Cedars is still in its original location, enclosed by the larger Harvey Cedars Bible Conference. Warren spelled it "Kenzie" but as the man was an ancestor of mine I have corrected the spelling.

3. *Sneak boat*: Now known as a sneakbox, this shallow-draft boat is indigenous to Barnegat Bay and could be sailed or poled in a few inches of water and easily converted into a duck blind.

4. *Life-boat station*: The Chadwick Beach Lifesaving station number 12.

From *Shooting, Boating and Fishing for Young Sportsmen*, New York, Charles Scribner & Co., 1871.

1870
Ocean Grove

James A. Bradley

By 1875 about 600 tents sheltered devout Methodist vacationers in Ocean Grove.

The elders of the Methodist Camp-Meeting Association had been search-ing up and down the Jersey coast for a suitable spot to establish a planned summer retreat. They almost settled for Seven-Mile Beach, now Stone Har-bor, but rejected it because of the scourge of mosquitoes. Finally in 1869, *under the leadership of founder Dr. William B. Osborn, the men chose some dry land near the ocean that had a "high beach, thick grove of pine, cedar and hickory trees, and the absence of disease-bearing mosquitoes." They called it Ocean Grove.*

James A. Bradley, who eventually founded Asbury Park, ran into the treasurer of the Ocean Grove Association on the sidewalk in Manhattan in May 1870; he impulsively committed himself to buying, sight-unseen, one of the first lots for $85. Since the age of twelve Bradley had worked hard and built up a considerable business. By the time he was forty he had become a workaholic: his health suffered and he planned a long, recuperative holiday to Europe during the summer of 1870. But his Methodist friends convinced him that what he needed was sea air, and in one of those fortuitous twists of fate his plans changed. A few days later Bradley journeyed south to choose his lot. He boarded a boat from New York to Port Monmouth, then took a train to Eatontown, and finally a carriage to Ocean Grove. Bradley subsequently wrote, "The turnpike company had just commenced operations and from Great Pond to Ocean Grove was one of the worst roads that could well be imagined." But once he got there, the devout Methodist was captivated by the wild, solitary surroundings. About five years later Bradley recalled that first visit.

Having for some time previous been in poor health, I decided I would try what I had heard recommended — sea-air. So, taking two horses, carriage, and tent, and John Baker, my colored man, I left the hum of the busy city behind to become an inhabitant of the wild woods, where my wearied body and brain might rest, lulled to sleep by the murmuring sea at night, and awakened in the morning by the song of the birds in the pine trees surrounding my couch.

John and I arrived at Ocean Grove just at nightfall, and, having got our horses under shelter, we hastened to erect our tent. It was getting too dark to get poles, so we hung the tent on the beams of what is now the Association office, the first building ever erected at Ocean Grove. The building at that time was without roof. We were without light, and soon after lunching on some crackers we lay down to sleep, our heads resting on the carriage cushion, and our covering being the carriage blankets; so we spent our first night at Ocean Grove.

In the morning Baker sighed and said, "Mr. B., this is a wilderness place."

He was homesick; for let the reader who has been on this same spot during the past four or five summers, and heard the continued click of the telegraph instrument, and seen the vast throng of men and maidens call for their letters when the mail arrives, remember it was far different on the morning of which we are writing; although it was the tenth of June, not a soul was within hearing distance of us. I cheered him up by saying, "Oh! don't be cast down," and soon we were eating our morning lunch. That finished, we proceeded to my lots on the lake and pitched our small tent on the ground. So began our Crusoe life. During the day we occasionally saw Mr. Franklin's men, who were working about the grounds, and at night we were left to our solitude. Mr. Franklin's men tented on the lots now covered by the Hayward cottage, but on Sundays went to their homes in the interior of the township.

One evening Baker and I took a stroll along the ocean, and I proposed a bath. Baker smiled and said, "No, no."

"But remember, John, cleanliness is next to godliness."

I took an ocean bath; but, oh, how different from the way bathers usually enjoy surf-bathing, the waves dashing over their heads. I laid down on the soft sand and allowed the water to just touch my body, and I can tell you, it is somewhat lonely to trust yourself in the great ocean, in the twilight, and alone. After I had been lying on the beach for a little while I looked around to see what had become of Baker. He had plucked up courage by my example and had really divested himself of his clothes, and coward, like myself, barely allowed the water to touch him. His dusky skin was somewhat in contrast to the white sand, and never before did I realize the relation that must have existed between Robinson Crusoe and his man Friday.

From *Historical and Biographical Atlas of the New Jersey Coast,* H. C. Woolman and T. T. Price, Woolman and Rose, Philadelphia, 1878, reprinted by Ocean County Historical Society, 1985.

1870 to 1871
Cape May

Frank Willing Leach

The Cape May Daily Star, *advertised on the side of this cart, merged in 1907 with the* Cape May Ocean Wave. *Frank Leach's father was editor and publisher of the* Wave.

Frank Willing Leach began his diary in September 1870. The tattered, *oblong ledger is one of six in which he regularly recorded his life in Cape May and Philadelphia until 1881, when the entries dwindled, then ended, three weeks after the woman he had been courting refused to marry him. One of nine children, Frank grew up in Cape May, where his father owned a general store on Washington Street. The house into which the family moved in May*

1871 still stands on Lafayette Street. At seventeen he went to read law with his brother Granville, an attorney in Philadelphia, where Frank was eventually admitted to the bar. Writing and politics appealed to him more than studying, and during his student years he wrote poetry, essays and news accounts for the Philadelphia Press *and the* North American. *Throughout his long life Frank Leach was devoted to the Republican Party and was private secretary to U.S. Senators Matthew S. Quay of Pennsylvania and Joseph F. Frelinghuysen of New Jersey; he was said to have met every president from Grant to Coolidge.*

When we meet Frank he is an intelligent, fun-loving 15-year-old caught up in gunning, sailing, loafing, horsing around and flirting with girls.

1870

OCTOBER 8: I decided to go gunning today. Crossed the railroad and met Dan [Mayhew]. We walked through Leaming's Woods but saw only small birds. I killed three, but threw them away as they were of no account. At Leaming's, Dan killed a thrasher and a cedar bird. I got two catbirds and one woodpecker. Dan and I crossed the railroad and went over to Shunpike.[1] We found some persimmons, but they were not yet ripe. We went to Levi Johnson's and met Bob [Hand] and his brother. We all hiked to Cape Woods where Bob killed a thrasher. At the swamp, we heard a noise like a rabbit in the bushes. Up jumped about fifty quail. Just as I aimed, someone yelled, "There's a $20 fine for killing quail." We made tracks out of there and came finally to an orchard, where we saw a lot of woodpeckers. A notice of a fine for trespassing sent us running for the fences. I heard a rustling in some brush, got down on my hands and knees and crept up on it. I shot a sapsucker and a nice lark, and just as I went to pick them up, a robin flew right at me, and I shot the robin. We packed the gamebirds in our bags and started home.

On Sunday after a good sermon at church, we came home to a delicious pot pie dinner of the birds we killed on Saturday.

OCTOBER 10: First day of school this fall. In the morning, I have Mental Arithmetic, Practical Arithmetic, Geography and Writing. Afternoons I have Algebra, Physiology, Grammar and Spelling. Alternate afternoons are History and Etymology. My seatmate, Joe [Leaming] and I were given a project to make a box to hold our pencils on our desk. After school, Joe and I went to find some walnut. We went to a new store on Washington

Street between Jackson and Decatur. The workmen told us to find "Strat" Ware, the boss. Mr. Ware said if we come back tomorrow afternoon, we could have all the wood we want. Next day, after school, Joe and I worked on our pencil box.

OCTOBER 12: I went to school this morning and found no fire. I asked Mr. Haynes[2], the teacher, if there would be a fire. He said, no, that he thought if he could stand the chill, I could, too. I could not see it as I did not fancy taking a new cold. There had been a hard rain all night. I thought we needed a fire. So, I gathered my books and went home. I went out and bought one and a half yards of blue chintz to cover my books. Finished that about noon. Stopped at Father's store and asked him to write a note excusing my absence from school in the morning. I returned to school and there was a fire in the stove.

OCTOBER 14: Overslept myself this morning. Nothing special happened at school. Some girls gave Joe and me some candy. After school, Joe and I went to his home and did quite an amount of work on our box. In the evening, I walked with Joe around to Perry Street. We met George, looking in a candy store window. We asked him if he was going to stand treat. He went in and bought twenty cents worth of burnt almonds and gave us each some. Then we met some other boys who said there was a ship on fire at the breakwater. We ran to the beach and saw over at Lewes what we supposed to be a woods on fire. We took a short walk, then I went home and crawled into bed.

NOVEMBER 8: After supper, about six and a half oclock, I went down Washington Street and met a lot of fellows. Some of them went back of Church's store and hooked some barrels. We then headed for the beach, up past the Stockton House. We here found about twenty boys assembled. They already had about twenty-four barrels, boxes, etc. They had an open wagon which they had pulled out of some stable yard. We went around and got a lot of seaweed and brush. We unloaded this on the beach and went for another load of barrels. In a little while we had a large load. We rolled the barrels down the beach to the water's edge, where we were going to have our Election Day Fire and Celebration. We piled the whole lot in a great, huge mass and set it on fire. It burned brightly for three-quarters of an hour. We enjoyed the show exceedingly. I should think there were at least one hundred boys there. About a quarter past nine, the fire smouldered out and we all went to our homes and then to bed.

NOVEMBER 16: About ten oclock, Charley [Clark] came around. I took my gun and we started off to see if we could kill a few robins. I shot at a blackbird but missed it. Charley also missed a blackbird. He said it was the fault of the gun, but I knew it was his own fault. Charlie put his hat on a post and I shot at it. Ed [Sayre] came along and he tossed up my cap and Charley shot at it. Then Charley threw up his hat and Ed cut it to pieces. We did not get home til after dark. I was home by eight oclock and soon went to bed with Ellie.[3]

DECEMBER 23: This morning I was rather late about my breakfast so I did not go to school. George and I went around to the church to help fix it up for Christmas. I was short of box-wood to trim with so Millard Ware, Will Moore and I went down to Thomas's cottage in the snow and dark and got a good load of it.

DECEMBER 24: We closed the store at six oclock and got to church at seven. The performance began at eight. I think I had more fun tonight than I have for a long time. While the Sunday School scholars were singing a piece about Kriss Kringle, out he popped from behind the curtain, dressed in a costume. He talked some time, said he had found some creature in the woods, but did not know what to call it. He asked us if we would like to see it. We said YES! So he went to the curtain and out jumped a regular Indian. When they both came forward, the audience laughed, yelled and clapped their hands. It was so funny. They took the candies and oranges off the Christmas tree and passed them around. The program was over at nine-and-a-half oclock. I staid with George and a few others, cleaning up the church til nearly midnight.

DECEMBER 25: This morning I went to church. Mr. Wilson preached a Christmas sermon. (That's all! Christmas Day for a fifteen-year-old boy is too full to spend much time writing about it.)

1871

MARCH 23: I worked at Father's store today, but, as I had no putty, I could not put in window glass. Therefore I had nothing to do but read. Although I had the *Wave* to read, I had the "Spring Fever" terrible. I finished the *Wave* in the morning, and, as there was nothing else to read, all I could do was gaping and yawning. About seven and a half oclock in the evening, I went to the Post Office with the fellows. About eight oclock, it commenced to sprinkle, accompanied by violent winds, and the atmosphere was exceedingly warm. This was noticed by a large number of people who were commenting on it. Some were superstitious enough to think it was a forerunner of an earthquake. We went into George Smith's candy store and Will Hughes treated us all to ground nuts.

MARCH 27: Most of the morning I was at Father's store, putting in window glass. Sam Bailey came in and helped me. After dinner we worked some more and Sam left at three oclock. Around four, I went down to the beach and fooled around, jumping and wrestling with the fellows. Then I went back to the store and fooled around cutting up with Sallie [Mecray] and a lot of the other girls. I went to the Lodge and staid til close to ten oclock. I then went home and crawled into bed.

MARCH 28: Sam helped me work on window sash again at the store. We expected Lizzie tonight on the train but were disappointed as she did not come. About eight P.M. I went to the Post Office with the fellows. I took the mail home and then we went down to the beach to see the Pilot boat men off. After that, Charlie and Eddie [Clark], Will [Hedges] and I went into Smith's Candy Store and staid til about ten oclock playing a new game called Parcheesi.

MARCH 29: About nine A.M., Sam came to the store and we went down to the beach to an old vacant shanty near the Government Boat House.[5] We went to work and made a good stove in the sand out of bricks, with a regular stovepipe and draught. We ransacked the "Sebang" and found an old grate. We went in again and found a wheelbarrow full of kindling so we took a few armloads and duly made a roaring fire. We then took some black mussels (which we picked up on the way), washed them and put them on the grate and put this on our stove. In about half an hour, they were done and we waded into them. While eating we thought it would be a good idea to come down in the afternoon and invite some girls, when we could have our own fun. So at eleven and a half oclock, we went up to the school and waited til it was out. Sam went up to Lena [Hand] and Lizzie [Downs] and asked them. This just suited them; they said yes. He told them to ask Nell Schellenger. We then asked Dick Ware so there would be the same number of boys and girls. I went to Father's store and got some crackers and went to find Sam. We went down to the stove on the beach and made up a new fire and put some mussels on to boil in a boiler that we found in the hut. We ate these and then loafed around in the shanty and outside waiting for the girls. We waited til about four oclock. By this time, we thought they were not coming so we put out the fire. We were on the point of leaving when we saw them coming. We hurried up and got up a new fire and had some mussels boiling when they came up. We soon after went to work eating mussels and crackers. [Here Frank put six lines of diary notes in code.[6]] At six oclock we went home well pleased with our little beach party. After the arrival of the train, I went with the fellows to the Post Office. Joe Leaming and I walked around caching glimpses of two goodlooking city girls. About nine oclock I went home to bed.

APRIL 10: About eight-and-one-half oclock, I went up to the schoolhouse. I met Emlen [Ralston[7]]. We went up to Sloan's store where Em bought a straw hat. We then went back to the schoolhouse and met Dick and we all went to Emlen's boathouse and got his sailboat and forthwith took a sail down to the inlet. Em went in to swim on the way but as it was so cold he soon came out. We landed on Poverty Beach and fooled around, jumping, running, etc. We staid some time and then started home. Dick and I rowed about a quarter of a mile. A nice little breeze sprang up and we sailed the rest of the way. We arrived at the landing at ten oclock. We put the boat in the boathouse and I went home. I had my dinner and went up to Father's store and staid til 3:30 P.M. I met Joe at the schoolhouse and we went down on one of the bridges near the Sea Breeze House[8] and shot at small crabs. We killed and wounded quite a number. Maurice Powell gave me some India rubber to make a new sling shot.

APRIL 18: Mr. Haynes was sick today so we had no school. I passed my time at the store. I got a torch light out of the shed, cleaned it and filled it with oil for tonight. At the usual time, I went to the Post Office and got the mail for the store. I soon after went home and got my old plug hat, put a rag around it and put it on. I walked around the streets for awhile with the fellows. About eight and one-half oclock, the Cold Spring and Cape May Bands, with Jim Stites as Marshall, assembled at Angell's Cigar Store. I got my torch light out of the store. Will Hedges also got one and we headed the procession. The instruments consisted of fiddles, drums, triangles, flutes, bones, flutinas, etc. A number of players had gongs, bells, horns and washing machines.[9]

About nine oclock we started the line of march. We marched around the streets serenading and then arrived at the Tremont House which was our stopping place. I will now explain. A daughter of Mr. Hughes, the owner of the Tremont House was married to a gentleman from Philadelphia this evening and we were serenading them. We got on the porch and the band struck up a tune. They played a number of pieces and then the washing machines commenced. They were all playing, jumping and yelling like demons when all of a sudden, down went the porch. Nothing daunting, they just moved farther down the porch and commenced playing again. And such a noise! I spoke to someone beside me but could not be heard as the noise was too dense. Some of the men in the hotel came out and expostulated with the musicians but it was no go, for no sooner had the men turned around when the players struck up again. As there was no appearance of getting a treat, the band, and I with them, left about eleven oclock for Dennis Shield's place. As it was a tavern, I did not go in, but they treated me to a cigar. I went home and crawled into bed, well pleased with my night's sport.

APRIL 19: In the morning, I met Will at the Atlantic House. We harnessed one of McMakin's horses up to their carriage. We drove it around to Hildreth and Taylor's where we left it. In the evening, Ed Clark and I went down to the beach. I here lit my cigar (that I got last night) and I smoked it til we got to the Post Office; by this time it was half gone. The remainder I gave to Ed. I got the mail and took it to Father's store. About this time, I began to feel rather dizzy from the effects of the cigar. So I went home and got a cool drink and it all passed off in a half an hour. I then went around to Clark's and met Ed who was not feeling too well by then. But we went around to the Council room and staid for a quarter of an hour. I then went home to bed.

APRIL 27: About ten oclock I went down to Washington Street. I met Dave Crowell and we walked over to the Engine House. Then we went to Dave's father's house and I shortened my sling while Dave split wood until noon. After dinner at noon, I took a sheet iron range shelf door to Benezet's to get mended. I commenced to build another knife cleaning box which I finished by six oclock. It was quite a fancy contrivance. When I showed it to Mother she thought it was splendid.

About eight oclock I started for the Post Office but had got no farther than Washington Street when some fellows told me that some dogs were fighting up an alley. I got my sling shot and then followed the crowd. I had not gotten far when I fell PLUMP! into a mortar bed. I then saw the trick. There were no dogs at all. The fellows only wanted to get me in the mortar. They set up a yelling and laughing. I was about as mad as I possibly could be. I came near laying some of them out. But I soon got over it and laughed with the rest. We then went to work and got about a half-dozen more people into the mortar. About nine and a quarter oclock, I went home and read awhile and then went to bed.

APRIL 28: As George was at the building all day cleaning up, I had to work at Father's store. I did hardly anything all the morning except to read *The Star of the Cape,* etc. and shot my sling. Dave Paul came by and we shot at a wagon. Dave bet one cent that I could not hit a lamp-post (a good distance off) two shots out of three. I bet that I could — and lost. I bet again and lost another cent. I then won them both back. I kept shooting and when Dave left I had won the sum of one cent. At the usual time, I went down to the Post Office for the mail. I shot at a window down on the other side of the street and distinctly heard it break but did not stop to examine.

MAY 1 (MONDAY): I wrote and read most of the day til five oclock when I went around to Mr. Beardwood's and got measured for a pair of gaiters. After supper, I got washed and dressed and then went around to the Lodge. It was called to order about seven and a half oclock and went through with the regular business. During the evening, four persons were proposed for membership. I proposed Sam Bailey at the request of his mother. About eight oclock the Lodge had a recess. Soon after, the doors were thrown open and the persons who had assembled to witness the installation poured into the room. The meeting was again called to order and the officers-elect were duly installed, I, among the rest, as Worthy Marshall. After the installation, an essay was read by the Worthy Chief Templar, A. L. Haynes. Speeches were made by Rev. G. B. Wright and Rev. E. P. Shields, and by Messrs. Price and Davies, interspersed by vocal and instrumental music. At ten oclock the visitors departed and the Lodge was once again called to order. A little business of minor importance was transacted and then the Lodge adjourned.

MAY 2: At eight oclock, I started up to the building to get the horse and wagon. I'd gone nearly half-way when I met Mr. Moore driving the horse down. I climbed aboard and rode down to the store with him. I then went down to the train depot and hauled three wagon-loads of sash weights up to the store. After dinner at noon, I jumped a little out in the store shed with my dumbbells, but did not jump very far. I then went in the store and tried jumping up a stepladder. After a number of trials and a skinned shin, I accomplished my objective. I then tried to jump up on the store counter which is nearly a yard high. I tried some time and at last made up my mind to do it. So I gave a great spring and landed "high and dry" on the desired spot. Frank Hildreth came over and we went to the lumber yard to order some lath. Going back to the store, I had an opportunity to talk to Frank on the subject of Temperance. I tried to get him to join the Good Templars, but did not succeed.

MAY 3: Most of the morning I spent fooling around Father's store, doing nothing in particular. About three and a half oclock, I went up to the printing office and got a *Wave* and read it until about five oclock. I then went to work and covered the desk stool with oilcloth. After supper I went over to the store and got two cigars and then went down to the Post Office but there was no mail. Ed and Charley and I went down to the boardwalk. I gave Charley one cigar and lit the other for myself. I smoked it til we got back to Washington Street. I then threw away the stump. I commenced to feel rather dizzy, so I went into Clark's house and got a drink. Then I felt the need of air, so I went back outside. After a while, I went home, but I staid outside sometime, not wishing to alarm Mother or Father. Then I went in quietly and straight up to my room. I felt very sick and soon I threw up in my chamber-pot. I threw the contents out the window and climbed into bed to sleep away the effects. Cigars are very difficult.

MAY 15: We had a man moving our things up to the new house[10] all day. I spent the day putting glass in window sash ready for glazing, til after seven oclock. I then went home, washed my hands, ate tea, dressed and went to the Lodge. Emma Shaw was invited. Mrs. Wight told me that Sallie was coming down for certain next Friday. The Lodge closed at ten oclock. I had an idea of going home with Emma Shaw but I concluded not to. So I went home with myself and soon went to bed and to sleep.

MAY 16: We had two men moving our furniture today. I did a little work around home such as taking down beds, etc. I then went down to open the store. I commenced glazing window sash which was left last night. (We had a glazier here last night at work on them, but he did not finish this one.) After dinner at the old house, I went to the store and got a putty knife and went up to the new house. Almost all the folks were there. George and I spent the afternoon glazing two east doors. Later I got the horse and wagon and went around to the old house for some coal for the fire and took it to the new house. At seven and a half oclock, I went to the Post Office and then went up home for supper. About eight and a half oclock, Ellie and I went up to our new bedroom. It is on the third story, fronting the street. I soon got into bed and went to sleep.

MAY 17: When I first awoke, I hardly knew what to make of it, seeing a strange room. But as soon as I got fairly awake, I understood it all. After breakfast, I walked down to the store and opened it. Joe and Frank came in. Soon after, a man named Farrer came in. He asked the price of a hoe. I told him seventy-five cents. He asked if I would take seventy cents for it. I said no. He then said that he always expected to pay two prices for anything here. That made me mad. I told him he had better not peddle any more stinking butter. He called me a young liar. I told him he was another one. I gave him particular fits. I told him he better not come in here trying to cheat me, or I would kick him out. I said there's the door, make good use of it, I do not want to waste breath on you. He said "I will see your father." I told him alright. He then left. I rather expected that he would let me have it, but if he had, I would have tapped him with my black-jack. Joe and Frank had a good time laughing about it. After supper, I went out and met Will and Ellie Roseman. We had a long talk about making an excursion to Atlantic City in a yacht next fall.

JUNE 9: At the usual time, I went up to the store to help Father. He brought out the horse and George and I drove down to a cottage family[11] to leave a circular. When I went to get the mail, I saw the girls at Wight's on the back porch. Charley came in the store and I tried to persuade him to go riding this afternoon with Laura and Sallie and me, but he could not go. About eleven thirty, I went to the harnessmaker's and got one of the sheaths that I ordered some time ago. It cost forty cents. On my way home, I stopped at Mr. Wight's and asked for Laura and Sallie. They had just come in from bathing a few minutes before. I asked them if they had an engagement this afternoon. They said no. I asked if they would like to take a ride. They were delighted with the prospect. I told them I would call for them abut three and a quarter oclock.

At two oclock I went home, got dressed, went to the stable and got the horse, took it up to Harry Farrow's, harnessed it up to Firm Richardson's buggy. I then drove down opposite our house and fixed the buggy up a little. I drove to Mr. Wight's and the girls were ready. I helped them into the buggy and we drove off. We first drove out to the light-house. Mr. Foster took us to the top. I went way out on the top railing. I had a magnificent view of the surrounding country. Cape May City looked to be about one tenth of a mile away instead of two and a half miles. Mr. Foster explained all the machinery and how it works. By the time we got down, we were quite tired. We again jumped into the buggy and drove to the Steamboat Landing. We then rode up the Old Turnpike and then down to the City. We rode over the new Schellenger Landing bridge. After going a long distance past Joe's, we turned around and I took them home. I made an engagement for this evening. I left the buggy where I found it and put up the horse.

After supper, Charley and I walked over to Wight's. Sallie and Laura were on the porch. We started off for a walk over to the Sea Breeze and sat there for an hour or so. We then started uptown. I told Sallie she had better take my arm. She did so. Laura took Charley's arm. We stopped at Smith's Ice Cream Saloon and Charley treated to ice cream and cake. On going along the street an Irish by the name of John Maguire hollered something at me. I marked him. We went up to Mr. Wight's porch and Sallie, Laura, Charley and I were left alone to sit and talk. About eleven oclock, we bid them goodbye and left. Our house was locked when I got home. Father had to come downstairs and open the door. I then went directly to bed.

JUNE 17 (SATURDAY): I was busy in the store all morning. Joe came in and bought some lemons and we made lemonade. At noon, I closed the store and went home, put up the horse and went to the Post Office. There was no letter from Sallie. Joe came back after dinner and we took a pull at our lemonade. We thought we would have some fun. So we drove down a stake near the pavement. We then took an old pocketook of mine and nailed it to the stake. We then went to the corner of the store and watched. Presently, two old women came by. One of them saw it and she went for it heavy. She jerked and tugged but it was no go. We then commenced to laugh and she dropped it and skulked off. We fooled about a dozen. It commenced to drizzle about five and a half oclock. At eight oclock, I closed the store and went to the Post Office, but there was again — no letter from Sallie. I went home and went to bed.

JUNE 19: About eight and a half oclock, Frank and I went up to the stables after the horse. We delivered quite a large amount of things to the cottages. Charley came into the store in the afternoon and we talked a lot about Sallie and Laura. I wrote my resignation as Marshall of the Good Templars. I also wrote George's (at his request) as Financial Secretary. I took the resignations over to Sallie's father. About eight oclock, Ed and Charley and Joe came into the store and told me there was a letter for me at the Post Office. As soon as possible I went and got it. I took it to the store and read it. It was hardly a letter. It was more an answer to my note. It nearly brought tears to my eyes. Her last words were "Goodbye, goodbye," as if she thought she had seen and heard the last of me. I took a walk with the fellows. At ten oclock, I left them. I met Dave [Crowell] and he treated me to two plates of ice cream at Smith's. I then went home. I read and reread my letter and then went to bed to dream of it.

JUNE 20: Early in the morning I went to work writing a letter to Sallie. After I got this done, I commenced copying it on small note paper. It occupied six pages. I was all the morning writing and copying it. About quarter to noon, I started home for dinner, first I stopped at the Post Office and left my letter. In the afternoon, Charley came in the store and showed me two letters he had gotten from Laura. Putting all the facts together, I came to this conclusion. Sallie had got my first letter Saturday afternoon. She showed it to Laura who thought she had better write to Charley, or she might get a bad one from him. So she wrote it and posted it. Then Saturday she got Charley's (which was sent the same time as mine was). She must have been hopping mad at herself and Charley, too, for in her letter she had said that Sallie had gotten an unsatisfactory letter from me. As if she did not expect one herself. I expect that she wished more than once that she had not written. She again wrote Charley yesterday, so he got both letters today. This was my idea of it. Charley staid at the store most of the afternoon writing to Laura.

About five oclock I started home with the horse and carriage. I'd gotten about halfway when I overtook Louise Ware and Annie Hand. They got in the wagon and I took them riding. We talked "Polertricks" most all the way. [Here follow two lines of Frank's secret code.] After supper I went with Ed and Charley and some other fellows down to the railroad bridge where we went in to swim. Soon after, an extra freight train came in loaded with horses, carriages, omnibuses, buggies, wagons, etc. for the Stockton House. I went around to the Stockton to see them put up the horses. I then went home. It had been thundering and lightning for some time past. I had not been in the house five minutes before it came down in torrents. I soon went to bed.

JULY 13: On looking at the Philadelphia papers I saw that there had been a great riot in New York City between the Catholics and Orangemen, police and militia. Sixty persons reported killed and two hundred injured. After supper I went to the Post Office and then over to Townsend's store. I got nicely fooled on the way. I met Joe and some of the fellows. They asked me if I wanted some cakes. I took some and commenced eating. At the first bite, I found that they were full of red peppers. I never let on but took a few bites and slipped them in my pocket. I then took some more cakes. They expected me to ask for water and make a big fuss, but I said nothing. They did not know what to make of it. They kept watching me, but I made believe nothing was wrong. We walked on and soon Dave treated to ice cream. Then Joe treated. At last, Dave asked me if I ate all the cake. (By the way, there were two kinds, cakes and ladyfingers.) I told him I ate all but a few which were mashed and dirty. He then said that they had filled the cakes with red pepper and dipped the ladyfingers in pepper. He did not know what to make of it. He was worse sold than I was!

JULY 16: On the way to church, I heard that James Kennedy, my old friend and schoolmate who had been sick some time, died at seven oclock. After church, I went down to the Stockton House. I met Mrs. Samuel Swain. She asked me if I would be a pallbearer at James' funeral. I readily agreed.

JULY 19: I went to Leaming's and borrowed a pair of Joe's black pants. I went down home and dressed and then went over to Kennedy's. We carried James' coffin out to the hearse. The pallbearers walked three to a side. In this manner we walked around to the Methodist Episcopal Church, followed by mourners and friends. Mr. Williamson preached the sermon. It was very effective. A large number were in tears, I among them. I could not help it. Mr. Wright spoke a few touching words. After the service, we took the body and put it in the hearse. We got into a carriage and soon started out. We crossed the Island bridge at twelve oclock. We then slowly wended our way toward the Cold Spring graveyard. After arriving here, all that remained of my friend and schoolmate was lowered to its final resting place. I was very sad as I could not help being. We took our carriage and started home.

AUGUST 2: About six in the evening I saw two policemen taking a man to prison. His clothes were torn and bloody. He was an excursionist. I learned that he had killed his wife at the Sea Breeze while in a drunken frenzy.

AUGUST 3: I learned today that the woman who was reported killed was slowly recovering. At home later, on going to bed, I found a little fellow up in my room asleep on the floor. He had no home. My little brother Ellie had brought him in. I thought it risky as I did not know him, therefore I slept all night with my blackjack under my pillow.

AUGUST 18: As soon as I got to the store in the morning, I heard of a terrible murder[12] that had taken place last night "up the road." The victim was Mr. Jonathan Hoffman. He had been visiting and as he was going home, he was shot. No clue as to the murderer has been obtained. It is something startling and unusual to hear of a murder here. About five and a half oclock, I went around to the Alderman's office where they were examining some news boys in reference to the murder.

AUGUST 19: I met Emlen and Dick. They each gave me a ticket to the Children's Ball at the Stockton House. I went directly to the Stockton. I found that it was free for children, but adults had to pay. The Grand March was very nice, but the fancy dances of the children were charming. They consisted of hornpipes, etc. I left for home at ten oclock and had just got opposite the Columbia Hotel when the Philadelphia coach came by. I jumped aboard and rode home. I then jumped off and went in the house to bed.

AUGUST 20: I went up the *Wave* office to see Mr. Magreth to tell him to put our name on the list of cottages receiving the paper. Later, I went home and sat out on the front porch. I sat here, wrapped in meditation. The crickets and locusts around me kept up an incessant chirp and buzzing. The sun had just set, leaving the dusky and shrouded earth. The atmosphere was mild and delightful, just such a time as a person would want to sit down and dream and build air castles. I was dreaming of the future and what it would bring forth. After it had gotten rather cool, I went in and read Longfellow's poems for about an hour before going to bed.

AUGUST 26: Today is my birthday — sixteen years old! It seems but a few short weeks since my last birthday. How fast the time flies. I hope the next year will be more profitably spent and that I will gain more knowledge.

NOTES

1. *Shunpike:* To avoid turnpike tolls twenty years earlier, John Tomlin had built a wagon track through the woods called the Shunpike.

2. *Mr. Haynes:* This wasn't the last run-in Frank would have with his teacher. By early spring Frank was expelled. He then worked in his father's store and continued reading on his own.

3. *Ellie:* Elbridge, Frank's 8-year-old brother.

4. *Wave:* In the 1850s Frank's father had been the activist editor of the *Ocean Wave,* Cape May County's first newspaper. It is one of the forerunners of the Cape May *Star and Wave.*

5. *Government Boat House:* Probably near the site of the U. S. Coast Guard training station.

6. *Diary notes in code:* Frank devised his own code for passages too personal to write openly. Anne Biddle Pratt, who edited segments of the diaries for publication in *The Star and Wave,* showed it to a cryptographer, but the hieroglyphic-like scratches remain a mystery.

7. *Emlen Ralston:* Emlen's mother's last name was Ralston because of a second marriage, but Emlen was actually Emlen Physick, whose house still stands.

8. *Sea Breeze House, Tremont House, Stockton House, Columbia House, Atlantic House:* All hotels, most of which were destroyed in the fire of 1878.

9. *Washing machines:* Washboards.

10. *The new house:* The double house which still stands on Lafayette near Madison remained in the Leach family until 1955.

11. *Cottage family:* Summer persons.

12. *Terrible murder:* At least three murders were recorded in Cape May County between 1871 and 1873.

From the diary of Frank Leach, reprinted with the permission of the Greater Cape May Historical Society.

1874
Beach Haven

Theophilus T. Price

Beach Haven's Parry House was built further from the ocean than it appears in this 1878 print.

 The men who developed Beach Haven had in mind that their resort would be like no other — not on the edge of the mainland as Cape May and Long Branch, but almost five miles at sea, where vacationers could be completely pollen free. As soon as rail service to Tuckerton was completed, 2,000 acres on

Long Beach Island's southern end were divided into lots, and in 1873 con-struction started on the Parry House. By fall of the following year several cottages and one other hotel, the Bay View House, were welcoming guests.

Theophilus T. Price,[1] a Tuckerton resident and a stockholder in the Camden and Burlington Railroad Company, wrote this letter to his son, Theophilus P. Price, shortly before the young man graduated from Haverford College.

June 18: My Dear Son, I went to Beach Haven yesterday with an excursion gotten up by the Directors of the Camden and Burlington Co. RR. About 60 persons, ladies & gentlemen, young men and maidens, composed the party. It was quite an opening for Robert Engle, and although he was at great inconvenience on account of the unfinished and unfurnished state of the house yet he got up a very nice dinner for the party in the new dining room, at which his new cutlery and spoons (heavily silver plated) were exhibited to good advantage. He served four courses, viz.— 1, oysters (raw) on half shell; 2nd, boiled sheephead (very fine); 3rd, roast beef or lamb with full vegetables, green peas &c; 4th, strawberries and two kinds of ice cream, with raisins and nuts to close. Wine, for those who partook. There seemed to be nothing lacking at the table that you would find at a first class old established hotel, and yet he and his family only went there last Seventh Day. They have worked very hard to get ready. He will be ready for boarders on the 25th, but will the *Barclay*[2] be ready? I fear not.

Our sail over was delightful. Our return decidedly wet. The wind was northwest and blowing a stiff breeze — Five yachts[3] carried the party, The Wave, Sylph, John Burton, and two Marshalls. The only young man of the party that I knew was Charley Harker. The larger number were married people — old folks, mostly. Your Uncle Arch & family will go to Beach Haven tomorrow for a sail. All are well. Affectionately yours, Theo. T. Price.

NOTES

1. *Theophilus T. Price*: Dr. Price wrote the history and compiled the statistics for Woolman and Rose's 1878 *Historical and Biographical Atlas of the New Jersey Coast*. He was also the grandfather of Eleanor Price, who discovered Sarah Thomson's diary.
2. *The Barclay*: A 124-foot paddle-wheel, shallow-draft steamboat.
3. *Five yachts*: 25- to 30-foot gaff-rigged catboats carrying huge canvas sails taxied passengers back and forth across the bay from the rail terminal at Tuckerton.

From an unpublished letter in a private collection.

1875
Sea Bathing

Anonymous

The latest in rented bathing finery on display in front of a portable bath house.

The most important attraction of a shore resort was, obviously, sea bathing, a very new and somewhat forbidding activity for most people in the 1800s. The ocean was often ferocious and scary, and almost no one knew how to swim. But even just to wade into the water was a thrill. But what to wear? A bathing suit could not be bought, it had to be made. And at this time in the 19th century, "suit" is the pertinent word; indeed, bathers were very fully *suited, and for women, because of the weight of the cumbersome clothing, actually swimming could be dangerous.*

Guide books, pamphlets and magazine articles advised vacationers not only what to wear but what to do and how to act. A pamphlet entitled "Summer Days in New Jersey" gave the following advice: "Before bathing in surf, run briskly up and down the beach for ten minutes. If you wear any lacing around the chest, throw it off and let your lungs have a hearty chance for all the air they can take. If any cheerful and willing muscular fellow is willing to race with you, have a foot-race on the sands. "Don't use soap in salt water. It will make you dismally sticky. "If your teeth are of the kind which did not grow in your mouth, beware lest a wave knock them out. "Now bounce through the surf with a hop, skip, and jump. Hold your fingers to your ears and your thumbs to your nostrils. Now dance, leap, tumble, swim, kick, float, or make any other motion that seems good to you."

A slim book published in Princeton, Life at the Sea Shore, *discussed for the novice beachcomber the benefits of bathing in sea water; cleanliness, prevention of disease, and cheerfulness of spirit are promoted. It warned against the dangers of solitary bathing - cramps, heart disease, undertow, sharks and stinging jellyfish — and advised readers what type of bathing costume to acquire.*

Where persons go to the shore alone, or with only their families or intimate friends, and they and none others there, they may use their own every day and commonest clothes with which to go into the water. If practicable, as to weather and those present, they may go in naked. This latter may be the better way. But where there is a mixed company and strangers, a suit appropriate to and specially designed for the purpose should be used. This may, in some cases, be hired on the ground. Hiring relieves of trouble in carrying and taking care of the garments: but, if a suit is to be used many times, it is least economical. Persons had better take their own suits. They will look better in them, feel better, and it will be cheaper. This costume should consist of twilled flannel, strong, and colored brown, blue or gray. The garment should be in one piece of light goods, and consist of pantaloons and coat over them. It should fit loose, be buttoned not tied, and have no unnecessary appendage. It should be made strongly and in good style, according perhaps to the fashion of the locality. Some would add a broad brimmed hat. This acts as a protector from the sun and wind. But as it is desirable to plunge the head under water in bathing, this also is an encumbrance and is unnecessary.

A correspondent for the Illustrated London News *visited the new seashore resorts from Maine to Cape May, studiously observing the northeast coast's expanding tourist industry and the women's bathing costumes, comparing them to the more revealing dresses seen at English and French resorts. He commented especially about Long Branch, which he termed the "Summer New York," because that city's fashionable society moved with all its decadent habits to the shore.*

The American customs in sea-bathing resemble those of the Continent more closely than those of England. A correspondent writing from Trouville, on the coast of France, described there "the canvas bathing houses whence issue at high water the ladies in 'bloomer' costumes and broad straw-hats, who are careful not to let either their faces or their locks come in contact with salt water, and who never bathe without an escort of male friends."

The American ladies wear bathing-dresses covering the entire person, from closely-fitting neck-bands to loose trousers buttoned carefully about the ankles just above the instep: even the sleeves are long and fasten at the wrists. The skirt of the dress falls about to the knee, or a little lower. This costume, it will be seen, differs materially from that worn by our [English] ladies, who disport in the waves, out of sight of the other sex, with much more of their persons exposed to the cool water. If aquatic pleasure were the only object sought, the dress of our countrywomen would certainly have the advantage. But the American ladies, like the French, are willing to sacrifice a little of their physical freedom in the water to the enjoyment of social converse, so their bathing-dresses are adapted to the proprieties of mixed society.

It is not strictly true that they "never bathe without an escort of male friends," like the French ladies; but American gentlemen and ladies meet each other in the waves as freely, and with as little restraint, as on the beach or in the drawing-room. A young gentleman offers his services to a young lady friend in the surf as gallantly as he would offer his arm for a quadrille, and she accepts the attention with as pretty a smile. Parties of ladies and gentlemen take hands, and fumble up and down among the breakers with merry laughter and amidst general hilarity. Seeing the same party in the evening, arrayed in the richest attire of the latest fashions, conversing with all the dignity of social etiquette, an observer would hardly imagine them the same beings.

An American damsel shows no unwillingness, like the French-woman, to have her face "come in contact with the salt water," for she dives into it with the utmost abandon; there is a rough straw hat upon her head that must share in the ducking. Her locks are usually bound up carefully, and protected by a closely-fitting oil-silk cap. The feet are bare except where the ladies fear the effect of shells or sharp stones; light, thick-soled sandals are then worn.

The "bathing-houses" at an American resort are usually primitive structures of boards, arranged in long rows, sometimes two or three deep, just beyond the reach of the waves at high tide. They are never moved from their places, and the bathers always walk to and from them over the beach. In each bathing-hut is a pail of clear water to wash the sand from the feet before dressing.

There is no American institution more popular than the summer resort for surf-bathing. Along the coast, from Maine to North Carolina, are found more than a hundred such places, all provided with hotels of greater or less pretension. The more celebrated of them are Mount Desert, on the coast of Maine; Nahant and Rye, near Boston; Newport, the summer residence of many New York millionaires; Narragansett, New London; Long Branch, the immediate refuge of heat-exhausted New Yorkers; Atlantic City and Cape May, the last named a special retreat of Philadelphians. Besides these, there are so many others of less celebrity that it is almost impossible to mention them all, even in guide-books devoted to the purpose. It would be difficult to find a stretch of good bathing along the northern Atlantic coast for seven hundred miles which has not its large or small hotel and its regular or transient visitors. Indeed, there are very few mountain nooks, pretty lakes, shady dells, or other places where the heat of summer can be comfortably endured in the Eastern States, that have not been utilized as "summer resorts" by this half-nomadic, ever-traveling people.

Long Branch is the celebrated of all the surf-bathing resorts of America. The beach extends for a distance of two miles without interruption under a high sand bluff. Along the edge of this bluff runs a wide carriage-drive; and within that extends, at irregular intervals, a line of immense frame hotels. People from all parts of the United States crowd to this place for a few days, a week, or longer during the season, which extends from about the first of July to the first of September. There is constant communication between Long Branch and New York, about twenty miles distant; and many citizens of the metropolis go down every evening after business hours, leaving their families there permanently. The 'Summer New York,' as it is sometimes called, is given up to social gaieties which extend to absolute dissipation. All fashionable distractions are as numerous and constant here in summer as during the height of mid-winter society life in the city.

From *Life at the Sea Shore, Where to Go, How to Get There, and How to Enjoy Public Resorts on the New England, New York and New Jersey Coasts, Princeton, 1880; and Illustrated London News*, September 4, 1875, quoted in *Another Look at Nauvoo to the Hook*, George H. Moss, Jr., Ploughshare Press, Sea Bright, 1990.

1875
Long Branch

Olive Logan

Beach flirtations and the surf were two of the main attractions in fashionable Long Branch.

The first railroad to Long Branch was extended four miles east from *Eatontown in 1860, and in 1865 the seashore line was built, setting off a post Civil War land boom. Long Branch, now an elegant resort spread out along the grassy bluff 20 feet above the strand, reached its apogée when President Ulysses S. Grant arrived in 1869, and for the ne xt three decades was the "gayest, sportiest, most fashionable" shore vacation destination. Monmouth*

Park racetrack opened its gates on July 4, 1870, and the president took a box. Eight years later the track was upgraded and Long Branch responded by building elaborate new hotels. Gambling[1] was introduced in 1876, and a decade of showy opulence followed. Four more U.S. presidents made Long Branch their summer capital: Rutherford Hayes, Chester Arthur, William McKinley and James Garfield, who was brought to nearby Elberon in an effort to save his life after he was shot by an assassin in 1881.

Olive Logan, an actress, journalist, playwright and lecturer, spent the summer and fall of 1875 in Long Branch and wrote about her stay for Harper's New Monthly Magazine. *Her haughty tone matched the snobbishness of the resort.*

Long Branch is like the lady's foot of *Punch's* shoe-maker — remarkably long and narrow. The fashionable watering-place reaches from Financier Jay Gould's cottage on the north to President Grant's cottage on the south, a distance of two or three miles, and somewhat suggests a carpenter's set scene at the theatre; it is painted on a straight piece of canvas: what is behind it, the audience neither knows nor cares. Those who have taken the trouble to look behind the scenes at Long Branch are aware that there is a little New Jersey village back there, with some pretty farms and parks, a race-track, and a few such trifles. But the crowds which come and go in the season, on pleasure bent, do not for the most part take cognizance of any thing but the gay scene along the shore, with its straggling hotels and abundance of piazza looking over out to sea. The popular drive is along the beach road called Ocean Avenue, which is the main artery, the Broadway, the Boulevard, of the "summer capital."

It has been a newspaper fashion lately to call Long Branch the American Brighton[2], but a Brighton it certainly is not, and will never be until the barn-like frame buildings which serve it as hotels are pulled down and others are erected of a material more solid, substantial, and imposing. It is these sprawling wooden structures which give to Long Branch that cheap and tawdry air — the place is very suggestive of a circus.

When the dinner train arrives from town just at that delicious lazy hour of mid-summer eve when the sun is gone but the dusk not fairly come, and Ocean Avenue is lively with fast-flying horses, driven by men in livery — conveying loads of human freight to places of residence, cottage, hotel, or boarding-house; when numberless flags in brightest red, white, and blue flutter from liberty-poles on lawns and hotel-tops;

when brass-bands blare on the grassy lawns, and here and there side-show-like tents for the sale of pop and gingerbread, or practice with air-guns as striped targets flap their canvas sides in the breeze from the swashing sea — indeed, the whole thing is irresistibly suggestive of saw-dust and a ring.

The bands and the flags and the fast-flying horses are no doubt intended by the innkeepers, who principally plan and shape the manners and customs here, to awaken a mad feeling of hilarity in the bosom of the arriving guest; but they are destructive to the sentiment of quiet and elegant repose which should no doubt inspire the existence of an altogether high-toned summer resort.

Long Branch is perhaps better in accord with the spirit of American institutions than any other of our watering-places. It is more republican than either Newport or Coney Island, because within its bounds the extremes of our life meet more freely. It is not so aristocratic as Newport, yet the President of the United States lives there, and so do many other prominent examples of our political, literary, artistic, commercial, and social life. It is not so democratic as Coney Island, yet the poorer and more ignorant classes are largely represented throughout the season.

On hot Sundays there come to Long Branch great throngs of cheap excursionists, small tradesmen and artisans with their families, with a sprinkling of roughs and sharpers. Long Branch has equal attractions for rich and poor. It is quite astonishing with what ease the millionaire can get rid of dollars there, and it is almost equally astonishing what cheap and comfortable quarters are at the command of the humblest purses. The same magnificent sea view which is put so heavily in the bill of the lodger on the first floor of the big hotels can be enjoyed by the poorer lodger near the roof of the cheaper houses at a comparatively insignificant cost.

Some of the most crushing dandies who loaf in the parlor door at the fashionable hotels when the Saturday night "hop" is on, faultless in attire and killingly eyeglassed and mustached, might be traced to humble abodes in the back region behind the theatrical scene when they saunter homeward in the hour approaching midnight. They are just as well-bred, well-mannered, and well-appearing gentlemen as any at Long Branch, and are just as well received by what is there called society.

Long Branch further illustrates a side of American character in the fact that it is a direct result of business energy, enterprise, shrewdness, and "push." It did not grow up slowly, year by year, an outcome of the natural fitness of things as Newport and Saratoga did. Twenty years ago it had no fashionable existence, which is saying it had no existence at all. There was nothing there but a lonely stretch of sandy shore, against which the surf beat unhonored and unsung. And even now one seeks in vain for the reason why this particular spot was chosen for this purpose, until his seeking brings him to the simple truth that certain speculators willed it so. They willed that the tide of New York's summer-resort seekers should pass by the charming Highlands of the Navesink, which now blink dully at the long whizzing trains flitting past them five or six times a day, loaded down with merry throngs all the summer through.

Along the road from Sandy Hook to Long Branch lie beautiful little villages which have their yearly throng of summer patrons, but they are not "the Branch," and their strongest recommendation as watering-places is that they are within easy driving distance of the summer capital. The glory and gain of transforming Long Branch from a deserted stretch of New Jersey coast into *the* sea-side city of to-day, and of familiarizing its name to the popular ear to such an extent that Chicago itself is not more celebrated, undoubtedly rest with a few capitalists who bought farms in Monmouth County for thirty or forty dollars an acre, and set about turning their corn fields into villa plots.

By one device and another, legitimate and illegitimate, by building a new railroad, by improvements of various sorts, and divers plans for attracting public attention to their pet and pride, the capitalists forced the growth of the place in public appreciation, and achieved a veritable *coup d'état* when they induced President Grant to go and live there in the summer.

There have been unfavorable comments made upon the President's course in accepting his handsome cottage by the sea, and for living in it a portion of his time in summer; but the American public must always have something it can scold its Presidents for, and I do not suppose General Grant slept less soundly, lulled by the murmur of the waves upon the beach, because of his critics. Probably Presidents get used to being scolded.

It is a lovely home; and when the President sits on his back piazza of a summer evening to smoke his after-dinner cigar, with his gentle and amiable wife and his comely children about him, it is a sight which no lover of his country need feel uneasy at seeing. At such a time, doors and windows all wide open, and the interior furnishing glimpses of a comfortable but not showy home, with pictures and books about and lamps burning, perhaps a group of carriages will come rolling down the road from the hotel region, and a crowd of friends and fellow-citizens with a band of music will invade the lawn. Then the dulcet strains of a serenade will rise on the evening air, and the family group will sit listening, to break into a little ripple of applause now and then, and Mrs. Grant, leaning over the piazza railing, will chat familiarly with whomsoever chances to be standing near, and press her visitors to come in.

"Do come in," I once heard her say on such an occasion; "we can give you a cracker at least in our little cot." Simple, unpretentious, and kindly, a scene like this is worthy to live in the records of our republican land, a type of its best spirit.

A flavor of Baden-Baden[3], as it was in the days before gambling was prohibited, is furnished at Long Branch by Chamberlin's club-house, an elegant "cottage" — for every building is a cottage here, unless it is a hotel — situated within a stone's throw of the West End Hotel, and within sight of the President's home. In the club-house there are tables for roulette, *rouge et noir,* and other games of chance, and I am told the scene late at night, when the place is thronged with Wall Street men and other skillful skirmishers with the goddess of luck, is a very brilliant one; but unlike the games *salons* of Baden-Baden, the gentler sex do not mingle in the scene at Chamberlin's.

Those ladies who wish to indulge their passion for winning or losing at hazard can do so on stated days at Monmouth Park — a racing ground a short drive back in the country, where the "Jersey Derby"[4] holds its "meetings."

Fashion is a queer moralist; and the same people who would be horrified at the thought of joining the throng in Chamberlin's club-house to toy with its tiger, go without a qualm to the races at Monmouth and bet their money on the running of horses instead of on the turning of a card. It is true that a large proportion of those who go to the races go as lovers of horseflesh and never gamble there; but it is equally true that betting is freely and openly indulged in by many ladies as well as gentlemen who have been taught to look upon gambling as a terrible vice.

The season of Long Branch is supposed to open about the 15th of

June and to close about the 15th of September — at least this is the period fixed by the hotel-keepers, who would, however, willingly extend it. But the fact is, the weather regulates the matter, and it has happened that Long Branch has been less full in the middle of July than it was at a far earlier period in the summer. A sudden storm came up one day last summer which played queer pranks in the parlor of the Ocean House. This parlor is used for dancing, and its carpet is covered over with a linen cloth; the furniture is of willow; and though the servants made all haste to close the windows and fasten the blinds, the wind swept in under the dancing cloth and blew it up like a huge bladder, upon which tables and chairs rode high in air, like little ships upon a rolling sea. Children were in ecstasies of delight at this phenomenon, and went wading out upon this airy sea, which tumbled them about shrieking with laughter and excitement.

Stormy weather by the sea-side is not without its charms to the thought-ful mind, however. A grand storm at Long Branch, if one is not too timid to relish the novelty, is a glorious experience; for thus one may enjoy one of the most thrilling sensations of an ocean voyage without the unpleas-ant accompaniment of seasickness or the possibility of shipwreck.

The first week of August was characterized by a prolonged series of storms which vied in intensity with those of winter. The great waves roared and plunged upon the beach, a gigantic wall of foam, noisy as Niagara, and the sea was white with rage as far out as the eye could see. Bathing was put a stop for several days, and the huts on the sands were so drenched with water that they were hardly dry again that season, but set one to sneezing whenever they were ventured into for disrobing pur-poses. Many of them were washed away; and after the storm was over, the shore was strewn for miles with strange objects, *débris* of shipwrecked craft, great piles of the slimy vegetation of the sea, dead fish and ani-mals. It set us thinking to walk on the beach that Sunday morning after the long storm and view the snapped masts, broken spars, baskets, boxes, and other *disjecta membra* of foundered craft — among them a defunct camel, water-swollen and hideous.

At the opening of the summer season, the shore in front of each hotel at Long Branch is taken possession of by certain men of semi-seafaring appearance, who proceed to set up on the sands, just under the bluff, rows of bathing huts of an architecture so contemptible that even Uncle

Tom and Topsy would have turned up their noses at them — shanties, of course, weather-browned boards, unpainted and often even unplanted, rudely nailed together, sides and roof of the same material, as incapable of keeping out wind and rain as so many paper boxes.

The same men also set up a shanty of a larger sort, with a roof that is water-tight, which they occupy in company with piles of faded woolen garments which they facetiously denominate "bathing dresses," and which they still more facetiously let to ladies and gentlemen throughout the summer at the rate of half a dollar for each bath. I suppose these men do not really look upon this transaction in the light of being the huge joke it is, but it certainly would not surprise me to learn that a beginner at the business was tortured with mad longings to rush behind the shanty and relieve his pent-up risibles in writhings of laughter after each successive letting of a damp woolen shirt and trowsers tied with string as a "bathing dress." Those who pass any considerable time at the Branch, and bathe with regularity, of course provide themselves with bathing suits of their own; but transient visitors do not find it convenient to do this; and how greatly in demand the garments of the bath-keepers are, is shown by the fact that they are often furnished damp and clammy to the new-comer, having had no time to dry since their last tenant paid for their occupancy.

If the Witch of Endor[5] had presided at the construction of these miraculous bathing suits, they could scarcely be more ugly and fantastic than they are. That so many Americans are to be found who are willing to put them on, and walk unflinchingly across the stretch of sand between disrobing hut and surf, under the fire of hundreds of glances from the ladies and gentlemen present, is proof that the bravery of the nation should not be lightly impugned.

The semi-seafaring Jerseymen who lease the bathing dresses are the only guardians of the beach. Sometimes they are two in number; at the larger hotels, three; but they ought to be a dozen. They loiter on the sands when not otherwise occupied with their tenancy work — and keep a good-natured eye upon the bathers, ready to go in and help should there be a cry for help. But it is easy to see that when their presence is most needed, when the bathers are most numerous, why, precisely then their garment-letting trade is liveliest and absorbs all their attention. There should be men to guard the beach, like watchmen, at all hours, with no other duty than to dissuade persons from bathing at unsafe conditions of the tide, and watching those who do bathe, assiduously and unceasingly. Lifeboats should be constantly plying. This is done in France, and it can be done here. The only protection our bathers have is a rope fastened to stakes on shore and in the water — a great convenience certainly, but puerile indeed when viewed as a measure of safety. When the surf is strong, the rope becomes useless to women and children, whose hands are torn violently from it by the power of the waves.

The bathing hour at Long Branch is generally in the earlier half of the day, but occasionally it falls in the afternoon. It is regulated, of course, by the tide; when the tide is lowest, bathing is safest. The signal to hotel and cottage people is a white flag which is seen flying from a short staff at the head of the wooden staircase that leads from the grassy summit of the bluff down to the sands. Each of the great hotels includes in its grounds a strip of beach, as do those cottages which look on Ocean Avenue. There is nothing exclusive about any of the hotel bathing grounds. Ostensibly for the "guests" of the hotel, they are actually open to any one who chooses to avail himself of their limited conveniences.

When the white flag is seen flying, there begins a general hegira of men, women, and children who go streaming down to the beach in crowds, some to bathe, some to look on. The scene when the day is fair and the bathing good, the water mild in temperature and the surf rolling gently in with a long shallow stretch, is a very animated one. From a central point, like that of the Ocean Hotel grounds, one may look up and down the beach for miles, witnessing schools of bathers at frequent intervals throughout the entire distance. Some days one may see two or three thousand bathers in the water at once, making the air vocal with shouts and laughter, the nervous shrieks of the timid and the boisterous merriment of the brave. The sexes mingle freely and it is no uncommon experience for the belles and beaux of the ball-room to make appointments between the figures in the Lancers[6] for the next day's bath.

The morning being usually devoted to the bath, the afternoon is set apart for excursions and drives. At a special festivity at Pleasure Bay[7], such as a clam-bake or a regatta, you are liable to meet the most important people at the Branch. The President himself has at times deigned to attend a clam-bake. Pleasure Bay is a charming drive from the centre of gayety at the Branch, just a mile and a half through a lovely open country to an old-fashioned New Jersey tavern in the midst of a green grove on the bank of a placid sheet of water. There is a flavor of combined Bohemianism and rustic simplicity about the place which contrasts delightfully with the ostentation of luxury of the sea-side hotel where you are staying; and it is but a carping critic who would discuss, while enjoying the cheap delights of the Old Pleasure Bay House, whether the landlord maintains its primitive simplicity out of a sentimental, poetic love of nature, or merely because (as some assert) he is too stingy to spend any of his profits in modern improvements. Be this as it may, it is pleasant to sit at the weather-beaten tables under the green trees and eat his crabs, and then go and catch some.

A fairy-like yacht with spreading sail receives you at the water's edge, and you are blown over to the opposite shore, where, with a chunk of fish on the end of a string, and a net at the end of a pole, you find that catching crabs is as easy as eating them. The sail gives you a glorious appetite, and if there is a clam-bake when you return, you will proceed to eat ravenously of a conglomeration of green corn, clams, crabs, potatoes, and yellow-legged chickens.

The excursions to Ocean Grove, like those to Pleasure Bay, are both for special and general reasons, the special being the camp-meetings which are held there at intervals during the summer. Ocean Grove is a summer city of Methodists, an hour's brisk carriage drive from Long Branch, through a somewhat monotonous country. It is on the sea-shore, and its bathing habits are precisely as those of Long Branch; in most other respects there is a complete dissimilarity. No balls, no billiards, no bars, no late hours, no dissipations of any sort are permitted at Ocean Grove, and existence there is carried on inexpensively. It is a sort of poor man's paradise, though there are rich people there; but even the rich dwell in modest cottages, while those who must practice a close economy live in tents or in cheaply constructed cabins in the woods. The place is curious and interesting in many respects, and visitors to Long Branch do not feel that they have seen all the "lions" until they have driven down to Ocean Grove. The gates of the community are closed at an early hour in the evening and on Sundays; but as one side of the Grove is not fenced in, but looks on a pretty sheet of water, visitors to the Sunday camp-meeting quit their carriages on the shore of the little lake[8], and are smuggled over — not very surreptitiously — in row-boats for a one-cent fare. The meetings are sometimes held on the seashore, right down where the surf makes music in harmony with the human chorus, and sometimes under the trees in the grove.

The amusements of the evening at Long Branch are varied: not to speak of such favorite diversions as lovers' strolls in moonlight or starlight on the beach, there are dancing parties every evening in the parlors of all the large hotels, with occasional concerts, dramatic entertainments, etc., usually given by amateurs and for some charitable object. Occasionally, too, a circus comes along and pitches its tent on the vacant lot near the Ocean Hotel, and, strange as it may seem to those who know not the ways of the fashionable world, the circus is packed full, not with the Jerseymen from the back village merely, but with the leaders of the *monde* at Long Branch.

The favorite night for dancing is Saturday; custom has made this the most brilliant night in the week in the parlors of the hotels; more people arrive on Saturday than on any other day, and in the height of the season on a Saturday night the piazzas will be so thronged that it is almost impossible to move about, thousands of men and women in gala attire sitting by the open windows to listen to the music and see the dancers. They have the best of it too, for dancing in midsummer ball-rooms is hot work, and the sterner sex invariably maintain that they thus make martyrs of themselves only to please the fair. Dancing is always concluded at half past ten except on Saturday nights, when it is sometimes prolonged till the stroke of twelve.

On Saturday nights, at some of the hotels, an instrumental concert — called "sacred" by courtesy — is given on the balcony, the piano being wheeled out there for the occasion. On other nights, after the dance is over, parties will sometimes be made up to go and serenade the President, or some other person of consequence, or lady of social popularity. Groups go strolling on the grassy bluff or gather in some favorite nook to sing hilarious songs, with wine and wit and spirits bent on driving dull care away.

Beyond all question, the most delightful time of the year at Long Branch, but not the most fashionable, is the autumn, when then comes upon the shining face of the sea a soft haze which is most agreeable to the eye, and the air is full of balmy odors. To many people the sight of the sea with the sunlight beating on it in the bright days of summer is painful and wearisome.

"Oh, I can't bear that sea!" cried a poet of my acquaintance, one day, as we stood on the bluff; "it puts my eyes out."

But in the mellow days of autumn, though the ocean then grows smoother than even in the hottest of the dog-days — though it will sometimes lie for days together like a mirror, it is not a mirror which flashes back dazzling sunbeams, but absorbs them, and the eye is rested. Then the lapping waves woo the shore so gently and playfully that bathing therein is an Oriental luxury not to be resisted. The atmosphere is so sweet and pure you can almost taste it, and the waters, warmed by the long heats of summer, are as balmy as the air. When the tide is low, there lie exposed such long reaches of shallow bathing ground as the bathers of the midsummer would hardly believe possible. On the same spot of shore where, in July, the surf buffeted strong men and tossed them, panting with exhaustion on the hot sands, now, in September, they might wade out half a mile from shore before they would meet a surf sufficiently strong to knock them off their feet. But in September, when the surf-bathing was like this, there would be no more than three or four lonely bathers in the sea at the hour when formerly there were a hundred. I remained at Long Branch last season until near October. The hotels were utterly deserted; cows pastured on the lawns in front of them; the windows were nailed up with boards, the bathing huts were torn to pieces and lay piled, mere every-day lumber, in heaps on the grassy bluff; no carriages rolled up and down the Avenue; no lovers strolled upon the sands; yet the days were simply heavenly, and passed by like dreams of fairy-land. Long Branch was at its loveliest, but the crowds were gone.

NOTES

1. *Gambling:* A wave of puritanical reform swept New Jersey in the 1890s; the race track closed and gambling was outlawed. Long Branch's popularity started to slide.

2. *Brighton:* The British shore resort famous during the late 18th and 19th centuries for its riotously extravagant and exotic pavilion commissioned by the Prince of Wales, son of George III. It is still a popular year-round resort.

3. *Baden-Baden:* A southwest German spa, known for its curative waters.

4. *Jersey Derby:* After the track closed, this race was moved to Kentucky.

5. *Witch of Endor:* The reference is from 1 Samuel:28-7.

6. *Lancers:* A variation of the quadrille, danced by four couples.

7. *Pleasure Bay:* An apartment complex is now near the site of the steamship landing on Pleasure Bay.

8. *Little lake:* Wesley Lake.

From *Harper's New Monthly Magazine*, September 1876, volume 53, no. 316.

✺

1877
Sandy Hook to Atlantic City

William Rideing

William Rideing and Granville Perkins sailed from West Creek to Beach Haven to Atlantic City and back to Barnegat Inlet in this 30-foot catboat captained by Bill Pharo.

▨ *Traveling south by carriage, train and sailboat into the relative wilderness of the central New Jersey coast was a real adventure in 1877.* Harper's New Monthly Magazine *assigned a writer, William Rideing, and an illustrator, Granville Perkins, to explore some of the developing shore resorts. The pair* left Manhattan by steamer, stopped briefly at Sandy Hook, then continued by train to West Creek, where they hired a boat to sail them across the bay to Beach Haven, then south to Atlantic City.

Beach Haven was only three years old, and the voyagers had a limited choice of lodging: the oceanfront Parry House, the Engleside Hotel (newly opened by Robert Engle, who three years earlier had been manager of the Parry House) or the Bay View House on the edge of the marshes. Rideing did not state in which hotel they stayed, perhaps maintaining journalistic neutrality. But, judging from his story, he did appreciate the natural setting of this nascent resort on the outer beach, even if he didn't seem to hold out much hope for its future development.

Atlantic City in 1877 was in the process of transforming itself from a tiny shore village with rough accommodations catering to fishermen and sportsmen to an urban center by the sea. The Philadelphia and Atlantic City Narrow Gauge Railway was completed that year, bringing packed carloads of one-day excursionists. Atlantic City had become accessible to Philadelphia's working class, eager for an outing by the ocean, even if they had to put up with saber-toothed mosquitoes and voracious greenhead and black flies. About 34,000 visitors came that summer to stroll on the handsome, new, eight-foot-wide boardwalk.

We join Rideing and Perkins as they are asking the government agent stationed in Sandy Hook where they can find a place to eat.

"Is there a restaurant?"

The signal-man's face lengthened with amazement. "Restaurant!" he repeated, incredulously — "restaurant!" and then he smiled provokingly.

"Well," I continued, "is there any place where we can get some pickled mussels, or something of that kind?"

The suggestion of this appetizing delicacy gave the signal-man's mind a more serious turn, and enabled him to answer my first question with the gravity which its importance demanded. "Don't know about pickled mussels," he answered; "but you see that little house over the sand, just beyond the plank-walk?" We saw an unpainted, forlorn, orphan-like shanty in the direction indicated. "Well, you may be able to get a bit of something to eat there."

Where were we, that the idea of a public larder was so preposterous? In a tower some fifty or sixty feet above the ground-level, out before us beat the Atlantic — a great quivering plain, upon which ships were short-ening or making sail, and over which they were stealing so noiselessly and mysteriously that they seemed to be intangible shadows in a dream. It all seemed like a dream: that immense platitude of green-gray irregu-larly speckled with the white of combing waves; that serene arch of blue rising above the illimitable basin of water with a few shreds of cloud hanging from it; that low line of glittering white fretted with ermine surf; the fish-hawks that swept down from a self-sustained perch and flapped up again with something silvery in their beaks — yes, it was like a dream; and the breathing of the wind and the beat of the sea increased the lull. That was the picture as we looked seaward. Landward it was different.

We surveyed a crooked neck of cedars, sand hills, swamp, and beach, washed by a bay, every ripple on which was tipped by a diamond-like point of reflected sunshine; and the bay led into a river guarded by a line of bluffs moodily wrapped in dusky foliage, save where a clearing showed a scar of crimson earth. There was nothing like this in Newport, whence we had recently come; nothing like the solace and recreative quietude; nothing nearly so beautiful as this low-keyed symphony of wind, water, and sky. This sequestration from restaurants and hotels, from bathing houses and Saturday-evening hops, from summer excursionists and modern improvements of all sorts, was the idealization of a holiday vaca-tion. Here we might muse and rest, renew and review ourselves, expiat-ing (with a pipe of good tobacco) the errors of the past in a mental way, and easily forming better plans for the future; here our nearest connec-tion with the active world seemed to be that phantom-like procession of sailing vessels, which exquisitely illustrated the rhythm of nature, though less than three miles away was the landing of the Long Branch boats with their loads of social butterflies.

We were on the extremity of Sandy Hook, that narrow peninsula which stretches into the ocean like a hand of greeting and farewell to the ves-sels that pass into and out of New York Harbor through the deep-water ship channel which it borders and our stand-point was the tower of the United States Signal Service Station.

We trod back to the steamboat landing along the narrow, much-in-dentured edge of beach, upon which large numbers of horseshoe crabs had stranded, and thence we went southward in a train, most of whose passengers were city people returning from business to their summer homes at Long Branch. That fashionable resort had no inducements strong enough to detain us, who were in search of the picturesque, and we continued in the cars to Whiting's, some thirty-six miles farther down the coast, where we transferred ourselves from the New Jersey Southern to the Tuckerton Railway, by which we arrived at West Creek.

There is an implication of remoteness and queerness in the very name of West Creek. The traveller who finds it in his time-tables is quite sure not to make the mistake of supposing that it is much of a town, or a mushroom outcome of real estate speculation. It is old, probably; its inhabitants are fishermen, and the sea washes up to it through a slough in one of the wonderfully green saltwater marshes. That is the idea the name would convey, and it would not be very much out of the way.

The inhabitants are fishermen, farmers, and boat-builders properly, but in the course of a year they turn their hands to the harvesting of salt hay and ice, the cultivation of oysters and clams, or to almost any thing else that will yield an honest penny. Many of them are old sea-captains, who in their day have taken large vessels on voyages to the farthest countries, and who, because the sea when it once takes hold of a man never wholly relieves him of its charm, or allows inland life to be endurable, are satisfying their lingering cravings for the element by short and safe yacht cruises, spiced by the small profits and gentle adventurousness of blue-fishing. Others have been fishers from babyhood, their cradles seines, and their mothers' apron strings trolling lines. By thrifty living the best of these have acquired the proprietorship of small cat-boats or sloops, and are enabled to exist comfortably and respectably.

To understand the geographical position of West Creek, it is necessary that the reader should know one remarkable and uniform feature of the Atlantic coast. From Long Island southward to Cape Fear, a distance of some six hundred miles, the main-land is separated from the ocean by a belt of dazzling white sand, intersected and broken into islands by narrow inlets, and at the portals of New York, Philadelphia, and Baltimore, by the New York, Delaware, and Chesapeake bays. In some places this outer beach is not more than a quarter of a mile wide, the surf almost drenching it from side to side, and in other places it is five miles wide. The sea encroaches upon it or extends it from year to year, widening here and shortening it there, and sometimes leaving dangerous shoals still farther out, upon which the waves break in terrific tumult. Few of the inlets are navigable, and most of them are constantly changing positions, new ones appearing after violent storms, and others being as suddenly filled in by sand. The water between the beach and the main-land is navigable to small vessels, and when the sea is heavy outside, it affords safe sailing to the many sloops and schooners trading between village and village along the coast. On the inner border the main-land meets it with a long, low, melancholy fringe of salt meadows, which retreat into cedar swamps and firmer ground.

From the dusky cedars and through the meadows West Creek flows, and on its banks, where it is not more than twelve feet wide, the village stands. The fresh-water of such land-born streamlets, mingling with the salt of the ocean, and the flat reaches of sedge and rushes, make a paradise for birds, and in the gunning seasons sportsmen from the city drop into the village, but other visitors are seldom seen.

Leaving it by the way of the creek, the village looks its prettiest. Its white houses are compactly knotted in a clustering wood, and above the topmost waves of green a church spire impales the sky. It resembles an island, the low meadows pressing against it without a shrub or tree among the tall rank grasses, whose swaying is the only relief to their prostrate verdancy. Drifting through those meadows on a brilliant August day in the smallest of sloops; a warm sun and a sapphire dome of sky; the heat of the sun modified by a sea-breeze, and the blue feathered with distant waifs of cloud; a pile of salt hay strewn in the stern for our comfort in reclining — such were the accessories that made idleness sweet, exertion vanity, and care a vapor, as we hoisted sail at the little landing and moved toward the ocean.

The artist[1] had been quiet so far, but now he burst into rapturous exclamations of delight at the colors, the shadows, and the forms, exacting attention to this object and that, as an artist will when he strikes a phase of nature to which his imagination is harmoniously responsive. The creek is a zigzag, and its straight reaches are so short that in whichever direction the wind is, the tacks must be frequent and abrupt. Each turn brought something new in view to arouse the enthusiasm of my artist friend, and one moment he eagerly directed my observation to the queer sail of a passing sloop and its flickering reflection on the water, or to the indolent attitude of the sunburned man at the tiller; the next moment to an old battered scow lying against the muddy bank with the long grass hanging over it and trying to hide its unloveliness; the next, to a mass of drift-wood washed into a little bay, upon which the sun, breaking through a bed of rushes, cast long yellow bars; the next, to the village wrapped up in the foliage, that was now quite distant; the next — but his discoveries were continuous and his raptures inexhaustible. Meanwhile a whole fleet of fishing boats were passing us on their way to the village, and our captain sitting astern was talking to us incessantly.

We had intended to hire the boat of Aaron Pharo for our cruise; but as he was away fishing, we accepted the offer of his brother to take us to him. Brother Bill is a celebrity from Cape May to Squan², and his character is so luminous that I think it would project itself in any community. A little boastfulness; a good deal of a certain kind of knowledge; a clear perception of what is wrong, and a total inability to live up to the precepts which he reiterates oftenest; much good nature, and no means to substantially gratify it; a flood of profanity and irreligion, with a Gulf Stream of sentiment mellowing parts, and putting around his nature some of the pleasant mistiness through which we now see it — these are some of the boldest headlands in his moral coastline, and they are, after all, the salient features of many others; but what leaves him in one's memory as a gleaming point of humor is the very oddest face I ever saw, and a most wonderful pair of trousers. The trousers he wore rose from the knees with a spring-tide to within a few inches of the shoulders, where a pair of determined-looking suspenders caught them, and they were as voluminous behind as a Chinese novel. His face is long and red, two high cheek-bones pressing against two saucer-like, deep-set eyes, with a craggy forehead hanging over them, and a comical seriousness flashing in them. His conversation covered a wide variety of subjects; it was his opinion that what is now New Jersey was recently, geologically speaking, part of the bottom of the sea, and in proof thereof he adduced the fact that oyster shells had been found very much farther inland than the present coast-line.

We passed out from the mouth of the sinuous creek into Little Egg Harbor Bay, separating the outer beach from the main-land, and sailed across to Beach Haven, the newest of watering-places, where we proposed to spend the night. Behind us was that emerald expanse of meadow limited by a broad blue line against which West Creek village rose; a fleet of small sailing vessels was in sight, and beyond the beach, which threw off a blinding reflection from its intensely white sand, was the ocean, with larger sailing vessels gliding north and south.

The landing at Beach Haven is inviting, but its promise is not fulfilled by a more intimate acquaintance with what is called "the only practical sea-side resort in America." Pleasure-boats with white hulls and high, slender masts are harbored around the wharf, and more serviceable sloops and schooners find anchorage in the adjacent waters. The beach is not more than half a mile wide, and it fronts on the bay with an edging of salt meadows, which are half submerged and redolent of brine.

A long path leads up to three overgrown caravansaries — these with a row of bathing-houses, comprising the settlement, which is unique in several ways. It is called a "practical" sea-side resort because it is actually on the ocean, and the bay removes it from any thing more than a mere suspicion of land air. The surf on the outer beach is boisterous, the waves throbbing in overwhelmingly, and the wind spends itself over the low reach of sand without a tree or elevation of any kind to break its force. For the first few hours of a visit one is amazed at the unaccountableness of the taste which brings people here in search of pleasure. The light is intolerably glaring; the shore is flat and verdureless; in times of storm the hotels are bleak and unsheltered, and in calms they are filled with mosquitoes. It is not accountable at any time, indeed, unless we give the visitors credit for a keener susceptibility to a very subtle and poetic form of nature than most watering-places *habitués* have. Charles Kingsley[3] once said that marshes were one of the kinds of scenery he liked the best; a quick appreciation of color and a sensitiveness to the inarticulate pathos of the "mighty mother" are necessary to their apprehension, and it is in the marshes that reward will be found by those having such qualifications. But what most visitors came for and staid for were the evening hops, the bathing and yachting, all of which are much better at many other places we could name; and it is in view of this fact that Beach Haven is unaccountable.

We arrived on a Saturday evening. Fiddles were scraping and feet shuffling in the halls of the big hotels; the broad piazzas were crowded with loungers and promenaders, mostly fair maidens and stately matrons in refrigerant summer dress that reached their necks in diaphanous snowy muslins; the men were happy in a surfeit of tender attentions; and at the close of day, all the yachting parties having come home to supper, the wharf on the bay was left to us.

The sun was setting on the brilliant plain of sedge as we looked landward and beheld the spires of West Creek and Tuckerton rising out of the distant woods, which changed from blue to purple, and from purple to a smoky crimson, until the great globe of fire sunk well behind them and left them a chilly black. But before this, the whole sky was transformed into a sea full of flaming shoals; a mass of cirro-cumuli had become detached, and the fragments floated against the pearly blue of the sky and burned with the reflected glow. Green never before seemed so green, or so capable of many shades, as it did on the marshes, which, as the sun disappeared behind the woods, were momentarily tipped with gold, and then left to brooding green and blue.

In the far north a storm was bursting of tumultuous clouds, which had also caught some of the rosy magnificence of the sunset, and were laced with the vivid thrusts of forked lightning. The night came upon us, advancing from a tender pearl blue to a steel blue, and from a steel blue to an unsympathetic gray, which grew darker until the last light from the west had been extinguished and the stars pierced the sky with incisive brilliancy. The myriad stars that shone in the opaline moonlight night were as nothing compared in numbers with the gnats and mosquitoes; but who would not have endured even greater torments for a sight so memorable? It was such a sunset as can be seen nowhere else than on those plaintive marshes and barren sands of the Jersey coast.

The sandy strip upon which the "practical sea-side resort" is situated is nearly twenty miles long, and is called Long Beach, its northern extremity being formed by the Barnegat Inlet, and its southern extremity by the Little Egg Harbor Inlet. The next island south is called Brigantine Beach; the Barnegat Shoals are northward. Along this desolate coast so many vessels have come to grief, and so many bodies have been washed ashore, that it is known among fishermen as the Grave-yard.

Treasures from many lands are gathered from wrecks, and a fisherman's family is often helped through a trying winter by the provisions which the sea casts up. When an orange schooner is wrecked, there is dessert after every meal in the cottages; or should the cargo be prunes, that fruit becomes a common article of diet. A visitor is sometimes surprised to see foreign brands of olives and canned stuffs on the shelves of the village stores; he learns that they have been secured from a wreck; and the host of one inn at which we spent a night had some excellent Maria Benvenuto claret, labelled, with grim suggestiveness, "Importation direct *via* Barnegat Shoals."

Much queerer things than these are occasionally picked up. A forlorn old parrot, feeble from its un-English complainings, drifted in on a spar, and at another time a pair of Manx[4] cats were saved from a wreck by a noted old beach-man, Caleb Parker, of Harvey Cedars, near the Barnegat Light, who has raised a family of eleven more, and meets a visitor at the door of his cottage with a purring retinue of his furry friends, one of them perched on his cap, two others playing on his shoulders, and the rest brushing his legs. "Dad" Parker is one of the heroes of the coast, and carries a silver medal presented to him for life-saving.

Fashionable summer resorts are new things to the outer beach. Formerly a small house was erected here and there for the accommodation of sportsmen and parties of fishermen, who came over from the main-land with their wives, daughters, and sweethearts for an evening dance. The gayety of one of these gatherings at Harvey Cedars was eclipsed by the startling announcement that a ship had gone ashore, and was making signals of distress; whereupon the whole company made for the beach, including the women in all their holiday finery, and not a ribbon or a flounce was thought of until the last man had been landed from the wreck.

Bill's brother Aaron came to Beach Haven for us on Sunday morning, and we embarked in his yacht on a cruise up and down the coast. Parting with Bill, who was most affectionate, he gave us an account of an unlucky venture which he once made in prunes. A vessel from the Mediterranean was wrecked, and a large part of her cargo of fruit washed ashore. The sands were strewn with prunes, several cart-loads of which were gathered by Bill and peddled through the country in a carry-all with great success, until he was arrested for selling without a license, and condemned to forfeit his earnings.

"The shark's a derned greedy fish, likewise the octopus, and the 'skeeter' in August," he commented, at the end of his story, "but they ain't nothin' aside of an Ocean County constable."

We sailed down the bay, and out on to the ocean through the Little Egg Harbor Inlet, which separates Long Beach from Brigantine Beach. It was a white, windless day, and the sea was only disturbed by a silent, sleepy swell; even the water over the bar was unruffled; and white as the day was, the whiter beaches cast dazzling reflections in the lucid air. A fleet of small boats were fishing, and two or three larger vessels were at anchor over the wreck of the steamer *Cassandra*, which foundered some ten or twelve years ago, and from which they were still taking iron. Now and then a picturesque sloop drifted past, and the captain's wife projected her head above the cabin entrance to look at us; or a comrade of Aaron's went sailing into the bay with a load of blue-fish, one of which he held up for our admiration.

Few other parts of the coast are as populous with food fishes as New Jersey. Nineteen different species are caught in abundance, and not less than one million dollars' worth is sold annually, the principal markets being New York and Philadelphia. The tautog or black-fish, weighing from one and a half to four pounds, is taken with bait in large numbers both in summer and winter; the porgee, weighing from one-quarter to two pounds, is taken with bait in July and August; the sheep's head, weighing from two to twelve pounds, is taken by hand and net from June to October; the weak-fish, weighing from one-half to two pounds, is taken by hand and net; and about fifty thousand mackerel a day are caught during June and July. The other varieties that are more or less common include the drum-fish, the Lafayette fish (so called from the fact that it first appeared on the coast during the revisit to America of the French marquis), the blue-fish, the sword-fish, the cod-fish, the haddock, the winter flounder, the oblong flounder, the salmon, the anchovy, the smelt, the fall shad, the herring, and the menhaden or moss-bunker.

We went southward to Atlantic City, the popular watering-place of Philadelphia, with whose homes it is connected by two steam railways, the distance being about fifty-four and a half miles. Seen from the ocean, it is quite captivating, the striped tower of the Absecon Light rising to a stately height from a low belt of foliage, and only the handsome turrets of the leading hotels being visible. But the beauty vanishes on closer acquaintance, and we find a hot noisy flat covered with buildings and devices for the entertainment and recreation of multitudinous excursionists. The streets are wide, straight, and well paved. A praiseworthy effort has been made to line them with trees, but the desert-like heat and aridity coat the leaves with yellow early in the season. The hotels, saloons, restaurants, and boarding cottages of all sizes are innumerable; and along the beach, which is semicircular, there are photograph galleries, peep-shows, marionette theatres, conjuring booths, circuses, machines for trying the weight, lungs, or muscles of the inquisitive, swings, merry-go-rounds, and all the various side shows which reap the penny harvest of holiday crowds. These extrinsic attractions, which are so familiar in the second-class watering-places of England, make Atlantic City much gayer than the popular sea-side resorts of New York, such as Coney Island and Rockaway Beach; and were it not for the enormous beer pavilions, inestimable flow of lager and the Teutonic waiters, one might easily fancy himself to be on the other side.

Admirable precautions are taken for the safety of bathers. Some men with life-saving apparatus at their control are stationed in a tower from which they can observe the movements of the people in the water; and boatmen, whose duty is to avert cases of drowning, paddle watchfully along the outer line of surf. A plank-walk[5] extends along the beach; and there are many other things that command Atlantic City to us, and place it above the resorts of excursionists near the metropolis.

A fair wind carried our little yacht seven or eight miles north in an hour, and at sunset we were gliding, with a faint ripple at the bow, through a narrow "thoroughfare" of the bay. The marshes were on each side of us; behind and ahead a motionless sea, varying from a most vivid emerald to a dusky cedar green. A curtain of gray concealed the city, but a flash of gold suddenly emblazoned the western windows, and the lighthouse, whose tower rose in pathetic isolation against the horizon, sent forth a pallid ray. A heron projected itself in silhouette against a sky of red, gold and amber, in which the sun had left a sinuous trail of fire, and a flock of plovers whistled mournfully as they winged themselves home. The water was like a mirror, except where a school of small fish broke it into a thousand ripples, and our boat was inert, the sail hanging loosely from the mast. As the sun fell closer to the blue line of the main-land woods from a heaven of unspeakable color, the evening star and a crescent moon were growing more radiant in the pale gray-blue east, and cast a reflection on the water while it still held the imprint of the more passionate orb. We were alone in the world at that moment, and the world was motionless. There was a wan, pitiful look on the meadows, which, lying in a death-like lull, gave the scene its salience, and despite the rosy ardor of the western sky, nature desponded and fell into a sad sleep. Sunsets at second-hand are not satisfactory, but those that we saw night after night along the Jersey coast were so individualized in their contrasted splendor and melancholy under-tone that they really seemed to belong to its topography.

The wind fell altogether at dark, and as we drifted through the winding reaches of the thoroughfare, our ecstasies were overcome by a plague of mosquitoes and gnats, which attacked us so seriously that one member of our expedition was threatened with delirium. We had to propel the boat with poles. From time to time we grounded, and it was after midnight when we reached Bond's[6], a summer hotel south of Beach Haven.

The next day was cloudy and gray, and a variable wind took us through the bay to Barnegat Inlet, off the Barnegat Shoals. It was sunset when we reached our boat, and great flocks of birds flew out of the reeds, uttering wild and melancholy cries. A schooner lay at anchor near the inlet, and the wreck of the steamer *Mediator* was visible. One wreck is no sooner out of sight than another happens, and in such terrible evidences the few inhabitants of the settlement at the inlet are constantly reminded of how inhospitable a coast theirs is. Barnegat Light is famous, and we stood under it as it was ignited. The shaft towers from a bed of sand which has formed a ridge twenty or thirty feet high around the base, and out of which a few cedars grow. The great brilliancy of the lantern, which makes it visible to vessels some twenty miles away, is lost to people standing at the base, and the only indication of it is in the prismatic glass. The keeper's house is nearby, and the children sleep while the father watches and works in that radiant crown on the tower.

The wind was now in our favor, and we ran up to Tom's River past Waretown, where an old grave-yard sadly overlooks the sea, and past Seaside Park, another of the fashionable places which have appeared within the last three or four years on the outer beach. Tom's River is charming, and the village is one of the prettiest in America. Then we took the railway again and went to Sea Bright, where we spent a happy day with the fishermen. There is no settlement more picturesque or interesting than this along the shore, although summer boarding-houses and hotels are crowding the old huts[7] away. Small boats, white, green, and red, line the beach, their bronze sails flapping idly in the wind. Here an old fisherman sits mending his nets; there a boat with a load of shining mackerel has just been beached, and a lot of tawny men, bare-legged and bare-armed, are transferring her cargo to small hand-carts. The huts are built among the sand hills, and the peculiar, conical roofs of the ice-houses give the village a foreign look.

When we reached Pier No. 8, North River, where we ended our journey, we landed with faces as brown and weather-beaten as Bill Pharo's.

NOTES

1. *The artist:* Granville Perkins, in addition to working for *Harper's* as an illustrator, was a maritime artist who traveled to paint in this country and Cuba.

2. *Squan:* Manasquan was often referred to this way.

3. *Charles Kingsley:* English clergyman and writer (1819-1875) who was particularly fond of the Derbyshire Fens, similar to New Jersey's marshes.

4. *Manx cats:* Descendants of these felines were alive and purring in Harvey Cedars as late as the 1960s.

5. *Plank-walk:* A second portable boardwalk was laid in 1880. A storm in 1884 damaged oceanfront buildings — the boardwalk had been taken up for the winter — so as a precaution a sturdier one was built the following year and raised five feet above the strand. A hurricane in 1889 washed out that walk and a fourth was installed, 24 feet wide and elevated to the extent that railings were required. In 1896 the fifth boardwalk was completed and formally designated a street. This one lasted until a hurricane in 1944, when it was rebuilt partially of planks from Beach Haven's ruined boardwalk.

6. *Bond's:* Thomas Bond had been a regular guest at the Philadelphia Company House and bought it in 1851. He renamed it Long Beach House and operated it until the rambling structure was sold at foreclosure proceedings in 1883. It closed three years later when the railroad was extended to the more fashionable Beach Haven.

7. *Old huts:* Sea Bright was a small fishing village before vacationers built huge cottages and squeezed out the picturesque fishermen shacks.

Harper's New Monthly Magazine, February 1878, volume 56, no. 333.

1878
History of the Beaches

Theophilus T. Price

Dr. Theophilus T. Price in 1888.

 *H. C. Woolman and T. F. Rose's lavishly illustrated* Historical and Biographical Atlas of the New Jersey Coast *was the first comprehensive study of the state's 127-mile shoreline. From the beaches to ten miles inland, the region is minutely described as it was in 1878, county by county: Maps, city and village plans, biographies, history, populations, lighthouses, shipwrecks*

and more than 50 detailed drawings of homes, hotels, inlets, gardens, farms, businesses and boats. Also included is the following observation of nature's opening and closing of inlets and the migration of barrier islands.

The New Jersey coast is that part of the State which faces the Atlantic Ocean. It extends from the north point of Sandy Hook to the south point of Cape May. It is flanked on the north by Raritan Bay; on the south by the Delaware. It stands at the entrance of the gates of traffic. It stretches along the breast of the continent one hundred and twenty-seven miles.

A low sandy barrier, the set bounds of the sea, curved in the form of a bow, constitutes its outward rim. Its several divisions, formed by the intersection of inlets and small rivers, are known as beaches. These are raised but a few feet in average height above the tide-level.

They consist almost exclusively of fine white sand, piled up in hills like snowdrifts. Some of them are of comparatively recent formation, and produce only a coarse grass and a few shrubs. On these the hills are still forming and shifting their positions.

Others are of older date, and are covered with oak, cedar, and other timber, in some cases of one or two hundred years' growth. The soil of these latter contains a small percentage of clay, and the sand having become incorporated with some vegetable mould, no longer drifts with the winds.

The hills, or dunes, on the older beaches lie in long ridges parallel (or nearly so) to the shore. They present an appearance as if in their original make the ocean had gradually receded, and new ridges had formed outside of the older. Several successive ridges, such as are described, are found on these old beaches, separated by long narrow valleys, in which are found coarse grasses, rushes, low bushes and vines, in addition to oak, cedar, and holly timber. The hills, as well as the valleys, are covered with a like growth of trees. Wild fruits, as beach plums, fox grapes, huckleberries, and similar kinds, are found abundantly in some places. The valleys, or *swales,* as they are sometimes called, have in the lower places ponds of fresh water, which during the winter and spring are filled, but which frequently dry up in summer.

These ponds are popularly known as "slashes," and are favorite resorts of wild fowl at those seasons of the year when they are migrating along our shores or living in the bays and sounds. Large numbers are annually killed by sportsmen, who lie concealed in "blinds" near the slashes, and shoot them when they come to drink.

Some of these ridges, and the valleys between them, are from one to two miles in length. They are highest and more heavily timbered on the northern parts of the beaches.

The peculiar features, above described, of the older beaches are more prominently exhibited on those bordering the county of Cape May than on any others along the coast. Notable examples are the Seven and Five Mile beaches.

The same condition existed on the northeast end of Absecon Beach before the streets of Atlantic City had been graded. It may have been the same at the "Great Swamp" on Long Beach before it was washed away, and may probably now exist at Sandy Hook.

All the beaches are continually undergoing changes. Those south of Barnegat Inlet are wearing away on the northeast ends.

The inlets move southward. New ridges and dunes form on the south and southwest ends of the old. In some cases they work seaward, extending outside of and overlapping older beaches. A recent instance is that of Long Beach, having made two or three miles of new beach within a few years, shutting up entirely the old Little Egg Harbor Inlet, sweeping outside of and around Tucker's Beach, and crowding the surf back a quarter of a mile from its former bed.

North of Barnegat the inlets work in an opposite direction. The old Cranberry Inlet, opposite Tom's River, moved nearly a mile northward during its sixty years of continuance. The Shrewsbury Inlet also moved from opposite Shrewsbury River a full mile towards the north before it was closed, and this it had done twice.

Sandy Hook, the only beach with a free extremity north of Barnegat, has extended northward a mile since the Revolutionary War. In all cases there has been considerable wear on the outer border of the beaches, and some of them are much narrowed; but this wearing away on the broadside is comparatively a slow process.

It is resisted by the formation of shoals a short distance from the shore, which break the force of the sea and protect the strand. It is often compensated for by the shore itself recovering through a series of favorable years several rods in width of its former ground. Absecon Beach, in front of Atlantic City, has made off twelve hundred feet since 1852. Boarding-houses now stand beyond where the low-water mark then was, and new shoals are still making further off.

The changes, therefore, which are occurring seem to be like the ebb and flow of the tides, each advance and retreat occupying an undetermined series of years. No certain law has been discovered on which positive predictions can be founded.

The awe with which the ocean strikes the beholder who looks upon it for the first time awakens the impression that in its angry moods so slight a defence as these beaches present would be insufficient to stay its irresistible power. Accordingly, a sense of insecurity is felt. A lady, who had reached the age of sixty years without seeing the ocean, stood for the first time at its edge a few months ago, on the strand at Beach Haven. "And what is there," she inquired, with manifest uneasiness, "to prevent the sea from rising over this flat beach, and carrying us, with all these houses, away?"

The friend who stood at her side replied, "That so long as civilized men had known this coast, the ocean had lain in that same bed, checked by the same low, sandy wall," and reminded her of the Almighty's challenge, expressed in the Book of Job, "Who shut up the sea with doors, when it brake forth, and said: Hitherto shalt thou come, but no further; and here shall thy proud waves be stayed?"

Those parts of the coast where a slight elevation of the mainland extends directly to the ocean are bluffs or banks. Properly speaking, there are no beaches in front of these, only a strand. Long Branch, and a part of the front of Cape May City, are of this kind.

At other places along the coast the upland slopes off gently to the sea. Sandhills form above high-water mark on these slopes — in some instances a number of rods from the strand — and in many respects they exhibit the features of the beaches proper. Deal, and the shores south of it as far as Point Pleasant, present this appearance. Monmouth Beach, above Long Branch, and the beach at Sea Grove, as well as the greater part of the eastern shore of the Delaware Bay, are of this class.

From *Historical and Biographical Atlas of the New Jersey Coast*, H. C. Woolman and T. T. Price, Woolman and Rose, Philadelphia, 1878, reprinted by Ocean County Historical Society, 1985.

1878
Point Pleasant

Anonymous

Bluefish were hauled out of the surf on hand lines until early in the 20th century.

Most beachgoers have seen a bluefish blitz: The swirling, feeding-frenzy as a school of blues pursues bait fish close to shore; and the frenzy of following fishermen brandishing their poles in hot pursuit. Fishing equipment was comparatively primitive before 1900; rods and reels did not have the strength or *technological sophistication to do successful battle with the powerful, wily bluefish. But in 1878 hardly a house on the beachfront was without its coil of tarred bluefish line, which was twirled like a lasso by experienced anglers. The anonymous author of this story is trying it for the first time.*

I was seated on the bench of the piazza which runs around the house. A pleasant summer murmur filled the air. The shrill busy hum of insects, the soft sighings of the southwest wind, and for bass the roar of the surf on the beach completed the harmony. I was doing nothing but thinking, thinking and pitying in my heart those who were compelled to live in the busy, noisy, dusty city.

I was seated on the piazza, an old decaying one round a farm-house in Point Pleasant, rightly so named. Settling myself down for an after-breakfast smoke, and dismissing as much of the machinery of thought as showed signs of motion from my brains, I lit my pipe, blew a long cone of smoke out into the still summer air, and looked up at the calm blue space above my head, in which the swallows were skating with swift and graceful turns. I had just settled myself when I was suddenly and unexpectedly interrupted.

"Oh, land of Goshen, what are you about? The fish are come down to the sea and every man and boy in the place is out after them!"

"Grandmother, where is my squid and line?" I asked.

"In the back kitchen, I reckon," was the answer.

To rush there and catch the line off a nail, seize my hat and start was the affair of a moment.

Down I ran along the banks of the Manasquan until I came to its inlet. There, on coming to the beach, I found an excited, eager crowd of some thirty or forty boys and men running up and down it, and stopping every now and then to throw their line into the rolling surf, as yet, however, without success.

I stood on a sand-bank at the mouth of the Manasquan River and watched. Presently there was a loud shout from the opposite bank, and I saw them running. There was a strange sort of boiling appearance in the water, and then a whole host of small fish, moss-bunkers, flung themselves wildly on the sandy beach, flopped about thereon, gasped hysterically, and then, after a few more fruitless leaps, lay still, choked by the hot air and burning sun. The men and boys were meanwhile swinging as fast as they could their squids, and sending them, some of the best throwers, fifty yards into the surf. No sooner did the squid touch and disappear beneath the water than they ran up the sand-hills, and lo! a large blue-fish came leaping and tumbling out of the sea.

We on our side could only stand and look on. There was no boat to put us across, and we had to stand and see them hauling out the fish as fast as they could heave a squid. I felt like swearing, but I did not, as I found plenty of the old fishermen give vent to their injured feelings in terms more than amply sufficient for all. Heave, heave, heave! and each and every time a fish — large ones too, some ten pounds' weight over there — and not a sign of one near us. It became almost maddening. All in vain I tucked up and finally pulled off my pantaloons to attempt to wade across. A laugh of mocking derision from the other side was the issue of the attempt (for swim I could not) as I turned despairingly back.

"Won't you come over and help us now?" tauntingly queried a man on the opposite side.

Well for him a swift and rapid stream intervened, or I should have forthwith struck my squid into one of the angular parts of his person, if I had not brained him on the spot. I sat down sad and well-nigh despairing, and counted — yes, actually counted — twenty-eight, twenty-nine, thirty fish, in as many throws, to the lot of that man! How I began to hate him for his invariable success! Mockingly, at seeing me so forlorn, he hove, and tauntingly he hauled each one of the finny prey, and then held it up to the intense disgust of all us on the wrong side.

As I sat I saw Nemesis drawing near to that man with slow, sure, and stealthy step. Saw, and rejoiced greatly. Quietly the flowing tide swept in and neared every minute that bad man's boat. There, her nose lifted a little with that last wave. Now it moves a little, a very little; and then a sudden slide of the sloping sand and the scow is afloat! Nor man nor boy on our side spoke or moved, as, with bated breath, we watched her drift off into the stream, and, borne on the wings of a propitious breeze, gradually draw toward us.

I looked at my abomination — that man — fearing lest he too should see it. No, he was far too busily intent upon his squid.

Nearer and nearer it comes — across the channel now — in shoal water on our side! Three or four of us make a dash at it, while a loud, victorious hurrah burst from my lips as, line in hand, I seize the boat's side and scramble in: the others quickly follow, and a few vigorous strokes with the oars, which are luckily in it, carry us to the other side. Each one for himself, in vain the others called to us to send the boat again across. We all prepared to make up for lost time. I looked at my line — looked, and again felt like swearing; it was all in a tangle and snarl. Patiently I unrolled, untwisted, unknotted, and, without one single word for nearly twenty minutes, tried to unravel that horrid line. Didn't I *think* swearing, however! At length I got it cleared, and then — why then the fish had gone — all gone, and there they were hard at work on the very side we had just come from.

I looked reproachfully at my line: I appealed mutely and beseechingly to the man with the boat.

"Come along, old fellow," said he, "I'll give you a start across agen." I liked him forthwith. Again we crossed, and this time I was all ready. All ready, with the exception of never having thrown a squid before. I tried, however, and hurling it three or four times round my head, I threw. It pulled up short. I found I had hitched myself with the hook in some unknown posterior region. Fortunately it was only through the pantaloons, and my friend quickly cut it out there and then, and still more quickly retired from my immediate vicinity as I undauntingly again attempted to send the squid flying to the place where I wished it to go. Once, twice, thrice I threw, and each time fell short. The skin had taken its departure off my forefinger with the efforts of my futile attempts. A little lad some ten years old is my next neighbor, and he catches at every throw.

Shame gives me fresh skill, and again I send the hook abroad — *Evoe! Io triumphe!*[1] I feel a check, and the line very nearly escapes me. Proudly over my shoulder I place it. Up the beach I run and feel as if I was dragging a hundred-weight behind me. On I rush, shouting in the triumphant excess of my joy, and my first fish is caught — caught, but still unhooked.

I sat down and smoked a pipe — a libation, an incense to the gods, to Neptune in especial, for my success. Then came the unhooking process. I placed my bare foot shudderingly on the cold-blooded, slippery beast — a sharp snap of the jaws very near my great toe made me as quickly remove it. After some little maneuvering I at length got my thumb and finger up its gills and cruelly and unremorsefully wrenched out the hook.

Again and again, after wrapping my finger with a piece of my pocket-handkerchief, I threw and each time caught a fish. I got four, and the little lad, my neighbor and my landlord's son, had six. Ten in all. I think of home a mile away, and the ten fish to be carried there under a burning June's sun.

A shout startles me, and I hear my name called. Come here — here quick! Lloyd has got a squid through his foot. I look, and the little lad is on his back; and another lad over the hill, out of sight of the sea, thinks he has got a fish, and hauls away with all his might at the poor lad's foot. There a wave comes up and covers him, and he rolls on toward the sea, borne away by the undertow. O God! how nearly he was gone, for the men have stopped the other boy and the line is slackened. Almost sick with fear I rush to the place and pick up the lad. A moment and my rejoicing is changed to grief and sorrow. I look at the foot, dreading the operation I know will have to be performed. To my great relief and joy it has gone only through the outer side, and no muscle or vein will interfere with the cutting it out. I take out my penknife and ask the men to cut while I hold the lad. They all refuse. Those big, strong, sun-browned men, who venture out every week to sea, holding their lives in their hands and fearing not the winds or storm, can not cut a hook out of a little child's foot but turn sick away. Half angrily I ask them to hold him while I do it myself. The lad, a fisherman's son, neither winces nor cries during the operation. I at first was going to file off the hook, for I had a small file in my pocket. "You'll spoil the squid!" was the lad's quick answer; "cut it out!" And cut it out I did. Taking my handkerchief I tore it into strips and bound it up.

I then started for a farm-house I saw two or three fields off, and borrowing there a wheel-barrow, returned to the spot. Piling thereon my fish I put the boy on the top and started once more homeward. The sand was loose and deep, the wheelbarrow, an old one, would not bear the weight, so taking the lad on my back and resuming once more the barrow and fish I toiled my weary way home, where I duly arrived heated and tired, and more than satisfied with my experience of blue-fishing.

NOTE

1. *Evoe! Io triumphe!* In Greek mythology, the triumphant cry of the Dionysian revelers during their orgiastic festival.

Harper's New Monthly Magazine, 1878.

1879
Atlantic City

Walt Whitman

An early postcard view of Atlantic City's first permanent boardwalk, looking toward Absecon Inlet.

Walt Whitman preferred the shore in winter and found inspiration there for his 1880 poem "Patrolling Barnegat." The famous poet had been living in New Jersey since 1873, after leaving his federal job in Washington, D. C., following a stroke that left him partially disabled. He moved to Camden to stay with his brother George and slowly recuperated, spending much time writing and reading at the nearby Stafford farm on Timber Creek. In 1882 David McKay, Whitman's Philadelphia publisher and personal friend, brought *out a new edition of* Leaves of Grass, *the royalties from which enabled Whitman to buy his own house on Mickle Street in Camden. It is now a museum dedicated to his life. This journal entry was the basis of an essay that appeared in the* Philadelphia Times *just two days after the poet had taken a day trip to Atlantic City on a mild, sunny Sunday.*

JANUARY 24: As I went to bed a few Saturday nights ago, it entered my head all of a sudden, decidedly yet quietly, that if the coming morn was fine, I would take a trip across Jersey by the Camden and Atlantic Railroad through to the sea.

Luck for me! A bright clear sunrise — after a good night's rest — crisp, champagne-like winter atmosphere —brief toilet and partial bath — a trill of song to welcome the day and clinch my own contented mood — and then a good breakfast, cooked by the hands I love. (How much better it makes the victuals taste!)

Walking slowly, or rather hobbling (my paralysis, though partial, seems permanent), the hundred rods to the little platform and shanty bearing the big name of "Pennsylvania Junction," were not without enjoyment to me, in this pleasant mixture of cold and sunbeams. While I waited outside the yet unopened hut, two good-looking middle-aged men, also journey-bound, held animated talk on gunning, ducks, the shore, the woods, the best places for sport, etc. Each had a long story to tell about "his gun," its properties, price and history generally. Their anecdotes of wonderful shots, bird events, and such — all with many idioms, and great volubility. (Have you ever heard two sportsmen recounting their opinions and experience that way? To me it is not lacking in interest or amusement for a change. And perhaps there is no more innocent style of blowing.)

From the car-windows a good view of the country, in its winter garb. These farms are mostly devoted to market truck, and are generally well cultivated. Passing the little stations of Glenwood and Collingswood — then stopping at old, beautiful, rich and quite populous Haddonfield, with its fine tree-lined main street (Revolutionary, military reminiscences too — a tradition that the Continental Congress itself held a session here).

Some four or five miles south of Haddonfield we come to the handsome railroad station of Kirkwood. (This place looks to me like home, but I am not intending to stop now.) Here is a beautiful broad pond or lake. They are getting the ice from it, and a good sight it is to see the great, thick, pure, silvery cakes cut and hauled. In summer, the pond with its young groves and adjacent handsome pavilion, forms a favorite destination for Philadelphia and Camden picnics.

Not far off is my own choice haunt, Timber Creek, with its primitive solitudes, its flowing, fresh winding stream, its recluse and woody banks, its cool, sweet feeding-springs, and all the charms that, in genial seasons, the birds, grass, wild flowers, nooks, rabbits and squirrels, old oaks, walnut trees, etc., can bring.

Domiciled at the farm of my dear and valued friends, the Staffords[1], nearby, I have passed good parts of the last two or three summers along this creek and its adjacent fields and lanes. And indeed it is to my experiences and my outdoor life here — conquering, catching the health and physical virtue of Nature, by close and persistent contact with it at first hand — that I, perhaps, owe recovery, or partial recovery (a sort of second wind, or semi-renewal of the lease of life) from my paralysis of 1873, '74, '75 and '76.

Five miles from Kirkwood we strike the thrifty town of Berlin (old name Long-a-Coming, which they had much better kept). We reach Atco, three miles further on — quite a brisk settlement in the brush, with a newspaper, some stores, and a little branch railroad to Williamstown. At the eighteen mile post the grade of the railroad reaches its highest point, being one hundred and eighty feet above the level of the sea. Here is what is called by the engineer, "the divide," the water on the west flowing to the Delaware, and on the east to the ocean.

The soil has now become sandy and thin, and continues so for the ensuing forty miles; flat, thin, bare gray-white, yet not without agreeable features — pines, cedars, scrub oaks plenty — patches of clear fields, but much larger patches of pines and sand.

I must not forget to mention that there are some manufactories both off and on the line of the road. At Williamstown, Tausboro, Waterford and Winslow junction are glassworks, and at Gibbsboro, two miles west of Kirkwood station the white lead, zinc and color works of John Lucas Co., and the pleasant country-seat of Mr. and Mrs. L. and their large family. Beside a few cloth and cotton mills through these counties, working in ice, charcoal, pottery, wine, etc., give a little variety to agriculture, which is of course the vastly preponderating occupation.

We steam rapidly on to Hammonton, about thirty miles from Philadelphia (half way on the route) and the liveliest looking town on this part of the road. Then, after touching at De Costa, arrive at Elwood — rather pleasant appearing.

A thin-soiled, non-fertile country all along, yet as healthy and not so rocky and broken as New England. The fee-simple cheap, vines and small fruits eligible. The whole route (at any rate from Haddonfield to the seashore) has been literally made and opened up to growth by the Camden and Atlantic Railroad. That has furnished spine to a section previously without any.

It all reminds me much of my old native Long Island, N.Y., especially takes me back to the *plains* and *brush* — the same level stretch, thin soil — healthy but barren — pines, scrub oak, laurel, kill-calf, and splashes of white sand everywhere.

We come to Egg Harbor City, settled about twenty-five years ago by the Germans, and now with quite a reputation for grape culture and wine-making — scattered houses off in the brush in the distances, and a little branch railroad to May's Landing; then Pomona, and then another lively town, Absecon, an old and quite good-sized settlement, 52 miles from Philadelphia.

After this a broad region of interminable salt-hay meadows, intersected with lagoons and cut into everywhere by watery runs — the strong sodgy perfume, delightful to my nostrils, all reminding me again of "the mash" and the continuous South Bay of old Long Island. The Atlantic City *Review* says: "We believe the day when some effort will be put forth to reclaim the meadows between this place and Absecon, or which span almost the entire Jersey coast, is not far distant. It can be utilized by a system of dyking and drainage, for where the experiment has been tried the soil has been discovered to be remarkably rich and productive. The salt water drained away, the meadows are no longer miry, but form a solid bottom, the soil resembling that of Illinois."

Passing right through five or six miles (I could have journeyed with delight for a hundred) of these odorous sea prairies we come to the end — the Camden and Atlantic depot, within good gun-shot of the beach. I no sooner land from the cars than I meet impromptu with young Mr. English (of the just-mentioned *Review* newspaper), who treats me with all brotherly and gentlemanly kindness, posts me up about things, puts me on the best roads and starts me right.

A flat, still sandy, still meadowy region (some of the old hummocks with their hard sedge, in tufts, still remaining) an island, but good hard roads and plenty of them, really pleasant streets, very little show of trees, shrubbery, etc., but in lieu of them a superb range of ocean beach — miles and miles of it, for driving walking, bathing — a real Sea Beach City indeed, with salt waves and sandy shores *ad libitum*.

I have a fine and bracing drive along the smooth sand (the carriage wheels hardly made a dent in it). The bright sun, the sparkling waves, the foam, the view — Brigantine beach, a sail here and there in the distance — the ragged wreck-timbers of the stranded *Rockaway* — the vital, vast monotonous sea — all the fascination of simple, uninterrupted space, shore, salt atmosphere, sky (people who go there often and get used to it get infatuated and won't go anywhere else), were the items of my drive.

Then, after nearly two hours of this shore, we trotted rapidly around and through the city itself — capital good roads everywhere, hard, smooth, well-kept, a pleasure to drive on them. Atlantic avenue, the principal street; Pacific avenue, with its rows of choice private cottages, and many many others. (I had the good fortune to be driven around by William Biddle, a young married man — a hackman by occupation — an excellent companion and *cicerone* — owner of his own good team and carriage).

Then after dinner (as there were nearly two hours to spare) I walked off in another direction (hardly met or saw a person), and taking possession of what appeared to have been the reception room of an old bath-house range, had a broad expanse of view all to myself — quaint, refreshing, unimpeded — the dry area of sedge and Indian grass immediately before and round me — space, space, with a sort of grimness about it — simple, unornamented space. In front, as far as I could see, and right and left, plenty of beach, only broken by a few unpainted houses, in piles, here and there — distant vessels, and the far-off, just visible trailing smoke of an inward bound steamer. More plainly, ships, brigs, schooners, in sight in the distance. How silently, spiritually, like phantoms (even in the midst of the bright sunshine and the objective world around me), they glide away off there — most of them with every sail set to the firm and steady wind. How the main attraction and fascination are in sea and shore! How the soul dwells on their simplicity, eternity, grimness, absence of art!

Although it is not generally thought of, except in connection with hot weather, I am not sure but Atlantic City would suit me just as well, perhaps best, for winter quarters. As to bad weather, it is no worse here than anywhere else; and when fine, the pleasures and characteristic attractions are inimitable.

Cape May I must reserve for another screed, Gloucester, Salem, Cumberland and Cape May counties to the south — the whole line of the West Jersey Railroad, with its occasional fertile spots and the towns it reaches — Woodbury, Glassboro, Salem, Bridgeton, Vineland, Millville, and so the staunch old (both popular and "aristocratic") summer resort and watering place, Cape May — surely, as soon as the spring opens, beginning the foundation of better attractions and accommodations even than before the terrible fire of three months ago.[2] Bad as that disaster was, it may be I say (out of the nettle danger plucking the flower safely) that Cape May, even from it, will start on a prosperity, popularity, attractiveness, beyond any and all of the past.

General New Jersey Character

Of course New Jersey character is in the main the same as all other human character. It must ever be borne in mind that the facts of resemblance between any people, place or time, and any other, however distant, people, place or time, are far closer and more numerous than the facts of difference. Of course, too, in New Jersey humanity there are many places or strata. Materialistic, very set and obstinate, but good sterling ore, native qualities — good material for the future. If we were asked to strike an average for the morality and intellectuality of the people, it would be neither the highest nor lowest. Thrift, wariness, stolidity prevail. The women are the best, as everywhere. There is a quality in the men analogous to open air, to barns and earth-fields and sea-shore — on a low plane, but real and breezy — most welcome and delightful to me. (I am speaking of Camden, Atlantic and Burlington counties, and the middle and southern parts more particularly.) The Jerseyite has neither the sharpness of the New Englander nor the enterprise of the West. From the situation of the State, not from any native impetus, it has been cut through by railroads and travel-forced into a connection with the busy, bustling world — yet the common ranges of the people are sluggish, content with little, and hard to rouse. With all this I like them much, and some of my best times of late years have been passed with them. Character is, indeed, on a low key, but it is fresh, independent and tough as a knot.

No doubt the nature of the soil has had to do with advancing certain personal traits and repressing others. Flat, much sand, few forests worthy the name, so natural wheat land, immense lines of sea-sand, vast wilds of dwarf pine and scrub oak, mostly describe it. The northern portion of the State is hilly, even mountainous, with mines and furnaces, and doubtless would require a different portraiture. I hope to explore it one of these days and perhaps report.

But to me it is the sea-side region that gives stamp to Jersey, even in the human character. I am counting with eagerness next summer (as the Yanks say, "make reckoning") on a special long-contemplated exploration of this creek-indented and sea-beat region from Cape May to Sandy Hook — 100 miles — a stretch offering both the people and the places most interesting to my taste, in which salt and sedge are inborn.

NOTES

1. *The Staffords:* The Staffords were close friends of Whitman. He admitted to his journal that while he was recovering at their farm he'd get "some old edition of no pecuniary value" and tear out the portion he wanted to read, stuff it in his pocket and ramble out along Timber Creek, by a pond, or in a warm nook under an oak tree, resting and reading.

2. *Terrible fire of three months ago:* Nine large hotels were destroyed in a wind-driven firestorm on November 9, 1878. Cape May did not fully recover its position as a major resort until late in the 20th century.

Proceedings of the New Jersey Historical Society, October 1948, volume 66, no. 4, reprinted with the permission of the New Jersey Historical Society.

1880
Ocean City

Robert Fisher

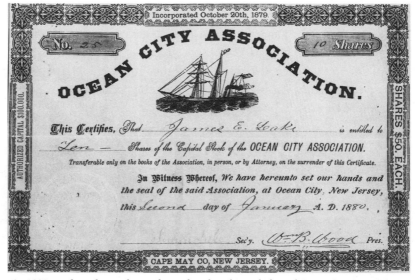

Incorporated October 20th, 1879.

No. 25   **OCEAN CITY ASSOCIATION.**   10 Shares

AUTHORIZED CAPITAL $100,000.   SHARES $50. EACH.

This Certifies, That *James E. Lake* is entitled to
Ten — Shares of the Capital Stock of the OCEAN CITY ASSOCIATION.
Transferable only on the books of the Association, in person, or by Attorney, on the surrender of this Certificate.

In Witness Whereof, We have hereunto set our hands and the seal of the said Association, at Ocean City, New Jersey, this *Second* day of *January* A. D. 1880.

Sec'y. *W. B. Wood* Pres.

CAPE MAY CO, NEW JERSEY.

An 1880 certificate for ten shares of capital stock in the newly formed Ocean City Association is signed by Simon Lake, patriarch of the town's founding family.

Robert Fisher landed on Peck's Beach in February 1880 to work as a member of the Ocean City Association's first crew to survey the city and lay out the streets. Fisher was an Irish nobleman, educated at Belfast's Royal Academy, and came "incognito, to live the simple life and cure a nervous condition." Fragments of his diary are quoted at length in a journal kept by William Lake, cousin of the Lake brothers who founded Ocean City.

Fisher, a gifted writer, painted a romantic yet graphic picture of Peck's Beach before the land was cleared. He also recorded visits by various clergymen — Lake and his colleagues — to inspect the newly purchased land. The "owners and friends" Fisher refers to in the following incident are probably the Lakes. Parker Miller, a bayman who had settled on the island 20 years earlier, built a crude boat landing on the shoreline; if visitors happened to arrive at low tide, they were picked up and carried ashore across the mud flats.

MID-FEBRUARY: The landing could be readily accomplished if you came when the tide was up, and if you came when the tide was out it remained for you to wade ashore or be carried pick-a-back by the captain of the boat. Many a passenger, male or female also, has the writer seen carried thus to land. On one such occasion, a party of owners and some friends came as far as the boat could be pushed up on the flats. Captain Amos Lewis took off his boots, rolled up his pants and got overboard to back his passengers ashore; one by one he toted them slipping and sliding over the mud — those in the back like to split at those being carried, and those that had gotten ashore laughing at those whose turn came next.

When all but one was landed he also prepared for the trip but was so full of laughter at the comical situation that he could scarcely control himself or keep his seat on the back of his carrier; still he would utter words of caution and tell how little he desired mud baptism. When they got pretty well toward shore, the captain's foot slipped and the dominie was dumped heels over head in the mud; the tall hat flew several yards ahead of him while the safe ones on the shore laughed uproariously at the plight of their friend. In a few minutes, however, his Reverence was picked up and divested of what mud could be readily scraped off, and with some remarks about the unpleasantness of bathing at low water the party moved off on their visit.

FEBRUARY 23: A party of stockholders and managers of the enterprise came over to select the site for the Camp Ground and found a very difficult job, the underbrush being so dense that a few feet, in most instances was as far as you could see; paths were cut in various directions to enable the investigators to spy out the most desirable spot with plenty of shade. Having finally decided on the location, a flag pole and flag were secured to the top of the tallest tree and an informal dedication made.

The gentlemen of this party were obliged to remain over night and that evening all hands enjoyed a general conversation, speculative and prophetic of the future, until bedtime. On preparing to retire, Mr. Miller advised hanging our boots to the ceiling if we expected to find them in the morning, as the rats were so plentiful they would either carry off or destroy them before we next saw them. On this hint we acted with much mirth to think it was our shoes and not our money that was in danger.

A sound sleep and a good breakfast put us in proper form for another day's activity; but as we were about to sally forth one of the Reverend gentlemen of the party began hunting for his gloves which could not be found; the good brother (the same one who had the mud bath experience) had protected his shoes but not his gloves and the rats had taken the opportunity to protect themselves against the cold at his expense. "It was too bad," he said, "almost new, a present from a friend"; their owner was sorry to lose them, but they were gone.

LATE FEBRUARY: We had no experience in the matter of "cave dwelling" and so some shelter had to be contrived. We had noticed in some of our strolls along the beach a quantity of boards lying near the water line, and found that they were the remains of a one-time bath house which Mr. Miller had put up to preserve the decencies when parties used to come over on picnics to enjoy the pleasure of an ocean dip. Their owner freely donated these old boards; they were Jersey pine of the crooked grain variety, tough as whalebone and contrary as an army mule. To get two of them to come together you had almost as much success as reconciling two politicians. Well, when a space about nine feet square had been enclosed, there was no necessity for making any further arrangements for ventilation.

When everything was about completed, Capt. J. S. Willets, then in charge of the Life-Saving Station, came along and seeing one board left lying on the ground with a knothole in it about the size of a bucket, asked what place that was being kept for, and we told him it was for part of the roof and the hole was just right for the stove pipe. He laughed heartily and gave us a fine endorsement for practical economy. "Now," said he, "you've got her up, what are you going to call her?"

We told him this was "Hope" cottage, as hope at that time seemed to be our greatest asset.

In this cottage we had three sleeping apartments, one above the other, and being of humble disposition I selected the under berth, Somers S.

Smith chose the second tier, and Elijah Steelman for some time held his mighty revels in the sky-scraper. He was a man of larger proportions and a full-sized nose, and as the rafters came pretty close to the upper edge of his resting place, it was a matter of considerable skill and tact to reach his perch in safety and when once in bed he had to wake up to turn over without skinning his nasal organ.

We had a fine heating plant installed in the shape of a tin plate stove and when we got her fairly going in the evening the radiation was perfect. Here we did our cooking, washing and ironing. We were the simple life. Rabbits were abundant, clams and oysters were had for the labor of gathering, and the carcass of many a fine young heifer hung from the limb of an adjacent cedar for a period, then occupied the pickle barrel for our sustenance.

[Later] The murmuring Pine and Cedars, the Holly in garments green and with coral decorations, the sassafras with its pungent perfumed breath and a scant sprinkling of gum and oak were the sentinels guarding this sacred shrine. Interlacing and spreading in every direction, binding tree to tree and trees to earth again, strung taut as shrouds of a ship, the briars were everywhere climbing along and making each object a path on their way to sunlight. They dominated the situation and many a tree has defied the strength and the axe of the workmen, for even when its trunk was severed, it still stood upright, held firmly by these briar braces.

A vast undergrowth of Beach Plums, Wild Roses and Bayberry covered the ground which in many places was richly carpeted with a velvety moss or lichen through which Teaberries and Rabbiteyes forced their way and in rich profusion made this carpet a rare Turkish design woven on nature's loom.

The tops of the trees as they rose above the ranges of sand hills had a uniform slope from seaward to landward and while none of them had attained any considerable height they had held the fort for centuries; and often, while leveling the hills, whole trees would be dug out completely swallowed up by the drifting sands.

These ranges of sand hills with the intervening valleys, small plateaus, rivers and lakes, made up a miniature continent in itself, and when one rambled off to the top of some of these sand dunes and looked about there was that charming variety and beauty of scenery that we find described by landscape connoisseurs inspired by larger and more comprehensive views, but shone with equal charm in this limited compass.

I could stand on one of these mountain tops and look into the clear limpid lake at its base with its margin of reeds and Indian grass; I could trace the stream from its source back of the ocean front dunes as it wound its sinuous course ever westerly, around knolls and obstacles to the marsh and the bay. A great "Santa Fe trail" was deeply trodden by the herds of wild cattle, whose pleasures led them to wander often from their fat pastures to get a view of the passing ships, their only dissipation.

The Bay Shore indented with creeks, thoroughfares and inlets had an interest all its own, shielded by all we have described from the turbulence of the mighty mass of ocean. The creeks and inlets furnished safe harbors for boats from almost any storm, and from the northern end good landing in deep water up to the bank, which provided the means of getting to land.

Still further toward the northern end a high natural boulevard extended for a considerable distance, from which one of the finest landscape and waterscape views was obtained, twenty feet above where the water lapped and splashed again the rock-like sand wall. Basking in the shade of some giant cedar, I looked up the bay with its many channels interspersed with emerald green islands [and] away off to the rolling savannah of the Tuckahoe and further west to the sombre woods beyond. Following the line of the Atlantic County shore [I overlooked] the Middle and Egg Harbor Rivers northward, over Patconk and Brick Kiln Creek to the Somer's Woods at Somer's Point with the sweep of the bay to Lousy Harbor, where a score of vessels lay in indolent ease awaiting favorable winds, [and] eastward down the Anchor Point shore to the waterways back at Longport and extending up to Lake's Bay and the navigable channel to Atlantic City, then back over the boiling surf on the bar of the inlet, and the glorious glistening mass of tumbled flashing breakers out of the bosom of the great Atlantic.

Round the sweep of the Great Egg Harbor Inlet the encroachment of the Ocean had washed down a considerable slice of the bluff, and with it some of the finest cedars the island had produced. These had been cut off by pirates for fence posts, and being all heart, these red cedar posts came as near being everlasting as anything that grows; the roots of these trees lay partly imbedded in the sand, the exposed part, washed clear of bark, looked like the bones of some extinct race. A great stretch of sand with numerous waterways lay north and east of this point covered, however, in whole or in part by every high tide. The most inland channel hugged close round the point and running south joined the ocean some distance down the beach.

The bay was populous with wild fowl, geese, ducks, brant, loon and others of their kin and it was no uncommon sight to see flocks of "blue bills," acres in extent, moving up and down with the tide, and at evening the homecoming of the geese from their day on the ocean, was as regular as the sunset. The woods were filled and thrilled with music, song birds everywhere, from the thrush and robin down to the incisive and persistent mosquito. The sweet voiced birds were the cheerful companions of all our labors.

The herds of cattle roaming wild on the island were both picturesque and interesting, picturesque as you stood at a safe distance and watched them feeding in the valleys or standing like Titan statues on the hill tops facing the setting sun; interesting as you came suddenly upon them in one of their narrow trails and halted with your heart in your mouth as you faced them, not knowing what attitude they might assume towards you, but feeling so far as you were concerned it would be one of peace for the time at least and trusting that their better nature might prevail and the incident close with mutual good feeling all around.

The Ocean Beach from Great Egg Harbor Inlet on the north to Corson's Inlet at its southern end, a stretch of about seven miles, was a splendidly beautiful sight as first seen by pioneers, smooth and hard as adamant, where the ebb and flow of the tide covered and uncovered it. The beach was strewn thickly in many places with large conch shells with their delicately colored and enameled surfaces, and fringed with a space of soft glistening sand, shells and pebbles, backed with a hem or binding of the drift from old Ocean's stores, fragments of once proud ships and samples of cargoes from every nation and every clime swathed in seaweed. Here was the dial of a compass keeping company with the battered remains of a brass lantern; a piece of ship's rail still holding in its jaws a couple of belaying pins; a lidless copper kettle, companion to a broken frying pan, all enmeshed in the tattered remains of a mattress, etc. Anything, everything that could be of service to a junkman.

Back of this hem rose the seawall hills sloping westward, but in some exposed spots where the breakers had struck they were cut off perpen-

dicularly as if hewn by hand. These hill ranges rose up fifteen to twenty-
five feet above the ordinary level and spread out many times their height
at the base; the deep-rooted Indian grass covering their sides and domes
helped to hold them securely from drifting and lent a charm of color to
their otherwise uninteresting appearance, as well as refreshing the eye
from the sand's glare.

Cape May County New Jersey Magazine of History and Genealogy, June 1953, reprinted with the permission of Cape May County Historical & Genealogical Society.

1881 - 1889
Sea Isle City

Richard Atwater

*Abby Atwater (seated in white dress) and her husband, Richard (in profile wearing cap),
surrounded by their nine children on the porch of their bungalow, 1884.*

*After Richard and Abby Atwater's daughter Betty was born in 1880 Abby was
very ill, so Richard took mother, child and nurse to Cape May where the ailing
mother recuperated. The Atwoods discovered that there was "great benefit and
enjoyment from the sea bathing" and resolved to have a seashore house where
their eight children could experience a "free life on the beautiful beach." The growing family lived in Millville and wanted a location convenient to home.*

Abby wrote to her sister: "We are talking now of taking all the family to a place just started on the Jersey coast called Sea Isle City. While it is getting under way to be the grand watering place he [developer Charles Landis] intends it to be, we might spend July there for a year or two quietly and pleasantly. There are no mosquitoes, and still-water bathing inside, and surf outside the island. It is near enough for Richard to come down every night and bring all the fruit, and so forth."

Before Landis bought Ludlam's Beach, the island on which Sea Isle City was built had been used for little but foraging cattle, horses and sheep. The cattle were pastured on beach grasses in spring and barged back to the mainland in winter. A lifesaving station stood near Corson's Inlet, but beyond that was an expanse of wide beach, marshland, magnificent dunes and areas of lush growth with copses of holly and cedar trees sheltering a rich wildlife. Landis envisioned his island community as a utopian escape from polluted industrial centers. His plans included a protected harbor, a thousand-foot wooden pier and a pavilion. Sea Isle City would be a "seaside city with elaborate canal and drainage system, public baths and fountains, public buildings with Renaissance artwork, sculpture, and statuary."

In the spring of 1881 the Atwaters read a circular announcing the sale of lots on Ludlam's Island. The Cape May railroad was opening a branch from Seaville to Seaview on the mainland, and access was assured. They bought land and built a house; over the years Richard recorded the growth and changes in their home, family, and town.

1881

The island itself was far from inviting — a low marshy stretch, flooded by stormy tides and in several places swept through by surf — an irregular and broken range of sand dunes at the high water line and a few patches of fast land — on which however were fine old cedars in a jungle of holly, sassafras and undergrowth. The one redeeming and hopeful element was the beach — broad and smooth and hard — with a surf which made one forget all that was behind it.

A few weeks after the first Circular was received on April 21, 1881, Christy and I went to Seaville. A letter of introduction to Capt. Thomas Townsend was sufficient to give us his valuable services and advice. In his boat we sailed to the island and took a survey of its good and bad elements and noted the desirable lots. A number of street posts had been set up — a path had been blazed through the jungle — a wilder spot could hardly have been found on which to plant a colony of little children.

I attended the Auction of Lots in Philadelphia on May 2 and bought the first lot fairly sold. It was the central front lot in the block containing the largest clump of cedar trees on the island. I acted on the advice of Edward Cooper to buy a front lot or none. I sent the details of my plan to John K. Yarnall on May 3 and on May 11 received the drawings and specs from him. On May 23 I made the contract to build with Chas. Preston of Seaville and on the same day bought lumber and materials in Camden. Preston began his work on June 9.

On June 8 Arnold and Eliza Chace, Abby and I sailed with Capt. Henry Corson through the creeks and thoroughfares and entered Ludlams Bay at noon of a hot day, but the sea breeze met us as we touched the shore. We walked across the dry inlet, lunched on oysters on the beautiful strand, took a bath in the surf and returned home, meeting the lumber for our house as we sailed up the creek.

We had been discussing plans for a simple house for several weeks. A description by my mother of Dr. More's house on Lake Ontario seemed to us to afford the desirable elements of coolness, ease of running, good views and cheapness. We took the general idea of the cross sections in a square house and developed the details, using the rug in the nursery for ground work. The time was short, and if the house was to be occupied that year it must be built quickly.

On July 6 Abby started for Sea Isle and moved into the house, such as it was. Besides our own number, there were with us Mrs. Greene, Emily Angell and two servants, Maude and Morly. From Seaville station carriages took them to the creek. They lunched at Cedar Landing and in the afternoon sailed to the island, a scow in tow carrying the goods. I came down in the evening and was carried in Aley Hildreth's stage to the Turnpike Bridge which was not yet completed. Roger [?] was ferryman and Henry Ludlam was on the opposite side bringing the first load of goods.

The confusion in the house was great. A long carpenters bench covered with tools filled the front part. The floor was covered with lumber and shavings and it was dark before the furniture was brought and piled in the back part of the living hall.

An accident with an oil lamp nearly set the house on fire and the arrangements for supper and sleeping were of a primitive character. When we were left alone the weirdness of the place and the wildness of the surroundings was very impressive.

The life this first year was unique and can never be repeated. We were nearly alone on the island. A few prospectors during the middle of the day were the only disturbers of our solitude. The beach was rich with shells and strewn with old wrecks, some high and dry and others showing the timbers at the fall of the tide. The flowers and berries were luxuriant and in great variety. We used to take long strolls in bathing costume. Boys and girls alike went barefoot and were clad in the simplest garments. A pair of goats with their kid afforded much amusement and some annoyance as they ate clothing, stole food from the fire and climbed the stairs in quest of food or fun.

1882

We moved down June 11 with Alice Atwater and two servants. We came to Seaville Station and rode to the house in carriages, an improvement over the previous year but we looked enviously at the railroad not yet quite completed to the island.

The elements of breeze, sky and sea which we had sought to obtain in full force proved too strong. The dampness of the sea made a driftwood fire necessary every night; the wind kept a stream of sand playing through the house, and clothes and hair were in disorder. A partition ran across the dining room and in the back room the women had planned to do the cooking with an oil stove. This was found to be impracticable and a kitchen was established under a sail near the back door.

The bay room was divided into two rooms, one a pantry opening from the kitchen and a clothes press opening by the great door. The house was unpainted and unbattened. The wind whistled through it and at night the tight ropes holding the weights of the lifting doors kept up a shrill music which with the ground swell of the ocean gave the effect of a hurricane. Inside we sat about the roaring fire, separated from the world as Crusoe on his island.

On July 11 the trains ran[1] and the transit to the island became a far easier matter. Since this event, although the island has lost its peculiar charm of isolation, it has gained in many substantial ways.

As our commissariat, starting from Millville at five o'clock P.M. with a can of milk and a basket of meat and groceries, I landed at Seaville and was met by the stage specially provided by agreement with Mr. Landis, the founder. At Seaville I bought berries and bread. At Henry Corson's I added vegetables. At Ezekial Bossi I added ice. I filled our water can and took in melons, etc. The stage was usually well filled by the time we reached the thoroughfare and the transfer of the freightage from the stage to the ferry boat was thence by cart to our castle. It was no easy task.

After August 1 the bridge was completed and the butcher and baker wagons came over twice a week. Public wells supplied water for washing and cooking. We had no communication with the shore at night until the bridge was completed. Fortunately we had no sickness nor accident during the whole season requiring a doctor or other help from the mainland. On September 13 we moved back to Millville.

1883

During the interval of 1882-3 the three lifting doors having become much worn were replaced, the one in front by the wide swinging doors, the one on the south side by the locker, the north only large sash. These sash were all taken from the bedroom windows which were now fitted with French sash, a great improvement. In front, the piazza was built and outside a bulkhead was built to prevent the encroachment of the sea. Boardwalks were laid, a good deal of gravelling done about the house and it was repainted inside. The ladder going up to the front bedrooms was replaced by a winding staircase.

We moved down May 31 with all the family but Sophie, who was in Winchester, and in addition Alice Atwater Carry and May Mason, Herr Reinhold, Sally Lawton, Quade and the donkey. I brought Sophie home at Commencement. Alice went home July 4 and during July, John L. Atwater and family spent a week with us and George L. Clarke spent three weeks. On August 24 in a terrible storm lasting several days which drove the sea past the house on both sides.

Marjorie Garrison Atwater was born. The next day J. E. Morse and wife and two children, mother and sister visited us. On August 26 Miss Burnham came. The next week Max was very sick with pneumonia and we had a drenching northeaster but all went well and we moved back September 17.

1889

We went down as usual in June, having for help five Indian students — girls from the Indian School at Carlisle, Pennsylvania.[2]

During this season I was at work in Philadelphia and only came to Millville and Sea Isle for weekends. David was very ill with typhoid fever in the spring and early summer of 1889 and was in a very weak, emaciated condition but rapidly recovered at the shore.

On September 12 the greatest storm in the history of the place occurred. A northeast hurricane held the ocean up regardless of tide for three days, and the town was flooded and the three miles of marsh to the Sea Side Road became a raging sea. Half a dozen houses above and below our house were undermined and fell into the ocean. I was in Philadelphia until the third day, Wednesday, when I went by train to Ocean View and crept on my hands and knees on the railroad ties which were stretched like a whiplash over the marshes, till I reached the shore. It was a scene of desolation but our house stood firm, only the front porch being swept away. The family were all safe and well, including two or three visitors.

The Indian maids were greatly frightened and on the following Friday deserted us, walking and wading to Ocean View. We all followed as soon as we could get transportation and closed the house.

The family lived abroad for almost 18 years and didn't return to Sea Isle City until September 1907, when Atwater planned a family reunion. The children, now grown and with families of their own, suggested to their father than the property be further developed to have enough space for their children to experience the shore as they had. Atwater, surely a loving patriarch, built a new house called "The Barracks." This barn-like structure accommodated four families who shared a kitchen. By the end of May 1908, three generations of Atwaters were summering together.

Atwater continued his journal where he'd left off, recording dozens of guests: "Including family servants and visitors we entertained 50 persons for an average of 30 days each and we had a tremendously good time." He noted the arrival of his sons: "The four boys seemed children again and played as they had done 25 years before. Dick, Max, Chris and Edward Smith took part in the canoe races and made a fine show. David was the sensation of the tub race and won it." Canoe races in the surf, tilting canoe tournaments, Sunday-morning singing, bagatelle, tennis, the opening of the yacht club and the introduction of motorboat racing to Sea Isle City filled his diary.

The 1916 season was unusual "on account of the plague of sharks on the coast," although no lives were lost in Sea Isle City, and the polio epidemic, which kept one branch of the family quarantined in New York.

In 1918 tragedy hit the family when a sand dune caved in on two of Atwater's young grandsons; but his son David and his other three grandsons, fortunately, returned safely from World War I.

Richard Atwater's last entry in his journal was made in 1921: "It was a very quiet, healthful and agreeable season."

NOTES

1. *On July 11 the trains ran:* A branch line of the Pennsylvania and West Jersey Railroad was built from just north of the South Seaville station (known as Sea Isle Junction) across the marshes to the island.

2. *Indian school at Carlisle:* As migration pushed westward, displaced American Indians were forced to live on reservations, and many children were separated from their parents and transported back East to special schools to learn to speak and read English. Congress passed a bill in 1879 authorizing their removal. *Harper's Monthly* in 1880 expressed the sentiment of many Americans when it editorialized, "Their uplifting may prove to be the most important factor in the Salvation of their race."

───────────

From the diary of Richard Atwater, printed in *South Jersey Magazine*, Summer and Fall 1991, and Winter 1992, used with the permission of the Sea Isle City Historical Society.

1887
Salt Water Day

Anonymous

Clams and oysters, watermelon, a jug of applejack, a wide sandy beach, and uninhibited high spirits were all that were needed for a joyous, unrestrained Salt Water Day.

▨ The origins of Saltwater Day have disappeared as surely as the oysters; but its existence shows that not only finely dressed ladies and gentlemen responded to the call of the sea. One 19th-century historian recalled a "sheep washing" day in the 1880s, when farmers made a pilgrimage to the sea. Even earlier, residents of rural areas within twenty miles of South Amboy celebrated "bathing day" on the verdant banks of Raritan Bay on the first or second

Saturday after the August full moon: In 1856 one observer counted during a three-hour period more than 2,000 persons of all ages, sexes and colors returning from the shore. Behavior, he noted, was "highly unconventional."[1]

The custom of observing Salt-water Day is so old that it's supposed to be of Dutch origin; but long before the Dutch came to New Jersey the Indians had a custom which might very well have furnished the model. It is a fact established in history that the New Jersey Indians were in the periodical habit of assembling in the neighborhood of the salt-water for the purpose of feasting upon oysters, and the gathering and eating of oysters was one of the chief features of the Salt-water Day observed among the Monmouth County farmers in later years.

Before oysters became private property, and when there were natural beds of them along the Jersey shore, farmers living within twenty or thirty miles felt a keen oyster hunger about the first of every August, and on Salt-water Day, which occurs at this season, the beds were made to suffer. They suffered so much that the New Jersey Legislature finally passed a law restraining people from taking oysters by any means except the unsupplemented feet and hands, so that for several years previous to the time when oysters ceased to be public property the farmers on Salt-water Day could obtain this delicate food only by "treading" it; that is, by working the oysters from the bottom, and skilfully bringing them to the surface with their toes.

South Amboy used to be a favorite place of gathering on Salt-water Day, and so lately as five years ago as many as one hundred tent-top wagons brought in their loads of people from the back-lying farms to assist in this celebration. At South Amboy the festivities are concluded in a single day, but at the other places — and notably at Point Pleasant, or Sea Girt, as it is now called, a part of the village of Squan — three days are devoted to them. Of course at these festivals at the edge of the sea there have come to be other joys than the joy of eating oysters. Bathing, dancing, and miscellaneous feasting are to be reckoned among the delights of Salt-water Day. There are stores of cold fowl, sandwiches, home-made pies, cider and pink lemonade, and some of the wagon-tops keep the sun off from a keg or a demijohn of apple-jack. The bathing suits worn by the farmers and their wives and daughters are home-made, the same as the pies, and are commendable for their comfort and serviceability rather than their fit.

But the observance of Salt-water Day is not what it used to be. Railroads have brought the sea and the oysters nearer to the farmers, and the reason for the celebration is largely gone. The colored people still observe the day with considerable fervor at Long Branch, but the festival, speaking generally, is one which is rapidly going out.

NOTE

1. Gustav Kobbe, *The New Jersey Coast and Pines,* Short Hills N.J., 1889 and William A. Whitehead, *Early History of Perth Amboy,* New York, 1856.

Harper's Weekly, August 13, 1887, volume XXXL, number 1599.

1888
Manasquan

Robert Louis Stevenson

Guests at The Union House, near the juncture of the Manasquan River and the ocean, over-looked the village, the river, and the ocean.

 The Scottish author Robert Louis Stevenson was tired in the spring of 1888, and "in and about The Slough of Despond." In late April he wrote a friend from New York City, "I do not know where I am going, yet I must get away right soon and get to work." [1] William Low, Stevenson's friend from a decade before in Paris, arranged for a trip to the Jersey Shore, where, it was thought, the healthy sea air would benefit the writer's declining health. During the first week of May Low and his wife, Stevenson, his mother and stepson took the train to Manasquan's Union House, a popular summer resort on the banks of the Manasquan River. Stevenson's wife, Fanny, had gone on ahead to San Francisco but the writer had to "rake together" some articles for Scribner's magazine before he and his family left for a cruise in the South Pacific.

Union House was about a mile and a half west of the juncture of Manasquan River and the ocean, opposite Gull Island. It was so early in the season that Stevenson and his party had the place to themselves. Low describes the hotel in his 1908 book A Chronicle of Friendships: "A lawn slopes down to the river bank, where there is a dock for the service of the many cat-boats and dories moored nearby, and the bank is shaded with large willows." Stevenson was ailing, Low wrote, and "clung to us with a singular dependence that measured the depth of his depression more eloquently than words," but was glad to spend most of his non-working time out of doors. "His interest was centered by the cat-boat, a craft new to his experience." Stevenson got hold of a manual on sailing the cat and put it to good use.

"We sailed up and down the river², Stevenson being greatly pleased with the manner in which the laws of navigation were construed in our behalf," Low recorded. "The draws in the three bridges which span the river opened promptly for our cockleshell craft, in response to the imperious toot of a tin horn which signified our desire to pass through the bridge. Once, when a train was detained on the railroad bridge that we might pass, Louis declared that the sense of our importance, shown by our having the right of way, was most gratifying."

A few days after Stevenson wrote the following letter to his longtime friend and editor Sidney Colvin, he finalized plans for the cruise from San Francisco to the South Pacific where he remained until he died of tuberculosis in 1894.

MAY 8[?], 1888: My dear Colvin, We are here at a delightful country inn, like a country French place, the only people in the house, a cat-boat at our disposal, the sea always audible on the outer beach, the lagoon as smooth as glass, all the little, queer, many coloured villas standing shuttered and empty; in front of ours, across the lagoon, two long wooden bridges, one for the rail, one for the road, sounding with intermittent traffic. It is highly pleasant, and a delightful change from Saranac. My health is much better for the change. I am sure I walked about four miles yesterday; one time with another — well, say three and a half; and the day before, I was out for four hours in the cat-boat, and was as stiff as a board in consequence. More letters call. Yours ever. RLS.

NOTES

1. *Get to work:* Letter to Ida Taylor from New York, late April 1888.

2. *Sailed up and down the river:* An anecdote Low tells in his book gives an idea of the kicked-back diversions the men enjoyed. One day they sailed up the river to a small island with a wooden bulkhead on one side: "As the island was nameless we proceeded to repair the damage and christened it 'Treasure Island,' after which we fell to with our pocket-knives to carve the name upon the bulkhead, together with our initials and the date." With the passage of time, some local historians and authors came to the erroneous conclusion that this island had been the inspiration for *Treasure Island*, which had been published in 1883.

From *The Letters of Robert Louis Stevenson, volume 6, August 1887 to September 1890,* edited by Bradford A. Booth and Ernest Mehew, Yale University Press, 1995, New Haven and London.

1892
Wildwood

Charles Conrad Abbott

A section of Wildwood's "W" tree — shown here before 1903, when Magnolia Lake was filled in and the tree cut down — is displayed at the Boyer Museum.

In 1885 Philip P. Baker, one of Charles Landis' partners in the Sea Isle City development, and two of his brothers bought about a hundred acres on Five-Mile Beach between Anglesea and Holly Beach, now the Wildwoods. The island was empty except for the fifty-room Anglesea Hotel overlooking Townsend's Inlet. Baker noted at the time that he was "surrounded by one of *the most curious groves of trees containing many of the most remarkable freaks of nature in living wood. Massive trees are wrapped around each other as though placed there by art." Even though Baker apparently was appreciative of nature's creations, he was, nonetheless, a developer. In 1886 he advertised a "charming resort, grand forest, beautiful sod and safe bathing for women and children," but promised "building and other improvements."*

When ornithologist Charles Abbott visited, the resort had a dance pavilion, more hotels and "beautiful cottages." The fifty acres of primeval forest for which the town was named was still largely intact. But not for long: A 1909 aerial view shows very little natural growth; streets, houses and a boardwalk had replaced the wild woods.

It too often happens in these latter days that a suggestive name proves sadly disappointing. We look in vain for the attractive features the mind pictured, and have good cause to criticise the unbridled imagination of forerunning visitors. Fortunately, a recent ramble had no such painful ending. I have heard of a wild-wood, and since have found it.

Clustered trees, though there be many, do not of themselves make a forest. Many a woodland tract is as uniform as a cornfield, or, at best, but indefinite duplication of the trees along a village street. If the rambler merely seeks the shade, then one tree is sufficient, and perhaps an umbrella is even an improvement, seeing we can plant it where we choose. But now I had found a wild-wood in the fullest sense of that suggestive phrase. Here variety ruled, and only the choicest of Nature's handiwork had foothold. Think of it! Century after century nature had had full sway, and turned out a finished piece of work. Every sense is charmed; eye, ear, and nose are alike regaled; the sense of touch delighted. Perfect trees to look upon; the birds' songs and the moaning of the sea to hear; the bloom of a thousand roses to smell; the carpeted sand to lie upon.

Yet, where all was nearing perfection, there stood out one grand feature overtopping all else — scores of magnificent hollies. I had seen many of these trees before, but never where they gave a distinct character to the woods. Elsewhere they occur in clumps of three or four, or perhaps a dozen, but here, on an island by the sea, there are hundreds. One that I measured was sixty-eight inches in circumference and forty feet high. The pale-gray trunk was well mottled with curious black lichen, and among the branches drooped long tresses of beard-like lichen.

The pathless wood about it was a most fit surrounding, the abundant birds its appropriate comrades, the murmur of the sea the music to which its branches gently swayed. To be able to throw oneself on a moss-carpeted sand dune and gaze upward at such a tree is abundant recompense for miles of weary walking.

But this little nook was not the whole wild-wood, and every tree was worthy of description. I would that I could write the history of a tree: the stories of these hollies would pass for fairy tales.

Irregularities in tree-growth are nowhere unusual features of a forest, but here the hollies are, or have been, on the lookout to break away from all restraint and become as wayward as possible. Here is one that has twirled about until now the trunk is a gigantic corkscrew; and not far off, another and larger tree has branched some ten feet from the ground, and then the two main divisions of the trunk have been reunited. A modification of this, where a stout limb has returned to the parent stem and re-entered, making "jug-handles," is a common occurrence, and, more marvellous still, a venerable cedar has some of its outreaching branches passing not merely into, but entirely through huge hollies that stand near by. Evidently the cedar here is the older tree and the hollies have grown around the now imprisoned branches. And, as if not content with such irregularities as these, other hollies have assumed even animal-like shapes; the resemblance in one instance to an elephant's head and trunk being very marked. Even the stately and proper-grown hollies have their trunks incased in strangely wrinkled barks, suggestive of a plastic mass that has suddenly hardened.

Why all this irregularity I leave to others. There was no patent explanation for him who ran to read, and I was puzzled at the outset to know in what direction to commence guessing. This is an entertainment, when idling in the woods, the rambler should not despise. Our best outings are when we wear other head-gear than a thinking-cap. So far as the crooked hollies are concerned, it will be time enough next winter to muse over the conclusions of the botanist.

Equally startling in such wonderland is it to see a thrifty blueberry bush growing from the trunk of a tree, so high in the air that you need a ladder to reach it. This bush annually bears a full crop of excellent fruit. That I am at last in a bit of Jersey's primeval forest there is little doubt. Had an elk darted by, or a mastodon screamed, it would hardly have been surprising. This not seriously, of course; but how promptly the present vanishes in such a wood; how vividly the past is pictured before us! Everywhere towering trees bearing evidence of age, and early in the day I found myself face to face with a huge cedar, dating back at least to the Norsemen, who it is thought reached America, if not the New England coast. Here was a tree that for centuries the Indians had known as a landmark.

It is a mistake to suppose that old trees do not remain in almost every neighborhood, for an old tree is not of necessity a big one. A dwarf will wrinkle and crook as surely as a giant. In many a swamp there are gnarly hornbeams that date back at least two centuries, and grape-vines are known that are even older. It is common to consider as old every object that has rounded out a single century, but this is nothing uncommon in tree-growths, and even some shrubs. Many a wild growth, if undisturbed, becomes practically permanent, and I am positive any number of insignificant growths in the undrained swamps and plough-defying meadows date back to Penn's treaty, and even earlier.

There is a familiar lilac hedge, or part of it, within the bounds of my ordinary rambles, planted by my grandfather in 1804, and so, in a dozen years, will be a hundred years old; but it looks nothing different from similar hedges planted fifty years ago. The old cedar in the lane was but eighteen inches in diameter, and I have documentary evidence that it was a familiar landmark much more than a century ago. A thunderbolt or tornado recently shivered the old tree beyond recognition, literally reduced it to splinters, and I found that the heart was very much decayed. There was no possibility of determining the age by counting the rings of growth shown in a cross section, and so I have but the poor satisfaction of merely conjecturing. At one place a narrow bit of the outer edge was smooth, and I counted forty-eight rings, one for each year of my life, and these had added but little to the tree's girth.

But here, at Wildwood Beach, is a cedar almost twelve feet in circumference, considerably more than double that of the cedar in the lane. There is no reason to consider that its growth has been forced by peculiarly favorable conditions. It is simply a magnificent example of what a tree may become if a fair chance is shown it. I have suggested that the tree may be nearly or quite one thousand years old, and I believe it. Peter Kalm[1], when wandering in the Jersey wilderness in 1749, noticed the cedars carefully, and mentions the fact of "very slow growth; for a stem thirteen inches and a quarter in diameter had one hundred and eighty-eight rings, or annual circles, and another, eighteen inches in diameter, had at least two hundred and fifty, for a great number of the rings were so fine that they could not be counted."

Of course, much of the beauty of this huge, lone, sea-side cedar is lost in being so hemmed in by other growths, and it is a startling fact that, if the rambler was not very open-eyed, he might pass it by unheeded. Think of what wealth of wonders are in every wood, and that so few persons find them; what a staggering array of marvels in a forest laid bare!

Why this luxuriant vegetation on a sandy island by the sea? The soil suggests barrenness only. Except the faint traces of decayed vegetation, it is a matter of pure white sand. It is known that the land along the Jersey coast is sinking, and we naturally look for a stratum of loam, once well above but now below or at the level of the sea. This, in our fancy, we hold necessary for timber growth; but if it is here at all, these trees' roots have not reached it. It is strange that such huge growths can find safe anchorage in these light and shifting sands. They have found some strength in union and close companionship, it is true; but, though they are built on a sandy foundation, the storms have not prevailed to their detriment even. Whence the trees' nourishment? Largely from the atmosphere: but why speculate? Suffice it to say, that, were we to take these same trees and shrubs inland and set them in pure silica, though Paul planted and Apollos watered[2] ever so carefully, there would be no increase.

The undergrowth, too, is everywhere equally luxuriant and gives a semitropical appearance to the landscape, this feature being emphasized by the vigor of fine growths that bind together the tallest trees and unite many an oak, cedar, and holly standing scores of feet apart. We are forced to smile nowadays when we read the glowing accounts of America's earliest visitors, and wonder how it was possible that they should have been so deceived; but the truth dawns upon me when I recall these early writers and see the wondrous conditions obtaining on this sea-side island.

This little island, I take it, is a relic of old New Jersey; this forest a living fragment of that now buried one, not far away, which has "given rise to a singular industry, the literal mining of timber. At several points ... enormous quantities of white cedar, liquidambar, and magnolia logs, sound and fit for use, are found submerged in the salt marshes, sometimes so near the surface that roots and branches protrude, and again deeply covered with smooth meadow sod. Many of the trees overthrown and buried were forest giants. In the great cedar swamp ... the logs reach a diameter of four, five, and even seven feet, and average between two and three feet in thickness."

In one case, one thousand and eighty rings of annual growth have been counted and under this huge stump was discovered a prostrate tree, which had fallen and been buried before the larger one had sprouted. This lower-lying log was determined to be fully five hundred years old. Here then, is evidence of fifteen centuries that have elapsed, and forests even before then had grown, flourished, and decayed. It is a series of surprises to dig into such strange earth. Think of passing through an underground cedar swamp and coming upon magnolias and sweet-gum still deeper down! What if there were tongues in such trees? Here is a spot whereat a poet might dwell to his and the world's advantage. Not all the grandeur of the world centers in the sea or rests upon a mountain. There are other beauties than those of a spreading landscape or a rocky gorge; a strange, peculiar beauty, worthy of a poet, clings to every trunk and broken branch of this sunken sea-side forest.

When we consider that for miles at sea, as we stand upon the present beach, we are looking upon waters that cover what was once, and not so very long ago, dry and habitable land, we can better realize the one-time conditions of this region when primitive man threaded the mazes of the primeval forest. Dr. Lockwood has told us of masses of peat and vegetable growth cast ashore during storms, and of a mastodon tooth that had long been buried in a swamp, and yet came from the bottom of the sea, waves breaking now where but a few centuries ago a forest had withstood the tempest's fury. Was man here then? How constantly this question comes to mind when we recall the past! One cannot reasonably doubt it, and it never would have been a debatable matter had not ignorance declared man's recent creation, and that our continent's quota of humanity had to force the ice-barriers of Siberia and Behring's Strait, and so finally reach the Atlantic coast of America. Happily, such nonsense is forever downed.

While, the island over, I found not even an arrow-head, yet other traces of early man were not wanting; traces contemporaneous with the buried swamps at sea and hidden forests on the mainland. I refer to submerged shell-heaps.[3] These are now a feature of the marshes, and would be puzzles, indeed, were it not that they rest upon hard-pan, and so were started upon what was then dry land. Now, the marsh has grown about them to a depth of several feet, and not far from the dark holly forest, wherein I am now resting, there is a long, narrow deposit of broken and burnt shells that is not exposed even at low tide. One need not fear that his fancy will run riot in picturing that early time when the broad marsh and shallow bay were scenes of human industry of a most primitive kind. While the gathering of shell-fish, for both immediate and future needs, was kept up by the Indians into historic times, it must not be concluded that the remains of their feasting are all comparatively modern and offer no differences among themselves.

These Indian shell-heaps or "kitchen-middens" vary considerably in one particular, some containing traces of Indian art in its highest development; others have little else than a few broken and battered stone hammers. This might be explained if there was no evidence of antiquity of a geological character; but this exists, and a very superficial tabulation of these shell-heaps, scattered over a few square miles of territory, showed that those most deeply buried in the marshes contained no pottery or evidence of skilfully-worked stone, while those that are still above the water-level do contain elaborately-wrought implements. Further, here, as elsewhere, I doubt not, if careful sections of the most extensive of these shell deposits could be made, their bases would show a lower stage of primitive art than is found near their surfaces. And what of the shell-heaps that have been washed away? Thousands of acres of habitable land have been engulfed. If this was forested, as is the little island over which I now wander, what a paradise for primitive man!

But the day was drawing to a close, and I had the long shadows in mind that dimmed the sun's glare upon the beach. Across lots through the woods was but a step, and in all its summer glory glittered the broad Atlantic. What a quick transition! Here, literally joining hands, a seaside forest and the boundless ocean.

NOTES

1. *Peter Kalm:* A Swedish botanist who visited the American colonies in the mid-eighteenth century. His experiences were translated into English as *Travels into North America.*

2. *Paul planted and Apollos watered:* Apollos was an Alexandrian Jew; he and Paul baptized the new Christians in Ephesus and Achaia, but according to the book of Acts, Apollos' baptisms were invalid and Paul had to do the job over again.

3. *Shell heaps:* Shell heaps resting on gravel around which marshes have formed have been excavated up and down the coast.

From *Recent Rambles, or In Touch with Nature,* J. B. Lippincott Co., Philadelphia, 1892.

1892
Ocean Grove

J. S. Hoffman

A postcard view of the boardwalk, where three tribes of parading Indians were denied entrance to the restrictive Methodist resort.

The Methodist resort of Ocean Grove was a quiet, spiritual retreat. Its stated mission was "to provide opportunities for spiritual birth, growth and renewal through worship, educational, cultural and recreational programs for persons of all ages in a proper, convenient, and desirable Christian seaside setting." The tent town that had inspired the affectionate name "little canvas village" twenty years earlier was gone, replaced by rows of small cottages around a central park and an auditorium seating 6,600 people. But the "blue laws" for which the town was known were still on the books and many would stay so well into the twentieth century: no alcohol, no theater, no organ-grinder, no parades, no dancing, no card-playing, no scissors grinder, no carriages on the beach, no bicycles on the walkways, no swearing. On Sundays, a day of prayer and meditation, the gates were closed[1] to all but foot traffic to services.

J. S. Hoffman, a press agent, was with Pawnee Bill's Historical Wild West Show in Asbury Park the Sunday the Indians — three tribes of them — wanted to see the ocean. This is how Hoffman described the event.

We got to Asbury Park on Sunday, the day before the show opened. After the Indians pitched their tents — make no mistake, they were the real thing and savage looking — they said they wanted to see the Big Water, meaning the ocean.

That gave me an idea. I herded a bunch of them and we set out for the beach with Pawnee Bill at the head. It was a picturesque parade. Pawnee Bill was a figure to attract attention anywhere with his frontier garb and long hair falling over his shoulders. The braves' costumes were gay and so were those of the squaws. Some of them had papooses strapped on their backs.

We hadn't gone very far in Asbury Park before we had a crowd following us and the farther we went the greater it grew. Finally we got to the beach and did those Indians look! It was their first glimpse of the ocean and they couldn't get enough of it.

"How big is this lake?" they asked. "Who owns it? Are there great fish in it?"

Their eyes popped when I told them it would take a lifetime for a man to paddle across it in a canoe. I pointed out the great canoes of the white man — big sailing ships with three and four masts. I told them of the great storms that came when Manitou would puff his cheeks and blow great blasts, and flash lighting from his eyes.

I had planned the thing as a stunt, but I got interested in my own show. So we walked along the boardwalk, feathered headdress, red shawls, yellow moccasins and all.

The crowd milled around us so that we could hardly walk. Finally we approached the boundary line of Ocean Grove at the foot of Wesley Lake and started to cross into the Ross Pavilion as the North End was then called.

Then Pawnee Bill was stopped by a policeman named Chamberlain who told him he couldn't bring his parade into Ocean Grove on Sunday. Bill's hand fell on his revolver — it was loaded with blanks, of course. "Who's to stop us?" he growled.

Looking nervously at the hand on the revolver, the policeman said, "Well, it's against all rules and regulations. It's breaking the Sabbath — and besides, you don't have a parade permit."

"This is no parade," replied Bill. "This is a peaceful group of Indians who owned this land before the white men stole it from them. They are peaceful visitors dressed in the garb of their race and are merely sightseeing and viewing the ocean for the first time. I defy you or any other man to stop us."

The policeman hedged, but told Bill the Indians must be quiet and orderly. So we proceeded along the boardwalk with the crowd following.

When we got to the foot of Pilgrim Pathway, up came Dr. E. H. Stokes,[2] president of the Ocean Grove Camp Meeting Association. He greeted us courteously and remarked that the Indians were very interesting but their presence in Ocean Grove was upsetting the peace and quietness of the place. Then he asked Bill as a personal favor if he would take his Indians away.

Bill agreed, and we marched back to Asbury Park where the Indians watched the ocean more. Then Pawnee Bill took them all for a ride on the trolley cars. But they sure loved that ocean.

NOTES

1. *Gates were closed:* The gates would not open Sundays until 1980.
2. *Dr. E. H. Stokes:* One of the founders of Ocean Grove.

From an unsourced clipping at the Ocean County Historical Society.

1892
Asbury Park

Stephen Crane

What Stephen Crane called the "observation wheel" was almost closed down when nearby hotel owners complained that its engine spewed sparks and ashes over their bed quilts.

 Stephen Crane was just 23 years old in 1895 when publication of his novel The Red Badge of Courage *made him an overnight literary celebrity. Four years earlier, during his final year at Syracuse University, Crane had been a stringer for the* New York Tribune. *By the summer of 1892 Crane was report-*

ing regularly from Asbury Park, James Bradley's booming new resort, where his mother had moved with three of her children when Stephen was eleven.

Bradley had bought the five hundred acres that would become Asbury Park in 1871. Inspired by his involvement at Ocean Grove just to the south, he wanted a resort that would encourage religious principles and temperate moral living. Thus, he named his town after Francis Asbury, the first Methodist bishop in America.

Bradley owned the oceanfront and all land surrounding the lake and he planned his town carefully, boasting, "There will never be another seaside town on the Atlantic coast, from Sandy Hook to Barnegat Inlet, with as wide streets and open spaces as Asbury Park." He placed the extra-wide streets at right angles to the ocean to gain maximum benefit from cooling ocean breezes and landscaped a generous amount of public parks and squares. In an August 1892 Tribune article Crane wrote, "Founder Bradley has lots of sport with his ocean front and boardwalk. It amuses him and he likes it. It warms his heart to see the thousands of people tramping over his boards, helter-skeltering in his sand and diving into that ocean of the Lord's which is adjacent to the beach of James A. Bradley."

Asbury Park's first boardwalk was laid in 1877; it was rolled up at the end of the season. Three years later a larger, wider, permanent walk with intermittent benches and covered pavilions was installed. A fishing pier with sea-lions in a saltwater tank, bathhouses with lockers, and a bandstand fronted the ocean. Vacationers could ride a roller toboggan — predecessor to the roller coaster — or New Jersey's first electric trolley.

Bradley maintained tight control over Asbury Park, including deed restrictions against gambling and alcohol — although any man who wanted a drink had a choice of saloons a mile from the city limits. Trains were prohibited from stopping at the station on Sundays, but by 1883 Asbury Park was so popular that on one peak summer day 103 trains brought in 5,500 day-trippers and 2,500 overnight passengers. Growth was rampant: in 1889 more than 200 hotels and boarding houses had been built; fifteen years later there were 800.

In a Tribune report datelined July 2, 1892 Crane described the incoming visitors: "Great train-loads of pleasure-seekers and religious worshippers are arriving at the huge double railway station of Ocean Grove and Asbury Park. The beach, the avenues, and the shaded lawns are once more covered with the bright-hued garments of the summer throng. The 'old timers,' evading the crowds of hackmen, take leisurely routes to their hotels, and gaze at the improvements and new buildings of the twin cities; the newcomer falls a victim to the rapacity of the hackmen because of his great astonishment at the vast length of platform, the huge pile of trunks, the wide roadways and the wriggling, howling mass of humanity which declares itself ready to take him to 'any hotel or cottage' at a moderate charge. Having escaped with the connivance of one of these weary toilers after the dollar of the summer traveller, he forgets the turmoil of the station as he rides through the high Main-st. gates and obtains a view of a long, quiet avenue, shaded by waving maples, with a vision of blue sea in the distance."

A month later Crane submitted to the Tribune the following story entitled "Joys of Seaside Life."[1]

This town is not overrun with seaside "fakirs," yet there are many fearful and wonderful types in the collection of them here. The man with the green pea under all or none of three walnut shells is not present, nor is any of his class. There is no fierce cry of "Five, five, the lucky five!" nor the coaxing call of "Come, now, gentlemen, make your bets. The red or the black wins." These men cannot pass the gigantic barriers erected by a wise government, which recognizes the fact that these things should not be. However, the men who merely have things to sell can come and flourish. There are scores of them, and they do a big business. The summer guests come here with money. They are legitimate prey. The fakirs attack them enthusiastically.

Those who are the most persistently aggressive are the Hindoos, who sell Indian goods, from silk handkerchiefs to embroidered petticoats. They are an aggregation of little brown fellows, with twinkling bright eyes. They wear the most amazing trousers and small black surtouts, or coats of some kind. Apparently they are, as a race, universally bow-legged, and are all possessed of ancestors who are given to waddling. The Hindoos have soft, wheedling voices, and when they invade a crowded hotel-porch and unload their little white packs of silk goods they are very apt to cause a disturbance in the pocketbooks of the ladies present. They parade the streets in twos and threes. They all use large umbrellas of the rural pattern to protect their chocolate skins from the rays of the sun. A camera fiend was the first to discover an astonishing superstition of fear which possesses these men. Once she perceived three of them reclining in picturesque attitudes on a shady bank. Their bundles and umbrellas reposed beside them and they were fanning themselves with their caps. She approached them with an engaging smile and a camera levelled at their heads. Astonishment and terror swept over their faces. With one accord they gave a great shout and raising their umbrellas, interposed them as a bulwark against the little glass eye of the camera. The fiend had her finger on the trigger, and she pulled it before she was aware of the bewildering revolution in the appearance of the objects of her ambition. As a result the picture is the most valued one in all the fiend's collection. There is the grassy bank and a few trees. In the foreground appear the tops of three large umbrellas. Underneath dangle three pairs of legs with also three pairs of feet. The picture is a great success and is the admiration of all beholders.

Of course the frankfurter man is prevalent. He is too ordinary to need more than mere mention. With his series of quick motions, consisting of the grab at the roll, the stab at the sausage and the deft little dab of mustard, he appears at all hours. He parades the avenues swinging his furnace and howling.

There is a sleight-of-hand Italian, with a courageous mustache and a clever nose. He manoeuvres with a quarter of a dollar and a pack of playing cards. He comes around to the hotels and mystifies the indolent guests. Nobody cares much to ask: "How does he do it," so the mustache takes a vain curve and the exhibition continues.

Tin type[2] galleries are numerous. They are all of course painted the inevitable blue, and trundle about the country on wheels. It is quite the thing to have one's features libelled in this manner. The occupants of the blue houses make handsome incomes. Babies and pug dogs furnish most of the victims for these people.

Down near the beach are a number of contrivances to tumble-bumble the soul and gain possession of nickels. There is a "razzle-dazzle," invented apparently by a man of experience and knowledge of the world. It is a sort of circular swing. One gets in at some expense and by climbing up a ladder. Then the machine goes around and around, with a sway and swirl, like the motion of a ship. Many people are supposed to enjoy this thing, for a reason which is not evident. Solemn circles of more or less sensible-looking people sit in it and "go 'round."

On the lake shore is an "observation wheel,"[3] which is the name of a gigantic upright wheel of wood and steel, which goes around carrying little cars filled with maniacs, up and down, over and over. Of course there are merry-go-rounds loaded with impossible giraffes and goats, on which ride crowds of joyous children, who clutch for brass rings. All these machines have appalling steam organs run in connection with them, which make weird music eternally. Humanity had no respite from these things until the police made their owners tone them down a great deal, so that now they play low music instead of grinding out with stentorian force such airs as "Annie," the famous, so that they could be heard squares away.

The camera obscura is in Ocean Grove. It really has some value as a scientific curiosity. People enter a small wooden building and stand in a darkened room, gazing at the surface of a small round table, on which appear reflections made through a lens in the top of the tower of all that is happening in the vicinity at the time. One gets a miniature of everything that occurs in the streets, on the boardwalk or on the hotel porches. One can watch the bathers gamboling in the surf or peer at the deck of a passing ship. A man stands with his hand on a lever and changes the scene at will.

These are the regular ways in which Asbury Park amuses itself. There is, however, a steady stream of transient fakirs, who stay a week, an hour or perchance go at once away. This week an aggregation of five Italian mandolin and guitar players came to town. They are really very clever with their instruments, and have already made themselves popular with the hotel guests. One "Jesse Williams" is a favorite with everybody, too. He is very diminutive and very black. He has a disreputable silk-hat and a pair of nimble feet. He passes from house to house, and sings and dances. He accompanies both his dances and his songs on an old weather-beaten banjo. The entire populace adore him, because he sometimes discloses various qualities of the true comedian, and is never exactly idiotic.

But the most terrific of all the fakirs, the most stupendous of all the exhibitions is that of the Greek dancer, or whatever it is. Two Italians, armed with a violin and a harp, recently descended upon the town. With them came a terrible creature in an impossible apparel, and with a tambourine. He, or she, wore a dress which would take a geometrical phenomenon to describe. He, or she, wore orange stockings, with a bunch of muscle in the calf. The rest of his, or her, apparel was a chromatic delirium of red, black, green, pink, blue, yellow, purple, white and other shades and colors not known. There were accumulations of jewelry on different portions of his, or her, person. Beneath were those grotesque legs; above, was a face. The grin of the successful midnight assassin and the smile of the coquette were commingled upon it. When he, or she, with his, or her, retinue of Italians, emerged upon the first hotel veranda, there was a panic. Brave men shrunk. Then he, or she, opened his, or her, mouth and began to sing in a hard, high, brazen voice, songs in an unknown tongue. Then he, or she, danced, with ballet airs and graces. The scowl of the assassin sat side by side with the simper and smirk of the country maiden who is not well-balanced mentally. The fantastic legs slid over the floor to the music of the violin and harp. And, finally, he, or she, passed the tambourine about among the crowd, with a villainously-lovable smile upon his, or her, features. Since then he, or she, has become a well-known figure on the streets. People are beginning to get used to it, and he, or she, is not mobbed, as one might expect him, or her, to be.

NOTES

1. *Joys of seaside life*: This unsigned article from the *New York Tribune* ran in July 1892. Stephen Crane died of tuberculosis when he was just twenty-eight and in an effort to document his short but prolific life, 20th-century scholars have combed newspapers, collecting his newspaper articles, some written anonymously, but credited to Crane because of the subject matter and his definitive style.

2. *Tintype*: Ferrotype, the technique of printing an exposed image on tin, was commonly known as tintype.

3. *Observation wheel*: George Ferris developed his amusement wheel between 1890 and 1893. It became popular after being exhibited at the 1893 World's Columbian Exposition in Chicago. The term "Ferris wheel" was more widely used after the inventor died in 1896.

"Joys of Seaside Life" from the New York *Tribune*, July 17, 1892, quoted in *The New York City Sketches of Stephen Crane and Related Pieces*, edited by R. W. Stallman and E. R. Hageman, New York University Press, 1966.

1894
Asbury Park

Sterling Elliot

The Asbury Park Baby Parade was a promotional coup for the resort, and the high point of the season. The parents of this young goddess transformed her winning image onto a postcard.

A seasonal baby parade was a feature of several Monmouth County resorts, but Asbury Park took the prize for the biggest and best. The first parade marched along the boardwalk on July 22, 1890, led by founder James Bradley carrying a large white umbrella. The band played such hits of the day as "Rock-a-Bye Baby," "Baby Mine," and "Peek-A-Boo." Almost 200 children participated, and one of them won the grand prize — a baby carriage. Ten years later more than 500 children paraded, and every state in the Union except two was represented. By 1910 Asbury Park's baby parade had become an institution, drawing 100,000 spectators. Express wagons were transformed into allegories, and children portrayed fairy tale characters. The parade grew exponentially; by 1919 the winner was awarded an automobile instead of the usual pony and cart. With the exception of the Depression and war years, the tradition continued until midcentury.

Sterling Elliot, the editor of the Boston periodical Good Roads, *was in Asbury Park for a convention when he happened upon the annual event, which he subsequently detailed in his magazine.*

The annual exhibition of babies at Asbury Park is not only a local issue but is the event of the season. The Fourth of July races drew 5,000 people to the grounds without diminishing perceptibly the appearance of the streets and avenues of that beautiful city. The fireworks on the evening of the national anniversary were well attended, but still here and there were to be found people who seemed to be following some regular business.

But on the morning of the baby show! What a change was there in the atmosphere of Asbury Park. The listless, tired out citizen of the day previous was suddenly seized with a new style of locomotion, and had in his or her eye a strangely luminous anxiety and all were looking and walking in the direction of the ocean.

Being a stranger within the city's gates and noticing the unusual excitement, I asked a policeman "what was up." His answer was short enough, but the look that went with it was expressive even for an Asbury Park copper. He looked as though not certain whether he was being made the possible victim of a joke, or whether he had struck a real backwoodsman. He gave the benefit of the doubt, however, and said

"Baby Show" in a tone which clearly indicated his opinion of so absurd a question.

On what a Chicago friend was pleased to term the "lake front" we found a large portion of the inhabitants of New Jersey, but it was impossible to see what they were looking at, owing to the density of the crowd. At one end of the pier was a sign which stated that "The pavilion was for representatives of the press only." A short talk with the doorkeeper took the place of the otherwise necessary badge, and I was placed in view of the long stretch of board walk over which was soon to take place the greatest show that the season affords.

We learned from an old resident that when this baby parade was started, it was provided that prizes should be given for the handsomest babies. He remarked incidentally that none of the original promoters of the scheme are now living. This, however, may be only a logical result of perfectly natural causes.

The prizes now are given for the best decorated baby carriages without reference to the occupant. It is said that when the personal appearance of the infants was what must be passed upon it was difficult to get judges, finally it became impossible, hence the change.

The parade consisted for the most part of baby carriages decorated in various degrees of elegance, and occupied in each case by the sweetest little youngster in town (This last statement may do in a report of this kind, but you can see how the judges might have to be more explicit.) The line was over half a mile in length and showed in a startling and not unpleasant manner how tastes differ. A beautifully and very expensively trimmed carriage contained a young baby whose face was entirely unprotected from the blazing sun. Another was so loaded down with decorations that the tiny passenger was nearly smothered for lack of ventilation.

A majority of these exhibits were evidently from those to whom fortune had been kind, yet there was also seen the gaunt hand of poverty. A few little cabs from which the shine of varnish had long since vanished, cabs which had in their time done duty for more favored babes, and which now had been turned over, let us hope gratuitously, to little ones who otherwise could not have known such a luxury. A few green leaves with here and there a penny flag showed as did also the light step of the neat but cheaply clad mother-nurse, that the spirit of baby day was by no means a matter of worldly goods but was born of that independent patriotism which makes of the American citizen what it will.

Who can predict the relative social and commercial relations of those two classes of little folks for the next fifty years? No one, and herein lies the charm of our American plan of doing things.

The display which most impressed me was the little four-wheeled patrol wagon bedecked with American flags, pulled by a goat, three tots in it, and the clanging of the little gong, and the dignity of the driver as well as the twenty inch mite who stood as straight as an arrow on the tailboard. A remarkable thing about these boys is that they are brothers aged three, five, and seven years and that their birthdays come on the same day. The dignified little "cop" who is holding the goat is a son of the mayor of Asbury Park. With his red "sideboards," he formed a very striking headlight to the parade.

"Asbury Park Baby Show," *Good Roads: An Illustrated Monthly Magazine,* volume 6, 1894.

1896
Asbury Park

Stephen Crane

James A. Bradley built a paved bicycle path along the Asbury Park oceanfront to satisfy the Gay Nineties cycling craze.

Stephen Crane's mother died in 1892, and his closest brother, J. Townley Crane, who had operated a summer news agency for the New York Tribune, moved from Asbury Park. Crane was now living in New York City, fine-tuning The Red Badge of Courage. While awaiting its publication in 1895, he traveled to the American West and Mexico, gathering material for a newspaper syndicate. After a camping trip "deep in the woods" in July 1896 he returned to his former hometown.

Crane, experiencing the journalist's boredom with the mundane, had hoped to find the town changed and searched for something unique to write about — "We seek our descriptive material in the differences." But he did not; and in an article entitled "Asbury Park as Seen by Stephen Crane," he again satirized the resort's founder, James A. Bradley, who was known for supporting puritanical restrictions on dress and distributing detailed dictums around town. Signs posted on the women's bathhouses read: "Modesty of apparel is as becoming to a lady in a bathing suit as it is to a lady dressed in silk and satin. A word to the wise is sufficient."

Asbury Park somewhat irritates the anxious writer, because it persists in being distinctly American, reflecting all our best habits and manner, when it might resemble a town in Siberia, or Jerusalem, during a siege.

A full brigade of stages and hacks paraded to meet the train, and as the passengers alighted the hackmen swarmed forward with a capacity that had been carefully chastened by the police. While their voices clashed in a mellow chorus, the passengers for the most part dodged their appeals and proceeded across the square, yellow in the sunlight, to the waiting trolley cars. The breeze that came from the hidden sea bore merely a suggestion, a prophecy of coolness, and the baggagemen who toiled at the hill of trunks sweated like men condemned to New York.

From the station Asbury Park presents a front of spruce business blocks, and one could guess himself in one of the spick Western cities. Afterward there is square after square of cottages, trees and little terraces, little terraces, trees and cottages, while the wide avenues funnel toward a distant gray sky, whereon from time to time may appear ships. Later still, a breeze cool as the foam of the waves slants across the town, and above the bass rumble of the surf clamor the shrill voices of the bathing multitude.

The summer girls flaunt their flaming parasols, and young men in weird clothes, walk with the confidence born of a knowledge of the fact that their fathers work. In the meantime, the wind snatches fragments of melody from the band pavilion and hurls this musical debris afar.

Coney Island is profane; Newport is proper, with a vehemence that is some degrees more tiresome than Coney's profanity. If a man should be goaded into defining Asbury Park he might state that the distinguishing feature of the town is its singular and elementary sanity.

Life at Asbury Park is as healthy and rational as any mode of existence which we, the people, will endure for our benefit. This is, of course, a general statement, and does not apply to the man with seven distinct thirsts in one throat. He exists here, but he is minute in proportion. He labors unseen with his seven thirsts and his manners are devious. He only appears when he has opportunity to deliver his ode to Liberty.

Besides the prohibition law, there are numerous other laws to prevent people from doing those things which philosophers and economists commonly agree work for the harm of society. It is very irksome to be confronted with an ordinance whenever one wishes for novelty or excitement to smash a cannon [canon?] to smithereens. Moreover, there are a number of restrictions here which are ingeniously silly and are not sanctioned by nature's plan nor by any of the creeds of men, save those which define virtue as a physical inertia and a mental death.

But in the main it is unquestionably true that Asbury Park's magnificent prosperity, her splendid future, is due to the men who, in the beginning, believed that the people's more valuable patronage would go to the resort where opportunity was had for a rational and sober existence.

On cloudy nights there is always one star in the sky over Asbury Park. This star is James A. Bradley. The storm forces discover that he cannot be dimmed. A heavy mist can vanquish gorgeous Orion and other kings of the heavens, but James A. Bradley continues to shine with industry.

Orion and other kings of the heavens complain that this is because they do not own an ocean front. He it was who, in 1879, purchased a sand waste and speedily made it into Asbury Park, the seething summer city. He has celebrated this marvel in a beautiful bit of literature in which he does not refer to himself at all, nor to Providence. He simply admits the feat to be an evolution instead of a personal construction.

The famous feature is not obvious at once. James A. Bradley does not meet all incoming trains. He is as impalpable as Father Knickerbocker. It is well known that he invariably walks under a white cotton sun umbrella, and that red whiskers of the Islandic lichen pattern grow fretfully upon his chin, and persons answering this description are likely to receive the salaams of the populace.

He himself writes most of the signs and directions which spangle the ocean front, and natives often account for his absence from the streets by picturing him in his library flying through tome after tome of ancient lore in chase of those beautiful expressions which add so particularly to the effect of the Atlantic.

Then suddenly he will flash a work of philanthropy of so deep and fine a kind that it could only come from a man whose bold heart raised him independent of conventional or narrow-minded people, and his grand schemes for decorating the solar system with signs will be forgotten. Withal, he never poses, but carries his sublimity with the calmness of a man out of debt.

Of course there has long been a flourishing garden of humorists here who owe their bloom solely to the fact that Founder Bradley indulges sometimes in eccentricities, which are the sun of the morning and the rain of noon to any proper garden of humorists. But he is eccentric only in detail, this remarkable man.

The people should forget that, for purposes too mystic, too exaltedly opaque for the common mind, he placed a marble bathtub in the middle of a public park and remember only that he created the greatest summer resort in America — the vacation abode of the mighty middle classes — and, better still, that he now protects it with the millions that make him powerful and with the honesty that makes his millions useful.

Of late the founder has been delivering lop-sided political orations from the tailend of a cart to stage drivers, newsboys, unclassified citizens and summer boarders who have no other amusement. "I own the pavilions and the bath houses, and the fishing pier and the beach[1] and the pneumatic sea lion, and what I say ought to go with an audience that has any sense." The firmament has been put to considerable inconvenience, but it will simply have to adjust itself to the conditions and await his return.

In the meantime the brave sea breeze blows cool on the shore and the far little ships sink, one by one past the horizon. At bathing time the surf is a-swarm with the revelling bathers and the beach is black with watchers.

The very heart of the town's life is then at the Asbury Avenue pavilion, and the rustle and the roar of the changing throng give the casual visitor the same deep feeling of isolation that comes to the heart of the one sheep herder, who watches a regiment swing over the ridge or an express train line through the mesquite.

As the sun sinks the incoming waves are shot with copper beams and the sea becomes a green opalescence.

NOTE

1. *I own the beach:* Bradley sold the beach to the city on April 15, 1903, for $100,000.

"Asbury Park as Seen by Stephen Crane," Kansas City Star, August 22, 1896, in the Crane collection at Columbia University's Butler Library. Reprinted in *The New York City Sketches of Stephen Crane and Related Pieces*, edited by R. W. Stallman and E. R. Hagemann, New York University Press, 1966.

1899
Atlantic City

Lilyan West

READY FOR A BATH

Bathing suits had become briefer by the end of the century, but respectable girls still wore stockings.

Lilyan West wrote on the inside cover of her 1898 journal: *"If you chance to read this book/ And should find it silly/ All blunders you must overlook/ For it was written by Lilly."* Lilly seems to be typical of the "respectable" young women who went to Atlantic City around the turn of the century: Fun-loving but well-behaved, giggly but haughty, chaperoned, but not all the time; and no more or less boy-crazy than any teenager of any era. Lilyan kept a diary regularly from 1895 to 1902, writing in lined, hardcover notebooks. However we know even more about her because her younger sister Mary Jane (Mamie) was even more rigorous in her journal habits, writing and clipping newspaper stories about the family regularly from 1903 until 1911, when she married, and again from 1916 until 1919.

Until they married, the girls lived with their parents in Ridley Heights, Pennsylvania. One clipping calls their father, George W. West, "one of the most substantial citizens of this county [Delaware] and a large taxpayer in the county and city." After graduating from the Swarthmore Preparatory School, Lilyan studied at the Philadelphia Training School for kindergarten teachers in Philadelphia. She then organized and ran a school in Chester. During July and early August 19-year-old Lilyan was setting up her school in preparation for a September 18 opening, while at the same time getting ready for her vacation to Atlantic City.

The West family went to Atlantic City or Cape May every summer, sometimes as a family, sometimes just the girls and their mother; and occasionally Lilly and Mamie visited friends who owned a cottage at the shore. This season, according to a clip from the local paper, "Mrs. George W. West and family leave tomorrow for Atlantic City, where they will remain for the next two weeks at the Leedom."

JULY 15: I stayed at home all morning and sewed to beat the band, we are preparing for Atlantic and have to hustle. I have finished my new duck & linen skirt during the last few days and Mama is making Mamie a very pretty new lappete lawn dress so we are busy. In the afternoon I had to go to Chester to get my parasol which Mamie broke Decoration Day.

AUGUST 12: Trimming my new leghorn hat, it is sweet.

AUGUST 16: Bought new trunk for Atlantic, $6.25.

AUGUST 18: Fixed over my dress. Jo called with his snowball nag "Phillip" and we all went to Andrews, lots of dances and splendid refreshments. Jo kept swelling my head with I was the best gowned girl there, etc. Oh! he can compliment. Lizzie says he liked me real well. People often say things to tickle your ears, you know.

AUGUST 19: The weather very hot, have arranged to go to Atlantic August 26th.

AUGUST 21: Washing and ironing preparing for Atlantic.

AUGUST 25: Chased around this morning and did some shopping. I answered up all my letters and we packed our trunks all ready for tomorrow.

AUGUST 26: We arose early and drove down to the train. We stopped and bid Uncle Billie, Aunt Mary and Uncle Jo's families goodbye. Mabel met us at the station and the Andrews in Philadelphia and we went directly to dear old Atlantic, about eleven o'clock when we landed. Went to the Boardwalk. Met Will Howarth and he took us down on the Steel Pier[1] where was Mabel, May Pomeroy, Harry Borden, Miss Krieble, Mr. Lot, Herman and Mr. Miller. We spent the morning there and had a fine time. We also met Hamilton Ewell and Dr. Sticker. After dinner they came around and took us out on the pier to hear Innes band. Ham made a date for the evening so we came home and had supper. At supper we met the Misses Nellie and Byrde Slayman of Altoona, awfully nice girls. Well after supper Dr. Sticker and brave Hamilton came around and informed us that the Dr. had made a date with some other girls and they would be unable to keep ours as theirs was of longer standing, etc. so I as usual got mad and sent Ham off. He begged to go around with me tomorrow but I said No, sir, I have it all engaged. I think he is a mean old thing. We went out on the pier and met Elsie and all the other girls with several new boys, the names I have forgotten. We danced some and saw the minstrel show[2] and came home about 11:30. Owing to the full house[3] we had to room with the Slayman girls and we talked nearly all night and by morning knew all about Altoona and they all about Chester. That's the way of girls. They seem to be very nice and wealthy from all appearances. This ends our first day. Good night.

AUGUST 27: Although it was Sunday[4] we donned our bathing suits and repaired to the beach. The same crowd was there with the addition of Mr. Pomeroy and our friends, the Slaymans. They also met two boys from Altoona, Mr. McCarthy and Melvin, so we added them to the ranks. Everybody seemed to like my bathing suit and I couldn't help seeing the people look at it and several remarked that's a pretty bathing suit. We went way out in the swells and were having a grand time but alas and alack one of the swells broke over our heads and down we all went in a bunch legs and arms heads and everything all mixed up together. Fortunately the boys regained their balance and fished we girls up as best as they could but Oh! we were holy sights. We certainly had a jolly time.

We all went up to call on the girls at the Ponce de Leon[5] and had a splendid time in the evening. Cholly Pomeroy came around and took me to hear Innes band and it was certainly great. The girls introduced us to their uncle and aunt, Mr. and Mrs. Cunningham, who are staying at one of the swellest hotels down here, the Waldorf Astoria, so we called on them too. In the afternoon the whole ten girls all dressed in different colored dresses and linked arms and promenaded down and up the Boardwalk. It is only proper to say we created quite a sensation, all colors of the rainbow, ten of us and on Sunday afternoon.

AUGUST 28: The first person we met going up the Boardwalk was Mr. Ham with a new girl. Nobody cares, I'm sure. He is going home tonight, anyhow. Well we all put on our suits again today and sat in the sand with the boys. They had their cameras along and took a lot of pictures. In fact, everyone took our pictures all along the beach. The same old crowd was together. In the evening we all went to Young's Pier.[6] The ladies, Mrs. Cunningham, Mama and Mrs. Andrew accompanied us. We saw the colored cake walk[7] and Pennsylvania was simply great in his red coat and lady in pink, of course he won first prize and I clapped until my hands were stiff and one finger swollen. We moved our clothes today into #15 away from the two Slaymans, but they are right below us. Didn't get in till late. In the evening our sunburn began to bloom and never such a glow was to be seen as that which graced the ends of our individual noses. Poor Harry was as red as a penny and required "witch hazel" as a remedy.

AUGUST 29: Well it rained today so we didn't get a chance to go under the pier but we all shouldered umbrellas and went hunting palmists.[8] We found Madam Shaw and she told our "fortunes." She informed me I was to have two husbands to marry, the first young for love and that I would also get money with it. At fifty-five a great change was to take place, I was to marry the second time receiving love and a large amount of money with my 2nd husband. I was also to have a very severe spell of sickness then. I would travel abroad. Never do anything in September of much consequence and oh! many things. Our chase wet my feet and I now have a peachy cold. Mr. Howarth and Mel met us in there and we went on the merry-go-rounds and don't mention fun! In the evening the push all went to the cake walk on Steel Pier and we had a great time, just 17 of us. Penna won again. Didn't get in until late, danced some afterward.

AUGUST 30: Donned our suits again and sat on the sand. More pictures taken, the same crowd and good time. Mabel and Will went home this afternoon. This evening we all met on the pier (Young's). We were hardly seated when in marched three boys "awfully cute" and tried their best to flirt with us but we wouldn't, so they soon left. We had a great time though. Saw the giant[9] and the wonderful Martel family bicycle riding, the passion play and the Minstrel. After the show we all went over to the Waldorf and had a nice chat with Mr. and Mrs. C. and met some very nice people. We all had our pictures taken in our bathing suits today and they look awfully cute.

AUGUST 31: We went in bathing today and met a Miss Moore, Miss Venderlen, Mr. Rohr & Atchinson Deckard and several others, among them the two boys we saw on the pier last evening, Mr. Miexel Hyatt and Straub, one of the cadet's brothers. They are awfully cute fellows and promised to come to the Euchre[10] tomorrow night. We spent the afternoon playing cards, getting in trim and in the evening all went up to Pomeroy's. Oh! Nan and Mrs. Bowers called this afternoon and we met them and Elsie at the merry-go-rounds and all went up to May's. She is just wild over Miexel too. He is certainly cute. Met Emily and John Pomeroy, they have a fine house. Cholly asked to take me to the Opera tomorrow night but I am going to the Euchre.

SEPTEMBER 1: We went down on the sand today and sat there, all the crowd was there and we invited them all to the Euchre tonight. Hyatt and Miexel, Straub and a Mr. Cross. Straub and Miexel brought Mamie and I home. In the P.M. Mary and I took a walk out to Heinz Pier[11] and had a splendid time. Mary had her fortune told again. The Slaymans are mad at Elsie because she did something and they called on her this P.M. In the eve the boys called for us. Cross and Robinson took me. Miller, Mamie. McCarthy, Nell. I won the 1st prize. Just think of it! Mamie third and Miller third man's prize. Six tables and four occupied by our 16. It was at the Waldorf Astoria and afterward we all linked arms and walked as far as the Ponce. The policeman stopped us for fun and we had a jolly time. Miller and Cross brought me home. They are two fine fellows. The 1st prize was a belt buckle and Mamie's a vase. Miller's a scull. Met a lot of new people. Elsie left today.

SEPTEMBER 2: Arose early this morning after the great Euchre and went down to bathe. Mr. McCarthy took me in and we had a fine bath. He is a "dear" fellow with light curly hair and blue eyes. Nan and Mr. and Mrs. Bowers came up and went in bathing with us too, so we had a large party. Nan made arrangements for me to go to the train to meet Jo who is coming at noon, so I promised. Mr. Hyatt and Miexel were with us today too. Hyatt took me in the water, too. I got my hair so wet that it didn't dry until too late for train time and who should come up but Miller to say goodbye. He stayed quite a while and just went when Jo, Dale and Lou West all came in on us. Shortly after Mr. Rohr and Atkinson from Virginia called with a box of salt water taffy so we had a merry party. In the eve we all went out on the pier to dance, out of eleven I only missed two and those I sat out. Dale had 3, Jo, 2, McCarthy 2, Miexel 2, Melvin 1 and Atkinson 1. McCarthy and Miexel to soda and Jo afterward to ice cream soda. Fine night.

SEPTEMBER 3: Jo was around the first thing this morning but we couldn't go in bathing because of Sunday — how nice!!! Everybody was down under the pier and I took some dandy pictures. Jo brought me home in the P.M. The crowning act was sailing. Papa and Mr. Sharpless came down and with Uncle John wanted to go fishing. We also wanted to go but they were afraid it would make us sea sick so put us in another boat to go sailing just for an hour. The sail was grand but my inner man was bound on taking an outing also and two of a kind don't mix well, you know. Oh! I was deathly sick. Jo, Dale & Pomeroy all came around again and took us all down the Bowery and we had some more ice cream soda and Jo bought me a box of chocolates and salt water taffy. Had a great time, didn't get in until quite late.

SEPTEMBER 4: All went in bathing today, had the best bath of the season. Jo and Hyatt took us in. I didn't get my head or hair a bit wet. Those boys are so strong, they took us in the swimming pool afterward. After dinner, McCarthy said goodbye. Oh! the promises he did make. Jo and Bradly who came this morning took Mary and I out to the Auditorium[12] but it was closed so we went to the minstrels. We had a picture taken, the boys look horrible. They treated us to ice cream soda and each a box of taffy. After supper we took papa to the train. Bradly and Jo came while we were away and when we returned took us to the Runnymede. We called on Mr. and Mrs. Bower and Nan. They hired a bus and drove us to the station. Jo, Bradly and Nan all went home. Mr. and Mrs. B treated us to soda and we came home. Had a date with Straub, Miexel and Hyatt, but had to walk up and break it with them and they were so disappointed. So was I. McCarthy, Krieble, Robinson, Melvin, all went today. Day of big G.A.R. parade in Phila.

SEPTEMBER 5: Arose early today but wouldn't go in bathing as we expected to go home this afternoon but Mama changed her mind in the morning. What is left of our crowd went together under the pier as usual. I took some more pictures and we managed to have a little fun. In the afternoon we went out shopping. Mama and I and Mamie packed our trunks. Dale called, also May Pomeroy who wanted me to go down to the Traymore to see Miss Stone but I was decollete so couldn't go. In the eve we all went up to the Minstrels, met Hyatt, Miexel, Straub and a new fellow, Riley — and afterward Dale and Pomeroy with the Slaymans. We saw the cake walk and had a dance or two, one with Dale and Hyatt and bade Miexel and Straub goodbye and got all their pictures. G.A.R. came to Atlantic in the morning.

SEPTEMBER 6: Arose early and after breakfast found Dale waiting for me on the porch. I promised him I would go with him to make him smile while his picture was taken so we went and they are real fair. He and I did the Boardwalk, then came back to "Leedom" where Mamie and Mama was waiting. We all walked up as far as the pier to say goodbye. I took Hyatt's photo and we, after many rash promises, bade farewell to all. After dinner we all took the 3:45 train from dear old Atlantic. First we had a big fight with some woman for swiping our seat and secondly we ran into and killed a poor old woman[13] near one of the crossings. We all saw her and it was a heart rending sight.

NOTES

1. *Steel Pier:* What would become "The Showplace of the Nation" had opened the previous season.

2. *Minstrel show:* Minstrel, vaudeville, opera and serious drama all played on the piers and in theaters.

3. *Owing to the full house:* When demand exceeded supply, the smaller, cheaper hotels would often double up their guests.

4. *Although it was Sunday:* Blue laws were not enforced in Atlantic City; the Sunday trade was too valuable to merchants.

5. *Ponce de Leon, Waldorf Astoria, Runnymede:* Three of the 621 hotels operating in Atlantic City in 1899.

6. *Young's Pier:* George Young's pier offered vaudeville acts, concerts, rides and games and had a huge ballroom. It was destroyed by fire in 1912.

7. *Colored cake walk:* The Cake Walkers were a black dance troupe on Young's Pier. The cakewalk was a combination march, strut and dance of African-American

origin in which the couple with the most intricate and eccentric steps won a prize. The popular feature continued for decades.

8. *Palmists:* Fortune telling was a fad at the turn of the century. According to Charles Funnell, "The ladies queued up to consult various 'professors,' 'gypsy Queens' and other savants 'just arrived from Paris.' The palmists had all sorts of queer-sounding cognomens, some of which are regular jaw-breakers, and were attired in 'some fantastic costume' to impress 'the fair patron with the weight of their marvelous powers.' " (*By the Beautiful Sea,* Charles E. Funnell, Rutgers University Press, 1975)

9. *Giant:* The Steel Pier specialized in "freak" shows, such as midgets, giants and Siamese twins.

10. *Euchre:* The name of this popular card game came to mean to cheat or swindle.

11. *Heinz Pier:* H. J. Heinz bought the Iron Pier in 1898 to popularize his 57 varieties of packaged foods. It was the only pier with no entry fee; indeed, free pickles and free pickle pins were offered as souvenirs.

12. *Auditorium:* Auditorium Pier was at Pennsylvania Avenue; it became Steeplechase Pier. Another hall or theater on Kentucky Avenue was also called The Auditorium.

13. *Killed a poor old woman:* A news clipping about the event was pasted into the September 6 page of the diary. "The 80-minute flyer from Atlantic City to Philadelphia over the Delaware Bridge road, struck and instantly killed an unknown woman near the Marlton pike, Camden County. The woman was about 70 years old, and has not been identified. She was walking toward the train and appeared not to see it."

From the diaries of Lilyan (Lillian) and Mary Jane West, 22 volumes, 1895 to 1919, donated to the Historical Society of Pennsylvania.

1907
Atlantic City

Sir Alfred Maurice Low

A peek of garter and thigh was quite risqué when this card was mailed home in 1906.

Atlantic City's early promoters had badly wanted a socially elite resort to compete with fashionable Cape May, but they'd had to settle for a respectable family one, with the added tensions of thousands of young, single, working-class men and women pouring in for their week in the sun. The city-by-the-sea offered a fantasy world where social formalities were relaxed. Single vacationers could meet on the beach, Boardwalk or amusement piers — an atmosphere not imagined in the structured city society where a shop-girl could never hope to meet a college man. Although the "mackintosh law" forbidding *the wearing of bathing suits on the Boardwalk without a coverall had just been passed, young women were learning to swim and discarding the yards of heavy material in favor of knee-length suits, and the most daring of them rolled or eliminated their stockings. Occasionally the temptation to exceed even the expanded social proprieties was overwhelming, as in the case of the young man who "stole" four kisses from a woman he did not know. The judge fined him five dollars a kiss.*

Such was the atmosphere when English writer Sir Alfred Maurice Low arrived in America's largest summer resort. "The Middle-Class Playground" is the phrase that Low used when he described the human beehive that was Atlantic City at the beginning of the twentieth century. He noted that the rich and fashionable didn't come because the "common people" were there in force, although he did concede that "persons of means and recognised position" had been known to spend a month or two. Low was bewitched with the women's daring bathing costumes, but realized that although, to his eyes, Atlantic City was "decidedly unconventional," it had the unaffected innocence of a little child that was "unabashed in the presence of its own nakedness." Low was comforted that the pleasure was innocent. Propriety may have been bent, but it was not broken, and Atlantic City was too essentially middle class for its folly to degenerate into wickedness.

While the very rich in summer are dawdling and philandering at Newport and Bar Harbour, the masses, the backbone of America, are enjoying their vacations in a more sensible fashion, and in a way that really gives them great enjoyment. The most famous seashore resort in America is Atlantic City, the playground of the great middle-class. It is a city of some thirty thousand people; and from the beginning of June until the end of August, it houses a population of never less than two hundred thousand persons. It is a city of hotels, boarding-houses, and summer cottages, and its chief industry is the entertainment of the summer vacationist. It is one of the finest beaches in the world; stretching for miles along the Atlantic Ocean is a smooth and sandy floor, ideal for bathing or for those persons who find their enjoyment in watching the water and the bathers.

It is a place where the god of pleasure reigns supreme, where people give themselves up to merriment, where for a week or month they spend there, they leave care behind and endeavor to get as much fun as possible out of life.

Colour and gaiety riot in Atlantic City. There is never a dull or quiet moment. From early in the morning until late at night the beach and the "boardwalk," the great promenade of Atlantic City, are thronged, and there one may see women beautiful in face and form and no less beautifully and expensively dressed than their more aristocratic sisters in Newport, but who are there for what the Americans call "a good time," and who have it. It has been said that not the ultra-fashionable go to Atlantic City, yet there are many cottages owned by people of wealth and station, and it has happened that an ambassador of an inquiring turn of mind has preferred the middle-class environment of Atlantic City to the aristocratic and exclusive dullness of Newport.

Everybody bathes in Atlantic City, and in the morning between ten and half-past twelve the beach is thronged with men and women in their bathing suits. The amalgamation of the sexes does not end at the water's edge. The Americans do not bathe from a bathing machine[1] as custom requires in England, but they undress in bathing houses, the majority of which in Atlantic City are a couple of hundred feet or more from the ocean, and men and women emerge from these bathing houses in their bathing suits. The effect at times is startling. The American woman, especially if she be young and pretty and proud of her figure, whether in the ballroom or on the beach, clothes herself in the most attractive way, and her bathing costume is not the unsightly and sacklike covering, always muddy blue in colour, one sees at Margate [England] but is a blouse and skirt and bloomers, black or red or green or blues of various shades, daintily trimmed, and the wearers are almost as critical about the fit as they are about that of an evening dress.

The Atlantic City sea nymph, attired in one of these bewitching costumes, with her hair coiled up on top of her head and hidden under a silk handkerchief of the colour of her suit, with her pink-and-white feet winking in and out of the sand, quite unabashed in the company of her male escort, whose manly form is about as well covered as a schoolboy's on the cinder track, leisurely strolls out from her bathing house, crosses the "boardwalk," goes down a flight of steps, walks a hundred feet or so across the sand, stopping frequently on her journey to talk to friends, and then finally makes her acquaintance with the ocean. The sea in front of the beach is a mass of men and women, boys and girls, and very young children, splashing about in the water, the majority of whom go out not more than a few feet from shore.

Bathing in America is not a quick dip or a long swim and a return to the normal garb of civilisation, but the Atlantic City Nereides are amphibious; and after they have been gently caressed by the surf for a few minutes, like modern Aphrodites they emerge from the sea, and crouch on the hot sand and with the still hotter sun beating down on them, lie there in supreme content until their clinging and dripping garments have been dried, when they return once more to the pleasure of being tumbled about by the waves. This leisurely manner of bathing makes the beach an ever-changing and animated picture. At all times during the bathing hours there are as many persons on the sand as there are in the water; and from the water arises a never-ending Babel of sound; feminine shrieks of the timid, as an impertinent or boisterous wave is too rough in its embrace, or the childish treble of little ones when they first feel the water; while from the beach there comes a mighty roar, as men and women and young people go romping about the sand, scattering it over each or burrowing in it and revelling in its heat.

The oldest and most staid become youthful at Atlantic City. The germ of light-heartedness is in the air and no one can escape from it, nor does anyone try very hard. It is no place for the melancholy or those with nerves. One must be sound mentally and bodily to catch its step.

To women — mostly young, usually good-looking, and not averse to attracting attention —who delight in doing audacious things and pushing propriety to the verge without quite stepping across it, Atlantic City offers the opportunity they desire, because there the boundary line between the conventional and the unconventional has never been delimited. One may do in Atlantic City what one would not be permitted to do anywhere else; and although occasionally a highly respectable and middle-aged matron from the West is shocked and watches with jealous care over her husband to see that he does not stray from the well-trod path of narrow routine, the middle-aged matron is in the minority, and the great majority, old and young, men and women, go to Atlantic City enjoying all that they see, even although they are virtuously thankful that such dreadful goings on would not be tolerated in the less rarefied atmosphere of their homes.

A young woman may walk the beach in the full light of day in the most abbreviated of costumes and no one thinks any the worse of her, because publicity is her protector and her every movement is made before a thousand eyes; but after the bathing hour, when night falls, there is a different code, and should she adopt the unconventional in dress, or make herself unduly conspicuous in a hotel or on the "boardwalk," she at once classes herself among the forbidden.[2] Atlantic City is free and easy, unceremonious and undignified, good-naturedly boisterous and unnecessarily loud, but it is respectable. It must maintain its respectability, otherwise it would cease to be the playground of the middle-class; and if that ever happens evil days will fall upon it, and the hotels that stretch in an unbroken row for miles facing the ocean would go into the hands of receivers and the glory of the city by the sea would depart forever.

People who go to Atlantic City and disport themselves for their own amusement or the enjoyment of the spectators must expect to receive the attention of the newspapers. Here, for instance, is what an Atlantic City correspondent writes to a paper noted for its disapproval of the sensational: "First among these are Two Little Girls in Green. That is what they have been called by the boardwalkers and the sand-flappers since they made their first appearance on the edge of the surf more than six weeks ago. But they are far from being little. They are strapping, handsome, fine-limbed young women. They are twins and dark.

"Their bathing dresses, like the girls themselves, are exactly alike. They are of Nile green mohair. The skirts are exceedingly short. The twins go stockingless, and wear sandals, the ribbons of which are of the same colour as their suits, cross their legs many times, and are tied in sizeable knots at their knees.

"The raven hair of the two girls is unconfined, and hangs below their waists. Their arms are bare to the shoulders, and on each arm they wear heavy bands, about an inch wide, of dull gold, and below these, on their left arms, slender circlets of gold terminating in serpents' heads with emerald eyes.

"They are as striking a pair of young women as have cavorted near these waters for many years. Trustworthy witnesses aver that the twins have been seen to moisten their sandals in all of four inches of water, but the ordinary run of beach-strollers declare that the twins haven't been within twenty feet of the sea's verge since they first made their appearance here.

"The two girls possess an immense amount of poise, and they don't appear to be in the least bothered by the attention and comment they invariably arouse when they show up on the sands. They often enjoy themselves by playing catch with a large green 'medicine ball.' They spend most of their bathing time in parading up and down the strand with their arms about each other's waist. While they don't appear to mind being stared at, they are averse to being snapshotted by the hordes of camera fiends, infesting the beach like sand-flies, and they keep a wary eye out for the kodakers. When they perceive that they're within range of a lens they quickly take to their heels, and none of the lens gunners has yet succeeded in catching them.

"A couple of pretty blonde girls, sisters, get themselves up in bathing dresses of vivid yellow silk, with yellow silk stockings, sandal ribbons, huge yellow bows in their hair, and all the rest of it. The only touch of any other colour in their make-up is the brilliant green sash which they wear about their waists.

"These sisters drive on the beach at the bathing hour every day in a double-seated trap of a bright yellow hue, pulled by a pair of small white donkeys rigged out in russet harness, to which many little tinkling bells are attached. Both of the donkeys wear straw hats, trimmed with green ribbon of the same tint as the young women's bathing dresses. The girls conduct themselves with great propriety, although when they first arrived on the beach in their trap they sent the donkeys along at a licketty-split clip, which caused them to be warned against fast driving on the strand. They, too, seem to regard the sea-water as something merely to be looked at, for they have not dampened their bathing apparel in the surf up to the hour of this writing.

"A quintet of actresses who have a cottage all dress themselves for bathing in baby blue mohair suits of the same cut, and they go through a performance every morning that makes them the focus of the eyes of the sand-loungers. They are all expert swimmers, veritable mermaids, and their little performance is a mute but eloquent protest against the heavy hampering skirts which women wear while bathing.

"After dallying about the sands for a spell, they all approach the water in a body. Just as they get to the verge, they get together in a close group. Then their skirts all drop off at once. A coloured maid gathers up the skirts, and the five women of the stage, skirtless and free to race into the flood in their bloomers, swim out beyond the breaker line, and cavort around like dolphins for half an hour or so without ever touching bottom with their feet.

"Then they make for the shallows again in a body, run out of the water, grab their respective skirts from the black maid, hop into them in something less than no time, and then make for their bathing house. They are all pretty, well and amply formed women, and their little act has come to be one of the expected and waited-for features of the kaleidoscopic bathing hour. The dictum of the authorities against the skirtless bathing suits doesn't apply to them, for the reason that they are not beach paraders. The rule against the skirtless bathing dress was framed for the purpose of forestalling women of the strand-strolling class who have an aversion for the taste of sea water."

Atlantic City by day is a huge mass of energy and volatile spirits ever seeking release; Atlantic City by night suggests a mammoth factory where a thousand looms keep up their ceaseless tasks, where to the hum and the clatter of whirling machinery, the shuttles in their insatiable greed fly back and forth weaving the threads into a complicated pattern, where the brain goes dizzy trying to follow the swiftly moving bobbin, wondering whether a thing so instinct with life ever tires or ever sleeps. Atlantic City never tires and never sleeps. At night the hotels, which range from good to very bad, whose tariffs would tax the revenues of a grand-duke or meet the pocket-book of a not over well paid mechanic, where one may eat for a shilling or dine for a pound, are thronged with their guests, who wear silks or fustian according to their class, who whether they drink iced water or iced champagne are equally enjoying themselves, and have no false pride about letting their neighbours see that they are on pleasure bent. The lights blaze, the music blares, the waiters rush about, women laugh and men talk, there is the perpetual energy and motion of the sea always heaving, always rising, always falling, never for a second still even in its gentlest moods.

After dinner all Atlantic City goes to the "boardwalk." The "boardwalk" is always crowded by day, but at night, in the height of the season, especially at the weekend, it is literally packed, and progress is slow. People stroll up and down, or they sit in the little pavilions that are found at frequent intervals, or they buy wonderful and weird things made of shells and lettered in gilt "A present from Atlantic City," or Japanese and Chinese curios that they can buy for much less at their homes, but which have an added value when brought back at the bottom of a trunk, or they go to the various amusements devised to coax the nimble sixpences and shillings from the pockets of the unwary. They ride on the merry-go-rounds, they shoot the chutes, they loop the loop, they do many other things that would horrify and disgust Newport — but they *do* have a good time, there is no doubting the genuineness of their laughter and the sincerity of their enjoyment, and Newport and the 'Four Hundred'[3] may go hang for all they care.

NOTES

1. *Bathing machine:* A private, curtained bath house that ran on rails from the back of the beach right into the water. The bather could then step discreetly into the water. Queen Victoria had one at Brighton.

2. *The forbidden:* A Victorian euphemism for a prostitute.

3. *The Four Hundred:* Society's top families, those who were listed in the Social Register.

From *America At Home*, George Newnes, London, 1908.

1914
Atlantic City

James Hannay

Rolling chairs were a popular diversion on boardwalks from Asbury Park to Wildwood.

James Hannay, an Irish novelist and playwright, came to this country to take one of his plays on the road; Atlantic City was a tryout location. Hannay was amazed by the city's gaudiness; he said that it was like all the seaside pleasure cities of the world rolled into one, then raised to the third power. His friends in New York warned him that he wouldn't enjoy Atlantic City out of *season, but it was Hannay's deliberate practice to visit "places of this kind" during a quieter time, when he could capture their essence: "I seem to get nearer that when the chief side shows are closed, when the hotels are being painted, and when the sea has given up the attempt to sparkle and look cheerful. One knows pleasure cities a little better when they have tucked up their skirts, put on old blouses and turned to the task of cleaning up after the festivities." Off-season or not, Hannay was sucked into Atlantic City's hype.*

I forgot how many piers Atlantic City has, but it is unusually rich in these structures, and I have no doubt that the builders of them were wise. A pier makes an irresistible appeal to the pleasure-seeker. He would rather dance on a pier, under proper shelter, of course, and on a good floor, than in a well-appointed salon on solid land. He would rather eat ices on a pier than in an ordinary shop, though he has to pay more for them, the cost of the ice being the same and the two pence for entry into the enchanted region being an extra. A cinematograph[1] show draws more customers if it is on a pier. The reason of this is that the normal and properly constituted holiday-maker wants to get as much sea as he can. When he is not in it he likes to have it all round him, or as nearly all around him as possible without going in a boat.

Boats, for several reasons, are undesirable. They sometimes make people sick. They are expensive. They demand an undivided allegiance. You cannot have a cinematograph, for instance, in a boat. The nearest thing to a boat is a pier. It is almost surrounded by the sea. That is why piers are a regular feature of up-to-date pleasure cities, and why Atlantic City has so many of them.

It is all to the credit of our revelers that they love to be near the sea, to feel it round them, to hear it splashing under their feet. The sea is the cleanest thing there is. You can vulgarize it, but it is almost impossible, except at the heads of long estuaries, to dirty it. It seems as if pleasure-seekers, who are also seekers of the sea, must be essentially clean people, clean-hearted, otherwise they would not feel as strongly impelled as they evidently do to get into touch with the ocean. And it is real ocean at Atlantic City. Far out one sees ships passing, the lean three-masted schooners of the American coasting trade, trawlers in fleets, tramp steamers, companionless things, all of these given to the real business of the sea, not to pleasure voyaging. The eye lingers on them, and it is hard afterwards to adjust the focus of the mental vision to the long wooden parade, itself almost a pier, the flaunting sky signs, the innumerable tiny shops where every kind of useless thing is sold.

Atlantic City has, indeed, some boats of its own, boats which go out from a haven tucked away behind the north corner of the parade, and pass up and down across the sea front. Their sails are covered with huge advertisements of cigarettes and chewing gums. They are manned, no doubt, by the kind of longshoremen who cater for the trippers' pleasure. They have in them as passengers whoever in America corresponds to the London cockney. Among ships which sail these are surely as the women of the streets. But you cannot altogether degrade a boat. She retains some pathetic remnant of her dignity, even if you make her sails into advertisement hoardings. It was good to watch these boats, their masts set far forward, after the American catboat fashion, making short, swift tacks among the sand banks over which the Atlantic rollers foamed threateningly.

It is easy to understand why the shops along seafronts of places like Atlantic City are for the most part devoted to the sale of useless things. Picture postcards I reckon to be very nearly useless. They give a transient gleam of pleasure to the buyer, none at all to the person who receives them. The whole class of goods called souvenirs is entirely useless. The photographs taken by seaside artists are not such as can give any satisfaction to the sitters afterwards. Yet the impulse to buy these things and to be photographed is almost irresistible. We yielded, not to the seductions of the photographers, nor to the lure of the souvenir-sellers, but with shameless self-abandonment to the postcard shops. I found it very hard to pass any of them without buying. I look at them whenever I feel in danger of growing conceited in order to reduce myself to a proper condition of humility.

We also — moved by what strange impulse? — bought several instruments for cutting up potatoes. Under ordinary circumstances a potato-chopper has no attractions whatever for me. I could pass a shop window filled with them and not feel one prick of covetous desire. And Atlantic City, of all places in the world, was for us — I suppose in some degree for every visitor — most unsuitable for the purchase of kitchen utensils. We knew, even while we bought them, that we should have to haul them with us round America and back across the Atlantic, that they would be a perpetual nuisance to us all the time, and in all probability no use whatever when we got them home. Yet we bought them. If the dollar we spent on them had been the last we possessed we should have bought them all the same. Such is the strange effect of places like Atlantic City on people who are in other places sane enough.

I can analyze and understand the impulse well enough though I cannot resist it. It is the holiday spirit of the place which gets a hold on visitors. All a whole long year we commonplace people, who are not millionaires, are spending our money warily on things of carefully calculated usefulness. We watch each shilling and see that it buys its full worth of something which will make life more tolerable or pleasant. Then comes the brief holiday, and with it the sudden loosing of all bonds of ordinary restraint. Our souls revolt against spending money on things which are any real good to us. We want, we are compelled to fling it from us, asking in exchange nothing but trifles light as air. In desperate reaction against the tyranny of domestic economics we even insist on buying things, like potato cutters, which will be an actual encumbrance to us afterwards.

The man who brought a load of potato-cutters down to Atlantic City was probably not a poet at all, but he had a profound knowledge of human nature. He knew that he would sell the things there. It was the place of all places in the world for his trade. It is a high tribute to Atlantic City as a holiday resort that it forced us to buy two of these machines. None of the other pleasure cities we have visited have had such a drastic effect upon us. Atlantic City alone could have sold me potato-choppers, two of them.

In towns and rural districts where men and women live their ordinary lives, work, love and ultimately die, it is the rarest thing possible to see any grown person wheeled about in a perambulator or bath chair.[2] Occasionally some pitiful victim of a surgeon's skill is lifted out of the door of a nursing home and placed tenderly in one of these vehicles. He is wheeled about in the fresh air in obedience to the doctor's orders, no doubt in hope that he will recover sufficient strength to make another operation possible. But a bath chair, even now when surgery has become a recognized form of sport, is a very unusual sight. In all pleasure cities it is quite common. In Brighton, for instance, or at Bournemouth, any one who can, with any chance of being believed, represent himself as an invalid, takes advantage of his infirmity to get himself wheeled about in a bath chair.

Atlantic City, the greatest of all such places, has devised a kind of glorified perambulator, something far more seductive than a bath chair. It has room for two in it, and this in itself is a great advance. It has the neatest imaginable hood, which you can pull over you in case of rain or if you desire privacy. It looks something like a very small but sumptuously appointed motor car.

You need not even pretend to be a cripple in Atlantic City in order to make good your right to enter one of these chairs. All sorts of people, brisk-looking young girls and men whose limbs are plainly sound, are wheeled about, not only shamelessly but with evident enjoyment. There are immense numbers of these vehicles, more, surely, than there are invalids in the whole world. Out of season they are absurdly cheap, almost the only thing in America except oysters and chocolates, and, curiously enough, silk stockings, which are cheap judged by European standards. I longed very earnestly to go in one of these vehicles, but at the last moment I always shrank from the strangeness of it. Girls and young men, certainly middle-aged men, would feel like fools if they sat in perambulators anywhere else, but it is a sweet and pleasant thing — according to a Latin poet who must have known — to play the fool in the proper place. Atlantic City is the proper place. Hence the enormous numbers of perambulators.

The hotels in Atlantic City are, most of them, as fantastic in appearance as the place itself. I imagine that the architects who planned them must, before they began their work, have been kept for weeks on the seafront and forced to go to all the entertainments which offered themselves by day and night. They were probably fed on crab dressed in various ways and given gin rickeys to drink. Then, when allowed to drop to sleep in the early morning, they would naturally dream. At the end of a fortnight or so of this treatment their dreams would be imprinted on their memories and they would draw plans of hotels suitable for Atlantic City. Only in this way, I think, can some of the newer hotels have been conceived. They are not ugly, far from it. Crab, dressed as American cooks dress it, does not induce nightmares, nor is a gin rickey nearly so terrific a drink as it sounds. The architect merely dreams, as Coleridge did when his Kubla Khan decreed a stately pleasure dome in Xanadu. But Coleridge dreamed on opium and his visions were of stately things. The Atlantic City hotel is less stately than fantastic. It is a building which any one would declare to be impossible if he did not see it in actual existence.

It will always be a source of regret to me that I did not stay in one of these hotels which captivated me utterly. It was just what, as a boy, I used to imagine that the palace of the Sleeping Beauty must be. It was colored pale green all over, and, looked at with half-closed eyes, made me think of mermaids. I am sure that it was perfectly delightful inside; but we did not stay there. A friend had recommended to us another hotel, of great excellence and comfort, but built before Atlantic City understood the proper way to treat architects. In any case we could not have stayed in the pale green hotel. It was closed. We were in Atlantic City out of season.

NOTES

1. *Cinematograph:* After about 1900 this word was commonly shortened to cinema.
2. *Bath chair:* Shill's rolling chairs originated at the 1876 Philadelphia Centennial celebration. At first they were rented to invalids, but by the early 1880s Harry Shill, himself handicapped, had designed graceful wicker models and was renting them to anyone.

From *From Dublin to Chicago: Some Notes on a Tour in America,* George A. Birmingham (pseudonym), George H. Doran Company, New York, 1914.

1915 & 1917
Tuckerton

Eleanor Browning Price

*Eleanor Price, her older sister Florence and an unknown man, possibly the captain, on board the
beamy, cat-rigged sailboat* Marjorie, *in which the Price family often sailed to Beach Haven.*

 Eleanor Browning Price kept a diary for most of her life, penned in a neat,
graceful script in lined school notebooks. It was Eleanor Price who transcribed
Sarah Thomson's diary, and she was the niece of Frank Leach, who read his
boyhood diary at the table and gave the family a good laugh when she was a child.

Eleanor was a member of an educated family and an avid reader; as a young woman she "kept" the library and in its solitary atmosphere devoured book after book, checking them off in her diary like battles won. But she was fun-loving, too, rejoicing in dancing, moonlight sails and excursions to the beach.

Eleanor was deeply concerned with the horror of World War I, even before the United States entered on the side of the Allies, and she regularly recorded the ups and downs of European battles and her emotional reaction to them. In July 1918 she answered the call to duty and went to Washington and took a government job, writing, "I need war work that will satisfy my restless soul and mind and tire my body." But she overtired her body and in mid-September came down with Spanish influenza.[1] By the end of October she was recovering in Tuckerton.

Perhaps Eleanor felt that the war touched her closely because the 825-foot German wireless telegraph tower had recently been completed a few miles south of town, and in January 1914 began receiving high-frequency messages from Germany. Eleanor often wrote that they would get the news first, through friends like Mr. Mayer, at "their" tower.

In some ways Eleanor was a progressive young woman, and she worked diligently for the women's suffrage movement. When we join her she is in the middle of the 1915 battle to get the vote for women.

1915

JULY 20: Sat. night I went with Anne & Gran[2], Clara and Mr. Ballou to a circus — Wheeler Bros. — up by the station and had quite a good time even tho' I was only chaperon. Mildred & Dorothy and I went to the woman Suffrage meeting which took place after the WCTU [Womens' Christian Temperance Union] meeting in the Fire House. We tried to get the women there to join us but only succeeded with a few. In bathing yesterday but was too tired and achy to go in today. My swimming is progressing quite beautifully. Tonight the same old crowd was in again dancing but it wasn't a whole heap of fun. The national situation is becoming more tense all the time. A German submarine tried to sink the *Grdina* which was a Cunarder[3] carrying only passengers from Liverpool to New York.

JULY 23: This afternoon Mrs. Mayer came down to watch us bathe and came home with mother. She and I got into a polite argument about the war — quite thrilling. Tonight went on a "moonlight" [sail], as they say here, over to Beach Haven. The war situation occupies the largest place in my thoughts — I try to forget it as much as possible for it does no good to go over it in my mind. Mrs. Mayer[4] said she hoped this country would stay out of it and I told her it certainly would unless Germany killed another American.

JULY 25: This afternoon called on Mayers and they took Florence and me to Beach Haven and back in their car. We drowned "r.r.'s" two new kittens today.

JULY 27: A cold — so can't go swimming. This afternoon Cousin Katharine took a motor party down to the Wireless. Mr. Mayer and Mr. Lichstenstein[5] showed them all over and when they came to the receiving house Mr. M came and got me — I had seen the rest before and was standing outside talking to Mr. Ballou who had driven up on his motor cycle — and I heard some messages being sent — Norfolk talking to Boston or vice versa.

JULY 31: My cold hung on so that I could not go swimming until today. Got up early this morning to see Vangie off for Brooklyn to visit her father and Mildred[6] off for Ocean Grove with her dad to attend a Progressive Convention. At nine o'clock we went out in the bay in the *Marjorie*[7] to crab and fish. In bathing late this afternoon. Tonight went to the movies with Claribel and Lotta for want of something better to do. It has been terribly hot these last two days — so that we have done as little work as possible.

AUGUST 1: A year ago the war started — and it seems only a short time ago! I wonder how much longer it will last — two years probably! A scorcher today until a shower came up this afternoon. Picked out crab meat and worked in the morning. I read also to Florence[8] for awhile in John Adams Diary which is very interesting and just as different from this one of mine as his fame and honors in the world are from mine. Still I am well content about the latter — I only want a life with few sadnesses and too-heavy burdens in it — and I'll not ask for any great happiness or experiences. Except that I would love a trip to Europe — even if it's only once.

AUGUST 2: Terribly hot. Sat and read most all day — finished *The Awakening* by Henry Bordeaux.[9] It is very interesting and certainly made me think. A story of a divorce that was never gotten. Some passages are splendid! But I am convinced more than ever that I was never made for matrimony.[10] About four o'clock Mr. and Mrs. Mayer took mother and father up to Whiting in their car and I had dinner to get. Was frightfully cross — and quite ashamed of myself. We couldn't hold the Suffrage meeting because of a very heavy storm that came up in the evening — and which we sorely needed for everything was drying up.

AUGUST 4: Tues. afternoon Mildred and I did woman Suffrage canvassing. At night Annie, Clara and Mr. Ballou came in and we played "hearts" and danced a bit. Last night a terrible northeaster came up and it rained and blew like Hades. It seems that Warsaw hasn't been evacuated quite yet as far as the papers know altho' they all seem to vary in the news. One day it is reported taken and the next that it is still holding out.

AUGUST 5: Tonight's paper announced that "by wireless to Tuckerton" word had come of the evacuation of Warsaw. Gran says that Mr. Ballou and Mr. Caulfield, two navy operators here, got word of it from the German operator in Eilvese an hour before the official report came over from Germany. Therefore they were the first two men to hear of it in America. They have morning chats with the operator over there quite often. Henceforth most of the German news will come thro' us. Another exciting thing is that Mildred got her first interest money since coming of age and she plans to deposit it herself in this bank and take charge of her own finances after this. Her father is furious at that and they had a row but Mildred knows she can "hold her own" now against him and he doesn't scare her any more altho' she hates the rows they have.

AUGUST 6: This afternoon Cousin Katherine took a lot of people over to Beach Haven in the *Marjorie* to see Mary Pickford in "Cinderella" for the benefit of the Red Cross. It was splendid and the best part of the whole show was the comments of the children.

AUGUST 7: Finished *Angela's Business*.[11] It is a splendid book and expresses my very sentiments and views on the subject of women. Strange to say I think both of the books I have read this week have tried to show a newer and better womanhood, altho Henry Sydnor Harrison's is much further advanced, as all American ideas are on that subject.

AUGUST 9: Church in morning Sunday. Father preached. This morning we went crabbing in the *Marjorie*. Donald and I had a dead-shrimp fight and enjoyed ourselves immensely. He is so grown-up and yet so boyish! I wish he were my brother. Swimming in the afternoon and got along splendidly.

Suffrage meeting tonight over at Mrs. Allen's. Quite good attendance — for us — but Mildred and Mrs. Allen rooted for Suffrage Festival in order to make money for getting a speaker in the county just before the 19th — and we finally decided to have it — much to my disgust and apprehension. The most of the work will devolve upon Mildred and me — I know!

When I got home from there found Virginia and Donald with the girls and Gran in the drawing-room in the dark having a good time. I hated to miss what I did.

AUGUST 10: My 22nd birthday. Mother gave me a "Movie" party tonight — Donald, Virginia, Janie, Florence and myself. Afterwards we danced and then went to Blackman's.[12] In swimming for only a short time today — the water was so low and so dirty.

AUGUST 11:Out sailing for a short time in the Marjorie this morning. Mildred and I did Suffrage work — preparing for the hated Festival.

AUGUST 12:In swimming this morning — all by myself and the water was fine but I was so tired I couldn't do much. Had Mrs. Mayer and Debbie in for bridge this afternoon.

AUGUST 14:Swimming yesterday afternoon. Helen Allen married Marshall Lentz at nine o'clock yesterday morning and caused a great excitement in the town. Last night we played cards over at Cousin Angie's — two tables bridge and 500. Kept Library today.

AUGUST 19: Sun. Florence and Janie, Gran and Earl went by boat to Seaside Park. Monday we went out on the bay in a party given by Cousin John, bathed in the surf at the Skeeters[13] in overalls and a man's "Jumper" for I left my bathing suit home. Suffrage meeting that night. Tues. afternoon Lola Moore stenciled some banners for us. Tues. night Cousin Katherine took us to Movies and Blackman. Yesterday we worked hard all day getting ready for the Suffrage Festival which we held at Willow Landing last night. It makes me shudder to think of the work and worry we did — so I'll not dwell on that any longer. Today Mildred and I did the cleaning up and were and are dead tired from it all. A speaker from North Jersey, Miss Morris, spoke in front of the movies tonight, while we distributed literature.

AUGUST 20: Florence gave an evening sailing party. We took our supper out and ate it on the boat while we were sailing. It was a lovely night altho' the moon was very hazy. Afterwards we came up home and danced a bit. The Germans have sunk the *Arabic* that was bound for America.

Two Americans are reported lost. It seems funny to be on friendly terms with the Mayers (they were on our sailing party) now and perhaps in a few weeks have them for National enemies.

AUGUST 27: Tues. we were out in the *Marjorie* for the day — over to Beach Haven and then lunch aboard boat in the Main channel just off The Cedars. A wonderful day and a wonderful time altho' Janie, Virginia and Cousin Katherine were the only girls besides myself. V. took us to the Movies that night. In swimming Monday, Weds. and Thurs. Helped mother put up peaches all day today. Weds. night were on a moonlight sail to Beach Haven and didn't get home till 1:45 A.M. Last night Florence took Vangie to the Movies and I went too. That is the extent of our social doings.

The international situation seems to be clearing up a bit. Von Bernstorff[14] declares, according to the Press, that Germany will give in to our submarine demands — but I won't believe it till history records it. I can't help but feel the Germans are fooling us.

AUGUST 29: Made a cake Sat. morning — my first aside from spice cake and Boston cookies. Library in afternoon. I love to start a new book sitting over in the Library all "by my lone" surrounded by books I have read and books I want to read. It rained hard last night and seemed awfully cozy and quite like old times to be spending an evening reading.

SEPTEMBER 7: Bathing these last two days — and the water was fine. Monday morning mother and I spent in scraping the paper from the walls of Gran's room preparatory to getting them papered again. Tonight attended Suffrage meeting which we didn't hold because of the few people there.

I get madder at Germany every day! Another liner was sunk — no Americans lost but it shows that Germany hasn't any intention of keeping its word and is making fun of us. I don't speak to the Mayers when I can get out of it without seeming rude. I s'pose it's narrow-minded and bigoted but I can't seem to help feeling that way.

SEPTEMBER 13: Pinkie came last Thursday, and we have been doing something ever since. That night we went to the movies. Friday in swimming where we had a big crowd, had lots of fun on the beach. I argued for woman Suffrage for all I was worth. In the evening, H., Samuel and the girls came in and we danced the new steps Pinkie has taught us. Sun. night met Samuel in church and he came on over and stayed till nearly one, when finally I had a terrible scrap with him over the war and tore his hair and ordered him home. This afternoon he came up to us on the beach and showed signs of making peace but I don't care to have any Benedict Arnolds in my list of friends, and don't want to ever see him again.

SEPTEMBER 18: Pinkie left this morning. Saw her off, hated to see her go altho' I'm plumb worn out with such late hours and my almost daily swimming. Yesterday at noon Mr. Ballou left for good. He stopped off on the way to say goodbye to us all and sat on the porch for about an hour showing us his maps etc. We hated terribly to see him go — he is such a dear!! He told Gran our friendship to him had been the pleasantest experience he had had since going in the navy. Gran told him the night before that brains and morals were our standard by which we judged people and he certainly had made a hit with us. When mother said "goodbye" and told him she was awfully glad she had met him he couldn't seem to speak and hardly dared to look at her he was so moved. The afternoon before, Thurs., we all were down on the beach for the last time and I took some snaps of the crowd. Later on Mr. B. and I had a long argument on Suffrage until everyone finally left us sitting close together and arguing to "beat the hammers" as Jim would say. He told Gran that night that he'd like another argument with me on Suffrage before he left. He certainly left a hole in this town. Now to bed for a nap if possible, to make up for lost time.

SEPTEMBER 22: Sat. night Clara Rose spent the evening here and told me all her history — both with Marshall Lentz and Mr. Ballou. She is very lonely since the latter left and needs a friend most horribly. I really do believe in her morals but I never saw such ignorance and lack of common sense in regard to men as she has. She appears to be my present duty and I hope I don't allow my selfishness to get in the way of it. Sun. after church I called at cousin K's and was invited to dinner in honor of V.'s birthday. She told me lots about being married — and I don't want any, thanks! Sun. night after church Florence, Mildred and I sat out on the porch in the most glorious moonlight I ever hope to see and talked and talked. Monday morning mother and I did apples for jelly — in the afternoon went bathing with Clara. That night attended Suffrage meeting in Fire Engine House. The crazy woman that Mr. Ballou saved from drowning last week was there. Yesterday morning did more apples — worked all morning hard — in afternoon Mildred and I collected dimes for the Suffrage League. Went bathing with Clara — altho' only for a very short time this afternoon. The water was icy and the air icier! It made me feel fine!

SEPTEMBER 25: In at Clara's last night. Mr. Ballou sent her a dozen pink roses for her birthday. Today Lila and her mother took me to Atlantic City. We got there about twelve o'clock, put the car up and walked up the boardwalk beyond Heinz Pier then out Rhode Island Avenue to where her aunt, Mrs. Clement, is spending the summer. After calling there for an hour we took a trolley back to Virginia Ave. and went on the Steeplechase Pier.[15] Watched the kids and danced a bit. Got home by eight o'clock — in a beautiful moonlight.

SEPTEMBER 29: Mildred and I have canvassed for Suffrage the last three afternoons — we hate it like the Dickens but do have some funny experiences occasionally.

OCTOBER 5: Nothing much doing lately except that I began my dancing class again last night and made $2.25, the best I have ever done but of course it will never happen again. One of the "Jockies"[16] came — an awful one — that was so tough he made you sick-at-your-tummy to be near him. I kept thinking of the 25 cents I'd get from him and that enabled me to endure. It seems as tho' I must be awfully mercenary to be willing to go thro' all that for the sake of the money!

OCTOBER 12: This afternoon went with Florence to Barnegat on the train to buy paneling at Conrad's. Tonight attended Bible class. Am dead tired.

OCTOBER 18: Mildred and I sent out 140 postals today for the Suffrage cause — our last effort.

OCTOBER 20: Our cause went down to defeat yesterday by about 51,000 majority but even at that we polled 140,000 votes which is very encouraging. I expected to be defeated but I did hope not quite that badly. Suffrage was only beaten by about 55,000 in Pennsy. — a remarkable showing — the other two states swamped it good and proper. Nevertheless I am more full of fight and zeal than ever and intend to begin now for the 1920 or 22 (whichever it will be) campaign. I expect to wear my suffrage button during all that time and try to convince people of the rightness of our cause whenever I can. We have a little stray kitten that we've named "Joffre"[17] and call it "Joffie" for short.

1917

MARCH 13: Evening. The national affairs are progressing rapidly. We are arming our merchant ships and they have orders to treat the [German] U-boats as pirates — which means war — with other nations anyway — and even with us this time, I imagine. Wilson's dander seems to be up at last. It's down with the pacifists now!

MARCH 17: Morning. Yesterday's papers announced the abdication of the Czar Nicholas II after a small revolution. Tonight's papers are uncertain about events in Russia. One report says it's a republic, another that Grand Duke Michael is regent. England fears it will be a big revolution and thus stop Russia's part in the war. Uncle Frank [Leach] is home; came in this afternoon and told us interesting bits of Washington news — what Congress thinks about things etc.

MARCH 26: Afternoon. Have just been reading the papers; they are full of war preparations and quite thrilling. Two Jersey regiments have been ordered out. Nothing exciting occurs in my life.

APRIL 3: Evening. Yesterday was a great day in the Nation's history. Last night at about nine o'clock Wilson made a speech in the Senate that will most likely go down in history — calling on Congress to declare that a state of war exists between Germany and America. The speech is a marvel — I only hope his subsequent actions follow it up as well. He was applauded from the time he left the White House till he returned, the papers say. Several flags are flying in Tuckerton and Cousin John says Trenton and Phila. are one mass of flags. The first armed ship has been sunk. Went to the Lakeside[18] to dance last night. I need something to divert myself from thinking too much of the situation, altho' I'm happier now that we've taken a firm stand.

APRIL 6: Morning. Florence and I think and talk of nothing else than the war and pore over the newspapers. I don't care how I look or what I do or whether I do more than exist — my whole interest seems concentrated on the national affairs.

APRIL 7: Morning. A result of the war that came near home occurred this morning when The Government "desired the presence" of all the Germans here at the Wireless in Newark. We are wondering if they are to be interned — poor Mrs. Mayer! We offered her a room here if she wished while Mr. Mayer was away. Cindy had kittens yesterday and we drowned them this morning.

APRIL 8: Mrs. Mayer admitted that Germany was in the wrong in the Zimmerman note[19] — the Mexican plot — and said it "certainly was a nasty thing to do." Some concession from a German! Poor soul! She is so worried over Mr. Mayer and isn't well herself. The rumor about town is that Mr. Mayer was conducting a secret wireless station at Manahawken, one that could be taken down in the daytime. We don't know how true it is. When the Secret Service men came for Mr. Mayer he asked if he could go upstairs and pack; they said "yes" but asked if the house had a back stair. He smiled and replied "Yes, but you needn't fear that I'll try to escape."

APRIL 17: Afternoon: It looks like the world is in danger of starvation or nearly that in a year or so. Florence and I want to have a garden where our old chicken yard used to be and raise beans for next winter. I have been cleaning up — or trying to — the old tenant house lot so that that can be utilized for later crops. Mrs. Mayer has been running in all the time to tell us the latest developments concerning Mr. M. and to get consolation. She has heard from him and her lawyer in Washington is trying to get him off on parole. Poor Mrs. Mayer is quite unnerved because of the awful stories going about the town concerning Mr. M. She came in yesterday morning and cried from nervousness. There is a submarine chaser stranded in the creek.

APRIL 20: Noon. A patriotic rally was held Wednesday night in the theatre to stimulate recruiting. Yesterday the recruits were examined — all for the Naval Coast Defense or Patrol. Five or six boys were accepted.

APRIL 21: Very early morning. Have just gotten father's breakfast for him. No one else in the house is up. I sit here at my desk with the windows up and can hear the birds singing and twittering outside. Spring is here at last, I guess. Yesterday afternoon Oscar and his wife and I worked clearing up the tenant house lot. My feet are almost like boils from that and dancing Thursday night with the whole pack of Guhles. "Never again" — for some time. I enjoy cleaning up the lot for it keeps me from brooding on the war and makes me feel that I am doing my bit — even tho' an infinitesimal bit.

APRIL 29: Morning. Uncle Frank came home Wed. night. He was full of the speech that Sen. Frelinghuysen[20] gave in the Senate this week. It was practically Uncle Frank's composition. Mrs. Mayer still declares she doesn't care who wins and I think she said that a German interned with

Mr. Mayer says the same thing. I haven't reached that state yet but it looks to me as tho' God were going to allow the humans to fight it out in all its horror to the bitterest end — just to show them what a terrible and atrocious thing warfare is. I think the world has more suffering ahead of it than has ever been witnessed before, and there are likely to be some horrible memories for the person who is lucky (or unlucky) enough to live thro' it all. We don't waste a scrap of food in our household and I don't eat much unless I'm actually hungry. Friday afternoon a Woman's Service was organized. We plan to help in Red Cross Supplies. An American freighter sunk a submarine (or so they think) this week. The first one we've had the honor to destroy.

MAY 3: Afternoon. Mother is in Phila., father is surveying. My thoughts are, as usual, entirely given up to the affairs of the world. It looks especially black for us, as Allies, just now. I'd rather have defeat than neutrality. We have eight rows of peas planted in our garden — the rest we want put in beans. I've been harrowing in it a bit today. My only happiness is in hard work and well-earned rest at night. It seems to me that I'd rather die if we are not to be victorious, and yet I s'pose life would jog along just about the same whichever side wins. My forehead is lining with work and worry.

MAY 5: A terrible northeaster (dry, just at present) has raged since yesterday afternoon and it is quite cold out. I do hope the crops will not be injured by all this damp and cold weather. We got word yesterday that Granville was coming home to try and get in an officer's training camp. He has a letter endorsing his application from Frelinghuysen. Mother paced the floor for awhile and moaned but by now she has gotten quite reconciled for she feels so proud of him as we all do.

MAY 7: Morning. Mrs. Mayer goes to Ellis Island today to see Mr. Mayer again.

MAY 17: Afternoon. Sunday we had Mrs. Mayer in to dinner. Mr. M. has been transferred to Gloucester, and has much better quarters. Mrs. M. is preparing to leave next week or this to be near him. Will probably board in Phila. The training camps for officers have opened and so far that is about all that has been done by this country in a military way. The press is keeping so dark about what we are actually doing in the war — the censorship seems to be pretty complete so far.

MAY 25: Afternoon. Mrs. Mayer left town. She came in Sunday to say goodbye and left us with tears in her eyes. Our tenant house lot is plowed at last but not planted yet. I wish I had money for a liberty bond.

MAY 31: Afternoon. Yesterday was a big day in Tuckerton. We had a huge parade consisting of Marines, Jockies, various Lodges and a long line of children carrying flowers and American flags, besides the G.A.R. and Tuckerton Band. After impressive services at the cemetery the marines went thro' the manual of arms in front of the Carlton[21] and then gave us a demonstration of a sham battle — village fighting. It was intensely interesting and exciting. The family — minus Florence — took meals in the Fire House at the Ladies Aid affair as in days of yore. I quite — or very nearly — got back my "before-the-war" feelings, an impossible thing to do now-a-days. I can't imagine what it would be like to have this awful war-anxiety lifted for good from my heart. And I just can't imagine ever being happy again if we don't win. I keep telling myself that the issue is in the hands of God — and whatever happens must be the best. But I also realize it is only too true that "Heaven helps those that help themselves" and my greatest fear now is that my people will not rise to the occasion and be big enough for the task that is before them. It is hopeless and nothing short of a tragedy unless God himself intervenes. May the world never have to face such a crisis in civilization again! The turmoil is terrifying — if one allows oneself to realize what it may lead to. I wonder if God means to end the universe soon? A recent tornado in the West which killed over 100 people made no stir at all!

JUNE 6: Afternoon. A beautiful day after a beautiful rain last night that the gardens sorely needed. I planted carrots today and Gran has put in watermelon and cantaloupe seeds. We have some egg-plants, cauliflowers, peppers and tomatoes planted in half of the chicken-yard but the cut-worm is ruining some of them. Florence stayed home this morning and worked in the peas, which aren't looking very scrumptious.

JUNE 14: Morning. We've had terribly damp weather nearly all of June so far. Just at present the sun happens to be shining but no one knows how long that condition will last. Tuesday there was a little excitement when three French officers came down to inspect the Wireless. I took four snaps of them at the station but I doubt if they turn out well for they were moving all the time and my hands were shaking from excitement. One was young and quite good-looking. He rather scowled at me when he saw my camera aimed at him.

JUNE 20: Afternoon. I'm all fresh, clean and tired. Have been weeding the bean patch and a lot of other work. The Liberty Loan was tremendously over subscribed. When I heard it my nerves eased up a bit!

JULY 3: Evening. I'm housekeeper and have had a hot time of it between that and picking peas to sell. Friday we sold a peck, Saturday two pecks and Monday three pecks. We really picked lots more than that for I gave atrocious good measure — almost a peck for a half peck. One day I am all down in the dumps about the war and the next I feel quite hopeful. My nerves are certainly being given a run for their money. I am so glad that I have so much work to do — for I get very little time to actually brood on conditions altho' I cannot help thinking about them even in the midst of my work. We had our first beets Sunday.

JULY 4: The slowest Fourth I ever remember but I have loved it. Picked peas, mended clothes etc. Dorothy treated to ice-cream. I went without supper so as not to have the ice cream go to waste and then I ate a shredded wheat biscuit just a short time ago.

JULY 8: Late afternoon. Florence and I went to Manahawken Fri. afternoon to order winter vegetable plants. Our peas are still producing enough for our use, and we have our own beets and potatoes now.

JULY 11: Early afternoon. We're having rotten weather, but there is promise of a splendid potato crop so I'm not complaining. Read O. Henry and trash the last few days. My nerves are rather naughty and I need diversion for them.

JULY 19: Morning. Planted 2 rows turnips and have put in 3 more since. Sunday went with Cousin Katherine in the *Marjorie* to Beach Haven and attended Episcopal Church. Five marines went away to report at League Island for duty in France. They were quite excited.

JULY 22: Afternoon. A peaceful day. Gran is in Atlantic City. He will not be called up in the first draft, I guess. His number, 1638, was drawn out among the latter ones. Quite a lot of Tuckerton boys were called, tho'. The whole town was intensely excited about it and could talk of nothing else for a day or so. In fact the whole country has had its interest taken up with that one subject. It most chases the regular war news off the front page. We are having our string beans now and Gran's garden is giving promise to eats at last.

JULY 25: Afternoon. Went on S.S. picnic yesterday — a sure sign I'm bankrupt in the amusement line. The green-heads and heat and Marshall Lentz's ukelele and Mr. Hansel's monotonous tongue spoiled the day for me.

JULY 27: Morning. Was up before five. Picked beets and beans and had them all prepared before mother got downstairs. Out in *Marjorie* yesterday, had dinner on board — awfully good as usual. I was only young person but enjoyed the quiet and peace and the wonderful sea breeze. We had a family row early in the morning in which it was decided that I receive an allowance out of which I should buy my clothes and stand for all my expenses if I could.

AUGUST 2: Morning. We are having a heat wave of the greatest intensity I almost ever remember. It began Monday and is still on, only we have got a rather cool breeze just at present. Tuesday afternoon at 5 P.M. our thermometer by the front porch was 98 — in the morning with the sun on it it had been 107. Thirty-nine deaths from heat in Philadelphia on Monday and Tuesday, and more yesterday and today, I suppose. Our vegetables are fairly cooking. Our lima beans and tomatoes will be done for I'm afraid.

AUGUST 6: Afternoon. We've had gorgeous weather since the heat wave broke on Thurs. Are having corn now and had one tiny "mess" of lima beans yesterday. Friday night played "500" at Cousin Katherine's. She had Mrs. Lewis as a guest. My nerves are a little improved I think. I am able to forget about the war for a greater part of the time than I used to be. My reading is helping a bit.

AUGUST 8: Morning. Saw lots of men in khaki in town — some very good-looking. Postal from Mr. Ballou last night saying he was to leave for England yesterday and would write.

AUGUST 10: Afternoon. Wed. night Mr. Hansel came over and he and father had an argument about Germany, ending on the porch where Mildred chimed in and Uncle Frank even threw across from his bedroom "Stop talking to that damned Dutchman!"

AUGUST 12: Morning. I don't really tell here of my mental life — which is all the life I have now. As Mr. Van Note and I agreed in the library yesterday, one can think nothing but War. So my thoughts waking and sleeping, working and resting (I have practically no "play") are dwelling on it — living in it rather — and working, working to try and find the answer to the Biggest Problem in the world. I am trying to attain the Christ spirit of Love — even for the Germans (those who are innocent or even "know not what they do") and also to acquire the knowledge in my soul — and not my head only that God really does know what is best, and he has allowed this Great Crime against humanity and Christianity to occur.

AUGUST 20: Morning. Will Leach is here, came yesterday morning. Sat. night I went on the Beach Haven party. Had a most unattractive Naval Coast Reserve man for a beau. We danced at the Engleside[22] and had drinks in the Wisteria Room of the Baldwin — my drink being a claret lemonade. Drinks are not supposed to be sold to Naval men but the nigger[23] didn't object except that he asked the men to put their cocktails "in front of the ladies." Didn't get home till nearly 3 o'clock A.M.

AUGUST 24: Morning. Uncle Frank Clark came Wed. night. He, Will and father have gone down Sapp's Creek to see what they can do as to crabs and fish.

SEPTEMBER 1: Morning. Yesterday Cousin Katherine and I went over to a Red Cross movie at Beach Haven. It rests me so to get on the bay for even a few hours. Have received an invitation to a birthday dance for Mildred Lane on Sept. 15 which I don't think I'll accept because of her character. The drought is almost broken.

SEPTEMBER 6: Afternoon. Our first national Army boy leaves town tomorrow for Camp Dix — Fred Shinn. I wish I were he — now.

SEPTEMBER 10: Kenneth left yesterday afternoon. Charlie Horner came up to hear him sing his patriotic songs that he has been teaching the boys at Allentown. We had a regular patriotic orgy ending with Battle Hymn of the Republic. Charlie is going to try for the aviator corps. We have been hearing and singing these songs ever since Kenneth came. Mrs. Mayer is down and came over for some things in her trunks Sat. morning. I was very cordial to her then but I think that will end my cordiality for Florence and mother went to call on her yesterday and Florence said among other things she said was that America's heart wasn't in this war — that the men didn't care to go!

SEPTEMBER 22: There are two suspicious looking men staying at the Carlton. No one knows their business but they are foreigners — and very German looking. It is reported that they have been talking in German and that they go crabbing near the wireless station quite often but one can never be sure of the truth of the reports in this section. They, no doubt, are either spies or secret service men. Our government has unearthed more German "dirty work."[24] They give out new bits every few days! It is getting funny!

SEPTEMBER 26: Have had good restful times the last two days. Wed. afternoon Cousin Katherine took mother and me over to Beach Haven in her new Buick and we inspected the Little Egg Harbor Yacht Club[25] — a very attractive building. Yesterday I went over in the *Marjorie* to meet the three girls and bring them over to dinner at Cousin K's. We had a good dinner and a good time afterwards on the front porch, later driving down to the Wireless.

OCTOBER 8: Last week was a terrible one for Florence and me. We gave up our dear little babies Cindy and Toto for our country's sake. They required so much food, especially Toto-boy, who had a tremendous appetite. Father shot them on Thursday. We are only just now getting over it. I missed them exactly as tho' they were humans — especially Cindy, my favorite. We almost hate the sight of r.r. whom we kept because she is such a good ratter. Did a crazy thing last Sunday night, wrote to a strange man down in Texas who said in the newspaper, while asking girls to write, that he was studying aviation. His name was Donald Osborne. Don't imagine I'll ever get an answer. It may even be a joke, but I was desperate for some new thoughts and this answered the purpose for a time anyway.

OCTOBER 15: Heard from Harold Ballou Sat. He is at Shourcliffe, England. We have been busy the last few days saving our vegetables from frost. Florence pulled up all the kidney beans by roots and we are drying them in the house — if they will dry and not rot.

OCTOBER 22: One of our transports was gotten by a U-boat at last, but I thank God that it was on its way home, so few were lost. Frank Mathis and Archie Pharo were home from Camp Dix yesterday and Gran brought them up in their good-looking uniforms to let us see them. Their spirit is fine and they are so well and happy!

NOVEMBER 11: Went on an auto ride today with Lila, Della Smith, Francis Ehle and two friends of the latter. Francis Ehle is one of the Radio men. Met him last Sunday and was up at Lila's with him and Mr. Martin, a Marine, Tuesday. We had a dandy time that night, didn't get home till 1 o'clock. I had them in Thursday for the evening. Lit the candles in the drawing-room and made it look quite fine. We danced, roughhoused and, at Francis' suggestion, read from "Rhymes of a Red Cross Man" by Service.[26] Later had supper in the dining-room, made it as Hooverish[27] as I dared, chicken salad, olive sandwiches, nuts and coffee. We sat around the table and chatted till 1 o'clock. Had an awfully good time. Both Francis and Mr. Martin are such gentlemen and it is a pleasure to be with some once more.

The war is hopeless. Kerensky[28] has been deposed, Germans are still overflowing Italy. The British have taken Passchendaele tho. The World is going mad, I do believe.

NOTES

1. *Spanish influenza:* This flu epidemic entered this country in the fall of 1918, spreading quickly throughout the forty-eight states. In October 1919 it was declared a pandemic. Journalist Mark Sullivan wrote: "In the age of microbiology, serums, and enlightened medicine, here were death lists three or four times as long as those of the Black Death in London, the terrible plague of 1665."

2. *Gran:* Eleanor's brother Granville.

3. *Cunarder:* The *Grdina* was one of Cunard's transatlantic liners.

4. *Mrs. Mayer:* Mrs. Mayer was the wife of Emil Mayer, German commander of the wireless station. According to Nunn, he was a popular figure in the community. A small naval detail was sent to censor all messages after the European war started in August 1914. In September President Wilson seized the wireless from the Germans and stationed a larger contingent to monitor operations, still being managed by Mayer and his men. When the U.S. entered the war a Lt. Lichtenstein came with a detachment of Marines, the Germans were interned and American control was absolute. After the war the wireless was turned over to the French, who in turn sold it to RCA.

5. *Mr. Lichstenstein:* This might be the same man as the Lieutenant, before he enlisted.

6. *Mildred:* Mildred Leach was Eleanor's first cousin and best friend; she lived next door.

7. *Marjorie:* This catboat, 28 or 30 ft., ferried passengers between Tuckerton and the island. According to Granville M. Price, it was not owned by the family, but they used it frequently.

8. *Florence:* Eleanor's older sister.

9. *Henry Bordeaux:* A minor novelist of the period.

10. *Never made for matrimony:* Eleanor Price never married.

11. *Angela's Business:* A popular novel written by Henry Sydnor Harrison in 1915.

12. *Blackman's:* A Tuckerton ice cream parlor.

13. *Skeeters and The Cedars:* Two vacation cottages on Tucker's Island owned by Tuckerton families; both were washed to sea during the stormy winter of 1918.

14. *Von Bernstorff:* Johann-Heinrich von Bernstorff was the German ambassador.

15. *Steeplechase Pier:* Steeplechase was modeled after Coney Island's pier of the same name. Until 1904 it was known as Auditorium Pier. It burned in 1932.

16. *Jockies:* Probably radio operators from the Wireless.

17. *Joffre:* Joseph Jaques Joffre was a French general.

18. *The Lakeside:* A hotel near the lake.

19. *Zimmerman note:* Arthur Zimmerman, Germany's foreign minister, sent an encoded cable to the German ambassador in Mexico stating that his country intended to begin unrestricted submarine warfare against the United States in February. The British had broken the German code and passed the cable to American

officials. The note was instrumental in convincing President Woodrow Wilson that the United States could no longer remain neutral.

20. *Senator Freylinghuysen:* Joseph S. Freylinghuysen was the Republican senator from New Jersey between 1917 and 1923. Frank Leach was his private secretary.

21. *Carlton:* A Tuckerton hotel at the northeast intersection of Green Street and Route 9.

22. *Engleside and Baldwin:* Beach Haven's two largest hotels. The Engleside did not serve alcoholic drinks; the Baldwin did. The Engleside was demolished in 1943; the Baldwin burned in September 1960.

23. *The nigger didn't object:* An example of how common this epithet was, even among so-called enlightened persons.

24. *German dirty work:* The government's propaganda agency, The Committee for Public Information, encouraged Americans to report all suspicious persons or behavior; in newspaper advertisements it warned that "German agents are everywhere, eager to gather scraps of news about our men, our ships, our munitions." Overly zealous Americans saw German spies lurking everywhere and rumor compounded rumor.

25. *The Little Egg Harbor Yacht Club:* This private club on Beach Haven's bayfront was formed in 1912. The clubhouse was completed in 1917.

26. *Service:* Robert W. Service was a popular Canadian poet, well known at the time for his adventures in Alaska.

27. *Hooverish:* Herbert Hoover, head of the government's wartime food administration agency, preached conservation of food resources and stressed no waste. His mandates were popularly known as Hooverizing.

28. *Kerensky:* Alexander Kerensky was a Russian revolutionary who briefly formed a government in 1917.

From the diary of Eleanor Price, reprinted with the permission of Granville M. Price.

1917
Little Egg Harbor Inlet

Van Campen Heilner

Channel bass like this "bull dog of the sea" were tenacious fighters.

 Van Campen Heilner, born in 1899, was one of America's outstanding outdoor writers and the author of a half-dozen books and innumerable articles. He grew up in Spring Lake and before he was twenty-five he had hunted, fished and explored the uncharted corners of the United States; participated

in museum expeditions to Alaska and South America; and dived into a school of sharks off Key West to prove that so-called man-eating sharks were "bunk." After his 1918 graduation from Phillips Academy in Andover, Massachusetts, he sailed in the Caribbean for five years.

Wherever Heilner traveled, his life revolved around fishing and hunting. He had a deep attachment to Cuba, spending many winters in Havana, and wrote articles and made films about that island nation. Heilner fished with Zane Grey off the coasts of Florida, California and New Jersey and with Ernest Hemingway off Key West. In the preface to the 1953 edition of Heilner's 1937 classic, Salt Water Fishing, Hemingway wrote, "Van Heilner was a pioneer in salt water fishing. He found out quite early that he had more fun with the bonefish on the flats and the tarpon up the jungle rivers and with surf casting than with the huge fish for which no labor-saving tackle had yet been devised. [He] is a fine sportsman and a beautiful duck-shot as well as an old-timer in fishing. He has much to teach and he is always learning. I do not know any-thing better to say about a fisherman."

This pioneering angler was editor of Field & Stream magazine during the 1930s and 1940s, although his name appeared on the masthead as early as 1918. The following article was written when Heilner was just 18 years old and appeared in the September 1917 issue of Field & Stream.

Channel Bass! A name to conjure with, surely, for those who have never undergone the experience of taking one of those "bulldogs of the sea" as they like to call them down in Jersey. And then again, it isn't only the channel bass that prove so fascinating. How many of us long to wan-der down the misty beaches on long, drowsy days in August, with the miles upon miles of lazy breakers rolling in across the bars at low tide; to run splashing across the ankle-deep flats, casting a speculative eye up and down the beach for a good "slough" where in a few weeks the "drum"[1] will be found. The fascination lies in the sea, the birds, the whispering dunes, and the loneliness and wildness that goes with the pounding surf and the gray sands from Jersey to the Carolinas and on and on to the palm-strewn coasts of Florida.

I have sought his majesty *Sciaenops ocellataus* in the Carolinas, in Florida, and his cousin the white sea bass on the Pacific, but somehow, no matter where I am, my thoughts keep turning back to the sandy wastes of my own Jersey and the restless tides of Barnegat.

I shall never forget my first trip to the inlets, those wild and lonely lands of sand and waters to the southward. It was in spring, that season of all times of the year when the angler's spirit, lying dormant through the long, cold winter months, breaks through its caterpillar existence and spreads its wings to the warmth and life of the coming golden summer. We had heard of one inlet in particular; heard that here was a paradise for the surf fisherman, a place remote from the mad, rushing torrent of civilized man where with the dunes and the sea one could hold communion with one's soul and dream away the days, fishing the currents to one's heart's desire. It seemed almost too good to believe, but we decided to venture forth and see if we could at least find that which we all needed badly just then — rest.

So our little party, with Teddy as the moving spirit, packed our tents and duffle, loaded them into our cars, and sped toward the southward. At Beach Haven all roads ceased, and here we embarked for our trip down the bay to the now famous "point o' beach." This part of Jersey has romance and adventure lying at every turn. At the Cedars[2], so the legend runs, a band of pirates once buried their treasure when pursued by a Government cutter. To this day, with a west wind, one can pick up old Spanish doubloons and pieces of eight in the sand, and a native of Beach Haven has in his possession a rare cutlass found many years ago at the enchanted spot. Many a night I used to waken, and getting up, wander down the moonlit sand, half expecting to be confronted at any moment by the ghost of some old buccaneer returning to reclaim his own. We never found any treasure, but who knows but what it was there in the beauty of the sedge, the wheeling birds, and the salt air from off the sea that gave us that which is infinitely more precious than all the gold of all the ages — health and contentment.

We pitched our tents in the shelter of the dunes far enough from the water to escape the high tides, near enough to hear the surge and hiss of the waves as we sat of nights around the dying fire, near enough, in the freshness and sparkle of the glorious mornings, to race madly down the sand, clad as nature made us, to plunge into the curling breakers, emerging tingling from tip to toe and with ravenous appetites.

We always enjoyed breakfast. It began the day for us, and of necessity it *must* be good! And it was, for Teddy was an excellent cook. There are few things I can think of more enjoyable than to sit down before a crackling blaze to a breakfast of planked bluefish, hot biscuits and coffee, while to the eastward the sun is just rising over the dunes, and down at the point the faint screams of the wheeling gulls foretell a long day of wonderful sport.

The conditions at this inlet from an angler's standpoint were ideal. A lone point projected into the Inlet and the inrushing tide formed on the north side of this point a great tide rip in which fish of all kinds seemed to feed. The outgoing tide created the same formation on the south side of the point, and in the slack water of this last-named rip from the turn of the flood to dead low water lay some of the greatest fishing we were ever to experience in southern Jersey.

That first morning, what a glorious sight met our eyes! The sun had just risen, filling the whole world with its warmth and rosy light, and the ocean lay, like a vast mill pond, sparkling and dancing in the golden rays. The gulls had commenced to gather over the point, and as we trudged over the crunching sand, we could see flashes of spray here and there where the big tide-running weakfish were breaking water in their mad rushes for the small bait fish. By the time we had reached the rip and assembled our tackle, the school had sunk, so we turned to the eastward where lay the surf, rolling in across the bars for miles, as far as one could see to the northward.

We waded, knee-deep, in the foaming breakers, and cast; some of us landing on the inner bar, others in the "slew"[3] which at this point ran parallel with the beach for several hundred yards. Almost immediately the sport commenced and we were kept busy reeling in the big tide runners, the gay little croakers, or the luscious kingfish. By noon we had landed sufficient to keep our larder well stocked for some time to come, so by common consent we called a halt and broke up to start off "exploring."

It was the spring of the year, the month of June if I remember rightly, and the beaches were very beautiful. For miles the great gray dunes lay facing the sea, like sentinels keeping an everlasting watch along the coasts, their flanks bedecked with the new green sedge, sweet smelling and fragrant. Miniature inlets and sloughs flowed back between them, converging and diverging in different directions. One of these, I remember, ran not far back of our camp and here we daily washed our dishes. This particular slough was infested with many horseshoe or king crabs and we amused ourselves by shooting at them with our revolvers, a harmless amusement, for they would either settle more determinedly into the sand or rush wildly for the outlet and the sea, causing us great laughter.

It was mating time, too, and from every dune and marshy place the plaintive cries of the nesting plover came to us, punctuated at times by the sharp bark of a fox of which the dunes held quite a few. And how wild and lonely it all was! During the two weeks we spent there we saw not a living soul. In fact, we only counted three sails in all on the distant horizon. The coast there is a fierce and dangerous one, with continually shifting bars, and woe betide the ship that ventures too near the shore. We might have been so many Robinson Crusoes, so far as the outside world was concerned. We were cut off from everything save our own thoughts.

Fresh water was scarce; we carried what we had with us. So Charlie and I decided to tramp to the nearest Coast Guard Station, which lay to the north, and get a shave in good, hot fresh water. It was a bluff and rugged station we found, peopled by keen, rough, blue-eyed men — men who at any moment must be ready, if necessity called, in the dark of night, to put a boat through a wild northeast surf and *make* it live. They greeted us kindly, inquired as to the fishing, and told us to help ourselves.

How good it felt to bathe in sweet water again! How good it seemed to cleanse the salt from our eyes, the beards from our faces, with the soft rain water, their only source of supply. As we left the captain handed us a red flare. "If you boys ever need assistance, burn this," he said. And we knew then, here lay the reason for the steadily lessening toll of lives taken yearly by the shifting shoals.

One morning we were awakened by voices, and crawled out of our tents to see two strangers warming themselves over the coals of our dying fire. At first glance I wasn't impressed. In after years they became two of the best friends and anglers I have ever known, and many a night and day since have we spent together down the wind-swept sands.

They talked that morning, in the cold gray light of the coming dawn, of channel bass and "drum," and of the great schools of the former the fishermen had seen far at sea, making for the Inlet. And they told us where to fish at the inlet — the tide rips. And as the day dawned, we all sat around the fire, cooking breakfast and planning. "Hal"[4] and "Lew" we learned to call them, and Hal and Lew they shall always remain, two of the best anglers that ever trod the dreary wastes of southern Jersey.

The morning proved uneventful, but as Old Sol swung overhead and started toward the west there were developments. Lew had the first touch. He was standing knee-deep at the point, his line straight out ahead of him in the swift current of the rip. He raised his hand as a signal and the next moment his rod commenced to nod, his reel to sing, and the fight was on. What a glorious battle it was! Up and down the beach, contesting every foot of the way, went the angler and the fish, until Lew became once more the master and worked his quarry near the beach. It was then that he broke water and a beautiful sight he presented, his scales glinting coppery bronze through the green water.

Lew watched his chance, waited until the right wave came along, and gently lifted his fish in front of it, whereupon the momentum of the inrushing water carried the bass within reach of his eager grasp. Thirty-seven pounds of red-blooded resistance! Enough to fill the craving of any angler.

I shall *never* forget that ebb tide. It stands out in my memory as one of those "lucky" days which comes so rarely in a fisherman's life. Teddy hooked a bass that carried him around the point and out of sight. Lew fought and landed another, a thirty-seven pounder also, evidently the mate to the first one. The tide ebbed lower and lower. A great flock of gulls were screaming over a school of bluefish about a half a mile out in the Inlet. We could distinctly hear their cries above the gurgle of the outgoing tide.

I hung a small bass and lost him. Then Hal drew the prize of the day. He hooked the grandfather of all channel bass. Dusk was coming on and he stood silhouetted against the sunset clouds, his rod swaying seaward, his reel humming in spasmodic jerks. He passed out of sight into the dusk, waving to us as he went. Long after he had vanished we could still hear him, hurling defiance at his antagonist. Then the tide turned, and the fish stopped biting.

We returned to camp, tired and hungry, and gathered eagerly around the cheery blaze while Teddy prepared the evening meal, a marvellous concoction of fish, mulligan, and what-not which we devoured like ravenous wolves.

A figure loomed up out of the ghostly dunes and Hal came into the light of the fire, dragging behind him a beautiful bass.

"Took me clean 'round into the surf," he said; "where are the scales, boys?"

We crowded close as he held the great copper warrior up in the flickering light, and watched the needle on the scales quiver at forty-eight pounds. We were not jealous; only proud that one of our comrades had been so lucky, had had the skill to land such a prize, and we congratulated him.

With a great satisfying feeling fluctuating through my soul I crawled into the little shelter tent which Charlie and I shared together.

Far to the north came the steady flash of the Seahaven Light[5], and on our own point, the little beacon steadily kept pace with it. Above us the stars maintained an everlasting vigil, and a lightness in the east showed that the moon was on her way to join them.

From somewhere out of the night across the embers of the dying fire, floated the sound of voices in "close harmony":

Oh, why don't you work like the other men do?

How the h___ can we work when there's no work to do!

Thinking this was pretty good advice, I rolled over and dozed off, lulled to sleep by the rustle of the wind through the dry grass and the roar of the distant breakers.

The old world seemed very beautiful.

NOTES

1. *Drum:* During the second decade of this century, the biomass of red drum was so large that this mostly southeastern-waters' fish spilled over into New Jersey waters.

2. *The Cedars:* The Cedars was a private home and gunning club near the bay on Tucker's Beach; it washed away in 1918.

3. *The slew:* According to John Bailey Lloyd, the slough was an arm of Barnegat Bay running between Tucker's Beach and Tucker's Island. (*Six Miles at Sea*, Down the Shore Publishing/The SandPaper, 1990, page 47.)

4. *Hal and Lew:* Hal Collison was a well-known guide in Beach Haven. According to Beach Haven oldtimer Joe Sprague, "Lew" was probably Lou Broome.

5. *Seahaven Light:* Seahaven Light was located on Tucker's Island; it collapsed into the sea in 1927. Although Heilner says this light is "far to the north," he may have confused it with Barnegat Light, twenty miles north, and the "little beacon" on the point where they were fishing would have been Seahaven.

"In Quest of the Channel Bass" from *The Call of the Surf*, Van Campen Heilner and Frank Stick, Doubleday, Page & Company, New York, 1924. Originally published in *Field & Stream*, September 1917. Reprinted with the permission of *Field & Stream*.

1917
Atlantic City

Hector MacQuarrie

The question of how much or how little to wear on the beach consumed Atlantic City's moral arbiters.

During World War I, Hector MacQuarrie was a second lieutenant in the British Royal Field Artillery on assignment to the United States. At the time he visited Atlantic City, he had been in Pennsylvania on a mission connected with armaments supplied by the Bethlehem Steel Company. Together with a friend, he drove to Atlantic City at the height of the season; but even with more than 500 hotels and boarding houses, the officers had difficulty finding a room. Finally, after pulling rank, they were given dormitory accommodations on an upper floor.

In an attempt to prevent "moral decay," Atlantic City had passed a law in 1907 forbidding women to appear on the beach without their legs covered by stockings, and required the skirts of swimming dresses to be of a certain length. The regulation was enforced by "beach police," who patrolled with tape measures and arrest warrants. MacQuarrie thought the women's outfits were "extraordinarily hideous" and seemed more taken with the way the young men, "burnt a rich shade of copper," looked in their bathing attire.

AUGUST 30: The other day Dickey C. and I went to Atlantic City for the week end. So many of my Bethlehem friends go to this place every year, that I felt my American experience would not be complete without a visit. We left this town at about three o'clock; we ought to have left sooner. The chauffeur developed caution to an almost unlimited extent and this worried Dicky, a furious driver himself. He told me with some pride the number of times he had been arrested on the White Horse Pike. The caution of the chauffeur was responsible for our arrival at our destination at about ten o'clock at night.

Being Saturday night, of course, it was impossible for a time to get either rooms or food. At the hotel where Dicky usually stopped we were turned down. His Majesty, the clerk, disliked the shape of our noses or our clothing or something. We spent one dollar fifty in telephone calls trying to get some hotel to take us in.

We started with the good ones, but even the fifth class houses were full. I therefore approached the clerk and explained that I was a British officer with nowhere except the sands upon which to sleep. This worked like magic.

We were shown into what was called a club room near the top of the building, where twelve beds were arranged hospital fashion. Our fellow guests were not there then, so we decided to sleep on the balcony in case any of them snored. The building is a beautiful one, having wonderful sort of battlements, and we fixed our beds out on one of these.

Then we sought food. We tried one fashionable place, but the head water was not impressed. He certainly looked at our noses and at our clothes. About these clothes — I had on a very good sort of golf kit. I almost know the sheep on the Island of Harris off of which the wool forming the material came. My stockings were thick and home made in the Highlands, and my brogues were made by Mr. Macwell in Dover Street. Dicky was turned out similarly and being a big handsome sort of chap looked fine. Perhaps if we had given the waiter ten dollars as his usual patrons do, we would have been ushered in with much bowing, but we preferred to starve rather than to give him a cent.

We sought restaurant after restaurant, but could get nothing, not even a poached egg. Dicky was getting crabby. After an hour we at last got into a hot, cheery sort of cabaret and drank small beer and ate all sorts of grills, also clams. After this Dicky became brighter, and I also felt more kindly, so we hired a comfy chair on wheels and spent an hour on the Board Walk, while the chairman told us with much enjoyment of all the sin and wickedness[1] existing in Atlantic City. His stories, very lurid, were mixed up with automatic "Pianners" into which one put a nickel.

Upon returning we found most of our fellow guests of the club room in bed, so we stole out on to the battlement and soon were sound asleep.

I awoke in the morning to find a terrific sun shining on my head threatening to melt my brain. I looked up towards the hotel and noted that we were sleeping on a balcony above which were roughly about eight stories. Immediately above us stretched a line of windows marking a staircase, and out of each window looked a head. It was really a study in black and white. There were black maids and white maids, and they were all interested in Dicky as he lay there with the sun turning his light coloured hair into gold. I awoke him, and we both got inside and dressed.

After breakfast, and as it was a table d'hôte we were not at all sparing in our choice of food, we sat for a time on a charming balcony overlooking the Board Walk. It was interesting to watch the people. I made a tremendous discovery, which was perhaps a little disappointing. I had always hoped that the British Empire contained the lost tribes of Israel. It does not. The United States of America has that honour.

We then sought a dressing room, and after removing our clothes and donning "fashionable bathing things" we sought the sand. There was a continuous procession of persons clad in bathing things, thousands of them. Few went into the water. There was much that was really beautiful. There were men burnt a rich shade of copper, beautifully built, with clean cut, good looking faces, walking along enjoying their youth. There were some priceless looking girls well decorated. I dislike women's bathing suits. They are theoretically meant for bathing in, but why on earth should they wear those extraordinary hideous garments: They look awful when they return from the water. Their stockings are all dragged round their legs and if they are shoeless the toe part of the stockings seems to escape and hangs over. However, most of the ladies had no intention of swimming. Their faces were often powdered and painted and their hair arranged in a most engaging way. Still many were delightful to look upon, notwithstanding their attire. I believe there are very strict rules about women's costumes at Atlantic City. My landlady assures me that she has seen the policemen measuring the length of a girl's swimming skirt.

The bathing suit here in America is exactly like the kit we wear for Rugby football. Perhaps it would be better for swimming if it were lighter, and in one piece, but as much time is spent promenading, it is obviously better that it should be as it is.

Of course, quite a number were not beautiful to look upon. There were thousands of men and women who had reached the unlovely stage of their existence. Large portly men walked about unashamed and women with large stout legs encased sometimes in green stockings could be seen. As one walked along the beach the society seemed to change. Towards the poorer part of the town the people were a little older and less interesting. We came to one section where most of the bathers and promenaders were coloured people. I must say at once that the effect was singularly diverting. The young coloured ladies and gentlemen were smartly turned out. These American negroes look like awfully nice people. One would see a young coloured lady with an expensive and sometimes a beautiful swimming suit walking beside a fine handsome coloured boy. They seemed so happy. I was thrilled with the little ones as they dashed about with their strong little limbs. Unfortunately we had little time for observation because Dicky had seen a huge fat man at another part of the beach in a bathing costume, the sort of fellow that one sees at a country fair, and he insisted upon returning to have another look. This fat man sat there with his huge fearful limbs partially exposed while a crowd stood and looked at him. He seemed to like it, too. Human egotism is truly wonderful. The whole morning was enjoyable. I loved the open air, the sea breezes and all that sort of thing.

I had heard a lot about the Board Walk. As a thing of use it is delightful. One can walk for miles along its length, seeing a strange procession of human beings, but its new look, the fact that it is made of wood, tends to give Atlantic City an uncertain and unstable foundation. It spoiled the effect of our hotel with its magnificent architecture. Still it provides a very restful way to walk, and I suppose it has its uses. I am a little astonished that Americans should come to this strange place and turn themselves into money fountains and, upon running dry, return to business; though of course it is fine to be with a crowd of cheerful people.

I have never visited any of our seaside resorts during the summer season, so I cannot well compare Atlantic City with any of them. I don't think that a similar place would be popular in England. Of course, we were there at a rather difficult time. I have been told that prices go up about twenty-five per cent, or even more during August.

Atlantic City seems to be a long thin town stretching for several miles along the Atlantic coast. The hotels are truly beautiful. Apart from their architecture they are beautifully decorated inside. Our hotel has a place called the Submarine Grill. The idea the artist wishes to convey is that the diners are spending a hectic time at the bottom of the sea. The general effect is rather lovely and the colouring suggests the inside of a very rich Mohammedan mosque, in spite of the sea idea. Perhaps the mermaids of Atlantic City make up for this; and there are many. However, we go down, pay the head waiter a large sum for three bows and a continuous smile and are ushered to the best seats. The food is beautifully cooked, but the bill grows very large, and one leaves quite happy but poorer.

Dicky and I had had about fifty dollars between us, but the price for our sleeping places had been small, and it looked as though we would return with about two dollars between us, until we met the chauffeur, and asked him for his expense account. Having paid it — it was one dollar more than my bill at the hotel — we possessed about three shillings, or seventy-five cents. This obviously left us but little money for food at Philadelphia upon our return, but we went into a mysterious automat eating house and managed to subtract a little nourishment from its shelves. We returned to Bethlehem owing the chauffeur about three dollars. I must say that I enjoyed the whole thing, but I have no intention and no desire to return.

It was the touch of nature that made the day enjoyable for me — the people, black and white, and the sea. But I objected to the hardly-veiled begging displayed by the numerous lackeys. I suppose they have got to live, *"mas je n'en vois pas la nécessité,"* as some philosopher[2] remarked.

When passing through the hotel on the Saturday evening I saw a lady quietly but beautifully dressed. She looked about twenty. I was certain that I knew her well, had met her in Washington or somewhere. I went over and said: "How d'ye do." We chatted for a time, but in spite of all my efforts I could not place her. Having rejoined Dicky, I remembered. She was the prim demure little lady from whom I have bought my "movie" tickets for the last six months. American girls are truly wonderful. We arrived at Bethlehem at about midnight.

NOTES

1. *Sin and wickedness:* As in any city of its size, plus cheek-to-jowl summer crowds, Atlantic City had its tenderloin: a scattering of bordellos, transient prostitutes and illegal gambling houses.

2. *Philosopher:* Charles Maurice de Talleyrand-Perigord, French statesman (1754-1838).

_____

From *Over Here: Impressions of America by A British Officer,* J. B. Lippincott & Company, Philadelphia and London, 1918.

1919
Wildwood

Christopher Morley

Salt water taffy was 20 cents a box when this photograph was made on the boardwalk at Maple Avenue in 1919.

 Christopher "Kit" Morley was a major player in the literary world of the first half of the twentieth century. He was born and educated in Haverford, Pennsylvania, and studied in Oxford, England, as a Rhodes scholar. A first novel in 1917 was followed by a successful life of letters in New York, where he wrote novels, essays, poetry and literary criticism, including the bestselling

Kitty Foyle in 1939. Between 1917 and 1919 Morley penned affectionate essays about Philadelphia that appeared regularly in the Philadelphia Evening Public Ledger. *"The Shore in September," Morley's report of a post-Labor Day excursion to a destination he not so subtly calls "Fierceforest," is the only out-of-town location included when the columns were collected in* Travels in Philadelphia, *which he intended as "snapshots of vivacious phases of life today." The atmosphere he captures has that spacious, peaceful essence still found at what is for many shore lovers the best time of year.*

The sands are lonely in the fall. On those broad New Jersey beaches, where the rollers sprawl inward in ridges of crumbling snow, the ocean looks almost wistfully for its former playmates. The children are gone, the small brown legs, the toy shovels and the red tin pails. The familiar figures of the summer season have vanished: the stout ladies who sat in awninged chairs and wrestled desperately to unfurl their newspapers in the wind; the handsome mahogany-tanned lifesavers, the vamperinoes incessantly drying their tawny hair, the corpulent males of dark complexion wearing ladies' bathing caps, the young men playing degenerate baseball with a rubber sphere and a bit of shingle. All that life and excitement, fed upon hot dogs and vanilla cones, anointed with cold cream and citronella, has vanished for another year.

But how pleasant it is to see the town (it is Fierceforest we have in mind) taking its own vacation, after laboring to amuse its visitors all summer long. Here and there in the surf you will see a familiar figure. That plump lady, lathered by sluicing combers as she welters and wambles upon Neptune's bosom, is good Frau Weintraub of the delicatessen, who has been frying fish and chowdering clams over a hot stove most of July and August, and now takes her earned repose. Yonder is the imposing bulge of the real estate agent, who has been too busy selling lots and dreaming hotel sites to visit the surf hitherto. Farther up the shore is the garage man, doing a little quiet fishing from the taffrail of a deserted pier. The engineer of the "roller coaster" smokes a cigar along the deserted boardwalk and discusses the league of nations with the gondolier-in-chief of the canals of Ye Olde Mill. The hot-dog expert, whose merry shout, "Here they are, all red hot and fried in butter!" was wont to echo along the crowded arcade, has boarded up his stand and departed none knows where.

There is a tincture of grief in the survey of all this liveliness coffined and nailed down. Even the gambols of Fierceforest's citizens, taking their ease at last in the warm September surf, cannot wholly dispel the mournfulness of the observer. There is something dreadfully glum in the merry-go-round seen through its locked glass doors. All those gayly caparisoned horses, with their bright Arabian housings, their flowing manes and tossing heads and scarlet-painted nostrils, stand still in the very gesture of glorious rotation. One remembers what a jolly sight that carrousel was on a warm evening, the groaning pipes of the steam-organ chanting an adorable ditty (we don't know what it is, but it's the tune they always play at the movies when our favorite Dorothy Gish comes on the screen), children laughing and holding tight to the wooden manes of the horses, and flappers with their pink dresses swirling, clutching for the brass ring that means a free ride. All this is frozen into silence and sleep, like a scene in a fairy tale. It is very sad, and we dare not contemplate the poor little silent horses too long.

Bitterly does one lament the closing of the Boardwalk auction rooms, which were a perpetual free show to those who could not find a seat in the movies. There was one auctioneer who looked so like Mr. Wilson[1] that when we saw his earnest gestures we always expected that the league of nations would be the subject of his harangue. But on entering and taking a seat (endeavoring to avoid his eye when he became too persuasive, for fear some involuntary gesture or the contortions of an approaching sneeze would be construed as a bid for a Chinese umbrella stand) we always found that it was a little black box full of teacups that was under discussion. He would hold one up against an electric bulb to show its transparency. When he found his audience unresponsive he would always say, "You know I don't have to do this for a living. If you people don't appreciate goods that have quality, I'm going to pack up and go to Ocean City." But he never went. Almost every evening, chagrined by some one's failure to bid properly for a cut-glass lady-finger container or a porcelain toothbrush-rack, he would ask the attendant to set it aside. "I'll buy it myself," he would cry, and as he kept on buying these curious tidbits for himself throughout the summer, we used to wonder what his wife would say when they all arrived.

Along the quiet Boardwalk we saunter, as the crisp breeze comes off the wide ocean spaces. Bang! bang! bang! sound the hammers, as the shutters go up on the beauty parlor, the toy shop, the shop where sweet-grass baskets were woven, and the stall where the little smiling doll known as Helene, the Endearing Beach Vamp, was to be won by knocking down two tenpins with a swinging pendulum. How easy it was to cozen the public with that! A bright red star was painted at the back of the pendulum's swing, and the natural assumption of the simple competitor was that by aiming at that star he would win the smiling Helene. Of course, as long as one aimed at the star success was impossible. The Japanese dealers, with the pertinacity of their race, are almost the last to linger. Their innocent little gaming boards, their fishponds where one angles for counterfeit fish and draws an eggcup or a china cat, according to the number inscribed on the catch, their roulette wheels ("Ten Cents a Chance — No Blanks") — all are still in operation, but one of the shrewd orientals is packing up some china at the back of the shop. He knows that trade is pretty well done for this season. We wondered whether he would go back to the beach for a swim before he left. He has stuck so close to business all summer that perhaps he does not know the ocean is there. There is another thrifty merchant, too, whose strategy comes to our attention. This is the rolling-chair baron[2], who has closed his little kiosque, but has taken care to paint out the prices per hour of his vehicles, and has not marked any new rates. Cautious man, he is waiting until next summer to see what the trend of prices will be then.

Across the fields toward the inlet, where the grasses have turned rusty bronze and pink, where goldenrod is minting its butter-yellow sprays and riotous magenta portulaccas seed themselves over the sandy patches, the rowboats are being dragged out of the canal and laid up for the winter. The sunburned sailorman who rents them says he has had a good season — and he "can't complain." He comes chugging in with his tiny motorboat, towing a string of tender-feet who have been out tossing on the crabbing grounds for a couple of hours, patiently lowering the fishheads tied on a cord and weighted with rusty bolts. His patient and energetic wife who runs the little candy and sarsaparilla counter on the dock has ended her labors. She is glad to get back to her kitchen: during the long, busy summer days she did her family cooking on an oil stove behind the counter. The captain, as he likes to be called, is about to make his annual change from mariner to roofer, the latter being his winter trade. "It's blowing up for rain," he says, looking over his shoulder at the eastern sky. "I guess the season's pretty near over. I'll get up the rest of them boats next week."

In September the bathing is at its best. Particularly at sunset, when every one is at supper. To cross those wide fields of wiry grass that stretch down to the sand, is an amazement to the eye. Ahead of you the sea gleams purple as an Easter violet. The fields are a kind of rich palette on which every tint of pink, russet and bronze are laid in glowing variation. The softly wavering breeze, moving among the coarse stalks, gives the view a ripple and shimmer of color like shot silk. A naturalist could find hundreds of species of flowers and grasses on those sandy meadows. There are great clumps of some bushy herb that has already turned a vivid copper color, and catches the declining sunlight like burnished metal. There are flecks of yellow, pink and lavender. A cool, strong odor rises from the harsh, knife-edged grasses — a curiously dry, brittle scent, familiar to all who have poked about sand dunes.

The beach itself, colored in the last flush of the level sun, is still faintly warm to the naked foot, after the long shining of the day; but it cools rapidly. The tide is coming in, with long, seething ridges of foam, each flake and clot of crumbled water tinged with a rose-petal pink by the red sunset. All this glory of color, of movement, of unspeakable exhilaration and serenity, is utterly lonely. The long curve of the beach stretches away northward, where a solitary orange-colored dory is lying on the sand. The air is full of a plaintive piping of sea-birds. A gull flashes along the beach, with a pink glow on its snowy under-plumage.

At that hour the water is likely to be warmer than the air. It may be only the curiously magical effect of the horizontal light, but it seems more foamy, more full of suds, than earlier in the day. Over the green top of the waves, laced and marbled with froth, slides a layer of iridescent bubble-wash that seems quite a different substance from the water itself — like the meringue on top of a lemon pie. One can scoop it up and see it winking in points of sparkling light.

The waves come marching in. It is a calm sea, one would have said looking down from the dunes, but to the swimmer, elbowing his way under their leaning hollows, their stature seems tremendous. The sunlight strikes into the hills of moving water, filling them with a bluish spangle and tremor of brightness. It is worth while to duck underneath and look up at the sun from under the surface, to see how the light seems to spread and clot and split in the water like sour cream poured into a cup of tea. The sun, which is so ruddy in the evening air, is a pale milky white when seen from under water.

A kind of madness of pleasure fills the heart of the solitary sunset swimmer. To splash and riot in that miraculous color and tumult of breaking water seems an effective answer to all the grievances of earth. To float, feeling the poise and encircling support of those lapsing pillows of liquid, is mirth beyond words. To swim just beyond the line of the big breakers, dropping a foot now and then to feel that bottom is not too far away — to sprawl inward with a swashing comber while the froth boils about his shoulders — to watch the light and color prismed in the curl and slant of every wave, and the quick vanishing of brightness and glory once the sun is off the sea — all this is the matter of poems that no one can write.

The sun drops over the flat glitter of the inland lagoons; the violet and silver and rose-flushed foam are gone from the ocean; the sand is gray and damp and chilly. Down the line of the shore comes an airplane roaring through the upper regions of dazzling sunlight, with brightness on its varnished wings. The lighthouse[3] at the Inlet has begun to twinkle its golden flash, and supper will soon be on the table. The solitary swimmer takes one last regretful plunge through a sluicing hill of green, and hunts out his pipe. He had left it, as the true smoker does, carefully filled with a match-box beside it, in a dry hollow on the sand. Trailing a thread of blue reek, he plods cheerfully across the fields, taking care not to tread upon the small hoptoads that have come out to hail the evening. Behind him the swelling moon floats like a dim white lantern, penciling the darkening water with faint scribbles of light.

But there are still a few oldtimers in Fierceforest, cottagers who cling on until the first of October, and whose fraternal password (one may hear them saying it every time they meet) is "Sure! Best time of the year!" Through the pink flush of sunrise you may see the husbands moving soberly toward the early commuters' train, the 6:55, which is no longer crowded. (A month ago one had to reach it half an hour early in order to get a seat in the smoker.) Each one transports his satchel, and also curious bundles, for at this time of year it is the custom to make the husband carry home each week an instalment of the family baggage, to save excess when moving day comes. One totes an oilstove; another, a scales for weighing the baby. They trudge somewhat grimly through the thin morning twilight, going back for another week at office and empty house or apartment. Leaving behind them the warm bed, the little cottage full of life and affection, they taste for a moment the nostalgic pang that sailors know so well when the ship's bow cuts the vacant horizon. Over the purple rim of sea the sun juts its scarlet disk. You may see these solitary husbands halt a moment to scan the beauty of the scene. They stand there thoughtful in the immortal loneliness of dawn. Then they climb the smoker and pinochle has its sway.

NOTES

1. *Mr. Wilson:* Woodrow Wilson was President from 1913 to 1921. He won the 1919 Nobel Peace Prize for his dedication to the League of Nations.

2. *Rolling-chair baron:* Although less well-known than Atlantic City's, Wildwood's chairs started rolling in 1904.

3. *Lighthouse:* Hereford Inlet Lighthouse.

"The Shore in September," from *Travels in Philadelphia*, David McKay Company, 1921.

1920s
The Northern Shore

Edmund Wilson

The bathing suits worn by these sporty flappers exposed more flesh than ever before seen in public.

 Edmund Wilson was born in Red Bank in 1895; he returned to the Monmouth County shore from Manhattan off and on over the years. After graduating from Princeton, Wilson started his literary career as a reporter on the New York Sun; *he went on to a career as a major critical writer. Wilson was managing editor at* Vanity Fair, *book review editor at the* New Republic, *a regular contributor to* The New Yorker *and a poet, novelist and playwright. He was one of the ablest intellects of his time and produced books in many fields. The following colorful vignettes are from* The Twenties, *a book derived from his notebooks and journal, which Wilson was working on when he died in 1972.* The Twenties *was completed by editor Leon Edel, who wrote in his foreword, "We discover how much Edmund used his eyes, his nose, his ears, his sense of smell. The notebooks are often the equivalent of a painter's sketchbook and as such are the intermittent record of a constant onlooker and an adventurous mind."*

1925

Asbury Park, Fourth of July

The girls were wearing long dresses and light coats lined with fur at the bottom and the men white knickerbocker trousers and sweaters checked tan and white. Hot dogs, dabbed with mustard from the common bowl with a little long-handled wooden trowel, and buttermilk; salt-water taffy, hot buttered popcorn. As day faded, the sands became palest buff and the ocean grayest blue, with the waves like white porcelain where they broke between — the moon was buff in the gray sky. As the sky darkened, the fireworks were started, and a rocket streamed violet and silver against the deepening gray — then it burst in brooches of red, gold and green, great bouquets that unfolded and shriveled, growing out of one another; the loud detonation of a cluster of white electric stars. Children held the bristling brass of their toy sparklers out to the enormous darkening sea — Before night, little blond bob-haired girls and boys, in pink and yellow pinafores, slid squealing down the smooth bumpy slides in an interminable succession. — The last random pops and shots of the Fourth. — The smell of gunpowder.

Atlantic Highlands

A garage man in corduroy trousers and the upper half of a bathing suit, from which brown arms bulged. — On the upper piazza of a "cabaret-restaurant," two tanned fishy girls with stringy bobbed hair and shreddy dresses, as if they soaked themselves habitually in the rank shallow water that lies between the mainland and the beach. — A green-blinded maroon summer cottage facing the breakwater of rocks, with crescents slit in the blinds of the first floor, a close row of pink and white petunias all around it and an old weather-worn children's swing on the porch. — Cottages rakishly designed as ships, with portholes and porches like decks. — Little sordid sandy sea-bleached bungalows, with people listlessly sitting about them in bathing suits.

Sandlass's[1]

A flaxen-haired girl, with legs and arms burned salmon pink in a turquoise bathing suit — afterwards she put on an orange cap and went in the water, where she stayed for a long time, swimming like a seal — she did an excellent crawl. — A little girl in lavender, with a purple bathing cap, was marvelously adroit at plunging with the waves — she would dive over them just as they broke or, looking expertly over her shoulder, make a quick flight forward. — Turquoise, robin's-egg blue, vermilion with a canary-yellow belt. — A fish hawk flapping above the water in its businesslike way — first flapping, then gliding a moment looking for fish — it makes a swift straight lethal drop when it sees one. — On the line of the horizon, flat against the sky, the white sails of a ship which seems to have almost the transparence of a phantom. The ugly silly crude light-green umbrella trees which everyone plants on their front lawns at Red Bank, Oceanic and all along the coast.

At Sandlass's — the sound of a solo with piano accompaniment from the radio inside the wooden enclosure where the keys are given out and where candy and beach toys are sold — the sweet melody and the bright piano notes between, slightly scratchy and effaced in spots, as if it had been affected by the sand and bleached by the dry sea air. It pervaded the bathing place naturally, as if in harmony with the sea-seasoned color of the bathing clothes and the brilliance of summer dresses put on without subtleties after the swim.

Swimming. Wading out, each successive swelling wave lifts a new rim of chill about the body.

1926

Seabright in July

A thin moving platform of glass — lucid water over the gray sand. I put my hand, sweaty from my face, in the water, as if I should be washing it fresh, and then tasted, when I wiped my face with it, that, instead of being freshened, it was seasoned with cleaner salt. — The sun dulled and the waves turned dark with the look of a mid-ocean sea, so different from the white curling crests and the shining blues and greens of the surf; and, presently, against the gray sky, appeared a small army dirigible, like the glassy iron-silver ovoid of a shark or a whale as we see them hanging stuffed in museums. It moved slowly toward the shore till, passing before and above us, we could see the number and the letters painted on it and the little black men in the car, one of them waving his arm. There were fins on its smaller end and, behind it, a small American flag, stretched out in the wind like a little steerer, and from its chin trailed a rope like a feeler. It tilted up, moving all in one piece, and moved off along the shore above the sea. — A girl in a green cap and a gray bathing suit with gray stockings and shiny black blunt-toed shoes, which she kicked off on the sand, after she had been sitting there awhile, went into the water. She was well filled out and swam quite competently. Her gray bathing suit became like a skin over her solid torso and molded her broad flat breasts, revealing the nipples as dark dots. This, as I later found out, was the beach for the rich people's servants, who were sometimes in their bathing suits unrecognizably better looking. — An engulfed sea crab, a purplish grainy gray, like the sand as one saw it through the water. I skimmed him out with a rusty wad of tin and put him over on one side in the shelter of a little breakwater which separates the Pavilion from the Beach Club.

A gray day at the shore — it was going to rain — sky and sea were both gray — a few gulls above the water — dry smell of salt dust in the nostrils above the breaking crests.

The next day, the girl on the sand whom I took at first for a boy — she had glossy black hair, boyish-bobbed, and wore a white shirt tucked inside a pair of black trunks like a boy — I first recognized her as a girl by the way she held her cigarette — her feminine gesture moving the upper half of her arm toward her body — later I saw the low roundness of her breasts. A young boy and girl playing ball across one of the life-lines in the surf, she a blonde in a turquoise bathing suit an with her tanned summer skin not quite continuous with the edge of the slip at the shoulders and thighs.

The New Jersey shore, etc.

Fully developed, heavily tanned girl and boy in bathing suits in delivery wagon-like Ford. — Straight slender-legged Swedish-looking blond girl in red bathing suit with sharpish nose, gray eyes, boyish-bobbed pale hair, well-developed pretty girl's breasts which were yet not excessive for her tall slim figure — unabashed independent manner and gaze, serious, except when talking to friend when she had a fine smile — proud. — Little children at Monmouth Beach in orange and pale green bathing suits, like flavors of lime and orange drops or bottled soft drinks. — Shredded seaweed swimming like spinach in the surf and when we got out, sticking to one's body in green transparent flakes. — A churning and crashing of wreckage — sticks and boards — by much too strong inhuman gray-green-colored waves breaking on the bias, which made swimming impossible and standing in the surf uncertain and uncomfortable. The rusty keys and locks of the humble and obscure bathing pavilion — and torn towels five cents extra — no separate men's and women's sides — between a wicked-looking breakwater and a limit.

AUGUST 21-22. The dark green leaves against gray-silver sky. —The rain from the gray-silver sky, as if it were being momentarily shaken. That feeling of indoors in the country on rainy summer days (reminding me of the Knoxes, when we used to sit indoors and play anagrams). A comfortable damp within doors, a wet by no means formidable outside — the summer wind of rain stirring the low sound of surf in the trees — blowing rain about the trees and gardens, darkening tennis matches, swimming and motoring for a moment, after which the brilliant glare

will reappear and the bright sun-broken surfaces of Seabright dry out again in a single night — a flurry of wind and wet and darkness to be comfortably, amusingly endured for the refreshment of the great lawns, which will have revived their green tomorrow.

1927

Seabright Beach

Pretty girl in rather a Germanic way, with plain white bathing-suit upper, belt and red trunks with white stripe down side — she had smiling darkish eyes and very white skin; her movements with her legs, first lying on her back and holding one knee up, with the thighs rather apart, her head on the man's chest; then running over toward me, so, as it were, to expose the pretty nest of the lap creased deep between well-rounded thighs — her movements with her legs were voluptuous. In the water, she swam beautifully and as if it were a natural element: she had a slow easy and elastic crawl. — They were one of those couples who do a certain amount of petting on the beach, he putting his arm around her, etc. Another couple: the girl would slip her hand under the man's bathing suit and caress his back.

Beautiful young blond slender girl, with plainer tanned mother and sister — they were sewing and reading on the beach — she would stand with her very long slender white legs apart, with movements unconstrained and unselfconscious, or rather with the calm assurance of the consciousness of beauty. Her shoulders, reddened with sunburn, were narrow, her low but properly developed, not flat, breasts beneath her white swimming shirt —she wore a belt and dark-blue trunks. Her towhair was bobbed straight off all around — there was something a little Swedish about her narrowish eyes, her pointed nose and V-shaped mouth, which was vivid and sharp against her blondness, perhaps by the aid of rouge. At last, when she was done with her sewing, she got up and put on a white wrap, broidered with a pattern of blue —she only put her arms half in, then stood, with her feet wide apart, looking out at the sea with the wrap billowing out behind her shoulders in the wind.

NOTES

Sandlass's: Sandlass's beach club was part of a development at Sandy Hook in-cluding Sandlass's large home and a community of small cottages. Sandlass had a 99-year lease from the federal government but it was canceled in the 1960s.

Excerpts from "Back in the East," and "New York" from *The Twenties* by Edmund Wilson. Copyright ©1975 by Elena Wilson. Reprinted by permission of Farrar, Straus & Giroux, Inc.

1922
Atlantic City

Arthur Conan Doyle

Famous escape artist Harry Houdini hung suspended from Atlantic City's Garden Pier, 1916.

Arthur Conan Doyle, the creator of Sherlock Holmes, lectured on spiritualism and led seances in the United States throughout 1922. He went from Manhattan to Atlantic City for a rest, but it's unlikely he succeeded because he stayed at the Ambassador Hotel, one of the liveliest, glitziest hotels on the Boardwalk. Sailing by moonlight was popular this summer and the famous entertainers of the day — comedian Eddie Cantor, singer Galli-Gurci, and actress Fritzi Scheff — were performing in the resort's theaters. Al Jolson, the great jazz singer, was there, too, swimming daily on the beach at Michigan Avenue. The famous escape artist Harry Houdini, a friend of Doyle's, both vacationed and performed along the Board-walk, escaping from improbable situations on Atlantic City's Garden Pier. Mexican squirrels were the latest in fashionable beach pets, and the Million Dollar Pier touted a display of "Infant Incubators with Living Infants." Prohibition was two years old and rum runners did their best to keep visitors from going thirsty while federal agents kept busy trying to intercept the high-powered garveys bringing in illicit liquor from schooners anchored offshore.

Doyle has the Delaware River running west of the city, but even if his geography is a bit skewed, we know what he means.

The weather was getting very hot in New York, with that peculiar brew of damp heat for which the island city is notorious, so we were glad to change our quarters, now that the work was done, to Atlantic City, the celebrated New Jersey watering-place. Our Ambassador Hotel had a daughter there, even larger and more wonderful than her mother, so that my only fear was that our party would become enervated from the luxury we were enjoying. It is difficult to describe Atlantic City, for we have nothing in England which is at all like it. The whole town is built upon a great sandbank with the Atlantic in front and the swamps of the Delaware River behind. It is so little above sea-level that it would be no surprise to me if a tidal wave some day were to wash it clean. Meanwhile, it is quite the liveliest place which we have found in our extended travels, and can only be compared to Manly near Sydney for the excellence of the surf-bathing. The Atlantic roller has not the glorious slow heave and roar of its Pacific brother, but it is big enough to give you a merry romp if you care to go out to play. The sea has always been a nurse to me, and I have spent two full years of my life actually on her bosom, so I was glad to be in her arms once again. To lie floating on a blue ocean and look up to a blue sky is the nearest approach to detachment from earth that normal life can give.

Though so pleasant, it is not a very safe beach, for there is a queer tricky goblin of a current which comes and goes, suddenly catching at your legs and sweeping you seaward. Several were drowned while we were here, and Houdini[1], who is one of the finest swimmers in the world, told me that he had to fight for his life on one occasion. They keep a patrol[2], however, of very competent men upon the beach, who are stripped and ready from morning to night. The constant exposure has burned most of them quite as red as an Indian and suggests the curious reflection that if we lived under quite natural conditions no such thing as the white race would be known. I am convinced that the Maoris, for example, are simply sunburned whites.

One of the favorite amusements of Atlantic City when you are not moving along the Boardwalk in the huge invalid-chairs — I thought at first that it was a population of convalescents — is to go down to Young's million-dollar pier[3] and see the fish-net being drawn. This occurs twice a day and is certainly well worth seeing. By some device which is beyond me the fish are led through a series of nets until they finally assemble in a *cul-de-sac,* which is duly brought to the surface. They are very numerous and very varied — indeed, it is rather a horrible sight, that mass of pullulating life, flapping and beating in its vain struggle against extinction. Crabs predominate, red crabs by the hundreds, and big king crabs, like huge horny tadpoles, never seen by me before save in museums and in palæozoic rocks. Then there are the fish proper, queer blowfish which puff themselves into spiky balls, and gasp through their parrot beaks, gurnards and char and hake, and comely sea-trouts, and big, stupid, heavy-eyed groupers, the fish which the diver fears more than he does the shark. Presiding over the whole scene, megaphone in hand, was Mr. Young himself, he who built the million-dollar pier, a democratic figure as he shouted small jokes to the crowd, and gave directions for the emptying of the net. It is certainly a sight to see once, though it leaves a repugnant feeling in the mind.

A Britisher passing through America is not, as a rule, impressed by hustle to the extent that Americans think. As a rule there is more snap and ginger in a London transaction than in an American one. There are, however, notable exceptions. When I saw on the Saturday the huge empty hall of the pier and was told that on the following Wednesday it was to be opened as a great railway exhibition, with engines which weighed a hundred tons and machinery all actually running, I was sceptical. But it all materialised according to schedule. On the Wednesday it was one long line of exhibits, and humming from end to end with turning wheels and sliding pistons. We were shown over by the Committee and were deeply impressed. Everything conceivable connected with railways was there, from the huge transcontinental engine already mentioned to the latest burglar-proof catch for a truck or the best cloth for lining a carriage. My head buzzed to match the wheels before I got out, for I have no brains for mechanics and it was a strain to try to understand it all. The most ingenious thing I saw was a little extra engine called a "booster," running by its own electric power, which had its own wheels, and is slipped under the big ordinary engine so as to give it extra power. Some genius had observed that there was unoccupied space under the engine and had thought that it could be filled like this. The "booster" is, I believe, being actually tried on the London and North-Western Railway, and it may prove one of those clever helps which come to us from the land of active brains.

I had come to Atlantic City for a much-needed rest but it was essential that I should get my travel impressions down while they were fresh, and up to this point many of them were mere jottings in a notebook. This work kept me busy for several hours a day. Still, what with my daily swim, and what with rides up and down the Boardwalk in the double bath-chairs, propelled by a one-negro-power human machine, I had a very restful time, and all of us found our fun in our various ways.

NOTES

1. *Houdini:* Famed magician and escape artist Harry Houdini was also interested in spirits and participated in a seance with Doyle. They talked about Houdini's power, and Doyle noted in his journal, "Very naturally he gives nothing away, for a trick explained loses its virtue." Doyle considers that it may be something spiritual — "of the spirit world" — which guides Houdini in his most daring feats. Houdini began performing his great escape on Garden Pier at New Jersey Avenue in 1917.

2. *Patrol:* Atlantic City hired a "constable of the surf" in 1855, who was paid $117 for the season's work. A volunteer force called "Rescue Life Guard Service" was organized in 1876, but the city's first official, paid lifeguards went on duty in 1892.

3. *Young's million-dollar pier:* Young's second pier opened in 1906; it was constructed of concrete and actually cost one million dollars.

From *Our American Adventure*, George H. Doran Company, 1923.

1926
Townsends Inlet

Jim Doyle

The village of Townsends Inlet in the 1920s, looking south over the railroad bridge toward Avalon.

Jim Doyle celebrated his sixth birthday getting stuck in the sand the day *that he and his family moved into his grandfather's house in Townsends Inlet. The house was the first one built between the railroad and the inlet; before Jim's grandfather bought it, the place had been the real estate office from which lots in that area were sold. In 1926 there was no development between the Doyles' and the inlet except Happ's stable on Ninetieth Street, where Jim and his friends went to barrage the rats with stones. Doyle's childhood expo-*

sure to a slot machine did not shift his loyalty away from his town when he became an adult.

Although Townsends Inlet was legally a part of Sea Isle City, the communities were separated by two miles of sand dunes, some towering as high as thirty feet. A road and the parallel railroad, now Pleasure Avenue, divided the dunes from the bay meadows, which would be submerged when high tide reached the tracks.

The truck driver and my father, Joseph J. Doyle, a lawyer from Philadelphia, were riding in the cab. My mother, Elizabeth Doyle, was in there too, along with my sister, Jane, on somebody's lap. In the back of the truck, a black, open, stake-bodied one, were a load of older furniture, my grandfather and I. It was a warm, sunny day, so he and I rode down from Philadelphia in the back of the truck along with the furniture, each of us seated on two lovely, old-fashioned, high-backed kitchen chairs that my grandfather had rigged up for us. My grandfather, Jim Tresnan, my mother's father, had bought a cottage on 89th Street, and that's where we were headed when we got stuck in the sand.

We drove south on Roberts Avenue (now called Landis Avenue), passed Shellem's store[1] at 86th Street, and then, with what we thought were two more streets to go, just after we passed Busch's at 87th Street and went up over the railroad, down we came on the other side of the tracks and immediately sank into sand!

We all got out and contemplated a while. With the situation assessed, a decision was made for everybody to get behind the truck and to push the truck out of the sand while the driver accelerated the engine. The whole family including me got behind the truck and attempted to push it out. But the faster my father revved up the engine, the more the wheels spun and spun and the deeper and deeper into the sand went the truck until it was in all the way up to the hub caps. A crowd of bemused onlookers gathered, and after watching us struggle futilely, disclosed to us the errors of our ways — literally.

First of all, we were pushing the truck the wrong way! What looked like a road ahead was a deception! The "road" was really only soft sand, a sand-filled and banked foundation for a future road. The future Landis Avenue was still waiting for the sand to "settle," after which heavy rollers would be pulled back and forth over the sand. Next the road would be "gravelled," that is, a top of gravel put over the settled sand, heavy rollers pulled over it again to pack it down further, and only then, after the sand and gravel had settled, could it be driven on.

The only thing to do, we were informed, was to "Get Mr. Happ." Mr. Happ was sent for and in due course, Mr. Happ arrived — along with his two sons, two horses, and whatever equipment was necessary for a pair of sons and a pair of horses to extricate any motor vehicle mired in sand.

The sons hitched the horses to the truck's rear bumper, then Mr. Happ positioned each of the two sons just behind the behind of a different horse, just out of the way of the rear hooves. When he was satisfied that all was ready, Mr. Happ hollered, "Gee!" as simultaneously each of the sons gave his horse a mighty slap on the rump and presto, the truck was yanked back into the middle of the tracks, sand pouring out of its underbelly. Everybody gave a cheer.

My father gave Mr. Happ a dollar. Although nobody had said it at the time, I had witnessed, indeed learned, the answer to the seemingly rhetorical question current in those early days of automobiling, "Why don't you get a horse?"

Since the truck's engine did not start after the mishap, Mr. Happ kept his team of horses hitched to the truck and they pulled us backwards down "gravelled" 87th Street toward the beach to the street that ran parallel to the beach just back of the dunes [and] along to our street, 89th, which had been filled with sand and graded, but not yet gravelled. There the horses were unhitched and taken across the sand to their stable, the only building on 90th Street. The truck, full of furniture, stood at the corner of 89th and the future Pleasure Avenue while we all pitched in, unloaded our furniture and carried it halfway down the block over the sand to our house. I carried my own small suitcase and a half empty box of Cracker Jack.

Our cottage stood about two or three feet above the ground and was built on wooden pilings driven down into the sand and was open to the air underneath. It had a three room arrangement and a front porch. There was a large living room/dining room which stretched across the whole front of the house and opened into a kitchen. Off the kitchen was a bedroom and on the platform just outside the back door, at the top of a landing which had steps leading down to the backyard, was a small room that had a flush toilet. There was no bath, only a cold water shower on the ground behind the house.

Though we had running water in 1926, we had neither gas nor electricity. We had kerosene lamps and a kerosene range in the kitchen for cooking. The front porch was not yet screened in and though my grandfather immediately tacked mosquito netting in place, mosquitoes got in anyway. Despite frequent and thorough immersions in citronella, my sister and I would get pretty well bitten.

Pests were a real problem in those days. First there were the regular flies. We had an assortment of fly swatters and hand held spray guns filled with Black Flag or some other insecticide. There were also the rolls of fly paper which dangled down from the ceiling. It was coated with a sticky substance so that when an unsuspecting fly landed on it, its feet stuck and it died there. These were unsightly things with all the dead flies stuck to them and my mother rarely used them, though they were commonly used at the hot dog stands as well as by other outdoor vendors.

The Stouts ran an ice cream parlor in a building on 85th Street. When I wanted an ice cream cone I went to Stouts. One Friday night I was sitting there at a table with my father and mother and sister eating a chocolate fudge sundae and watching a man standing at this silver machine behind my father. This man kept putting nickels into this machine, then pulling the lever and waiting while the machine did something. What?

From where I was sitting, I could see the things going past in the machine's little windows, but I couldn't tell what they were. Now generally I'm a slow eater. Except for two things, spaghetti and ice cream. With either, I'm the first one up from the table. Not the first one done. I'm the first one up for a second helping! This night, with the slot machine whirring, I had no trouble being the first to put away that fudge sundae in nothing flat, but instead of asking for more, I leapt up and went over to that machine.

Standing right in front of the machine, I could see that when the man put a nickel in the slot and pulled the arm, three pictures went by inside the three little windows, pictures of lemons and Liberty Bells and small bars. Most of the time when the machine stopped, there was a different picture in each window and this man would simply put another nickel in and pull the arm again. But once when the machine stopped, all three lemons stayed there in a line. There was a tinkling noise and four nickels came out. I was stunned. This was magic! The man, however put the nickels back into the machine, one by one, and nothing happened until the last nickel. This time when the machine stopped, there were the three bars side by side in the windows and ten nickels poured out of the machine. I couldn't believe it! I had witnessed a miracle.

As the man was taking the money out of the machine, a nickel dropped and rolled along the floor. I scooted after it, retrieved it and attempted to give it back to the man. He wouldn't take it, telling me to pocket it for good luck. I looked at my father. He nodded. I thanked the man and put the nickel in my pocket.

I stood there and watched as this man put back into the machine one after another all the nickels he had just won and not once did the machine give him back any nickels. He got change for a half dollar from Mrs. Stout and put that into the machine too. He won once more. The three lemons. He fed the four nickels back in and lost them too. Then he quit playing, took a seat at the counter and had Mrs. Stout mix him a coke.

Now nobody was playing the machine. I put my hand into my pocket and felt the nickel. I looked at my father. He knew what I wanted. My father looked at Mrs. Stout. She shrugged her shoulders and my father nodded OK.

I remember everybody watching as I took out my nickel, Mrs. Stout, the man who was sitting there sipping his coke, my father, my mother and my sister. I put my nickel into the slot and pulled at the lever. It wouldn't come down. I tried again. It still wouldn't budge. The man got up from the counter and came over to help me. My father stopped him.

"Let him do it himself," my father said.

They all watched while I struggled. Finally I put both hands on the lever and pulled with all my might. Down came the arm. The machine began to whirr, the bars and lemons began to spin past until a Liberty Bell stopped at the first little window, then another Liberty Bell in the far window, and I held my breath until a third Liberty Bell settled and stopped in the middle window. Three Liberty Bells! Five dollars! A hundred nickels spilled out! The machine began to play The Star Spangled Banner. The man at the counter shouted, "Hot Damn!" and jumped down on the floor beside me to help me pick up nickels. Eventually we were all down on the floor rounding up nickels. Mrs. Stout brought over a paper bag for us to put them in.

When we had picked up all the nickels, my father told me to give the bag to the man. I began to cry. The man pushed the bag away.

"Nope," he said. "They're the kid's." He continued to push the bag away.

"Keep them, sonny," he insisted. "They're all yours. You won them fair and square." And despite my father's protestations, he absolutely refused, shook my hand, wished me good luck and left. I never saw him again.

I was allowed to keep my nickels, but I wasn't allowed to play the machine any more that night even though I really wanted to and made quite a fuss.

When we got home, my father put the bag of nickels up on the top shelf of the kitchen cabinet. He ruled that I was not to be permitted to play the machine alone, but was to be allowed five nickels from the bag whenever we went to Stouts. He said I could do whatever I wanted with these, buy ice cream or play the slot machine. So whenever we went to Stouts, the bag was taken down from the top shelf, I was doled out my five nickels and the bag was put back up there. I'd take my five nickels in my inside pocket. Once in a while I'd buy ice cream cones for myself and maybe for my sister, but usually I opted to play the machine. So I played the machine every time we went to Stouts that summer, occasionally winning, usually losing, but each time playing until I had no nickels left. My bag of nickels was empty long before Labor Day.

Another great fun-feature of the beach for us kids was the formation of gullies which would begin to appear as the tide went out, leaving these lovely little lakes with sand bars arising on the other side of them. The water grew quite warm, often ten or more degrees warmer than the ocean temperature, and I loved to play in that warm water.

These gullies could be a foot or two deep, frequently having holes even deeper. Fish would be trapped in them as the tide went out, particularly minnows, but also an occasional small sand shark. Often we found a starfish in the gully and, if we did, we'd run out onto the sand bar, locate a buried clam by its breathing hole in the sand, dig it up and then put it in the water next to the starfish. Boy, did that clam move! Somehow the clam knew that the starfish was there and after it. The clam took off like its life depended on it. Which, of course, it did.

The gullies also made great wading pools for little children; kids played in them with safety and got to know the water and be unafraid of it. They were great places for learning to swim and I think that we all learned to swim there.

The bay was deep. The big kids swam in the bay off Vansant's Pier.[2] I really wanted permission to swim there too. The water off the pier end was deep, probably fifteen feet or so at high tide and a good dozen feet at low, besides which there was a strong current which could be three or four knots or more when the tide was coming in or going out. So I had to be a strong swimmer.

I begged my father to let me swim off the pier with the big kids. I complained that I really couldn't swim in the ocean, that all I could do was bathe and play in the surf. Besides I wanted to swim where the water was over my head, to show everybody how well I could swim, which was impossible in the ocean since my father had long ago forbidden me to go into water any deeper than up to my chest.

So one day, my father put on his bathing suit and went out on Vansant's pier with me. Some big kids I knew were cavorting there, diving off the tops of pilings on the south end of the pier and then swimming and letting the tide carry them across the front of the pier to the boat landing where they climbed up the steps and did it all over again. I could see that the tide was coming in and it looked pretty strong. My father told me to go ahead and dive in. I went around to where the kids were diving and stood there. I didn't know how to dive yet, but they were watching and I didn't want anybody to know I felt a little afraid. The kids started to yell at me to go ahead, jump. So I jumped. I jumped out as far as I could, hit the water and down I went, pretty deep, but I didn't hit bottom, which I think I was afraid of. I simply stopped going down and shot up to the top again. I felt the current begin to carry me along the front of the pier, so I took a couple of strokes towards the landing and grabbed the steps, breathless. I felt great. I did it!

I ran up the steps and asked my father if I could do it again. He told me to go ahead. So I did it again. This time he was waiting for me on the landing. He told me to swim back to the end of the pier, against the current, around to where I had jumped in. I really had to struggle to swim against that current, but I made it back to where they were diving.

I hung onto a piling to rest and then my father signalled me to come back. I just drifted back to him at the landing.

My father helped me out of the water and we sat there on the steps, talking about the current. It wasn't new to me, but he wanted to make sure I understood how strong it was, how hard it was to swim against, and how I had to treat it with respect, and be careful of it, and if it did start to carry me, not to panic and fight it, but to go with it, see where it was taking me, and to stroke a bit and gradually work my way in to the shore, just as I had learned to do in the ocean. And that was it. I was allowed to swim off the pier with the big kids in the deep water.

NOTES

1. *Shellem's store*: Shellem's was a general store; a market is still in the same location.
2. *Vansant's Pier*: Vansant's Pier was at the end of 86th Street.

———————————

Diaries of Jim Doyle, excerpted in *South Jersey Magazine,* Winter 1993 and Spring 1994, reprinted with the permission of Jim Doyle.

1930 & 1935
Cape May and Keyport

William L. Lathrop

Impressionist painter William Lathrop building his 24-foot sailboat, Widge, 1927.

On a warm Sunday afternoon in July 1926 William Lathrop told his son-in-law Rolf Bauhan that he was going to build a boat and asked for his help. Lathrop, a 67-year-old landscape painter[1] from New Hope, Pennsylvania, said he needed "some exercise to keep me outdoors, but not too strenuous." Because of a heart condition he had been warned by his doctors not to overexert himself. But, according to Bauhan, "he was full of enthusiasm for life and wanted to do something both physically and mentally stimulating." The two men right then and there drove across the river to a property just north of Lambertville where Lathrop had seen a stand of white oak. They found a "grand, big one," almost four feet at the base, sixty feet high with a spread of about a hundred feet. The farmer sold them the tree for fifteen dollars. Lathrop arranged with a sawmill to take the tree down and cut the lumber. The keel was laid the following spring, and Will Lathrop's dream began to take shape.

For the next three years father and son-in-law worked in a makeshift shed on Lathrop's property near the Delaware River. The gaff-rigged sailboat was modeled on a double-ended North Sea fishing boat, nine feet across the beam, twenty-six feet at the waterline with a 4 1/2-foot draft. Lathrop got the 35-foot spruce mast from Slade Dale's[2] boatyard in Bay Head. On Labor Day 1930 Widge was rolled on her side out of the shed, across the lawn and down to the Delaware Canal, where she was launched with much ceremony.

Six weeks later Lathrop began his journey, motoring south in the canal through the locks at Yardley, Morrisville, Bristol, and into the Delaware River. On this first run down the river Lathrop and Bauhan were plagued by a northeast storm, strong tides running against them and, when they tacked to avoid a tanker near Wilmington, Widge ran aground in the soft mud. By October 23 they had holed up in a protected harbor near New Castle, Delaware, where Lathrop penciled in his log: "She is in very gallant and swagger company; two 50 foot DuPont yachts in snow white paint, gleaming mahogany and polished brass lie on the other side of this little basin." The next day he "arose with an unconquerable determination to paint" but instead went to town and returned with a can opener, clothes pins, knife, a bunch of grapes and a 35-cent fog horn, noting that it was too cold to paint outdoors.

On October 31 Lathrop logged Bauhan's departure: "Rolf left me yesterday at a little cleft in the interminable marsh called Mahon's Ditch. But it has a lighthouse and is a port of shelter for the oyster fleet." The next day, sailing *before a fresh northwester,* Widge *headed east-southeast for Cape May: "We were soon out of sight of this low coast and for two hours we might have been in open sea, except for the oyster bed stakes which are everywhere except in the steamer channels." The wind and seas were increasing, so Lathrop reefed his mainsail and when he found himself in the midst of the oyster fleet he followed them into the Maurice River rather than continuing to Cape May.*

1930

NOVEMBER 2: Maurice River. Bright day but bitter cold north wind with thousands of sea gulls soaring, plunging and squealing about the river. If you dump a bucket of garbage overboard they mob you.

This is a most extraordinary place. Hundreds and hundreds of snow white schooners moored for miles along the shore! Huddled about the warehouses until their masts look like forests and shooting out into and from the open water at high speed from their powerful engines. They are very gallant and handsome crafts. The slowly developed perfection of a type. Almost all of them carry great weather-beaten gray trysails at their work in the bay. Beautiful!

I was invited to move *Widge* alongside of one of the oyster boats. Made some new friends — fine fellows! They have to be virile to endure this work, or even to choose it in the first place.

Got under way at 11 A.M. for Cape May, strong north wind, ebb tide, foresaw a quick and easy passage of perhaps four hours. If I had only known! What really happened was twenty-two hours of as strenuous sailing as I ever did. The strong north wind reversed itself, became a light south wind, a head wind. An hour later the tide did the same thing, so I spent the entire afternoon beating back and forth across the bay, and at nine that night found myself abreast of Brandy Wine Shoal in a dead calm, but with the tide again in my favor, so through the night partly drifting, sometimes sailing gently.

About 1 A.M. I was out in the open Atlantic on a dark night trying to unravel the mysteries of Prissy Wicks shoal. Unforgettable name! I was anxious, but from a study of the chart and such beacons and buoys as I had been able to identify I believed myself safely outside of the dangerous places. There was little wind, so that the boat was hardly manageable, but there were the usual big Atlantic rollers.

Suddenly in the quiet darkness on my port bow, not a hundred yards away, one of them burst with a thunderous roar into a *breaker*. I did some quick work with helm and sheets and slid away from there like a scared hen. I worked myself a good mile further off shore before I dared again turn eastward.

Sometime before dawn the breeze freshened a little. I was working east and in toward shore. That dawn was worth living for. It began very early in the night and lasted a long time. As the coast became visible I worked in and found myself abreast of Cape May City, with the harbor two miles further up the coast. It looked easy, but the breeze which had freshened with the dawn suddenly took on a vicious strength NE. *Widge* was carrying whole sail and I had a strenuous time making that last two miles, luffing when I had to and sailing when I could.

I was very thankful when I finally rounded the end of the south break-water and let her go with lifted sheets straight up the harbor, to come to and drop anchor handsomely before the Coast Guard station, then into my blankets and sleep for three hours before I thought of breakfast, though I had had nothing but bread and cheese since breakfast the day before. So ended *Widge's* first encounter with the Atlantic Ocean! Humiliating as to Prissy Wicks — but that was not her fault.

NOVEMBER 3: Roaring northeaster all day. Put chafing gear on my hawser[3] and slept all day.

NOVEMBER 4: Renewed chafing gear and slept all day.

In the evening Capt. Kent Moffett Redgrave of the C.G. service here, came out in his surfboat and offered to tow me in to his dock, which offered shelter from the gale, gladly accepted.

In the evening the northeaster ceased and the skies cleared; the wind beginning to blow lightly from the northwest caused me some uneasiness, as my berth at the dock offered no shelter from that quarter and I was so close to the beach at the short dock that it would be impossible to get out under sail. Captain Redgrave reassured me however and went home to bed.

In a couple of hours it became evident that we were in for a rip roaring northwester and *Widge* began to pound badly against the spiling[4] of the dock. I fended her off as best I could by placing my back against a pile and bracing my feet against the cabin top, but by midnight my back was raw and my strength beginning to fail, so I hauled out my tin fog horn and blew lustily for help. For a long time nothing happened. The gale blew my feeble toots off into the winter night, and I began to fear that *Widge* or I, or both of us, were to end our careers right there. But the Captain at last had heard me and came tearing down to the dock at 2 o'clock in the morning, followed by his whole crew. They started their motor boat and towed me off to the north side of the inlet where I anchored in a good lee, and not a word of grumbling or ill humor at being routed out of their warm beds at 2 o'clock of a winter's night to play nurse for a silly old idiot who liked to play at sailorizing. Truly a wonderful breed!

Word of Will Lathrop's solo battle with a northeaster on his first cruise into the ocean reached his mother in Ohio. She chastised him in a letter: "Well, Will, you've been at it again. This is the third time you have nearly lost your life in a boat... 71 years old with a weak heart... and a mother of nearly 92 to mourn her little golden haired boy tossing about in the sea. I was in hopes when I first saw this boat that you would never finish it. You are too old to spend such a night and not suffer for it. Come out here and paint pictures. Why don't you keep your boat on the rivers?" Will responded, assuring his mother that he had gained weight, renewed his youth and had gathered enough good sketches to keep his paint brush busy all winter. For the next four years he had smooth sailing, cruising from Keyport to Larchmont to Montauk to Martha's Vineyard, visiting family and anchoring for weeks on end to sketch and paint. We rejoin him in Keyport.

1935

AUGUST 16: Left Keyport 10:30 A.M., fair, warm, light easterly breeze close hauled to Seguine Point, Staten Island, then close hauled for Atlantic Highlands, wonderful sense of peace and refreshment in this quiet sailing for hours together, rudely broken in this case by running aground on a shoal off Atlantic Highlands, quarter mile off shore! A quick jibe, some pole work and a slight lift from the swell enabled me to sail off. But the jibe broke my cord on the gaff and spilled most of the parrals[5] overboard, so I squared away for New York at 2:30 P.M. to get new parrals. Will I make it before dark?

I write this enroute while *Widge* steers herself very sweetly. The wind is dying but I should catch the flood tide thru the narrows. Hoffmans Island is right ahead about 2 mi., and it is now 4:15, wind very light, can't sail at night for I have no light for my compass. But there will be more or less of light for four hours yet.

5:55. Tide has turned and we are moving right along.

AUGUST 17: Spent the night away up in Gowanns surrounded by huge rusting hulks of idle freighters. No population except watchmen, who looked on me with suspicion, and a waterside crowd whom I viewed with so much suspicion that I did not dare leave the boat to do errands in NY, so sailed back to Keyport.

AUGUST 25: Have done nothing since the 17th except pleasant work on the rigging outside of the boat and improving the stowage inside, with some sailing about the bay to explore its painting possibilities. Am beginning to feel like painting again. I was more tired than I knew. It has been a strenuous summer.

AUGUST 26: Did a good sketch at Perth Amboy.

AUGUST 27: Did another at Keyport.

SEPTEMBER 3: Noon. This begins the third day of easterly rain and cold fog that I have spent at anchor in Perth Amboy harbor. I arrived Sunday evening, went ashore at the yacht club and got a Sunday *Times*. Since then I have not been off of the boat. No sign of a break in the weather yet, pretty tedious. But I have slept a lot and am getting well rested. The small boat gave me a lot of trouble last night — wind against the tide! I got out of bed and went on deck in my pajamas in the drizzle and hauled her bodily up across the foredeck, oars, gratings and half a tubful of rainwater! She lies there still, a monument to my renewed energies.

I forgot to mention that I am taking some interest in fishing. I got a simple outfit on Saturday and a few crabs for bait. The first result was a large, healthy and very vivacious eel. He was all over the boat! Entangling 50 feet of line with sail sheets and halliards and finally lassoing the deck broom which followed him into the cockpit where I cornered him. I had trouble getting the hide off of him, but dipped in Aunt Jemima's pancake flour and fried with bacon he made a beautiful supper. I haven't fished since! Suppose that eel had been bigger? The natives tell me of eels six feet long! I would have had to leave the boat. Raritan Bay is shallow, I know, but not that shallow. So ends the saga of the eel.

5 P.M. "The Saga of the New Raincoat." Still raining! Wind still NE. I would give something for an evening paper and some fresh food, but have no waterproof coat, and feel shy about going ashore at the yacht

club in this weather without one. This silly self-consciousness which makes you suspect you are being observed and no one really is paying you the compliment of any attention at all!

6:30 P.M. Still the cold drizzling rain, still the east wind and the fog. Three days lost except for a few pencil sketches of harbor life. When this does clear it will probably be with cold wind from the northwest from which I am well sheltered. My anchor is probably foul with two or three turns of the hawser. But I am so closely surrounded with other boats that I do not dare lift it in this tideway.

SEPTEMBER 4: Cloudy, colder, sharp wind from NE. Slept in my clothes last night, partly for warmth and partly because of anxiety as to my ground tackle, foul anchor, etc., uneasy night. Boat pitching and wallowing violently, various things breaking loose in the cabin and calling for chase and capture with the spotlight. Used my last shredded wheat for breakfast! And the pineapple jam is gone! That is the worst!

4:15 P.M. Still raining, wind shifted to SSE. But the sky has more light in it. Must get ashore, food getting scarce, pea soup for lunch. Next will be tomato! Made a sketch this morning, but the boat was hopping about madly. Looks like the work of a Japanese, a crazy one.

5:30 P.M Went ashore after bailing a tubful of water from the dink and launching her from the foredeck. Still raining, but lightly. Bought a good substantial black rubber cloth raincoat, long and large, put it on with joy — $4.70, then a newspaper. Terrible storm in Florida — our disturbance here no doubt the last flick of its tail. Bought two cans of pea soup, one pineapple jam, dozen peaches, got back to the boat 6:30, found wind and rain increasing, getting dark, prospect of one more terribly uncomfortable and anxious night.

Thought of Keyport as a millpond of peace, which it is in all southerly and westerly winds. Decided to go there. Did not reef, thought she could take it and she did, though I often had to luff to ease her. Made a good get-away from the crowded anchorage in the sheets of rain and growing darkness. The compass light worked perfectly, sailed by courses and timed them. That early in the evening Keyport was more or less lit up, so I had no trouble in locating the town, and my anchorage was found by a cross bearing of the red and green lights of Keyport Yacht Club due south and some bridge lights due west. I hit it within a hundred feet!

In spite of the new raincoat my trousers, shoes and woolen socks were sodden with water. I had neglected to put on my sou'wester so the rain had poured down my neck and soaked my undercoat and shirt. But such peace! The boat hardly stirred all night. I got rid of my wet clothes — stacked them in the foredeck — rolled myself in dry blankets and slept.

SEPTEMBER 5: Still raining, light wind from NNE, a bad quarter for Keyport. If it should increase much I should have to seek shelter again!

I have an alcohol fire burning in the galley trying to dry out shoes and socks and trousers. I find that two tablespoonsful of alcohol in a Sterno container makes just as good a fire and lasts as long as the Sterno. Perhaps a little more smoky, but much cheaper.

SEPTEMBER 6: Has been an exciting and wearying day. Too tired to write until tomorrow.

SEPTEMBER 7: Have not yet had time to write of yesterday. Have found a quiet and retired place for an anchorage. Made a good sketch today and see more in prospect. Celebrated by going uptown and getting a steak dinner at the restaurant. I write this by the light of my little kerosene lamp. As the radio man says, "So long until tomorrow."[6]

SEPTEMBER 8: The NE wind which made me anxious on September 5th continued to increase during the night and by the morning of the 6th was blowing a gale, about 10 A.M. the dinghy broke her painter and went away. I was worried. Put a reef in mainsail and thought I would sail out of it. But found I could not haul the boat up to her anchor against wind and sea, had no spare anchor so could not buoy the other and leave it. Besides, lacking an anchor and dinghy I would have been like the wandering Jew, sailing and sailing forever, unable to stop anywhere. However, just at the worst, two men from Kofoed's in a stout motorboat came to me and between us we got the anchor and escaped to a safe shelter, and the little white dinghy and I and *Widge* were reunited. The small boat had drifted down straight into the harbor unharmed. Hardly had I been snaked up the creek to complete safety where even the worst hurricane could not disturb me when the sun came out and the wind died down, and I felt a little ridiculous. However, it really was serious for a while. A large motorboat out of the yacht club anchorage parted her mooring and was partially destroyed in the breakers.

The creek is the place for me, complete safety! Plenty to paint! Bluecrabs to chase, and good fishing if I am hungry!

SEPTEMBER 9: 9 A.M. Early morning gray and foggy, but sun is now coming out with a good barometer and promise of a fine day. Had a strange experience yesterday late in the afternoon — the boat was suddenly invaded by a horde of barnswallows from boom and bowsprit clear to the little pennant at the masthead. They took possession of every halliard stay and topping lift. They scarcely paid any attention to me moving about on the deck. They repeated the performance this morning and my deck carries the evidence of their good digestions. They have gone now but I can see them swarming over the marshes to the westward and they will probably be back, so it is no use trying to clean up.

SEPTEMBER 10: Yesterday morning applied elastic cement liberally around and over the mast wedges and across the forward end of the cabin where it joins the deck. Heavy rain and squall last night proved that a persistent leakage, especially around the mast, had been cured. At least for the present. Fine day today, but windy and cold.

Rigged a down haul for my staysail this A.M. It works from the cockpit. Much needed when you are sailing alone.

Remodeled my Samson post yesterday so that in my next "hurricane" can haul and *belay*, which I was unable to do in the gale of the sixth.

12 minutes to 9 P.M. It is the most beautiful evening possible. A full moon, a cloudless sky, the first since I sailed out of the boatyard on the 16th of August. There has been an exceptionally high tide, as always at full moon, and all the world — at least all of world of salt marshes, river and estuary — is flooded with shining water. There is no motion except the smooth roll of the tide speeding out to the sea.

I wanted to wash a pair of woolen socks yesterday. Put a tablespoonful of Rinso in basin of water. Put in the socks. No suds! Must be very hard water! Put in two more spoonsful of Rinso. Still no suds! Began scientific analysis of strange phenomena — finally discovered that what I had supposed to be a carton of Rinso was really a carton of Aunt Jemima's pancake flour! The socks, I am sure, will never recover. They are starched for life.

SEPTEMBER 11: Calm bright, cloudless, faint smoky haze. But the night was almost frosty. Tinkered all day. No painting.

SEPTEMBER 12: Foggy, partially cloudy morning, clearing later. Washed towels, rinsed them in sea water.

Took the small boat out and explored the marshland to the north, found a fine wilderness accessible at almost all stages of the tide where I can paint in privacy to my heart's content. I have not yet been able to use my sketching easel, for the lack of that privacy. All my work so far has been done in the cabin, a sort of impression from memory, helped out by peeps thru the small portholes.

SEPTEMBER 13: As I opened my eyes this morning saw a pale pink moon just setting in the west. Dawn sky clear and cloudless in the east. Sharp wind from the east, cold. Crawled out of bed, lit a Sterno and put on the coffee. Washed (with a rag), dressed. Ate two bales of shredded wheat, their asperity softened somewhat by dunking in the coffee au lait, with bacon and pineapple jam.

I forgot to say that my first chore in the morning is to go out on deck in pajamas and stockinged feet and extinguish the lantern which has burned all night, hanging from the headstay. The deck is always dewy, the cabin floor always more or less dirty, hence the frequent need for Aunt Jemima's washing powder!

SEPTEMBER 14: Just saw a weird looking beast on the mud in the shadow of the 8-foot tall reeds. Something like the sketch. A kingfisher uses the top of my mast as a perch from which to dive for fish.

Today has been cold, raw and cloudy, east wind. However, I did a 25 x 30 inch of the marsh from memory. It is pretty good, I think, tho, of course, I will think otherwise tomorrow!

SEPTEMBER 15: Foggy morning, rained some, clearing later. Shipped my bowsprit which had been lashed on deck. About noon, wind and tide being favorable, hoisted my staysail and sailed out of the creek and Keyport Harbor. Found the boat sailed well under staysail alone, about eight points off the wind. Got up my mainsail and went on close-hauled up the bay with fresh NW wind. From Great Bed Light came about and sailed down into Cheesequake Harbor, shift of wind to NNE, went in flying with boombroad off, met tail of ebbtide running out like a millrace. Nearly got into trouble trying to round to an anchor in the narrow harbor under those conditions. Should have come to outside the harbor, lowered mainsail, and run in under staysail alone. Know better next time perhaps. Very interesting place, got a good sketch. Could spend a month here!

SEPTEMBER 16: Cold 50 degrees in the cabin (morning *Times* says 40 degrees). Stiff wind from NE, high sea running in the bay. The two rough stone jetties of this little harbor are so low that at half tide they are completely covered, so as I lie here at anchor between them I seem to be in the open bay. The motorboats go under the bridge to the inner harbor which is well sheltered. I can't, of course, because of my mast. I was out on deck many times in the night just to make sure. It certainly feels and looks like winter this morning. The farmers will be anxious about an early frost in the cornfields.

The boat's lively motion forbids any painting. Will try to get out of here on the first of the ebb, about noon.

3 P.M. Got out. Drifted out stern first on the rushing tide. Once outside hoisted jib to get an offing from the shoals, then all sail and away for Keyport and my safe anchorage in the creek.

SEPTEMBER 17: Fair, but with a chilly east wind.

Bought two suits of warm underwear for $3. Need them. Bought a butterfish, all cleaned, for five cents. Cooked him (with the help of Aunt Jemima) for lunch.

Here is the "Saga of the Kingfisher." He sat on my mast head as usual while I got breakfast, the hatch was open. I measured the coffee, laid down the empty spoon, when click! Clear from the mast head straight into the spoon! A perfect bulls-eye! I closed the hatch! As I close it now metaphorically.

Made a good sketch.

SEPTEMBER 18: Day begins fair. Sunshine slightly veiled. Good breeze from SW. Barometer 30 16. Thermometer 65 degrees. Did a thorough clean up of my "cuisine." Filled and polished lamp and lantern.

Good sketch again. Bought a weakfish for fifteen cents. Fried half of it for supper. Put the rest in the cockpit for lunch tomorrow. In this weather it will keep. Had to put it under cover, else the gulls would carry it off in the early morning.

SEPTEMBER 19: Barometer 30-04. Thermometer 70 degrees. Cloudy, chilly, strong wind WSW. Breakfast coffee, two shredded wheats, bacon, pineapple jam, as usual. Made a fish chowder of the remains of the weakfish for lunch. Did no painting, can't tell why, some deficiency of character, no doubt. Cleaned a little. Sewed a little. Slept. Went to bed in a bad temper.

SEPTEMBER 20: Barometer 29-80. Thermometer 78 degrees. Beautiful day, clear, light clouds, warm west wind. Must get more water, kerosene and Sternos. Also jam is getting scarce.

Midafternoon. Barometer slowly falling, thermometer 85 in cabin. Took off my new underclothes. Tomorrow is the equinoctial. Some bad weather in prospect, no doubt. Will not need mothballs for the underwear. Did not feel like painting but got out a canvas. One of the big ones. Sat and stared at it and at the out-of-doors for an hour. Could not see anything to paint. Could not think of anything to paint. Put the canvas away and took a nap. Thought perhaps I needed a change of diet. Went uptown and got myself a steak dinner, fifty cents. Also a pound of delicious Spanish grapes, five cents, devoured them all!

Went to bed.

SEPTEMBER 21: Barometer 29-80. Thermometer 67 degrees. Sun shining but misty and feeble. Wind light, still SW, chilly.

No painting again today. Cleaned and polished furiously. Took a long walk in the afternoon. Marvelous sunset behind thunderheads. Violent thunderstorms all around the horizon. Keyport calm as a millpond, with a little patch of clear sky and stars directly overhead. Sat up late to watch.

SEPTEMBER 22: Barometer 29-94. Thermometer 76 degrees. Wind light NW. Clear sky. Perfect day. Am hoping that some one from New Hope will bring HBS⁷ for a sail.

Elizabeth and Rolf turned up about 2 o'clock. Stayed three hours. Their visit did me a world of good. Served them with hot coffee, brown bread, Swiss cheese and pineapple jam. Rolf begged or borrowed some bait from a nearby boat party and fished furiously, with his usual luck — nothing at all. Not even a bite. Promised to return Wednesday and bring HBS for a sail if possible.

Late afternoon light was very brilliant. Took the camera and rowed around the harbor making snapshots of some of the wonderful waterside stuff. But the camera does not seem to give you much. Must get some kind of small anchor for the dinghy, and perhaps use her for sketching. Have never tried it. Using small panels (about 8 x 10) it might work. Rolf carried away the panels I had done.

SEPTEMBER 23: Barometer 30-15. Thermometer 70 degrees. Wind E, cold.

Feel a new impulse to work. Started a sketch on a new plan of broad ground tones in crude color, to be refined with a second painting. Hope for better results than I have been getting. At least it promises to let me out of the jam I had got into. I am glad to have the old work out of the boat. Hurrah for a New Deal!

SEPTEMBER 24: Barometer 30-20. Thermometer 52 degrees. Clear, calm. Very sharp frost last night. Rolled up in two blankets but nearly froze my feet. Have barely succeeded in thawing them out with hot coffee, fried bananas and bacon. No painting!

SEPTEMBER 25: Barometer 30-25. Wind fresh SW. Perfect morning. Rolf and HBS appeared at about 10 A.M. loaded with beer, beef, and other bundles.

Started for a sail to Sandy Hook. Boat stuck in the mud at once, almost before we got the words out of our mouths, low tide, narrow channel, and a lack of gumption on the part of the Skipper. However, with the help of our hardy crew, and at the imminent risk of Rolf's life, who just missed being engulfed in the mud from the boom end, we finally sailed free and had a marvelous day.

With the boom broad off to starboard and the big balloon jib to port we had a memorable sail to Sandy Hook. The blue billows of the Atlantic tempted. But Harry refused firmly. He had a belated lunch of beefsteak, boiled potatoes, bread and butter and jam. Nobody thought of the beer! Which remained, and still remains, in the seclusion of the deepest bilge. Got back to Keyport and the outer anchorage at dusk. Supper of fried scallops in town. Great Day! The crowning hilarity of which was the loss of Rolf's keys to his automobile which necessitated much marching and counter-marching. No painting.

P.S. Not to be overlooked! Rolf caught two fishes! One as long as the somewhat worn pencil with which I am writing, the other smaller. We haven't weighed them.

SEPTEMBER 26: Fair, wind light SW. An eventless day. A long row up the coast to Cliffwood and a long walk exploring the country at the back. No painting.

SEPTEMBER 27: Spent the whole day in the cabin painting a 25 x 30, mostly sky with a stretch of calm sea and a rowboat with some fishers, a low line of sunlit shore in the horizon. Shifted to an old anchorage up the creek.

SEPTEMBER 28: Fog, no wind, some rain. Barometer 29-30

A dark, heavy, monotonous day. Low barometer presages a sharp change with strong winds for tomorrow. No painting. In afternoon went ashore to a movie. Forgot to mention that yesterday I bought some bright and shiny knives, forks and spoons for the galley, ten cents for each article. The rusty old iron things were no longer endurable, also two generous mugs for coffee, flat bottoms, not easily upset.

I am quite proud of my galley. It helps to preserve my morale when the painting fails me.

9:15 P.M. Tide at flood, on the turn, wind gentle but rising from NW. Will be a gale tomorrow and blow away this fog. Late hours for me. But this weather excites me although I have the safest anchorage in the world. The worst that could happen would be for the anchor to drag a few rods and deposit *Widge* and me in a soft bed of mud at the river edge.

NOVEMBER 14: A cold northeast wind, light snow on the hills beyond the marsh this morning. A low flame in the little oil stove, however, keeps the cabin comfortable even with the open companion. Am looking for a visit from Elizabeth, who telephoned the "clam man" to warn me she was coming, so I have done no painting. Got up late this morning, because the warm blankets seemed inviting. Breakfast pancakes, bacon, coffee and stewed raisins.

Gave the cabin a good clean-up in honor of Elizabeth. A little shopping also for her better entertainment. Sewed on a few stray buttons, and now turn to the old logbook to occupy my time until she comes.

It is 4 P.M., I begin to fear she will not come. She has been a wonderful help in these trying weeks. She has much of her mother's serene loyalty and good sense.

I have only one 16 x 20 panel left. I shall try to get a sketch on that tomorrow, and since winter is actually here I suppose I must lay the little boat up for the winter and go back to New Hope. I hate to go. If I had three or four hundred dollars in hand I would cruise south and stay out all winter.

I am having a wonderful time with my painting. I have made two major changes in my practice. Rich glazes over the light gray ground of the panel for my foreground, much of which I leave for color and the big quiet spaces as of sky, etc., I mix with the knife on the palette in generous quantities and lay it on bravely with a good sized brush. Very simple. Very speedy.

Elizabeth and Rolf turned up just at dark. Went to a restaurant and had dinner, steak, fried spuds, salad, pie and beer — a welcome change from fish.

NOVEMBER 16: This is the third day of bitter east wind. It has been blowing hard all day and tonight it is a real winter gale.[8] My anchorage is exposed to the east. Anchor dragged about noon, was painting in the cabin and did not notice until I was almost ashore. Then there was a rush to get out the other anchor and line, tumble them into the skiff and row dead to windward in the icy blast and toppling seas. I got well drenched with spray and nearly frozen, but with the new anchor down I was able to haul off to a good place, then I got up the old anchor, gave it a lot more line and rowed away up to windward and planted that. So I am riding to two anchors and very thankfully as I listen to the gale. The whole boat is shuddering to the vibration of the shrouds

I got my last panel painted today, in spite of all the excitement. A dramatic sequel to this is still to be written.

(Later by some weeks) The gale increased all afternoon of that November 16th. Both anchors dragged until the boat was within 100 feet of a surf beaten wall, where she would have been beaten to pieces in a few minutes. I had made all preparations to abandon ship when the wind fell! The tide turned! And three hours later the poor little *Widge* lay on her beam ends in the storm beaten marsh, and there she lay until the next spring, a hundred yards from the river.

For the next three years the aging Lathrop — now suffering some weakness and shortness of breath because of his heart condition — sailed Widge *mostly on Long Island Sound. In October 1937 he was moored in Big Pond, the harbor at Montauk, in the middle of a southeast gale. He wrote in his log that the foul weather seemed to stimulate his best paintings: "It was the prospect of bad weather that brought me here. Uncomfortable but stirring. So the worse the weather the better for me." The whole month was stormy, and finally he laid up* Widge *for the winter.*

Lathrop spent most of the next summer with his daughter and her family at Shepard's Neck, but on September 14, 1938, he was back on board Widge *in Big Pond. He logged continual bad weather. On the seventeenth he recorded, "I could sleep happily enough if I were only sure of my mooring. My life is in no danger, but I should lose my boat and all my equipment including my month's painting, if that old mooring let go."*

Three days later, at nine in the evening, a fisherman told Lathrop that the radio had reported a hurricane[9] north of Cape Hatteras and he made an immediate run for the lee shore. The next morning, September 21, the barometer fell to 29-65 and by one o'clock it was 29-36. Lathrop logged: "The

wind is ferocious. Two big trawlers have just come in to hug the eastern hills for shelter, others are here or coming." An hour-and-a-half later Will Lathrop wrote in large shaky letters the last entry he would ever make in his log: "Bar. 29!!" After the storm Widge *was found high and dry on the opposite side of the harbor; the log and latest painting were still on board. Lathrop's body[10] was later recovered from the marshes.*

NOTES

1. *Landscape painter:* While a young man, Lathrop had worked as a printmaker and watercolorist, providing illustrations for *Harper's* and *Century* magazines in the 1880s. By the end of his career he was considered an Impressionist. His paintings are included in the collections of the National Gallery of American Art, Corcoran Gallery of Art and Phillips Collection in Washington, D. C., The Pennsylvania Academy, the Philadelphia Museum of Art, the Metropolitan Museum of Art in New York City and the James A. Michener Art Museum in Doylestown, Pennsylvania, among others.

2. *Slade Dale*: F. Slade Dale was a noted New Jersey yachtsman and writer for boating magazines. He started out in 1927 selling outboard motors in Bay Head and twenty years later the huge Dale Yacht Basin was known up and down the coast.

3. *Hawser:* A heavy line, five inches or over, used for setting out an anchor.

4. *Spiling:* a group or mass of piles.

5. *Parrals:* A band of wooden balls, traditionally of lignum vitae, that connect the jaws of a gaff before the mast.

6. *Radio man:* In the 1930s and 1940s radio broadcaster Lowell Thomas ended his evening news show with "So long until tomorrow."

7. *HBS and Elizabeth:* Harry B. Snell was a fellow painter; Elizabeth was Lathrop's daughter.

8. *Gale:* Lathrop noted in his log that this severe northeaster completely wrecked the Keyport boatyard and that "the poor man" went out of business. This storm caused extensive damage all along the coast. It rolled 10-ton rocks out of the breakwater at the Manasquan River; cut a 250-foot inlet through Island Beach; destroyed the Pennsylvania Railroad bridge across Barnegat Bay to Long Beach Island; and washed out homes and damaged boardwalks from Cape May to Long Branch.

9. *Hurricane:* The 1938 hurricane raced north from Hatteras at 60 mph. The eye passed somewhat to the west of Montauk, placing *Widge* in the hurricane's most destructive northeast quadrant. The storm surge crossed Long Island Sound and submerged Providence, Rhode Island, under thirteen feet of water. Winds were clocked at 182 mph as the storm hit New England. Finally, 680 persons died and 19,000 homes were destroyed.

10. *Lathrop's body:* According to Lathrop's grandson, William L. Bauhan, a trawler might have inadvertently cut one of *Widge's* two mooring lines. The family speculates that Lathrop might have tried to swim ashore.

From the ship's log of William L. Lathrop, printed with the permission of William L. Bauhan.

1933
Atlantic City

Anonymous

Atlantic City Boardwalk Crushed by Surf. In the uptown section, showing how the heavy seas, lashed by a 65-mile-an-hour wind, uprooted the boards and twisted the railing.

Atlantic City Damage

WITH the wind reaching a velocity of 64 miles an hour at noon, and with 10 inches of rain already fallen by evening and the end nowhere in sight, Atlantic City yesterday watched helplessly while the northeaster continued to vent its fury on the resort city.

It was impossible to begin to estimate the damage, so vast and so widespread it was. The wind was blowing early in the evening at approximately 50 miles an hour and driving before it in a blinding spray a heavy rain.

The ocean was heaving and tossing as though tormented by demons, and was hurling giant waves up over the Boardwalk in some places

off from the mainland because high water on the meadows made it impossible for trains to get across.

This was denied emphatically by the railroads, and to prove the denial, trains moved in and out of the resort on fairly regular schedule.

Street cars, however, fared much worse. They were stalled all over the city, in some cases because of water in the motors, in others because of breaks in the power lines.

Motorists Stranded

An unmounted number of automobiles suffered similar fate on the streets in the city when their engines coughed and died and the drivers and occupants str...

This newspaper clipping, dated August 24, 1933, is from a scrapbook of storm reports gathered between 1903 and 1938.

More weather disturbances were recorded in 1933 than in any previous year; it was a bonanza year for northeasters and hurricanes. On the day that "E" wrote this letter, the Weather Bureau issued northeast storm warnings along the Atlantic seaboard, advising of a "disturbance of unusually great intensity" moving up the coast; another newspaper called it a "northeast hurricane." Although the Weather Bureau advisory did not use the word hurricane, a Philadelphia Bulletin *headline blared: "Hurricane Roaring Down New Jersey Coast." What the writer of this letter was experiencing was an extraordinarily bad northeaster; but what "E" didn't know as he or she was writing it was that within days the tail end of a real hurricane would give the coast a double-whammy.*

August 23: Dear Mom,

Don't worry about the reports of our hurricane. They say the out of town papers are making quite a fuss about it. The local papers try to make it sound as small as possible. It was the biggest thing of its kind I ever saw. It really started last Thursday and isn't entirely over yet. The rainfall has been tremendous, with the ocean rampaging around the streets every high tide. The water got into the cellars of all the ocean-front hotels. At the Claridge, which is 22 stories high, the water got into the elevator pit so they couldn't run the elevator without danger of drowning, so the people that couldn't walk to their rooms had to camp in the lobby. The gardens at the Marlborough were two feet deep in water when I passed on Tuesday; goodness knows where they are now. They said no one could get in or out of the Brighton yesterday.

The ocean was the handsomest thing I've seen for a long time, regular mountains of waves. Yesterday the wind struck us, blowing 75 miles an hour all day, and rain with it. Two big trees up the street were pulled up by the roots, taking a cement pavement with them. A jitney bus at our corner was picked up by the wind and literally thrown across the street. At about four o'clock in the afternoon the electric wires all down Pacific Avenue started to explode. From my window it made the most gorgeous display of fireworks, as I can see for blocks along the street, but for an hour or so anyone going out was in danger of being electrocuted as the live wires were switching about all over the street like spitting snakes. Sign boards were flying through the air. The second story balcony at Craig Hall, a block from us, blew into the street. It really was an exciting day.

I got out for breakfast with Miss Mills before the worst of the storm began. I had a chocolate bar and some popcorn in my room and thought that would do for lunch, but at twelve o'clock Mrs. Blakesley came upstairs carrying a tray with creamed chip-beef, sliced tomatoes, bread and butter and a pot of tea — wouldn't let me pay for it.

By supper time the rain had stopped, and I got across to the little restaurant where we have breakfast and got my supper by candle-light — all electricity in town being turned off. Miss Mills worked in the evening and, when she came home at 9:30 we bundled up and fought the wind down to the Boardwalk to look at the ocean. The wind had changed its direction, however, and the waves were not nearly so high as they were earlier in the week. If it is safe this afternoon, which is Miss Mills' afternoon off, we are going to walk down to the Inlet and see the damage. They say a large part of the Boardwalk is torn up there, and that the waves washed in the second-story windows of the apartment houses. Love, E.

Anonymous letter, printed with the permission of the Atlantic County Historical Society.

1934
Long Beach Island

Joseph C. Eckert, Jr.

The Beach Haven Terrace railroad station as it appeared 15 years before Joe Eckert rented it.

The Great Depression was bottoming out in the summer of 1934, but economic activity was, at best, minimal. Unemployment was high and summer jobs on Long Beach Island were as rare as foul weather gear on a sunny day. Although Beach Haven had a boardwalk, hotels and regular summer visitors, the rest of the island was mostly undeveloped, with miles of dunes to the east and bay marshes to the west of the narrow roadway that connected the string of small communities.

Joseph C. Eckert, Jr. had been coming to the island since he was a baby; his mother's family had built one of the first summer homes in Surf City. In 1934 he graduated from high school and came to the shore in search of work. His young Uncle Al answered Joe's prayers: he offered him a job at the Brant Beach Ice Company. With his newly minted driver's license, Joe could have his own ice delivery route. In addition, he could moonlight helping another friend, Al Arbuckle, truck fish up to the New York market.

On one special occasion, Al [Arbuckle] asked me to accompany him to New York as his helper. Since I had never seen Manhattan, I was delighted to accept.

The trip went well. About 2 A.M. we rolled through the Jersey City docks and aboard a Manhattan-bound ferry. In a moment or two we were underway, and that darkened but unmistakable silhouette came into view. How can I describe my feelings as the panorama unfolded? I just gazed in awe at the spectacular skyline as we glided across the dark waters and, to a rippling rhapsody of night sounds and harbor sounds, nestled against the dynamic heart of all the world. It was far more than a thrill. It was a once-in-a-lifetime experience. Perhaps I have attained a unique place in history as the first and only human whose first view of Manhattan was from a fish truck at two in the morning!

Soon we were bouncing over the cobblestones of the Battery and approaching the renowned Fulton Fish Market made famous by the cigar-smoking "Little Warrior" Al Smith. I was enthralled by the sights and smells as the unfamiliar drama of nightlife in the great metropolis came alive under my eyes. Union crews unloaded us with dispatch so that by three-thirty we were retracing our route. Al handled the Baby Mack very well. By five we were well down Route Nine and into open country. Suddenly Al pulled over on the shoulder of the road saying, "Joe, I'm tired. Take her in." I was flabbergasted as I was but 17.

Changing places, I took over, and not without considerable trepidation pulled out into the traffic lane. The darkness cloaked my nervousness in a merciful anonymity and I soon achieved a certain amount of confidence, particularly when I noticed that Al had fallen asleep, evidenced by the tell-tale noises emanating from the huge form braced against the opposite cab door. We hummed right along, slowed for Lakewood at first light, and again at Toms River at dawn. The balance of the trip was uneventful, and Al dropped me off just in time to start out on my day's run on the ice wagon.

I was very happily situated that year living with Al [Eckert] and my grandmother in Brant Beach. But as the season progressed the economic outlook worsened and my grandmother rented her beautiful cottage for the first time. By the time she climbed aboard a bus bound for the city and a visit with her daughter, Al had solved our acute personal housing shortage. What a resourceful guy! He not only found quarters for us, but free ones.

Admittedly, I was more than a little skeptical when I heard about his alleged bargain. However, it was just that — a tiny cottage of weather-beaten natural shingles facing the boulevard in Beach Haven Terrace. The interior consisted of a single, good-sized room. Windows on all four sides assured a continuous cross-ventilation from the ever-present and ever-refreshing sea breezes. There was a small lavatory which partitioned off one corner of the room, two vintage cots, a pair of nondescript chairs, a tiny table, and a much-used square of linoleum on the wooden floor. The window screens had reached a stage of advanced deterioration just short of complete disintegration. However, it was clean, orderly and cool. It was also well-lighted — in the daytime, that is, for there was no electricity. The long hours of daylight and a couple of flashlights solved that problem.

Over in another corner was a small icebox, but cooking facilities were as nonexistent as were the screens. We wondered who designed such a peculiar cottage, but the strange architecture became obvious when I learned that until a few years before, it had functioned as the Beach Haven Terrace railroad depot.

Mainland farms kept our little refrigerator well supplied with fresh milk and berries which, with cold cereal, added up to adequate breakfasts. Bread and luncheon meats from the Acme in Ship Bottom provided the makings for our midday snacks, after completion of our daily routes. Thanks to Al — the original Mr. Fixit — we enjoyed one good, cooked meal each evening. He accomplished this by making a "special arrangement" with Mrs. Pierce who operated Pierce's Restaurant in Ship Bottom. Mrs. Pierce was an upright, motherly woman and an excellent cook. She had opened the small dining room in an effort to eke out a living in those difficult days. "Captain" Pierce, her wiry, weatherworn husband, had retired from the sea. He occupied his time with the operation of an automobile garage near the restaurant. Private garages were rare in 1934. Proud automobile owners endeavored to preserve their vehicles from the ravages of salt air and wind-whipped sand.

Al had negotiated a very satisfactory deal. For a nominal fee, she would provide each of us with one dinner daily. As part of the deal, we ate at a large table in the kitchen of the restaurant, and she preferred that we come in before or after the peak traffic hour. Menu selection was no problem at all; we were served generous portions of whatever was in abundance at the time and I, at least, thrived on it. The homemade blueberry pies more than made up for the all-too-frequent small boiled potatoes.

Mrs. Pierce and I hit it off very well. Consequently, later in the season when my grandmother again succeeded in renting her cottage, Mrs. Pierce offered me the use of a very small room over the restaurant. After putting Grandma on a bus for another visit with relatives, I found myself with suitcase and alarm clock in hand climbing the long, long stairs to my new home.

A tiny chest quickly swallowed my meager belongings. Slipping off my gravel-stained shoes, I stretched out on the foldaway cot and glanced about me. My new "pad" was austerely furnished with all the simplicity of a sterile YMCA room; in addition to the bed and chest, there was only a gently flapping shade at the solitary window and a couple of chattering coat hangers on the back of the door. A five-and-ten paper wastebasket stood in a corner with a dust pan and brush alongside — a gentle hint that I was expected to gather up the inevitable sand and keep the room tidy.

The decor was definitely "seashore plain," as plain as a Franciscan's cell and just as appropriate for meditation. I stared at a lazy fly motionless on the ceiling, and reflected upon my extremely fortunate lot. For the first time I realized what it meant to have a good home and wonderful parents. Nor had I fully appreciated until then the extraordinary compatibility of three such unlike persons as my grandmother, my uncle and me. And for the very first time, too, I understood how full the world was with wonderful people — people like the Pierces who were so willing to share with another what little they possessed. It occurred to me that I would not have exchanged that little room for the finest suite. It was a most relaxing thought. The fly, I observed, was still dozing on the ceiling. With that, I dropped off into a dreamless slumber.

Papers of Joseph C. Eckert, Jr., printed with the permission of Nancy Eckert.

1936
The Sea Islands

Cornelius Weygandt

Mounds of ice piled up on the Cape May beach during the frigid winter of 1935-1936.

Cornelius Weygandt was a Pennsylvanian, an English language professor at the University of Pennsylvania, who said that having South Jersey next door was a real asset. He could turn there for "refreshment of body and heart, for health and recreation, for sea air and wide horizons, for good food and the lightening of what weighs on the spirit of man." When a child, Weygandt contracted typhoid fever and was sent to Atlantic City, where he gained strength from the "tonic air." As a young man he visited Beach Haven, Barnegat Light, Anglesea (North Wildwood) and Cape May. He sailed catboats, trolled for *bluefish in both gales and moonlight calms, and admitted that he was not a devotee of surf bathing or boardwalks. But what he loved best is obvious in the following chapter from his classic book,* Down Jersey.

In another generation the barrier islands off the Jersey coast will have wholly lost their glory. It is too much to hope that the State or the Nation will intervene and preserve certain stretches of strand and dunes, bayberry flats and stands of red cedar, holly thickets and salt marsh, as representative of the beauty our coast had for miles on miles down to a generation ago. Save for Atlantic City itself, the resorts had made few inroads upon the original condition of the islands in the days of my youth. From Seaside Park to Cape May, there was no resort save that on Absecon Beach that had wholly obliterated the charm our eastern littoral had for hunters and fishermen and summer folks during the two hundred years that European civilization had been established in this part of our country. And even here on Absecon Island, there were wonderful stands of aboriginal forest between Longport and Atlantic City. There were no Chelseas or Ventnors then, and Longport was but a huddle of houses. Fish hawks nested in these old trees and the ravens that had for generations raised their young just out of Pleasantville might be met on the beach on early mornings in summer and on winter noons as one walked where Ventnor and Chelsea are now.

The only long stretches left as waves and wind had made them are the southern portion of Island Beach from below Seaside Park to Barnegat Inlet, certain stretches, south of that inlet, on Long Beach. The sea and fire have done what they could to clear the immediate neighborhood of Barnegat Light of man-made ugliness, and by some chance the gnarled cedars and dunes have here been spared. The great lighthouse composes as beautifully as it did in my childhood with the great banks of grey sand about it and with the green hollies and the white-fruited bayberries, the andromeda and red cedars. A little to the south of Barnegat City, and along by Lovelady's, and for sections even down to High Point [Harvey Cedars] there is the old sweep of heath from the salt marsh to the sand hills just above high water mark.

As a child it was in summer I knew this end of Long Beach, but nowadays I love what is left of it best in winter. I have not forgotten the pink mallows and the roses as pink I picked with salt spray on them on the low dunes between the cedars and the sea. I found the same stand of roses, only the other day, where I had known them more than fifty years earlier. On the second of January, nineteen hundred and thirty-six, there was some two feet of snow about that bank of thorny stems, rosebushes of strong growth with their hips deep carmine against the whiteness of the snow. As I pottered about under the dunes trusting juncos continued their thrashing out of grass seeds from the tufts too tall for the drifts to cover. The cheering colors of the red cedars, the brightness of their boles, the dark greens and bronzes and clouded purples of their foliage, so took me I paid scant heed to the birds and missed the cat whose fresh track changing from the one paw mark after another to isolated groups of paw marks together, showed we had scared her off. I should have liked to note whether she was a bobtail. When I was a boy Manx cats bounced about in these thickets as if they were rabbits.

The sea had been forbidding to look at. There was little surf. Offshore were no whitecaps, only the roll on roll of wind-driven water making toward the beach and into the inlet which had for so long threatened to undermine the lighthouse.[1] The tide fairly raced by the stone pier thrown out to protect the foundations, and past the bulkhead of interlocking steel so close to its walls. Old automobiles, junked for years, had been brought here and thrown into the inlet to help hold the sand. They had served their purpose. Most of them were buried in sand, which they held from washing away.

It had been dropping rain all the time we had been poking about. Offshore that rain made a mirk on the water. No ships were in sight, only rolling water disappearing in the distance under the dimness. It was not fog, but just the falling rain making a curtain of fold after fold that finally ended one's vision eastward. You could just see the southern end of Island Beach across the inlet. A far skirling of gulls made itself faintly manifest, and grew in volume. A dory with outboard motor, towing a fellow, shot out of the dimness. Although the dories seemed to be going fast, the gulls could easily keep ahead of them, though they were revolving about the two boats in long ellipses. The dory that was towing dropped its tow, leaving the two men in it trying to crank their motor and to keep their hand pump going. Most of the gulls dropped into the water well away from the crippled boat.

As we idled back to our car in the idly falling rain, small birds began to drift across our path from the bayberries and willows and andromedas by the water side into the briars and smilax, the hollies and red cedars, of the rising dunes. There were white-throats among them, and a bouncing big fox sparrow, smaller sparrows that should have been seasides and sharp tails, and a tail-dipping plump bird with a white or yellow patch on its rump that I could not identify. It was too large for a myrtle warbler. At first glance I thought it was a pewee but it was not. There was a downy woodpecker in the group, and a bird as big as a robin that kept too far away and too close to the ground for identification. The rain seemed to delight them. It was not a warm rain, but no cold wind accompanied its falling, and it was no doubt grateful to them after the snowstorm of Sunday night and Monday that had covered the ground eight inches deep, and after the week of intense cold that had frozen Barnegat Bay[2] solid from shore to shore.

As we had gotten out of our car we had seen a big duck bobbing about on the waters of the inlet just offshore. As we returned to our car he was close inshore with his missus, both as tame as could be. The white on his sides made him look like a scaup, but I am not sure of his species. I was not near enough to him to pick out the blue bill that is his distinguishing characteristic. In the light in which we saw them we could note no white on the female.

The bird life on land and water was doubly cheery because of the rain falling and the dullness of mirky sea and sodden snow. The ducks looked snug as snug on the icy water. The gulls minded it no more than the air that was about them as they circled the boats. Icy rain in the air, icy water in the inlet were one to them. Their inward fire and their thick coat of oily feathers made them immune to all cold. The high temperature of the smaller birds kept them warm within their thinner and less oily coats of feathers.

There is hidden warmth and light everywhere on these heathy rolls of sand. There is a redness where andromedas predominate, but the grey black of the beach plum stems takes on an unaccountable purplish glow. The holly leaves glitter in the rain. The grass on the top of the dunes, a chill wheaten close to hand, warms to a low-toned greenish yellow where you catch it against the sky. Sand heath and all the other groundlings are too deep in snow to show at all, but despite the greying the rain brings to the landscape there are faint streaks of blue in the inequalities of the snow-covered dunes. Greys and whites, purples and dull reds, wheaten browns and the dune-top yellows all dull a monotone as the light lessens before the thickening rain. It is nearly a downpour now, but it thins again, the landscape lightens and the low tones disassociate themselves from the dull monotones. The roll of sea island eastward to the dune-tops is grey and white again, purple and reddish, wheaten and greenish yellow. Through a break in the dunes you catch again the leaden sea dimming off shore. You see no breakers, the dunes are so high they cut off the shore. You see just the leaden ocean and the mirk gathered over it.

Conditions are worse on the sea islands south of Long Beach. On a round of Brigantine Beach, Absecon Beach, Peck's Beach, Ludlam's Beach, Seven Mile Beach and Five Mile Beach I found in only three places, and each of limited extent, the beaches and dunes and salt marsh as I had once known them.

There was little left of what Brigantine used to be, no dunes, and no great patches of bayberry and beach plum. Only the strand was left. Everywhere everything was levelled because of bungalow building, or preparatory to bungalow building. There was nothing of the old forest between Atlantic City and Longport that I knew so well, that forest of old gnarled cedars and hollies and oaks. On Peck's Beach below Ocean City there was a stretch of virgin country, rather flat, that ran up to the base of the dunes, and then the low rise of those dunes themselves. There were no high dunes. There were numerous dips between the dunes through which you could see the ocean. On Ludlam's Beach, at Strathmere, there was just a little bit of low dune-land with sea-sand reed sparsely covering it. The first place that we struck a sample of the old beach preserved from yesterday was at Townsend's Inlet, the south end of Ludlam's Beach. Here there was a great dune to the right of the road almost at the island's end, a high dune with gnarled cedars and pines and sea-sand reed.

It was at the south end of Seven Mile Beach below Stone Harbor that we came on a real bit of the old seaside forest preserved. This was a forest of red cedar and holly, bayberry bushes and beach plums. The bayberry bushes and beach plums were, of course, not forest proper but outlying extensions of the forest proper, the forest of cedars and hollies. It was a bright day, bitterly cold, and of flooding sun. The hollies fairly glittered in the profusion of light and the cedars drank in the light and seemed transfused with it. They glowed almost palpitantly in that largess of light. It may be we enjoyed the forest more in that only a few acres of it remained. I hardly dare guess how much but perhaps ten to twelve acres. There were a few other places in which there were little stands of red cedars, maybe an acre here and two acres there. In the largest of these patches below Sea Isle City we saw a flicker. It looped across the road and lit in the top of a tall cedar.

One has to content himself with saying that though the glory of the dunes has departed, the sky and the sea remain unchanged and much of the broad salt marsh to landward. Year by year the bungalows creep farther over the few unoccupied acres along the sea islands. In another ten years, unless the government restricts a copse here or a stretch of sand dunes there, there will be nothing but bungalows and wharves and boardwalks on these once so beautiful stretches of dune-land and shore. When we had the beauty of the sea islands in old years we hardly realized it to the full. They hadn't been painted enough or celebrated enough in writing or enjoyed enough by the people who went to the seaside to give them a place in the affections of people and in the honoring that comes eventually to whatever takes a place in the affections of people. To me as a child they were places in which to play, in which to hide from other children, in which to suffer martyrdom from green flies and mosquitoes. I remember, too, how the sharp sea-sand reed and grass cut my bare legs. I remember how easy it was to be tripped by sand heath and by grass that had been looped by blowing sand so that it made a perfect snare for the feet.

Our February day of 1936 was a day of gulls and ducks and geese. I had seen hundreds of gulls in this place and in that before, but I had never before seen them in thousands on thousands. They were never out of sight over the long stretch from Brigantine to Five Mile Beach. Everywhere there were gulls, in the air, on the water, on the strand. At Brigantine the gulls were in the sea sliding slowly up the beach. They were floating so close to shore that when the waves receded they were left standing on their feet. There must have been seventy to a hundred of them here, some a few feet from the edge of the tide, some standing in the shallow water, some floating on the sea just off where it slid ashore. There were no breakers anywhere, no breakers as far as the eye could reach, not a whitecap on the sea. All the ocean was so quiet that when it came up on the beach it just rippled in. There was no smell of salt, for the wind was offshore. There was a wall of snow perhaps three feet high at high water mark at the foot of where the dunes once were. The levelling of the dunes has unquestionably brought about many of the inroads of the sea. The winds heaped up the dunes and the sea-sand reed rooted deep in them and knit them into solid walls that could withstand all but the severest storms. Nature took better care of man in throwing up the dunes that were a protection to the houses he built than he has been able to take by building sea walls and breakwaters. In many places up and down the coast we saw cottages that had been undermined and toppled into ruins, or thrown about in confusion, or carried in and left stranded quite a distance back from the ocean.

The beach at Brigantine where the sea was coming in so quietly was just one mass of shells. I have never seen so many anywhere. Perhaps the gulls were getting some sea creatures in those shells. They would dip down their bills every once in a while and when they were left standing as the tide lapsed they would poke down and eat something from the wet sand. They made very little noise. We didn't hear half a dozen skirls from these here or from their fellows farther down the coast. The bitter cold perhaps took the joy of life out of them so they didn't make that wild crying that always opens up such wide and lonely stretches of sea as it falls upon one's ears. In many places the gulls were hunched up on the ice. Except at the inlets, the bays and thoroughfares were everywhere frozen over, Little Egg Harbor, Great Egg Harbor, and the narrower bays back of Ludlam's Beach. The gulls huddled down so their feathers would cover their feet, but even at that it must have been very cold for those feet on that salt water ice. Their heads always pointed toward the wind coming in from the west. They were most of them in the adult plumage, very few brown or sooty birds were seen all day long.

There were so few unfrozen spaces in the thoroughfares that wherever we found one it was full of gulls or ducks. The ducks were almost all of them scaups, both the lesser and the greater scaup. We saw, too, offshore in the sea, some kind of fish duck, but whether sheldrakes or old wives I couldn't tell at the distance. We saw no geese on the water but again and again we saw their V's making from the sea toward, I supposed, the open tide creeks inland. We saw two straggling bunches of ducks flying here and there, but of what kind I am too much of a tyro to know. Some of these ducks were very tame. As we would run over the bridges or along the causeways between the sea islands and the mainland, they would be in whatever patch of water was unfrozen. In places we could have easily tossed a pebble on their backs. The gulls were even tamer, allowing us to come within fifty feet of them before they would take to the water or flop away.

I can remember old years at Atlantic City when the ocean was frozen out for at least a quarter of a mile and beyond that ducks in the open water. That was forty years ago. Once in those same old years I walked up the beach from Longport to Atlantic City when the ocean was similarly frozen. Then, too, there were immense congeries of ducks just beyond the ice. There were more ducks offshore on that walk than there were of the gulls in their thousands we saw this second of February.

Of all the beaches Five Mile Beach has been treated most roughly by man. There is nothing left of the old beauty of dunes and cedars from Anglesea down to Wildwood Crest. The dunes have been levelled and the cedars destroyed. I remember as a boy looking south from Anglesea toward Holly beach, and seeing the cattle, the wild cattle, standing in the waves, forty of them at least. Behind them I remember a great tangled wood of gnarled cedars and hollies. That has been cleaned away to the last tree. The only interesting thing that we saw on Five Mile Beach was the frozen slip into which the fishing boats come. They were frozen in solid here, most of them two-masters. It was very picturesque, this acreage of masts sticking up above white hulls frozen fast in the ice.

There were many men clamming through the ice along the causeways from mainland to sea islands by which we crossed to and from Seven Mile Beach and Five Mile Beach. In some cases they had already cut holes through the ice and were raking out the clams. In other places, one man would be chopping with an axe to make a new hole while another man would be raking out clams from the hole already made. It was interesting to see, with the tide out, the ice bent down but not broken in the ditches and thoroughfares.

One of the curious effects offshore was of frozen ice on the pilings of the fish weirs.[3] We couldn't make out at first what it was. I thought all this whiteness out to sea must be sails, but it didn't look like sails. It was diagnosed properly as ice frozen on the pilings of the fish weirs, but not by me.

It was strange to see turkey buzzards along Seven Mile Beach and Five

Mile Beach. I had seen them often, of course, in the mainland in South Jersey, but never before had I seen them on the sea islands. More than once we saw a bird over the very beach and in some instances one was taking a short cut across the sea from one side of a cove to another. There were crows, too, about on the beach, but no raven among them. We saw very few beach sparrows, either seaside or sharp tails.

The very best of what is left of the sea islands of yesterday is the stretch south from Seaside Park. Man has encroached less on this tumbled dune-land than on any other part of the sea front of New Jersey. There still you may see the white sails of an occasional schooner standing offshore, there are fish nets drying in the sun, there the beach plums break into bloom of stabbing white from black twigs and compose themselves with sure mastery against backgrounds of cedarn purple and bronze and dark green. There is as true a heath as any you will find on Long Island, or Nantucket, or Cape Cod. There you may forget that all the coast islands are not as this retreat of loveliness. There the scents of pine and salt marsh, of sand bogs and plum blossom mix with that of the sea in an elixir that sloughs the years from your shoulders. There in the April freshness your heart is the heart of a boy.

NOTES

1. *Undermine the lighthouse:* In August 1933, after a series of destructive storms eroded the surrounding land, the water was only five feet away from Barnegat Lighthouse.

2. *Frozen Barnegat Bay:* During the several months that the bays were frozen during the frigid winter of 1935-1936, "thousands upon thousands" of wildfowl were fed corn by the government, often dropped by Navy blimps out of the Lakehurst Naval Air Station. In some places the ice measured 37 inches thick. The cold winter had been predicted when icebergs were spotted in June by anglers fishing on the Barnegat Ridge, the fishing grounds 18 miles offshore.

3. *Fish weirs:* Fish pounds were set up two to three miles offshore in about 36 feet of water. To hold the heavy nets, 30 or 40 huge poles of North Carolina hickory, nearly 90 feet long, were used. Half of them stood in the sandy floor in a straight line running perpendicular to the shore for 1,600 feet, or about five city blocks. A series of long, weighted nets reaching to the bottom were strung out along these poles to form what was called the "leader line." The remaining poles were grouped to form the pound, an enclosure 50 feet square with a big net hung to form a pocket. The pound net had a bottom to it and a narrow funnel opening, which the fish could enter but from which they could not usually escape. Fish swimming along the coast would encounter the barrier of the east-west net. Instinctively heading for deeper water to get around this fence-like obstruction, they would be led into the heart-shaped funnel net and finally into the pocket. (*Eighteen Miles of History on Long Beach Island,* John Bailey Lloyd, Down The Shore Publishing/The SandPaper, 1994)

From *Down Jersey, Folks and Their Jobs, Pine Barrens, Salt Marsh and Sea Islands,* D. Appleton-Century, New York and London, 1940.

1940
Harvey Cedars

Dorothea Sjostrom

Carl Sjostrom and house guests in the surfboat he built. Dick Smith, back from the war, is standing.

🔲 *Dorothea Smith and her husband bought a small summer cottage in Harvey Cedars in 1928, but the next year he died, leaving the young widow with three small children, Dick, Dorothea and Steve. Five years later Dorothea married a naval architect, Carl Sjostrom, and in 1935 they bought an undeveloped ocean-to-boulevard tract at a borough tax sale. In her book, Dick Smith, Bomber Pilot, Dorothea Sjostrom wrote, "We stood up on the sand dune overlooking the ground, and both of us decided we could not hope to do better. Back to the Borough Hall we dashed and in fifteen minutes we had made our first payment." The whole family planned the cottage and drove down from Philadelphia during the winter to check its progress. Eventually, with two bunk rooms, one for girls and one for boys, they had enough space for 20 people at a time. For the next several summers the family used the new house to the fullest, packing it with guests every weekend until the United States entered World War II, and the oldest son, Dick, went off to war. The following excerpt is from the book Dorothea wrote after her son, who had been listed as "killed in action," turned up alive and well in Australia.*

Coming to Harvey Cedars week ends always means a lot of bustle and confusion on Fridays. We shop on Thursday so that Mrs. Ryan can prepare the food for our traditional Friday night supper at the Cottage — hamburg stew, little new potatoes, peas, hot rolls and devil's food cake. The stew is put in jars, the number of jars depending on the crowd that is going with us. The little new potatoes are cooked and tenderly wrapped in wax paper and the peas and rolls are ready to be warmed when we get down there. No trip is complete without one of Mrs. Ryan's devil's food cakes. We also take all the other food we will need for the week end except sea food which can be had in abundance on the Island.

This particular week end we had to provide certain frills and luxuries because of Dick's party and, to add to the general confusion, we also had to bring down summer formals for the men and evening dresses for the girls. Fortunately Dick had his car and we had ours, so not only was there extra luggage space, but there was no necessity for our usual fight about who should drive. Ever since Dick got his license there was always a rush for the driver's seat. Sometimes I would make it and sometimes he would.

The appearance of our living room just before we left would make one think that a great number of people were about to go on a long journey. As I stood in the doorway to greet Carl I could not believe that even two cars would hold all this.

"Carl, do you think we'll ever get them into the cars?"

"Yes, surely," Carl soothingly replied. "Nothing to it."

His eyes roved over the bags and boxes of food piled near the door; the ten suitcases of various sizes scattered around the room; the evening jackets swinging on their hangers from door knobs, lamps and curtain rods. It took us an hour longer than usual to stow everything into the luggage compartments, but we did get everything in, finally.

No matter how often we go it is always thrilling when we turn into our own lane and drive up to the parking space back of the house. (For years as we came in sight of the Coast Guard Station the children would start to sing "We're here because we're here" and keep it up until the car stopped.) Then all doors fly open and we emerge and make a rush for the boardwalk to get the first view of the ocean. We have much to see — whether the beach has changed, if the ocean is coming any closer to our precious sand dunes[1], how much the dusty miller has spread since we were down last, and whether the wind has done any noticeable damage. This inspection completed, Carl unlocks the front door. We troop into the living room and look around as if we were seeing it for the first time. It is new and wonderful to us.

After we realize we are really here, the unpacking begins. The bags are brought in the front door and left in the living room but all the food is brought up through the cellar and placed on the kitchen counter. I try to put it away as fast as it is brought up but I don't succeed, as I am also getting the food for our supper into the oven.

Now everyone is assigned to his room, bags and owners have disappeared from the living room. In about fifteen minutes we are ready for supper. No more city slickers! We are all clad in shorts and slacks. The girls this time had lots of fun getting the evening dresses hung in one closet and everyone was called in to see this array of finery, indeed a novelty down here. Dresses are usually something we arrive in and do not use again until we are about to depart.

We had lots of fun this night before Dick's birthday; everyone was in the best of spirits. We didn't have time for any long discussions around the table. Dick got up as soon as the last cigarette was lighted.

"Let's get the dishes done and some games started."

"Stage Coach!"

"No, Musical Instruments!"

"Numbers!"

We played all of them until exhaustion drove us to bed about midnight.

We have a ship's gong in our living room which is rung about half an hour before breakfast and the word "swimming" is yelled upstairs. All who wish, go for a dip. Our own family has always done this even when the weather seemed much too cold to most of our guests. Saturday started with a dip for most of us.

Carl had his surfboat and Dick, who gets seasick on fishing trips, had lots of fun taking Nancy, his particular date, and some of the other girls out through the breakers and riding them in on a long wave. Going out is more thrilling but not so speedy as coming back, because the boat rises almost perpendicularly into the air and you think everyone is going to be thrown out when it comes down with a bang. We on shore probably squeal louder than those in the boat because it looks so exciting.

Last Labor Day, just after a northeaster, someone on the deck said that there was a person out in the very rough ocean. Carl told me to jump in the car and hurry down and ask the Coast Guard whether he could see what the object was through his glasses, which I did, calling up to the man in the tower. He told me it was just driftwood and to tell those fellows down there not to attempt to launch the boat as it was too rough. I hurried back to relay the message, but Dick and Carl were already beyond hearing. They had already safely launched the boat through the heavy breakers, and, while we watched, went out and inspected the so-called "man clinging to a plank." It was, as the Coast Guard had said, a drifting piece of bulkhead. Carl and Dick just as safely, but very thrillingly, returned to shore.

I often wonder what the tower man thought. They have the reputation of being able to go out in the boat when everyone else said it was positively unsafe. Dick is a fine specimen of young manhood — a little short of six feet tall, broad shoulders, very pleasing expression, with dark hair and eyes. Carl is about the same height, built on slimmer lines, but with the same broad shoulders. The two of them looked like something that came out of a Viking book as they emerged from the sea in their swimming trunks.

The rest of the day was spent on the beach, coming in long enough at lunch time to have snacks at the kitchen counter. Then came the excitement of dressing up for Dick's dinner party. Each person was greeted with "Ahs" and "Ohs" as he or she came down for dinner that night. We spent the whole evening dancing and we'll never forget how beautifully

Dick and Dash did the Swedish schottische[2] together. It was a joy to watch them. Dash is sixteen, slim, fair and rather grown-up for her age. Dick has always been devoted to "Sister" as he calls her. When she became "Dash" (because both our names are Dorothea and we changed to "Dot" and "Dash" for identification purposes) Dick never changed his way of addressing her. She has never been anything but "Sister" to him, and a very devoted brother and sister they have always been. When they danced the scottische together, with many attractive variations which they seemed to work up as they went along, the rest of us just sat and watched them. We all danced, changing off occasionally to a Virginia Reel or a Paul Jones, with intermissions up on deck to look at the moon and the stars.

We are always hungry down here and soon snacks were in order. To this day we tease Dick about how polluted he got on root beer and milk. Dick loves his milk. No meal is complete without milk. No snack ever tastes good unless he has milk. If he drinks root beer he drinks milk first, and this night of his twenty-first birthday he drank both. Before long he was doing a fine imitation of a drunken sailor. The party broke up when we told Dick we would have to put him to bed. Root beer and milk just about proved his undoing.

As we relaxed around the dinner table Sunday the conversation centered on the war and whether we were going to get involved or not, just as thousands of conversations around tables all over the country were doing at the same time.

"I don't see why we have to get into war," I said. "Here in this country we have Italians, French, Germans, English, Slavs, Russians — all living together peaceably. Because they can't get along together in Europe is no reason for us to get mixed up in that mess."

"But what can you do with a bunch of international gangsters like Hitler and Mussolini?"

"Whose fault is it they are in power? Have you read Van Paasen's[3] *Days of Our Years*?"

"Here we go again," said Dick. "You and Sister read *Inside Europe,* Van Paasen, Vincent Sheean[4], and you know all about it."

"If England, France and the United States too hadn't helped Germany re-arm, Hitler couldn't have become so strong. We could have stopped this business when Italy went into Ethiopia, or before that, when we put an embargo act on Spain, but let Germany and Italy have all the war materials they wanted. Look at France now. Greed! Greed! Greed! Every big business wants to sell its products — the heck with the results!" cried Dash.

"More Van Paasen, I suppose," said Dick. "Why do you worry your pretty little head about such things, Sister dear?"

"I like that," responded Dash indignantly, "just because I am a girl I'm not supposed to think."

"Now that Hitler is in, what do you think we ought to do — just let him run the world, conquer and kill innocent people?" Steve broke in.

"Does war settle anything?" I asked. "There is nothing that is settled around a peace table after all the lives have been lost that couldn't have been settled before the blood was shed. We had one war to end war, to make the world safe for democracy. What are we going to do this time? We think of Japan as a potential enemy and we ship her all our scrap iron. We know that if we fight it will be Germany and Italy, yet we sent arms and ammunitions to both countries to use against the Spanish Loyalists."

"Blood has already been shed. Do you think Hitler will listen to reason now? He has had a taste of victory and power. He has nearly all of Europe under his control. He will go on and on. Nothing can stop him now but force. That is the only language he knows," Stevie was beginning to wax eloquent.

"All right, suppose we do get into the war and we stop Hitler — what then?" I answered. "Unless every person takes an interest in world affairs, knows what is going on, we'll have this same trouble all over again. I certainly am opposed to the persecution of innocent peoples and I can't think of any fate bad enough for those Nazi cutthroats, but I still think wars are a question of greed and profits and I hate war and all it stands for. I believe if it were not for lazy thinking and the apathy of all of us such things could not exist."

"Yet you are willing to have Dick go into training in the Army. How does that fit in with these peace ideas of yours? You're a fine mother. Just want him to get killed, don't you?" interrupted Steve.

"Just because Dick is going to learn to be a pilot doesn't mean that he is going to fight."

"Well, what do you suppose the Army's training him for?"

"As far as that is concerned, we have been having National Guards for many years and the colleges have been training reserve officers. They are not all necessarily going to war."

"Even if they are," broke in Dick, "or if I am, or if we all get into war, I guess I can do my part. But there is no use discussing it now, Steve. We're down here to celebrate my birthday, not to get me killed off."

NOTES

1. *Our precious sand dunes:* The Sjostroms were well aware that the dunes protected their home and built a boardwalk over them, avoiding the erosion caused by constant traffic to the beach. The dunes eroded during a hurricane in 1944 and the house was lost during the Great March Storm of 1962.

2. *Swedish schottische:* A folk dance popularized by the Scandinavian fishing community in Barnegat Light.

3. *Pierre van Paasen:* Dutch writer and bitter foe of fascism, van Paasen was forced out of Europe in the 1930s. *Days of Our Years* (1939) wove political history with autobiographical reminiscences and was a best seller.

4. *Vincent Sheean:* Sheean was a European correspondent for the Chicago *Tribune* who reported the Fascist march on Rome. In 1939 he wrote *Not Peace but a Sword,* a denunciation of fascism.

From *Dick Smith, Bomber Pilot,* Beach Haven, 1944. Reprinted with the permission of Richard S. Smith.

1942
Atlantic City

Alyce Crow

When soldiers trained on the beach, Atlantic City became known as Camp Boardwalk.

After the stock market crash of 1929, Atlantic City had languished; but during the Depression a renewed Miss America pageant helped keep the aging resort on the list of American favorites, for those who could afford it. When the United States entered World War II in 1941, the city struggled to maintain its popularity.

The war created many hardships along the eastern seaboard and the Jersey Shore was no exception. From early in 1942 beaches up and down the coast were declared off limits from sunset to sunrise: the Coast Guard restricted night fishing and beach parties. Tankers were torpedoed close off shore — one only three miles beyond Long Beach Island — covering the white sandy beaches with slimy clots of oil and the detritus of sunken ships. Mounted troops patrolled the beaches with German shepherds, on the alert for spies attempting to land from Nazi U-boats. Observation blimps hovered overhead, ready to drop depth charges on enemy submarines.

The war also affected the shore's economy. Electricity was limited; dark, oilcloth shades covered windows on the east side of all structures; automobile head lamps were painted with black eyelids, and food and gasoline were rationed. Many residents planted victory gardens and sold any extra produce to those few cottagers down for the summer.

Blackouts dimmed Atlantic City's Boardwalk, and instead of tourists, some half-million servicemen were billeted in the hotels and marched and drilled on the Boardwalk. Many of those grand "shore palaces" were also converted to military hospitals, where thousands of servicemen went for rest and recreation.

Summer jobs were not plentiful in Ship Bottom, the Long Beach Island community where Alyce Crow lived. So in July 1942 the teenager took the bus to Atlantic City. Young women were quickly moving into jobs previously held by men — before the war hotel restaurants had hired mostly waiters and Alyce was eager to be where the action was. She had been educated at Westtown Friends School in Pennsylvania and decided — or perhaps her parents did — that Alyce had peddled clams door-to-door long enough; it was time for her to become a useful member of society.

For a while during the particular summer of which I am speaking, I had tended store in a small shop in Ship Bottom which sold beach novelties and salt water taffy and rented boats. I hadn't liked it. In addition to my fifty-four-hour work week behind the counter — for which I received the magnificent stipend of ten bucks a week — other little chores were gradually added. I cleaned windows. I washed the breakfast dishes. In about a week, I was washing the proprietor's dinner dishes from the previous day's meal. I was scraping boats, etc. etc. You get the picture.

To worsen matters, I was receiving many letters from friends who were all excited about what they were doing. One had gotten an excellent job at Arthur Murray's Dance Studio in Philly and was buying a load of spiffy new clothes to start her fall term in the Cathedral School of St. Mary's. Friend George Buzby was working for his folks at the Hotel Dennis in Atlantic City, with an eye to Cornell and a course in hotel management. Ditto Kirby White at the Marlborough-Blenheim. Ditto the Cope boys at the Hotel Morton. Ditto the Mott kids from the Traymore. Even "Pecky," my next door neighbor in boarding school, was working at the Morton in Atlantic City as a waitress. She lived in an atmosphere that wasn't really very different from our boarding school. All the waitresses, she wrote, lived in a dorm, complete with watchful housemother; endured a rest period every afternoon called "Quiet Hour" and were required to write a weekly letter home. But there was enough free time every day and evening to make the whole deal seem thrilling, and loads of servicemen were in town — this was really thrilling. Pecky made waitressing sound so fascinating that I decided this, by gosh, was for me, and she hinted, maybe there might be an extra serviceman around for me, too. This was the clincher.

I found a real cheap room in a boardinghouse owned by a friend of my mother's (three bucks a week with cooking and laundry privileges). I didn't have a watchful housemother, but I did have a whole boardinghouse full of people who were interested in my welfare. The scorned "Quiet Hour" became a welcome treat after a few weeks of Atlantic City waitress work. As for the weekly letter home, I was at first so homesick that I wrote a postcard home every day. (Boarding school all over again.) And I had felt so smug about being on my own!

I filled out application forms in every place on Atlantic and Pacific Avenues where there was a window sign which said Help Wanted. I first applied for a candy coating job. When the lady asked if I were experienced, I crossed my fingers behind my back and said, "Oh, sure," positive I could fake it if I were hired. Luckily I wasn't, for candy coating, I found out later, is not an easy job. I then applied to every five and ten cent store on the Boardwalk. The application blanks were miles long; the pay, the managers explained, was a princely eleven dollars for a fifty hour week. Still, what I really wanted was a waitress job. Finally I walked from the Boardwalk down toward Pacific Avenue and on one pleasant street I saw a small, friendly looking restaurant. It was called the Bluebird. Best of all, like the Bluebird of fable, it was practically in the back yard of my own rooming house. I walked inside and the proprietor was standing there, small and faintly foreign looking, smiling.

"Would you need any summer help?" I asked timidly.

"When can you start?" he asked me.

"I can start tomorrow morning," I said.

"Good. You be here nine o'clock in the morning. You work nine in the morning to two, five in the afternoon till eight thirty at night. Seven dollars for six day week, plus your tips. That sound okay to you? You wear any kind uniform you want. You bring apron, any kind you want. I see you tomorrow morning."

That was my introduction to Angie, a Greek, one of the sweetest persons I ever knew whose name I could never spell, even if I could remember what it was. Well, I had a job at the Bluebird. Whether this particular Bluebird was going to be a bluebird of happiness remained to be seen.

I learned a whole lot of things in mighty short order. The first one was that the great American public will head like homing pigeons for the one and only uncleared booth in the restaurant. The dirtier the better. Papa will happily sit for hours, if necessary, grinding his elbows in bread crumbs while Mama contents herself with flicking at said crumbs with a pocket handkerchief and looking disdainful. Why in heaven's name they just don't move to a clean booth is something I have never fathomed.

The second thing I learned was that the public will forgive anything — even hot soup being spilled on a good suit — if only the waitress approaches them with glasses of water as soon as they are seated, hands them menus shortly thereafter, and then walks away for a short time. This gives them time for adequate perusal of the menu and a chance to decide what they can afford. Still another thing I learned was that when a patron is so ill advised as to make any kind of a scene, the sympathy of the onlookers is always with the waitress. But the most important thing that I learned while at the Bluebird was that by and large, people are essentially kind, say all you will about the Detached American. For a bumbling, inexperienced waitress, all one needs to do to get her customer on her side is to whisper to them that she is brand new on the job, and nervous. In nine cases out of ten the customers will outdo themselves in making her feel comfortable, and will almost invariably leave her an extra big tip in the bargain. In those first few days, I bumbled, I spilled things, I mixed up orders, and still the all-forgiving American Public tipped me royally.

The old time professional waitresses taught me a lot, too. I learned to take an extra pair of shoes to work for a "change-off" to rest the feet and prevent corns. I learned that cornstarch beats any kind of body talc on the market in absorbing B.O. and preventing chafing. I learned that people who at home never give a dirty ketchup bottle top or an unwashed ashtray a second thought find these two things singularly oink-y and distasteful in a restaurant. I learned that prissy old men dining alone and wearing very good clothes are usually very poor tippers. Ditto jovial sweet-faced old ladies. I learned that the average white collar worker has them beat a country mile when it comes to lavish tipping. I learned that a penny left underneath a water glass, in addition to the regular tip, is customary among certain cultures, and is in silent praise of extra good service.

In my sublime ignorance, I even learned from one of those old-time waitresses how to "play the numbers," but I didn't have the vaguest notion that that's what I was doing. Atlantic City was especially wide open, for it was still the Nucky Johnson[1] era, and every corner tobacconist was headquarters for the numbers racket. All the waitresses took a few cents in tip money for bets. When years later I told my mother about this she hit the ceiling. I told her I just thought it was some kind of a raffle — and I honestly did. And the summer, as summers do, sped by. I arose at eight-thirty to get to work at nine. By two I was glad to crawl home, get a bath, and take a nap. At four-thirty I'd get up and start getting ready for the next part of my split shift. By five-thirty the people were standing in line for the dinner hour.

The menu featured home made soup, all the hot rolls and real butter one could eat, as much coffee as one could drink, generous portions of meat and vegetables, and a bevy of delicious homemade desserts. These included the best brown betty I ever tasted. The highest priced dinner on the menu was filet mignon for ninety cents. We could eat whatever we wanted at any time, and did we ever eat!

In the evening after work, there were lots of dates and walks on the Boardwalk, dances on the Steel Pier, amusements on the Million Dollar Pier, and the wonderful Old Time Movie House on the Walk which showed silent films. It was there that I saw the original Dracula and Phantom of the Opera.

All too soon the summer was over, and it was time to come home and start thinking about school again. I hadn't seen as much of Pecky as I thought I would, but once in a while we'd get together and go out on a double date. We'd discuss the people we waited on, and giggle about some of the characters. It never occurred to us that maybe some of them thought we were characters, too. And we promised ourselves that we'd take our same jobs the next summer, but we never did. We were too young to know that the First Summer Job is a once-in-a-lifetime thing, and you can never really go back again.

NOTE

1. *Nucky Johnson:* Former sheriff and rackets boss, he controlled patronage, gambling and prostitution until 1941

From an article printed in *The Beachcomber,* Ship Bottom, August 1968, used with the permission of Alyce Crow.

1944
Atlantic City

Ray Hansen

The watch tower and wrecked Atlantic City Boardwalk near Absecon Inlet. The full length of the boardwalk was either repaired or replaced after the 1944 hurricane.

Ray Hansen spent his childhood in Atlantic City's Inlet neighborhood, where life, he later reflected, was an absolute joy. The Inlet was a predominantly working-class community with a great many commercial fishermen of Scandinavian descent. Hansen grew up fishing off the beach, off the docks, off the sea wall, and, when he was twelve, in his own small pond box. The youngster's adventures centered around the skiffs, the docks and the creeks meandering through the bay meadows. He felt as much at home on the water as on land, and like his father before him, would ultimately become a commercial fisherman.

The September day that the Great Atlantic Hurricane[1] came roaring up the eastern seaboard with little advance warning caught young Hansen and his buddy off guard.

I was about twelve when one of my pals, Buddy Starr, bought an old lifeguard boat from the city. We painted the boat with whatever paint we happened to find and it turned out black, red, orange, green — the ugliest thing you ever saw. Buddy and I had a lot of fun with that boat. We would row out to the bar off the inlet over on the Brigantine side and shoot seas. That is, ride them in. Sometimes we would catch a sea opposite Atlantic Avenue and ride it all the way into Brigantine beach. There was no jetty and the break ran for a half a mile. More often than not the Coast Guard would come out and try to get us to come in. Where we were, the water was too shoal and rough for their boat and all they could do was keep waving at us, which we just ignored. There wasn't anything more fun than when you were on top of a big comber zipping along; you felt like you were going thirty miles an hour. Sometimes we rowed that boat until our hands bled.

In September 1944 we had a pretty good hurricane and I had the scare of my life. The fall mackerel season was on when Bill Pebler of Pebler's dock approached me and another kid named Eddie Nevins. He told us one of the boats had lost its dory and that he had word it had washed up on the beach down by Convention Hall. He said if we went and got it he would give us five dollars apiece. There wasn't much a couple of us guys wouldn't do for five bucks.

We got two oars, eight-footers, walked down to Maine Avenue and got on the trolley. We had a little problem fitting the oars in the trolley but we managed to get settled. We found the dory full of water in the surf right in front of the hall. It took a while to get it bailed out and worked back to water deep enough to float it. When we first arrived we didn't notice that the seas were running so big, but as we started to try and launch the dory we realized the surf was really getting up there. We didn't have the slightest idea why, there hadn't been any storms recently. Well it took us at least an hour to get the dory out past the break. We rolled over a couple of times and had to bail her out again. We managed to draw a pretty good crowd on the Boardwalk considering the time of year it was. Summer was over and no lifeguards were left so we had the beach all to ourselves. Once we got outside the break things got a lot easier and with me standing and pushing and Eddie sitting and pulling we moved along very well. Laughing and joking about what a fun way it was to make five bucks, we got to the turn at Maine Avenue without much trouble. We didn't notice the sky getting blacker by the minute.

Rounding the turn to come up the inlet we ran into an outgoing tide; it was now that we started to wonder what was happening. The sky was really getting black, the swell was getting larger by the minute and the tide was running abnormally strong. We started to get a little panicky and picked up the beat of our rowing. It did no good; we could not make headway against the tide and, in fact, it was pushing us ever slowly farther out into the channel. Realizing we were losing the battle we picked up the stroke as fast as we could. Arms were beginning to tire, so we decided to change positions to me pulling and Eddie pushing. Even though that maneuver only took a couple of seconds to complete we lost valuable distance and moved farther into the channel. The farther into the channel we went the stronger the tide became and we were then just steadily going backward out to sea.

I looked toward the Coast Guard watch tower and didn't see anyone in it; the tower was empty. When we first started we were so sure of our capabilities of handling the dory; both of us had rowed dories on many occasions but we were now losing that confidence in a hurry. We both came to the realization at the same time that we were not going to make it and we started talking over our next recourse. I say talking like we were calm, but, hell, we were hollering at each other at the top of our lungs. The dory was now about a half-mile offshore and losing ground fast. We had just decided to give up, let the boat go until we were far enough out to sea where the tide would have a lot less effect and then head her back for the beach where we had started.

The L. M. Jeffries was a seiner that fished in Atlantic City and was owned by a good friend of my mother and father and, unbeknownst to me and Eddie, she was out that day. Eddie and I were just about done in when I looked astern and could see her coming in the inlet. They saw us and made in our direction. We were going toward them faster than they were coming toward us. The Jeffries had only a small four cylinder Cummins for power as she mostly used it for going in and out of the inlet. At sea she sailed; she had two large trisails as she was schooner rigged, and the engine only pushed her along at four to five miles per hour. As the Jeffries came alongside they had a man standing on the bow with a line. He threw it right at me, hit me with it and I dropped it overboard. They had another man on the stern and with the dory bumping along the seiner's hull I managed to catch the second line and make her fast. Three or four strong hands reached down to the dory and hauled us aboard just as the dory turned over. It had to be cut loose and that was the last we ever saw of it.

Eddie and I were soaking wet and shivering like lost puppies, so they put us in the engine room with a couple of blankets to warm us up. From where the Jeffries picked us up to the sea wall could not have been more than a mile but it took her almost two hours to get there; that's how strong the tide was. We were about to be hit by a hurricane.

NOTE

1. *The Great Atlantic Hurricane:* At 4 P.M. on September 14 the wind at Atlantic City was clocked at 105 miles per hour. This hurricane holds the century's measured record for the highest storm-surge tide, nine feet, which was recorded at Steel Pier. (*Great Storms of the Jersey Shore*, Larry Savadove, Margaret Buchholz, Down The Shore Publishing/The SandPaper, 1993)

From an unpublished memoir, printed with the permission of Ray Hansen.

1945
Mantoloking

Bertha Bates Cole

Two weeks after the end of World War II, Annsi, Alix and Danna Cole fly the "Flying Fortress" kite made for them by two visiting Australian servicemen.

The fighting in Europe and Asia was winding down during the summer of 1945, and it proved an exciting time for Bertha Cole. The Bucks County woman had been keeping a diary throughout the war years, and in her journal she intermingled the momentous with the mundane. When Winston Churchill was defeated politically on July 26 Bertha wrote, "Great changes are under weigh." Then with barely a missed breath she recorded cutting beans, a welcome present of fish, and two chickens received from a neighbor. The August 6 entry is printed in capital letters: "Today the Atomic Bomb was dropped on a city of Japan!" And also on the ninth: "President Truman's historic speech on his return from the Berlin (Potsdam) Conference. He seems to me a God given Man of the Hour!"

Bertha and Marshall Cole lived in the country, and had planted an extensive victory garden, which helped alleviate the wartime food shortages. Much of August 1945 was spent harvesting and canning hundreds of pounds of corn, peaches, green peppers, beets and lima beans. On the tenth Bertha exclaimed, "Tokyo broadcast its surrender acceptance!" Then, in her usual clear, refined script, "Canned the pickled beets. Worked on PTA sale." On August 12 she wrote, "Took in two RAF flyers for three days, Raymond Hooper and David Earl." It was not uncommon for families with the space and wherewithal to have foreign servicemen as guests in their homes.

A large, conspicuously scripted, "Peace has come to world today!" led the August 14 entry, and further down the page she penned, "Girls forbidden to swim [in a friend's pool] for fear of polio."

Before the war Bertha and her husband had summered on an island off the coast of Maine (but the shortage of gasoline had ended those excursions when hostilities broke out). Warm weather vacations were limited to visits in Mantoloking, a quiet village of weather-beaten summer cottages and Scandinavian fishermen. Bertha was enthusiastically patriotic and believed in her God-given duty to her country, but she was happy and relieved when gasoline rationing ended on August 15: "Somehow I can't adjust quickly to the thought of being able to drive anywhere I wish again!" Less than a week later she and her husband piled into their Mercury convertible and drove to Forked River for a day of offshore fishing on Charles Grant's party boat.

On August 25 the Cole family took in two Australian pilots; John Court, 20, and Don Dyer, 23. And with the heady joy of a full gas tank and the

freedom to go on a road trip, two days later found Bertha and her three daugh-
ters, Danna, 14, Alix, 11, and Annsi, 4, along with their Shetland sheepdog
Laddie, off on a jaunt to Mantoloking to visit a friend at her spacious, shingled,
oceanfront home. Back home later that evening Bertha confided to her diary:
"Molly Gibbs[1] invited us to take over the cottage, with maid and Butch [Molly's
5-year-old] for ten days after Labor Day. All home happy, singing lustily en
route and plenty sun burned."

SEPTEMBER 5: Spent morning gathering food and things for the shore
and the afternoon packing. Got off finally about 3:30, arriving 5:30.
Mercury convertible full as could be, with three girls, Laddie and I in
front seat. Saw Molly and Butch, then back for some organization and
bed making. Delicious supper of fresh mackerel, cooked by Janey. Quiet
evening, gals to bed early. Molly and I talking things over.

SEPTEMBER 6: Such a nice day! The weather continues ideal, tho' the
morning was misty. A run to Point Pleasant and thence phoned Lal, who
sounds most cheerful. We stopped at Beaton's boat yard across the bridge
to see the boat the Gibbs are scraping and conditioning — then back for
a lovely swim and sunbath before lunch. Janey's day out so we got lunch,
then put Molly on train to Phila. After "redding up," the boys and girls
all drove over to the yacht club with me. John, Don and I took the 20
foot cat boat out and I gave them a bit of a lesson in sailing, then left
them to try it for themselves, which they did, evidently quite satisfacto-
rily, until suppertime. Fran Harris and her two girls were crabbing and
gave us a lot of crabs (now fixed for tomorrow's lunch) and invited us for
a sailing picnic Saturday. The Muirs[2] dropped in as we were finishing
dinner then left to see "A Bell for Adano." Laddie and I gazed at the stars
for a little while prior to turning in.

SEPTEMBER 7: After dips and breakfast, John, Don, Annsi and I spent
an hour or so at Beaton's yard painting first coats on deck and bottom of the
cricket boat. Alix was making mayonnaise and picking the crabs to stuff
tomatoes for lunch. The usual good swim and sun, tho' today is spotty as to
wind and clouds. Annsi is gaining confidence in the surf and she and Butch
have a good time together. Butch beginning to miss his mother a little. The
boys took a sail, but are too green, really, to send out alone. Danna and Alix
did their Christmas shopping at Bay Head, spending lots of their well-earned
dollars and evidently really enjoying it. We all, except Danna, who is again

occupied in creating another doll, took a pleasant walk down the beach to the fish pound[3] and back. I read "The Roly Poly Pudding" to Annsi and Butch at their bedtime. We three finished a kite that Don and John were making for the small fry. Awaiting Lal.

SEPTEMBER 8: Boys and girls up for early swim. Lal breakfasted late and swam before the sail. We flew the kite "Flying Fortress" with great success on the beach and Don took some photographs. Then at noon all embarked on the *South Wind,* Joe Harris' lovely little yawl — sailed and lunched down the bay. Wonderful afternoon, a great treat to all of us. Back for dinner, delicious bonita mackerel. Annsi and Butch to bed on time, doubtless quite tired. The first sail of Butch's life! Lal and I found the Muirs out, so called on the Truitts and enjoyed an hour with them. On return girls and boys in bed after playing parcheesi. And so to bed. (Letter from Lissa in Offenbach, Germany — she received my second package of food.)

SEPTEMBER 9: John, Danna, Alix and I went to St. Simon's-by-the-Sea, morning service. Mr. Pitt conducted a moving, fine and sincere service: Lessons from Isaiah and Corinthians "Tho' ye speak with the tongues of men and of angels, and have not love..." and the sermon based on the hymn he had chosen, "God is working his purpose out." Swim, the Muirs and Eliz. Hubbard included. After quite a late and relaxed dinner, Lal and I enjoyed an hour together on the beach with Annsi and Butch sweet and self-sufficient nearby. "Tea" instead of supper and more kites in the making. John accepted our request that he accompany Danna to Virginia[4] tomorrow.

SEPTEMBER 10: Early breakfast for Danna, Lal and John, then they departed by car. Laundry to fix, etc., a stop at Beaton's, errands at Point Pleasant and a swim occupied the morning. Alix, Don and I and the two cherubs (they are so good and congenial and almost identical in size except for Butch's extra brawn!) rattle around with three absent. A letter from Molly, encloses ration points, and Don secured more from the ration board, welcome still for meat, margarine, butter, cheese and sugar. After lunch, at last, I had a talk with Janie — all difficulties seem to vanish away. She can be as nice as she has been disagreeable so hope the future will be rosy. She watched the children while I had a delightful two hour sail with Don and Alix, and cooked us a delicious dinner of our veal roast.

SEPTEMBER 11: Wash day for me, then the beach for all. But rough water, wind and overcast made it unattractive. We walked up and over to the little Bay beach, where Annsi and Butch had a bit of "swimming." After lunch the Bateses[5] came and discussed preparation for a two-day cruise in Molly's boat for Ted and Bob and we shopped for same, then a terrific rain and thunderstorm continuing intermittently all evening. I met John [at the train]. He successfully delivered Danna to Muddie last night and returned from Charlottesville this morning. "Australian Rummy" occupied the evening. After Alix departed to bed, Ted took a hand while I made up provisions for the cruisers.

SEPTEMBER 12: Fine and propitious weather. Ted and Bob off down the Bay in the big cat! Bless them! I have the curse so no swimming, but sunned and watched Alix, Annsi and Butch on the beach. Batch of mail from home: Janet writes that Tup[6] and other regular Army officers are not returning with their Divisions. Our hopes exploded. Lou came down and spent several hours. After Annsi and Butch were read to and sung to and tucked finally in bed Alix and I went to dinner at Bailey's Hall[7] with Lou. Very gay and Alix looking charming in that most becoming sprigged pale yellow dress! Played Australian Rummy (I won despite all efforts!) and Alix was presented the deck of cards as consolation prize. Small moon, stars, lovely night and the roll of the ocean, my favorite of all monotonies.

SEPTEMBER 13: A glorious day and actually an "answer to our prayer" for yesterday and today's weather made possible a lovely cruise to Forked River and back for Ted and Bob. They came over for a little while tonight. Just as they were leaving in walked John and Don, the most heartwarming sight I have seen! The wire this morning and phone this afternoon presaged departure and I felt very blue losing them. I made two little presents, my Jensen flower pin for Margaret, Don's fiancée, and my Spratling Mexican pin for John's mother, wanting to send something personal to testify to our affection for these two fine boys — "our Australians." Truly God is answering my little prayers most generously. "I seek God with my whole heart and he prospers me abundantly." A dear letter from Lal today.

SEPTEMBER 14: Showery, clearing later. John and Don swam before breakfast. I went to fish pound. Errands. Ping pong balls, car checked, while Don puttied the boat and John watched the children. Ping Pong and beach in afternoon. Reading LaFarge's "Laughing Boy." Cards in evening. John to bed. Don and I read. Message from Air Force Club to Don and John to report early Monday. Awaiting Lal.

SEPTEMBER 16: Back from Mantoloking this evening. At 4:30 we saw John and Don on the train for New York — said a fond farewell with oh, such a lump in my throat. Butch stepped on a nail, but is fortunately immunized by toxoid. This culminated a delightful couple of hours today, building a really masterful fort and fortifications in the sand, in which all joined. It was a charming scene, as I saw it from the window — Lal, Alix and Annsi, Don and John and Butch — all happy playing in the sand and the beautiful ocean background. A picture I shall long remember.

NOTES

1. *Molly Gibbs:* A close friend who had attended Pennsylvania Academy of Fine Arts with Bertha Cole.

2. *Muirs and Truitts:* Relatives with summer cottages in Mantoloking.

3. *Fish pound:* The Coles bought their fish at the Bay Head fishery; the fish pound was a bit south of Mantoloking.

4. *Danna to Virginia:* Bertha's oldest daughter was to spend the school year with "Muddie," her grandmother, Nannie Marshall Cole, in Charlottesville.

5. *Bateses:* Ted and Bob were Bertha's brother and nephew; Lou was Ted's wife.

6. *Janet and Tup:* John Tupper Cole was Bertha's brother-in law; Janet was his wife.

7. *Bailey's Hall:* A small hotel, it is now a bed and breakfast Inn.

———————————

From the diary of Bertha Cole, printed with the permission of the author.

1947
Atlantic City

E. J. Kahn, Jr.

The Easter Parade on the Atlantic City Boardwalk in 1945. This event originally celebrated the nation's centennial in 1876, and has remained an unbroken tradition since midcentury.

In 1946 the city fathers made a bid for posterity when they invited the United Nations to make its headquarters in Atlantic City. The fledgling international organization declined, but tourists returned in the years immediately following the end of World War II, yearning for that combination of relaxation and excitement that the self-proclaimed "World's Playground" did so well. Many former servicemen from around the country returned, too, but now often on honeymoons, to share with their wives the resort where they had first seen the ocean.

E. J. Kahn, Jr., a staff writer for The New Yorker magazine from 1937 until 1987, chose the opening of the season as his subject for the "Our Far-Flung Correspondents" column. The Easter Parade on the Boardwalk had been a tradition since 1876. The weather on this Easter Sunday was a bit iffy in the morning, overcast and drizzly, but by noon the sun was shining and a quarter-million paraders showed off the latest fashions. Women's skirts were still short even though wartime restrictions on fabric had been ended, according to one commentator, designers "went berserk with swirls and pleats." The Philadelphia Orchestra was playing at Convention Hall; the singer Dinah Washington and the trombonist Jack Teagarten headed a jazz lineup; the pianist Frankie Carle and five vaudeville acts opened the Steel Pier's new season and the hit song "On the Boardwalk in Atlantic City" gave notice to the vacationing world that the resort was back in business.

Before the war, Atlantic City had a reputation unmatched by that of any other community within a three hours' train ride of New York as a year-round haven for the convalescent, the weary, the aged and the furtive. During the war, the Army invaded the town in such numbers that civilian visitors were frequently hard put to it to find accommodations. The last military stronghold in the city — the Thomas M. England General Hospital, which consisted of two large requisitioned ocean-front hotels — was evacuated in September, and this spring's Easter parade on the boardwalk was the first since 1941 in which olive drab was not the predominant color.

Some of Atlantic City's permanent residents, I discovered when my wife and I arrived here for a holiday, are apparently not yet completely reconverted from the ways of war. For instance, the cabdriver who took us from the station to our hotel twisted his head around as we were riding along, and out of the corner of his mouth volunteered hoarsely the name of a restaurant in which, he assured us, we could get a good steak. As it turned out, not particularly to our surprise, we have found good steaks almost as plentiful in Atlantic City as souvenir ashtrays and salt-water taffy.

In a booklet entitled "Amusements," which was pressed into my hand the moment I had registered at our hotel, I read a friendly note of welcome from the mayor of the city, who extended to me the hospitality of what he called "The World's Greatest All-Year Resort." Despite this sweeping claim, Atlantic City seems to be as conscious of the weather as any old part-time resort. It, too, has its "season," which traditionally opens on Easter Sunday, when the many boardwalk concessionaires who seal up their premises for the winter come out of hibernation and preen themselves in anticipation of prosperous times ahead. As far as I am concerned, however, its season this year began at eight-forty-five a few evenings before Easter, in the boardwalk headquarters of the makers of Vitallan, a preparation that, I had learned by nine-forty-five, would do wonders for my hair. During our chilly first two or three days in Atlantic City, my wife and I had passed the spot several times while strolling along the boardwalk — still the principal all-year diversion of the resort — and we had noticed that it was always deserted, except for two employees who stood forlornly on a platform at the rear of the place. One was a lady who kept her back to the entrance in order to display to passersby a mane of hair that flowed almost to the hem of her skirt, and the other was a man, also with a fine head of hair, who faced the boardwalk and whose eyes, as he blew on his hands, searched wistfully for the nucleus of an audience. Passing the place after dinner on the night in question, a milder one, we were astonished to see that it was crowded. We entered and, joining a group of attentive tourists, listened to an eloquent lecture by the man, who, in addition to discussing the state of my hair and the sensationally more luxuriant state of the lady's, touched on such subjects as the absence of dental decay among elderly guinea pigs, obesity among sewer rats, the evils of radio advertising, the nutritive virtues of raw carrots, and the addiction of housewives to mah-jongg. (The Vitallan man said he had been in business on the boardwalk for nine years, and I gathered from the reference to mah-jongg that he hadn't changed his spiel much since his debut.) It was an hour before my wife and I could break loose from the spell of his oratory. When, enriched by a dollar and ten cents' worth of Vitallan, we returned to our hotel, we both felt that the sudden popularity of the hirsute couple's act was as good a sign as any that The Season had opened.

A crotchety minority of transients stay by choice in some of the smaller back-street hotels, complaining that they find the boom of surf, or even the lapping of waves, disturbing to their slumber, but most of the well-heeled visitors still prefer the big hotels that are perched right on the boardwalk, without which elegant footpath Atlantic City would have about as much allure for out-of-towners as would Niagara without its falls. The first Atlantic City boardwalk, a puny, narrow, mile-long affair, was built in 1870, and the growth of the municipality has since corresponded pretty much to the growth of its waterfront promenade. The present boardwalk, which was put up in 1906, is interminable (or seven miles long, according to my booklet) and sixty feet wide much of the way. It has undergone extensive repairs from time to time to undo the ravages of fires, storms, and shoe leather. During the hurricane of 1944, it collapsed at several points, but it has since been repaired for most of its length as any right-minded convalescent, weary, aged, or furtive citizen should want to cover.

More and more, there seems to be doubt in the minds of the people who run the resort as to whether the Atlantic Ocean, which, after all, was the boardwalk's original *raison d'être*, constitutes as much of a spectacle as the boardwalk itself. The clusters of benches that have been thoughtfully placed at intervals along the ocean side of the boardwalk for tired pedestrians to rest upon, free of charge, face not the soothing expanse of water but the bustling promenade, with its stream of rolling wicker chairs propelled by stooped Negroes, and the long row of hotels, penny arcades, Oriental-rug bazaars, neon signs, skeeball parlors, soda fountains, bars, bathhouses, hot dog and-cold-drink stands, handwriting-analysis booths, restaurants, and shops of all kinds that flank its landward edge. A winded stroller who wishes simply to sit in the sun and gaze without distraction at the sea is obliged either to seek a vantage point on the upstairs sun porch of a boardwalk hotel or to descend to the beach itself and, for a small fee, engage a deck chair.

I do not wish to imply, however, that the city fathers have disloyally forgotten the basic source of their prosperity. The municipal Department of Public Relations, which occupies a boardwalk store front just a fried clam's throw from the Miss America Pageant headquarters (an office in which a fully clothed typist sits primly at a desk, surrounded by enlarged photographs of bygone bathing-suited champs), has prepared a leaflet extolling the merits of thalassotherapy — a word that any Miss America can readily figure out by recalling, from her study of Xenophon's "Anabasis," that *thalassa* means "sea."

I was assured by an elderly barber in one of the ocean-front hotels, who posted me on local traditions one afternoon while cutting my hair, that by no means all the faithful who flock to Atlantic City season after season do so for thalassotherapeutic reasons, even in thalassotherapeutic weather. "They think of Atlantic City as the place to take it easy in," he told me. "Some of the old folks who come down here regular don't seem to care much about the ocean. They simply sit around their hotels most of the day and maybe play a little bingo. All they want to do is rest. Nowhere in the world," he added in ringing tones, "can you get a rest like in Atlantic City." A while later, as he whisked the sheet off me, he remarked that he hoped to have a vacation shortly, and I asked him where he planned to spend it. "Anywhere but here," he murmured.

Plenty of the visitors to Atlantic City are not elderly, of course, but I saw little evidence to support the composers of a popular song of the past winter entitled "On the Boardwalk in Atlantic City," who put forth the lyrical promise "Cinderella, you will find your fella, someone that you've waited for, in romantic, enchantic Atlantic City." It is possible, to be sure, that the song was written while the Army was still on the scene, at which time, for all I know, the midnight curfew may never have tolled for Cinderellas of any reasonable age. At present, though, most of the fellas here are undisguisably middle-aged, and many have a distinctly grandparental look. There is, moreover, an enormous number of widows in their sixties, or women who appear to be widows in their sixties, and it is largely because of their determined patronage that the community's vast colony of auctioneers manages to thrive. The persistent chant of the auctioneer can be heard at all hours along the boardwalk, and if you believe every sugary word of it, there must be more twenty-two-carat gold in Atlantic City than there is anywhere else outside Simpson's. "Now, ladies and gentlemen, *here's* something," a voice will croon from a cluttered antique shop. "This rare old Bohemian wine bottle — genuine Bohemian, mind you — came out of an estate. It's all real ruby and twenty-two-carat gold. Now, who'll say half a dollar for this beautiful Bohemian wine bottle?" And, a few doors down the boardwalk: "Just look at this pair of gorgeous bud vases. Did you ever see anything like them before? Now, did you, honestly? Just imagine these in your home, on your mantelpiece. Who wouldn't be proud to be a part of that picture? These bud vases, ladies and gentlemen, are trimmed with *twenty-*

two-carat gold. They are imported from the other side. Why, the customs duty alone on these priceless bud vases would ..." Still farther down, you see several more pairs of genuine, rare, gorgeous old twenty-two-carat-gold Bohemian wine-bottle bud vases, waiting for some considerate widow to bid the first half dollar for the privilege of giving them a home.

Atlantic City is struggling as gamely as ever to become known not merely as "The World's Greatest All-Year Resort" but as "The Convention City"; thalassotherapy is being hard pressed by gregariousness. There is nearly always a convention in session (my wife and I have rubbed elbows, for instance, with the members of the New Jersey Mosquito Exterminators Association), and in a few of the shop windows there are what look like permanent signs reading, "Welcome Conventioners." About midway along the boardwalk stands the city's Convention Hall, completed in 1929 at a cost of fifteen million dollars and big enough for forty-one thousand people to convene under its roof. It is difficult to stay in Atlantic City long without learning that the Hall is blessed with, among many other glorious fixtures, the world's largest pipe organ and that the floor of its auditorium is easily convertible into "the only full-size indoor football gridiron in the world" — a distinction that reminded me, when I first heard of it, of a billboard I once saw on top of a building in some Western city, which identified the occupant as "the largest laundry in the world of its size." Atlantic City is currently looking forward to conventions of the American Medical Association and of the Shriners. For a while during the past winter, the city had hopes of bagging this summer's American Legion frolic, and some of the local boosters were bitterly disappointed when the Legion decided to confer its spirited patronage upon New York. My barber told me, though, when I returned to him for a fresh-water shampoo before leaving town, that optimism had eventually been restored along the ocean front by an announcement that the city was thinking of negotiating for the 1948 reunion of the veterans of the Spanish-American War. "Atlantic City seems a more proper setting for them than for the Legionnaires," he said. "Those old-timers can probably stand a good rest."

1952
Ocean City

Edward Brown

Frank Schnepp and his family swim in front of Jernee's Bathhouse on Thirty-fourth Street.

 For many young men and women being a lifeguard is core to the summer experience. Edward Brown, a Medford writer, served on the Stone Harbor and Ocean City squads and recalls his summers on the stands with nostalgia, both for the elemental education in human nature, and for the outrageous, fraternal silliness. The routine of hauling small kids out of gullies or whistling

adventurous swimmers closer to shore was broken only occasionally by those moments of high drama, when "a lifeguard had to reach deep down to summon every bit of his strength and go all out to get to a drowning person in time." In this vignette, Brown writes of the off-duty hours, of low comedy, and moonlighting to make ends meet.

By a strange and illogical bit of mind-magic, somehow confusing the end of an immediate present with the finality of the long passed, summer's end always carries me back to my early days at the Jersey Shore. Surely gilding the past, and especially one's youth, is the most universal of human fancies. However, we submit youth, with its absence of phantom pains, mortgage payments not even on the distant horizon, and never a care for "second helping belly," coupled with a lifeguard summer stretching the length of the long beach, makes for paradise itself.

My peregrinations to the sea took me to Ocean City and when I remember that golden time, what a hectic flood of memories, one better than the next and each anxiously elbowing for attention, come crowding to mind. First, friends, of course, boon companions, fixed in memory as sunburnt youngsters, and the rollicking times with them, girls' smiles (even at this distance), places we lived, and much more.

The wildest lodging in memory was the "A House" in Ocean City, a hostelry rented exclusively to lifeguards. Known also as the "Ape House," there was no mollifying female influence there and most of the amenities had long since disappeared. In bursts of enthusiasm, the residents had broken up all the furniture of the hotel and had thrown it out the windows, carrying the glass along with it. There was nothing standing but a few rows of army cots in various stages of decrepitude; clothes were piled in the center of an upstairs room, and all items of apparel were regarded as community property. The last one up in the morning sometimes was penalized for being a slugabed by finding he had to stay indoors all day.

Though the A House was cheap, after a July of this, I moved to a rooming house with a second floor of summer waitresses and a third of dishwashers, guards, and icemen.

One of the young dishwashers had an odd hobby. He had been nightly collecting navel lint for some time, with a view to making a pillow out of the downy stuff when he finally settled down for good. By mistake, the

Acme bag containing the lint was thrown out. The dishwasher got the idea his roommate had done the bag in purposely and began a campaign of guerrilla warfare against him.

Short-sheeting was one thing but when the vengeful dishwasher pasted an unnerving, staring eye on the ceiling above his roommate's bed, the dispute erupted into a roaring fight, ending in a tumbling fall down the stairwell. By the time they both arrived at the bottom, the two concluded the source of the friction was hardly worth it, and arose from the floor as friends.

One of our friends on the beach patrol, an oversized jester with a shaved head and a striking resemblance to Buddha, livened up the Saturday night dances by periodically feigning monstrous "grand mal" seizures at climactic moments in the center of the dance floor. Continued practice made him quite good at it, and on the strength of his fit-throwing ability he left in the fall to try for an acting career in Hollywood.

Zinc skies and rainy days meant we could take the lifeboats and row out to sea to do some fishing, and after one northeaster we put together a hoax people might still be talking about. After we were well out and just when the storm was clearing, a dozen of us went over the side of the boats and swam ashore.

By the time we got into range of the beach, after-storm promenaders were taking the clear air, and seeing us stumbling out of the surf with no visible means of support, as it were, they were understandably curious.

But when we began babbling (in English accents) that there had been a "terrible shipwreck in the storm," and that we were the only survivors, the action really got heavy. Blankets, coffee, and brandy were produced for the shipwrecked men, and to our chagrin and discomfort, some officious person notified the Coast Guard of a sinking.

Incidentally, the same comic genius who concocted this scheme later drove the municipal ambulance into the bay after the lifeguard ball.

I was assigned to Twenty-sixth Street, known as the Kellys' Beach because that notable family's summer house was just in back of it. Here we didn't have to worry about importuning passing girls for lunch since one of the traditions of the Twenty-sixth Street station was that the Kellys' kitchen maid sent lunch up to us each day, a practice probably begun when Jack Jr. was a stalwart of the Ocean City Beach Patrol a few years earlier. Actress Grace Kelly was off in Africa making a film with Clark Gable, and hence, regrettably, would not be requiring any assistance, but her sister, Lizanne, who had a wonderful sulfurous beauty all her own, was on the beach most days along with assorted Kelly aunts, cousins, kids, etc.

Twenty-sixth Street was a good beach because the topography was straightforward and most of the bathers were knowledgeable about the surf. Lowest on most guards' desirability list for posting were beaches such as Ninth Street, which attracted hordes of "shoobies," day trippers or weekend visitors who didn't have a clue as to what the ocean might do in a fit of whimsy. A guard on a shoobie beach could count on runs galore and sitting around most of the day in wet trunks.

At one point there was a period of some four or five days in which two of us were waiting to get into a new apartment above a garage. Rather than hazard a week's rent, we decided to sleep under the lifeboat for the short interim, a pleasant enough idea given the state of the weather, but one with no provision for washing or shaving. By the fourth day we looked as hairy as a pair of spiders, but fate, in the form of a babysitting assignment, stepped in when we were at our most disreputable.

Most guards augmented their incomes with a variety of extra-curricular work, clamming, waitering, teaching swimming, etc. Besides swimming instruction, our specialities were tutoring and babysitting and we had a sign up at the back of our stand so indicating our availability.

We showed up that night for the job, threw our toilet kits in the bushes outside the house, and reported for work. As soon as the people left, we popped our charges into their trundle beds, scratched around outside until we came up with the dopp kits, and set to our ablutions.

By unfortunate happenstance, the owners of the children came back for a missed item, and found, to their surprise, two strange girls leafing through magazines in the living room (we had earlier invited them over for company), and no babysitting lifeguards. We were in the john, shaving, showering, and making ourselves presentable. It was touch and go, but quick talking and the fact the homeowners were mellow from before-dinner drinks saved the day.

The serpent in this 1952 paradise was the conflict in a distant place called Korea: far away, but not far enough. Our country was halfway through what would become known as "The Forgotten War," providing most of the troops for the United Nations side, and men were needed. Like others, lifeguards were being called up in the draft or signing up for the services of their choice. I was no exception, and left the Ocean City Beach Patrol before the sun set on that glorious summer for Marine Corps platoon leaders' training at Parris Island.

NOTE

1. *Kellys' Beach*: Grace Kelly was a famous actress who later married Prince Rainier of Monaco. She grew up in Philadelphia, and the family had a summer home on 26th Street. Princess Grace died in 1982.

Printed with the permission of Edward Brown.

1952
Island Beach

Shirley A. Briggs

Nine-mile-long Island Beach is one of the few undeveloped barrier beaches on the Atlantic coast.

 Shirley A. Briggs, a journalist specializing in nature writing, visited Island Beach the year before the state of New Jersey purchased the 2,694-acre tract from the Phipps estate for about $4.3 million, saving it from commercial development. In 1926 Henry Phipps, Andrew Carnegie's partner in what would become United States Steel Company, had bought the nine-mile strip of virgin barrier beach just north of Barnegat Inlet for $2.5 million. He envi-

343

sioned Island Beach — which had been an island until Cranberry Inlet[1] closed in 1812 — as an exclusive resort community. In 1929 his dream collapsed along with the stock market. For the next quarter century, Island Beach remained in its natural state, home to the state's largest osprey colony. With the exception of a Coast Guard detail and the federal government's using the beach as a missile testing ground in 1945, few visitors to Island Beach disturbed the wildlife — just fishermen, a few squatters, adventurous picnickers and the occasional naturalist. Island Beach State Park opened in 1959.

In the brilliant paintings of Audubon, the journals of the early explorers, and, rarely, in a small surviving fragment of virgin country, we can glimpse the original aspect of our land. Each generation has found fewer areas unaltered, as the most profitable lands were made to conform to our immediate purposes. But until our time the seacoast had, as a rule, been allowed to remain.

Within forty years or so, however, settlements of summer houses have spread down every stretch of accessible beach until the traveler who drives along the barrier islands of the Atlantic Coast, from New York to Ocean City, Maryland, will see few hints of the immemorial marshes and woods which survived there until recently.

An almost unbroken stretch of the ugliest sort of commercialized waterfront developments of stultifying monotony — with the exception of a few planned communities — covers almost every tract. The automobile has brought new hordes of vacationists to populate these places and the promoters have erased so thoroughly every trace of the original character of the shore that few realize what a poor substitute they have been given. To them a bulldozed, sterile expanse of sand must serve for the delightful variety of dune and pond, woods and heath, that once overspread the islands and made them fruitful.

We cannot restore these places, but we may hold back the destruction from the few surviving unsullied shorelands. From New York to Virginia, only Island Beach, New Jersey, and Assateague Island, Virginia and Maryland, remain, but both are in danger. Since Island Beach lies at the end of a densely populated island, with highways leading to its gate, the threat there is immediate.

Until recently, Island Beach has been known to few people, although it is surrounded by the thickly-populated Jersey coast resorts. Preserved by the foresight of the late Henry Phipps and his family, the area may be entered only by the few families who are permitted to maintain beach houses there, and by other authorized persons. This stretch of barrier island, ten miles long on the southern end of Barnegat Peninsula, is the only beach land north of Cape Hatteras remaining in its natural state, untouched by man, fire or grazing to an appreciable degree.

Once inside the gate, the visitor leaves behind the commercialized, teeming shore to the north. The island is less than a mile wide, but crossing from the sea to the bay the visitor finds a surprising variety of landscape. To botanists, Island Beach is a museum area, the only place where some species survive at all, and the only spot where native plants can be studied in their natural relationship to the land and to each other. From high tide line, plants begin the task of binding the dunes and creating a stable, varied vegetation that mounts from the beach grasses to the park-like woods on the higher land near the bay.

Experts the world over, wherever dunes are a problem, are trying to achieve such stabilization by plant growth. Here they may see it done without human assistance. Walking inland, we cross in a few steps the plant successions that have evolved through millenniums. Dune thickets, fresh and salt marshes, coastal plain forest, Southern white cedar forest, bog, and Hudsonia heath are found here in climax state.

The bird life at Island Beach is remarkable for its typical character in a region where everything else has been altered. Breeding populations may be assumed to have changed little since the earliest times, however much the transient and wintering populations of shorebirds and waterfowl have been affected. The relation of birds to habitat here has meaning of the greatest significance to the ecologist.

A general survey of the breeding bird population was made last June 23 by Charles H. Rogers, Curator of the Princeton Museum of Zoology, who has visited Island Beach for thirty years. Listening at intervals of .3 of a mile along the road down the center of the island, he noted the following breeding pairs: marsh hawk 1, king bird 11, barn swallow 9, purple martin 3, American crow 1, fish crow 9, catbird 43, brown thrasher 8, yellow warbler 12, yellow-throat 21, chat 2, red-winged blackbird 2, cowbird 2, towhee 32, and song sparrow 17.

Walking around the southern tip of the island, he found 12 American egrets, 3 more pairs of ospreys, 1 or more clapper rails, 2 piping plover, a dozen sanderling, 200 herring and 4 great black-backed gulls, a few laughing gulls, common and least terns, several more pairs of barn swallows, a long-billed marsh wren, more red-wings, 2 or 3 pairs of seaside sparrows and several more song sparrows. Of these, the sanderlings were, of course, not breeding, and the herring and black-backed gulls were immatures as a rule. Laughing gulls have a colony either in the Island Beach meadows or not far distant. Terns and black skimmers have been reported nesting at the southern tip of the island. The heronry west of the road had nesting great blues, American egrets, little green and black-crowned night herons.

On the basis of his previous experience, Rogers thinks that an intensive search might have yielded a pair or two of the house wren, Carolina wren, robin and cardinal near the cottages, and spotted sandpiper, Savannah sparrow and prairie horned lark nesting along the dunes. American bittern, black duck, and red-breasted merganser may breed in the meadows, with sharp-tailed sparrows, Virginia and black rails. An occasional pair of tree swallows and mockingbirds may be found, and killdeers are probable. Now and then, short-eared owls may nest in the meadows.

Transient birds form the most numerous bird life on the island. The often prevailing westerly and northwesterly winds cause the small migrants, most of which fly by night, to be concentrated along the coast. When they come down at dawn they need shelter and food in order to recoup their strength for the next lap. Island Beach is an incomparable resting place for these birds, an oasis along the solidly built-up beaches. The dense shrubs that give shelter also offer fruit. The Sassafras berries are eaten early by resident songsters, who share with the first August migrants the blueberries, huckleberries and blackberries. Lush growth of pokeberries, cherries and beach plums are available for the late summer and early fall migrants. And there are still large reserves for the late comers: red cedar, sumac, holly, poison ivy, smilax, and bayberries hold their fruits from fall to spring. Any small migrant coming down at Island Beach is assured an opportunity to live well whether his southward flight is resumed the next night or the next week.

Island Beach is a fine vantage point for the observation of other birds of passage. Along the outer beach, sanderlings run with the waves in company with willets, knots and ringed plovers. On the mud and grass flats are flocks of semipalmated, western, and least sandpipers, together with black-bellied plovers, both yellow-legs, dowitchers, and occasional Hudsonian curlews, marbled godwits and other less common shorebirds. Migrating hawks pass along the coast, notably the peregrine falcon and merlin. From mid-October it is one of the better places on the Middle Atlantic Coast for waterfowl. Winter brings Ipswich sparrows and flocks of horned larks and snow buntings, with an occasional Lapland Longspur.

Mammals in evidence are white-footed mice, meadow mice, cottontail rabbits, opossums, now and then a fox or deer, and a few bats. Intensive study would certainly reveal many of the more secretive forms. Indeed, for naturalists of almost any specialty, the area offers chances for fascinating study.

Commercialization of Island Beach, in the prevailing mode, would first destroy the most remarkable part, near the upper end of the area, where the Hudsonia heath and the interlacing woods are found. Waterfowl and nesting birds of the meadows could persist for some time, probably, but the unique value of an undisturbed beachland would be gone. The greatest loss would be to botany. (In the fully built-up sections, Mr. Rogers comments, the dominant plant is the petunia.)

But the scientific value of the beach, incomparable as it is, may not be the most persuasive argument for its preservation. The singular beauty of the area is not readily described. It is not dramatic — rather, it is serene, superlative in its detail and subtle variety. The dwarf oaks, a species found only here, and the handsome hollies and cedars make copses and tempting vistas over the Hudsonia-covered dunes, golden in their June bloom, silvery-green later. Little marshes, deep in pink mallow, flank the roadway. North of the gate, the buildings crowd to the beach, and people teem over the sand, but along the protected miles of Island Beach, the shore stretches to the horizon with only an occasional fisherman to punctuate the surf. The majesty of the ocean is found in a setting worthy of it.

NOTE

1. *Cranberry Inlet:* This inlet was about where Ortley Beach is now. During the American Revolution its location east of the port at Toms River allowed ships easy access.

"A Word for Island Beach" appeared in *Frontiers: A Magazine of Natural History,* no. 3, 1952, reprinted with the permission of The Academy of Natural Sciences, Philadelphia.

1955
Cape May

Edwin Way Teale

During the late fall migration, kinglets, thrushes and yellow warblers (illustrated) are often blown to sea by strong northwest winds.

Edwin Way Teale was a writer, naturalist and photographer who, according to the Saturday Review of Literature, *"excels in all three branches of his art." Between 1941 and 1960 Teale wrote numerous books on nature and outdoor life. The following excerpt is from a warm and mellow story of an adventurous, wan-*

dering, 20,000-mile journey across the advancing front of the season, from Cape Cod's far eastern tideline to Cape May, then westward across the northern United States. After exploring the underwater life off the eastern tip of Long Island, Teale — in the tradition of two centuries of naturalists preceding him — traveled the back roads of New Jersey, south to Cape May, the "great bottleneck" of the Atlantic Flyway, where he and his wife would catch the tail end of a hurricane and see clouds of birds migrating south.

The season of summer extends to about September 21 but the summer season ends with Labor Day. Then the newspapers begin referring to summer in the past tense. Vacations are over. Schools commence. To the popular mind, September belongs to autumn as December belongs to winter.

This unofficial beginning of the fall lay behind us as we ran down the New Jersey coast, advancing another 250 miles to Cape May and the drowned river of the Delaware estuary. The air was hazy and heavy under the blaze of the morning sun. We crept through the Long Island suburbs, threaded our way among the sweltering canyons of New York, dipped under the Hudson and emerged amid all the villainous smells of that caldron and retort and crucible of the east, the miles and miles of factories west of the river. Then we were out in open country, on U.S. 1.

Along that road Queen Anne's lace was going to seed, balling up like fingers closing into a fist. Already a few tupelos had turned a deep and winy red. And out of all the grassclumps arose the steely murmur of the insects, the song of autumn that was to accompany us from coast to coast.

By the time we reached the pine barrens of central New Jersey thunderheads had boiled up around the horizon and vultures pitched and banked in a stormy wind. We passed Forked River and Cedar Run and the purplish, gust-worried water at the mouth of the Mullica River under darkening skies. And when, south of the Mason and Dixon line, we came to old Cape May, the scene of Alexander Wilson's pioneer observations and a mecca for generations of autumn bird watchers, the rain was already a gray curtain over the ocean.

That night the tail end of a hurricane[1] that had headed inland through the Carolinas reached Cape May. We watched the seething white tumult of the surf from an upper room in an old inn facing the sea. All that wild and windy night the rain and spray, the flying foam and driven sand whipped and battered the windowpanes.

We had first looked from those windows nearly fifteen autumns before. Then we were making our initial visit to this far-southern tip of New Jersey, this eighteen-mile point of land thrusting, south-southwest with the Atlantic rolling in on one side and the wide Delaware Bay stretching away on the other. Here pirates had once landed to fill their casks with fresh water at Lake Lily. Here, in the heyday of its one hundred fifty years as a summer resort, had come Abraham Lincoln and Henry Clay and Horace Greeley and Ulysses S. Grant. Its spacious verandas and lacelike grillwork speak of another age of architecture. Henry Ford, near the turn of the century, had ridden at the wheel of a racing car on the packed sand of its miles of beach. In the swamps of the cape, "cedar mining" had once been a flourishing business with "shingle miners" unearthing blown-down, long buried trees that still contained sound and usable wood. At one time, it is said, Independence Hall in Philadelphia was shingled with cedar mined from the swamps of Cape May.

But to the naturalist Cape May means above all else birds in the autumn. It is one of the great bottlenecks of the Atlantic Coast Flyway. At the tip of the peninsula eleven miles of water extend across Delaware Bay to the high dunes of Cape Henlopen. West across the bay from Cape May Point the distance is twenty miles. To find a crossing of less than eleven miles a bird would have to travel forty miles up the wide Delaware estuary. So, at certain times the migrants, reluctant to venture over the water lest they be driven out to sea by the wind, pile up near the tip of the point in spectacular concentrations. On September 1, 1920, Witmer Stone, author of *Bird Studies at Old Cape May,* counted eighty-six species on a walk along the bay side of the point. Even as late as December 22, 1935, the Christmas census of the Delaware Valley Ornithological Club yielded 111 species. On October 27 of that same year members of a National Audubon Society field trip to the point piled up 123 species. Seventeen years went by before, on September 21, 1952, a party led by Julian K. Potter raised that figure by one to the present record total of 124 species seen in a single day.[2]

While the storm pounded the shingled walls and rattled the windows that night Nellie and I recalled our other visits in the fall to this historic cape. We remembered the time migrating hordes of monarch butterflies embrowned whole branches as they clung to the Spanish oaks within the circle at Cape May Point. We remembered a distant cloud of thousands of sanderlings that appeared and disappeared, flashing like a myriad twinkling lights each time the shorebirds turned and their white underparts caught the sun. We recalled a morning beside Lake Lily when we looked directly up into a revolving wheel of broad-winged hawks, 200 or more circling together, rising higher and higher until the wheel dissolved and all the buteos streamed away toward the distant dunes of Henlopen. We spoke of such things. Recollections of other autumns returned.

By morning the storm had largely spent itself. The surf was high but the clouds were breaking. September, a month that along the Middle Atlantic States has fewer days of rain than June, July or August, was reverting to normal. After a quick breakfast in a restaurant where the waitress asked us if we wanted "white or tan bread" we wandered down the side roads of a dripping landscape, into a day of swallow clouds.

By July, each year, the white-breasted tree swallows begin congregating in the coastal marshes of the northeastern states. Their numbers are so great that they sometimes festoon telephone wires, sitting side by side literally for miles on end. Hence a colloquial name: "Wire Birds." Their fall migration, beginning early, is a leisurely drifting down the map. Traveling by day, feeding on the wing, they loiter along the road. If a tree swallow's flight were straightened out it would cover a good many miles in a day. Harold B. Moore, a physician of Harrisburg, Pennsylvania, reported in *The Auk* in the early 1930s that a migrating tree swallow, flying beside his car down a straight road on a windless day, advanced steadily at a speed of twenty-five miles an hour. But most of the time the great flocks of the early swallows pause and advance, move south little by little.

During late August and early September, especially when the prevailing gentle, southerly breezes are supplemented for a day or so by winds from the northwest, tremendous numbers of tree swallows pile up near the tip of Cape May. This is the first spectacular bird event of fall. Roosting by night among the canebrakes of the phragmites, with as many as four or five swallows clinging to a single reed, and supplementing their insect fare by day with the frosty-gray berries of the myrtle, or bayberry, they build up the fat that will provide fuel for the later longer flights of autumn. Not only are birds at their peak in numbers in the fall but they are at their peak in weight. If you could weigh the southbound migrants of an American autumn, you would have more pounds of birds than at any other time of year.

We were heading for the western side of the point — where a concrete ship still lies where it ran aground in World War I and where water-smoothed bits of quartz, "Cape May diamonds," are scattered through the sand — when we came within sight of the first multitude of swallows. Over a wide expanse of open ground they formed a living cloud, acres in extent, continually in motion, continually changing form, swirling this way and that like windblown smoke. The cloud rose and fell. It elongated and contracted. It condensed and grew vaporous. It scudded low across the ground, zoomed as though caught in a violent updraft. Thousands of separate birds were lost in the group movement lifting, veering, diving, together.

There was something hypnotic, something deeply stirring in the sight. Swarm was the word that came instantly to mind. This teeming cloud of birds not only suggested a swarm of bees but there was something about their wild abandon, their holiday mood, that was akin to the spirit of the honeybees when they leave the hive on the great communal adventure of their lives.

We tried to estimate the number of birds in the moving cloud before us. Perhaps if, like some members of the Linnaean Society in New York, we had trained ourselves by dumping rice grains on a tabletop, estimating the number and then counting them, we might have had better success. As it was we settled for the rather vague term, "many thousands." Without doubt there are oftentimes more than 10,000 white-breasted swallows in one of these Cape May concentrations.

John James Audubon, in the first volume of his *Ornithological Biography,* describes how overwintering tree swallows along the estuaries of the Mississippi in Louisiana flew in dense masses low over the water at dawn. During these flights, he added, numbers of the birds were often killed by canoe men "with the mere aid of their paddles." These beautiful and beneficial swallows at one time were sold for food in the New York market. Alexander Wilson[3] recalls, in his *American Ornithology,* an instance in which a meat-gunner near Cape May fired into a cloud of tree swallows, killing or maiming 102 birds with a single shot. Such slaughter, once familiar to the cape, is now a thing of the past. But even today that ancient, and currently self-righteous, enmity of the human predator for the avian predator persists and every Cape May autumn is still tainted with the senseless slaughter of hawks[4] for sport and so-called food.

The cloud of the swallows drifted away. Later we saw this same concentration again and, driving northward up the cape, at least two other swallow-swarms — one over pastureland, the other above a wide salt meadow where a river entered the sea. All the evolutions on this day were comparatively low in the sky but sometimes a cloud of swallows will ascend up and up until the individual birds are nearly lost to sight. Several times, here and there, we came upon small groups resting and feeding on the bayberry bushes. So voracious are these autumn swallows for the gray, waxy fruit that as many as forty-one bayberries have been found in the digestive system of a single bird.

There were, that day, various other early migrants — red-starts, veeries, sharp-shinned hawks, red-breasted nuthatches. We saw them among the bushes and trees along the roads, near the seventy-foot Cape May Lighthouse and amid the sorry wreckage of the Witmer Stone Wildlife Sanctuary, blighted by chemical dust from the high chimneys of the neighboring magnesite plant. But this was our tree-swallow day. Above all else it was the swallow clouds, the thousands upon thousands of white-breasted, dark-winged birds swirling and scudding in unison, that made this particular one of the traditional "thirty golden days of September" so memorable. The swallows of Cape May formed our outstanding recollection of the Atlantic Coast Flyway, that first of the four great paths of migration down the North American continent.

While we would be working west toward and across the other three, the flood of migrant birds would mount at Old Cape May. Some, like the knots, would follow a narrow land close to the edge of the sea; others, like the thrushes and kinglets and warblers, would be moving south on a wide advancing front. It is these latter birds that are swept into the long pocket of the cape by northwest winds in the night. Many of them are carried out to sea and lost. Others, when dawn breaks, find themselves still within sight of land and are able to come ashore. I remember one morning when a steady parade of sharp-shinned hawks, hours long, came in from the sea. So numerous were they that we sometimes had half a hundred within sight at the same time.

On another occasion, when a great wind from the northwest was booming over the boardwalk at Cape May on a September night, I came upon a little kinglet fluttering against a lighted window of the Municipal Pier. I caught it, holding it loosely in my hand, and felt the violent pounding of its tiny heart. Suddenly it fluttered; the wind tore it from my grasp; it disappeared in an instant, whirled away across the white surf, out over the tumultuous sea, a small, doomed bird in the midst of a night of terror. In that moment I remembered the many times during these autumn expeditions when I had wished for a wind from the northwest to concentrate birds at Cape May. And I regretted every wish. At such times we see only the survivors. We miss the many small migrants that, helpless in the wind and dark, are carried to death at sea.

Although we found no "Cape May diamonds" along the sandy western shore of the point that day, we did glimpse something far more precious, an avian jewel once given up for lost, a bird that was listed half a century ago as totally extirpated in the state, a snowy egret passing overhead in buoyant flight. Another persecuted species at one time familiar here but now long gone is the whooping crane. With hardly more than a score of individuals in the world today, it is making a final stand at the Aransas Wildlife Refuge in southern Texas. Yet hardly more than a hundred years ago it sailed on seven-and-a-half-foot, white, black-tipped wings above this very shore. It fed among the sea meadows and marshes near by. Sometimes it even overwintered in the swamps of the Cape May region.

It was late that afternoon when, north of Great Egg Harbor, with swallow clouds left behind, we swung to the west, across the pine barrens, through a great gossamer shower where George Washington had crossed the Delaware, over the rolling land of eastern Pennsylvania with hills starred in the sunset by drifting thistledown. We were leaving the coast now, traveling toward the interior, as in ages past evolving life had crept from the waves and moved onto the land. The sea and the smell of the sea were behind us.

NOTES

1. *Tail end of a hurricane:* 1955 topped 1933 as the worst storm year of the century. "Connie was the first to rattle its way up the coast, spawning a few tornadoes on its edges, sloshing the waters of Chesapeake and Delaware bays, then heading overland to Lake Huron. But Connie wouldn't be more than an entry in the logbook had it not been for Diane, which followed along the same route a few days later. The Northeast was saturated with the waters of Connie. The ground couldn't hold any more, and the rivers were already fat. Diane set records in flood damage, hitting the billion dollar mark all by itself, a first in hurricane history." (*Great Storms of the Jersey Shore,* Larry Savadove, Margaret Buchholz, Down The Shore Publishing/The SandPaper, 1993)

2. *Record total of species:* According to Pete Dunne, director of the Cape May Bird Observatory, the record as of April, 1999 is 201 species spotted in one day.

3. *Alexander Wilson:* In 1793, Wilson emigrated from Scotland to Pennsylvania, where William Bartram fostered his interest in nature. Wilson edited the multi-volume *American Ornithology* between 1808 and 1814.

4. *Senseless slaughter of hawks:* The shooting of hawks became illegal in 1972.

"Swallow Clouds," reprinted from *Autumn Across America*, Dodd, Mead & Co., New York, 1956.

1955
The Parkway
And the Shore

Malcolm McTear Davis

The Garden State Parkway approaching the Route 37 exit as it looked in the summer of 1955.

 By midcentury major changes were underway up and down the Jersey Shore. A booming economy during President Eisenhower's administration allowed the middle classes to consider a summer vacation or even a second home. Families who before the war could not have afforded a car could now *own one, and sometimes two. A ferment of building ensued, and the first lagoon developments were carved out of the virgin bay meadows on both the mainland and the barrier islands, where a waterfront cottage might cost between $7,000 and $10,000, depending on location. A crush of vacationers, plus families moving to the area year 'round, burdened existing services; shore communities rushed to improve boardwalks and amusement centers, and to construct new hospitals and schools. Increased pleasure boating forced government agencies to maintain waterways and dredge inlets.*

Entrepreneurs bought cheap land and built restaurants, and motels offered rooms for less than ten dollars a night in the middle of small towns unaccustomed to short-term tourism. Speculators acquired large expanses of bayside land and quickly plowed under bayberry, cedar and holly trees. Creosoted bulkheads evened off the irregular shoreline and dredges buried the bay meadows under an avalanche of sand.

The migration to the shore along the Garden State Parkway was expected to strain access roads to the beaches, and local politicians jockeyed for state and federal funds to improve or rebuild causeways and drawbridges. One shore newspaper called it "a golden time."

Malcolm Davis was editor of Travel *magazine in 1955, a year after the first stretch of the parkway opened. The formal dedication and ribbon cutting was just before the July Fourth weekend, and Davis chose that holiday to see what was at the other end of the road.*

With both a newly opened highway and a long weekend dead ahead, we decided to buck the National Safety Council's chilling predictions and jaunt the length of New Jersey to its Cape May tip. A ribbon-cutting ritual at the weekend's start had put New Jersey's Garden State Parkway officially on the map — except for a one-mile stretch due to be finished almost momentarily.

We forced our way into the flow of the Fourth and, once through the turgid traffic that teemed into the Lincoln Tunnel, went the wrong way until we found a Parkway entrance.

The New Jersey people will be happy to pass you a packet of pointers about the Parkway — $305,000,000 in cost, 52,833,000 vehicles expected the first year, 114 entrance ramps, 112 exits — but what the details really mean is a miracle ride through a surprisingly scenic state. The Parkway is one of the rare modern superstrips we've rolled along that actually permits full and constant viewing of the adjacent real estate, and isn't merely an open-air artery to the end of the line.

Broad dividers separate northbound and southbound traffic streams, and you are hardly aware that travelers are moving in any other direction than your own, as some of these island areas are 600 feet wide. This extra-width distance aids in night driving, too, as approaching headlights seem to be in the next county.

A spate of service areas and restaurants are spotted along the expressway, plus a number of picnic groves and cutoffs for a little loafing or a nap during the drive. Despite expectations of bumper-to-bumper travel, we wheeled along the Parkway unhindered, except for a one-hour jam-up that mysteriously broke beyond a toll station as though the sun had melted every other auto. Indeed, on the southern segments of the Parkway there were times when no other car was in sight.

We reached Cape May around 4:00 P.M., having left Manhattan about 10 A.M., taking time off for trip-breaks at points en route. Along Beach Avenue, weather-beaten, expansive hotels are lined up for ocean views and breezes, most of the inns with a turn-of-the-century styling. Prices — the Lafayette wanted $17.00 per night, double — are closer to next century insofar as our informal weekend budget goes, so we cruised the town for something less pretentious.

Cape May is crowded with private homes, guest houses and similar small establishments along narrow tree-shaded streets within a sandal's throw of Beach Avenue. With little difficulty, despite the extra influx due to the Fourth, we were soon ensconced in a spotless home at a sensible $5.00 per night, double — or $2.50 apiece. Give or take a dollar or two and you'll find similar accommodations all over Cape May's near-beach residential district.

Cape May is not as rustic as we had imagined but most of the houses and converted cafes or shops are pleasantly aged. Except for a modern shopping section somewhat like a one-block version of Miami Beach's Lincoln Road that squats across from the boardwalk's midway point, you feel that grandad probably had the same view on his visit, minus a few neon signs.

A short drive out to Cape May Point puts you at the southern tip of New Jersey and gives you a close-up view of the lighthouse. An abandoned mansion, open to explorers and the elements, tips askew toward eventual destruction, although there's a fine view from its still-sturdy turret.

A Cape May evening is what you make it and can include the Cape May Theatre's stage presentation, followed by an evening snack or dancing, with intermittent sorties along the breeze-whipped boardwalk. The theatre could stand refurbishing, and perhaps better use of its technical facilities, but ahead of that is a need for stronger support. Only a handful of drama devotees were dotted through the house the night we were there.

Although the Garden State Parkway is the fastest route back to northern New Jersey and the exits to Manhattan, New York State and Connecticut points, we decided to diversify the run by taking the Ocean Drive homeward. It skirts the sea from Cape May to Atlantic City, and also destroys — if Cape May itself hasn't — any images you may have that picture New Jersey as closely packed with factories.

Along this ocean-edging avenue are still fishing villages, net-strewn and boat-filled, whose frame homes, set on stilts amid the wash of inlets and bays, etch themselves into captivating silhouettes as the sun dips to splash them in golden-streaked shadows. Ocean Drive's appropriate serenity is blasted only by Wildwood and its boardwalk battery of blatant amusement devices. Above this whirling raucous region, however, the Drive settles down to spanking sights that stretch out into the horizon as you bridge bays like Hereford Inlet, Great Sound and Townsends Inlet. East Coasters hie to Europe for lesser vistas of sail-spotted shorelines and spar-stacked harbors in tawny twilight.

Along Seven Mile Beach was our favorite site of the sea-splashed strip: Stone Harbor. A distinctive family resort, its setting is attracting growing numbers who hunt for a softly hued haven, and if zoning regulations remain in force the settlement should retain its salty tang and quiet charm for a long time.

We reached Ocean City well after dark and, although it appeared splendid for a short stay as we paused for inspection and boardwalk strolling, we made the masterful mistake of aiming at Atlantic City for an overnight halt.

Despite its tourist-based lures, Atlantic City can be an attractive area for an outing — at such famed palaces as Chalfonte-Haddon Hall or the Traymore. Without reservations on a holiday-happy weekend, however, you canvass the entire beachfront unsuccessfully and find yourself in the jammed jungle just a couple of blocks or so from the sea. We wish we'd stayed in Ocean City.

Taking U.S. 9 north the next morning, we cut off near Toms River on Route 37 for a drive up Island Beach, a narrow finger angled into the Atlantic. Private beaches border the brine along almost the entire isle, all the way to Point Pleasant. Except for side-street stops you might want to make for a quick look at the layout, you'll find that, with the ocean mainly hidden, you'll direct attention to the Barnegat Bay side for any scenic values, and home lovers will undoubtedly eye with envy the residential rows.

Depending upon your own schedule, you can strike out on Route 34 or continue up the coast, with possibly a pause at Asbury Park if just to underscore the appeal of less flamboyant townships like Allenhurst or Deal, and maintain the sea-circuit right on around to Perth Amboy.

Such a joyride through Jersey will introduce you to almost every aspect of the state's appeal — inland expanses of farmland, small fishing towns, giant resort cities, craft-crossed inlets, becalmed bays sprinkled with sailboats, and broad beaches fronting foamy surfs. And, unless strange gods cleared the lanes just for us, you won't be tangled in traffic, either, during a Jersey jaunt, for the State's highways rank among the finest in the country.

"Jersey Jaunt," reprinted from *Travel*, September 1955.

Acknowledgments

The research involved to assemble this collection was not a solitary pursuit. Many friends, colleagues, archivists and librarians aided my work. I would especially like to thank the following persons for pointing out productive paths as I chased both images and editorial matter: Vicki Gold Levi, George H. Moss Jr., Helen-Chantal Pike, Alexandra Warren, George Reiger, William L. Bauhan, James Fitzpatrick, Eleanor Smith, Marilyn Kralick, Debby Dooling, Phyllis Bur, Randall Gabrielan, Trish Schuster, Dr. Floyd Moreland, Pete Dunne, Barbara St. Clair, Lyn Martin George, Lucinda Hathaway, Polly Miller, Alix Cole Hansen, Jerome Walnut, Nancy Eckert, Fred Miller, Carolyn Campbell, Gail Redmann, Roy Pedersen, Robert Ruffalo, Polly Miller, Evelyn Shippee, David Foster, Cricket McGehee, Kathi and David Fertig, Peggy Davis, Adele Meehan, Granville Price, David Foster, Kathy Cangialose, Stacy Smith at The Noyes Museum of Art, Shirley Bailey at *South Jersey Magazine*, and Jean McKenna at *Field & Stream*.

Historical societies are a repository of valuable resource material. But the question "How do I find what I want if I don't know what I'm looking for?" plagued me. The persons, mostly volunteers, who staff these institutions were an immense help: Sid Parker, June Sheridan, and Jean and James Steelman at Atlantic County Historical Society; Ione Williams at Cape May County Historical & Genealogical Society; Anne Biddle Pratt, Deanna Brown, Jim Campbell and Pat Pocher at Greater Cape May Historical Society; Edith Holly at Gloucester County Historical Society; Laura Beardsley at Historical Society of Pennsylvania; Joanne Sencindiver, Marge Potosnak and the Tuesday kitchen gang at the Long Beach Island Historical Museum; Janet Rassweiler, Joe Lauterbach and the library staff at New Jersey Historical Society; Edna May, Marion Moore and Paul Anselm at the Ocean City Historical Museum; Dick Strickler and Betty Grant at Ocean County Historical Society; Carla Tobias at Monmouth County Historical Association; Marie and Mike Stafford at Sea Isle City Historical Society; Barbara Bolton and June LeMunyon at Tuckerton Historical Society/Giffordtown Schoolhouse Museum; and Bob Scully and Robert Bright, Jr. and Sr., at Wildwood Historical Society's Boyer Museum.

Also, staff members at the historical societies of Burlington, Camden, Monmouth and Salem counties and the state of Delaware were always quick to find the answers to my most obscure questions.

Librarians, both in person and on the phone, were unfailingly helpful and polite as I searched their stacks or requested books. I want to thank Julie Senack and Linda Jenkins at Atlantic City Public Library; Marge Cranmer at Beach Haven Public Library Museum; Lois Brown at Bishop Memorial Library; Susan Lyons at Cherry Hill Public Library; Linda Martin at Library of Congress; Nathaniel Reed at Long Branch Public Library and Nancy Weinberg at Philadelphia Public Library. Additionally, I thank the considerate, although anonymous, staffs of the public libraries in Asbury Park, East Orange, Manahawkin, Princeton, Tuckerton and New York City. The following three specialized archives provided material not available elsewhere: Butler Library at Columbia University, New Jersey State Library and the Rutgers University Special Collections and Archives at the Alexander Library.

Claire McHale, Edward Brown and Evelyn Rockhill deserve special mention for trusting me to take original art work out of their homes. And thanks to Van Thulin at Lynn Photo and Imaging Center for giving extra effort when restoring an old, torn photograph.

I am honored to have the noted New Jersey historian John T. Cunningham write the foreword to this book; additionally, he generously shared his knowledge whenever I asked for help. Mr. Cunningham's prodigious output — his books bank a long shelf at the State Library — is an inspiration to any aspiring writer.

An editor is a vital part of the writing process and I had two good men looking over my shoulder. Rich Youmans read and commented on an early draft of the manuscript and suggested several additional authors. Gene Lambinus, who honed his skills at The New York Times so finely that his red pen got him the moniker "The Butcher of Bank Street," shaped the final draft with skill, finesse and good will. I am very grateful to both of them..

My friends at the SandPaper and Beachcomber offices rate a special thank you: Anita Josephson and Jay Mann for technological support as I bounced from computer crash to system shutdown; Anita also for meticulous proofreading; Doris "Fast-Fingers" Horensky for transcribing early 19th-century script; David Gard for skillfully printing from old prints and negatives; Larry Savadove, who can always pull an obscure word or fact from his head; and Curt Travers, who made it all possible.

Credits

Page 22, 25 Courtesy Margaret Thomas Buchholz; 31 Map by Leslee Ganss; 34 from *Railroads in New Jersey,* John T. Cunningham, Andover, New Jersey; 44 *Harper's Weekly;* 52 John J. Audubon, *The Birds of America,* New York, 1946; 57 Cape May County Historical & Genealogical Society; 63 Cape May County Historical & Geneological Society; 75 "Souvenir of Long Branch" booklet, reproduced from photographs by Louis Glaser's process, Witteman Brothers, New York, from the Collections of the New Jersey Historical Society; 81 *Appleton's Journal of Literature, Science and Art,* 2 March 1872, from the Collections of the New Jersey Historical Society; 87 William C. Ulyat, *Life at the Sea Shore,* Princeton; 90 Cape May County Historical & Genealogical Society; 105 Courtesy Margaret Thomas Buchholz; 107 Atlantic County Historical Society; 112 John Karst after Winslow Homer, *Appleton's Journal of Literature, Science and Art,* 21 August 1869, from the Collections of the New Jersey Historical Society; 123 *Harper's New Monthly Magazine,* February 1878; 136 Courtesy Granville M. Price; 140 *Harper's New Monthly Magazine,* 1878; 145 Courtesy Adele Meehan; 152 Ocean City Historical Museum; 159 Sea Isle City Historical Museum; 166 *Harper's Weekly,* 13 August 1887, courtesy Larry Savadove; 169 *Historical and Biographical Atlas of the New Jersey Coast,* 1878 edition, courtesy Cricket McGehee; 172 Wildwood Historical Society; 180 Courtesy Helen-Chantal Pike; 183, 189 Courtesy Helen-Chantal Pike; 193 Cape May County Historical & Genealogical Society; 198 Courtesy Adele Meehan; 206 Courtesy Margaret Thomas Buchholz; 214 Courtesy Helen-Chantal Pike; 220 Courtesy Granville M. Price; 238 Courtesy Claire McHale; 245 from *Atlantic City, 125 Years of Ocean Madness,* Vicki Gold Levi and Lee Eisenberg, 1994; 251 Wildwood Historical Society; 258 Ocean City Historical Museum; 265 Photograph by Helen Harding Hunter/Vicki Gold Levi Collection; 269 Sea Isle City Historical Society; 277 Courtesy William L. Bauhan; 296 Courtesy Lynn Photo and Imaging Center; 300 Cape May County Historical & Genealogical Society; 309 Courtesy Debby Dooling; 316 UPI/Corbis/Bettmann; 322 U.S. Navy picture collection, New Jersey State Library/*Great Storms of the Jersey Shore*; 356 Courtesy Annsi Cole Stephano; 332 Atlantic City Public Library; 338 Courtesy Kathy Cangialose; 343 Courtesy Island Beach State Park; 348 Woodcut by Kathi Scholz Fertig; 356 New Jersey Highway Authority .

Bibliography

For the benefit of readers who wish to know more about the towns and times included in this collection, I have listed a selection of books about the history of the New Jersey shore. Most, but not all, were used while researching this book; older titles are out of print and available at libraries.

Allaback, Sarah, ed. *Resorts and Recreation, an Historic Theme Study of the New Jersey Coastal Heritage Trail Route.* Mauricetown, N.J., Sandy Hook Foundation and National Park Service, U.S. Department of the Interior.

Blackman, Leah. *History of Little Egg Harbor Township.* Greater John Mathis Foundation, Tuckerton, 1963

Colie, Frederic R. *Mantoloking 1880-1920.* Privately printed, 1970.

Cunningham, John T. *The New Jersey Shore.* New Brunswick, N.J., Rutgers University Press, 1994.

Dorwart, Jeffery M. *Cape May County, New Jersey, The Making of an American Resort Community.* Rutgers University Press, 1996.

Fleming, Thomas. *New Jersey, A History.* New York, W.W. Norton & Co.

Funnell, Charles E. *By The Beautiful Sea.* Rutgers University Press, 1983.

Heston, Alfred M. *South Jersey, A History, 1664-1924.* New York: Lewis Historical Publishing Co., 1927.

Horner, William Stockton. *This Old Monmouth of Ours.* Freehold, N.J., Moreau Brothers, 1932.

Jahn, Robert. *Down Barnegat Bay.* Mantoloking N. J., Beachcomber Press, 1980.

Kent, Bill, with Robert Ruffolo Jr. and Lauralee Dobbins. *Atlantic City, America's Playground.* Encinitas, Calif., Heritage Media Corp., 1998.

Kobbe, Gustave. *The New Jersey Coast and Pines.* 1889, reprinted by Gateway Press, Baltimore, Md., for the Ocean County Historical Society, 1970.

Lencek, Lena and Gideon Basker. *The Beach: The History of Paradise on Earth.* Viking Penguin, 1998.

Levi, Vicki Gold and Lee Eisenberg, Lee. *Atlantic City, 125 Years of Ocean Madness.* Berkeley, Calif., Ten Speed Press, 1994.

Lloyd, John Bailey. *Eighteen Miles of History on Long Beach Island*. Harvey Cedars, N.J., Down The Shore Publishing, 1994.

Lloyd, John Bailey. *Six Miles at Sea, a Pictorial History of Long Beach Island, N.J.* Harvey Cedars, N.J., Down The Shore Publishing, 1990.

Miller, Pauline S. *Three Centuries on Island Beach*. Ocean County Historical Society, 1981.

Moss, George H. Jr. *Nauvoo to the Hook*. Jervey Close Press, 1964.
— *Another Look at Nauvoo to the Hook*. Ploughshare Press, Seabright, 1990

Pike, Helen-Chantal. *Images of America*, Asbury Park, Arcadia Publishing, 1997.

Salter, Edwin. *History of Monmouth and Ocean Counties*. Bayonne, N.J., E. Gardner & Son, 1890.

Salvini, Emil R. *The Summer City by the Sea, Cape May, New Jersey, An Illustrated History*. Wheal-Grace Publications, 1995.

Schoettle, William C. *Bay Head 1879-1911*. Bay Head, 1966 .

Smith, Samuel Stell. *Sandy Hook and the Land of the Navesink*. Monmouth Beach, N.J., Philip Freneau Press, 1963.

Somerville, George B. and Nash, Charles Edgar. *The Lure of Long Beach*. Long Beach Island, N.J., 1914 and 1936 editions.

Studley, Miriam. *Historic New Jersey Through Visitors' Eyes*. New Jersey History Series, Van Nostrand, 1964.

Wertheim, Stanley and Paul Sorrentino. *The Crane Log: A Documentary Life of Stephen Crane 1871-1900*. New York, G.K. Hall, 1994.

Wilson, Harold. *The Jersey Shore*. Lewis Historical Publishing Co., 1953.

Work Projects Administration, Federal Writers Project. *Entertaining a Nation, The Career of Long Branch*, N.J., 1940.

Work Projects Administration, Federal Writers Project. *New Jersey, A Guide to Its Past and Present*. 1936.

Index

367

If you enjoyed this book, you might also like these related titles:

Shore Stories: An Anthology of the Jersey Shore
Edited by Rich Youmans

The first contemporary collection of short fiction, essays, and
poems about this celebrated shore.

*"It is hard to imagine a reader who will not find
something to delight in."*
— The Trenton Times

*"A compelling evocative collection of short stories, essays and
poems.. the unmistakable ring of authenticity."*
— The Asbury Park Press

351 pages, hardcover   ISBN 0-945582-50-1 $29.95

Under A Gull's Wing: Poems and Photographs of the Jersey Shore
Edited by Rich Youmans and Frank Finale

Sixty contributing poets and photographers capture the Shore in
a poetic journey from Sandy Hook to Cape May.

*"Every time I read from this book I come away with sand in my
shoes, salt spray on my glasses, and a new appreciation for a
stretch of shoreline that enchants millions."*
— Small Press Review

"A special pleasure to read."
— The Star-Ledger

207 pages, hardcover   ISBN 0-945582-36-6 $26

Down The Shore Publishing specializes in books, calendars, cards and videos
about New Jersey and the Shore. For a free catalog of all our titles or to be
included on our mailing list, just send us a request:

Down The Shore Publishing
P.O. Box 3100, Harvey Cedars
New Jersey 08008

or visit our website at **www.down-the-shore.com**